Lufkin

HOMELAND SECURITY

A COMPLETE GUIDE TO UNDERSTANDING, PREVENTING, AND SURVIVING TERRORISM

MARK A. SAUTER
Chief Operations Officer
Chesapeake Innovation Center

JAMES JAY CARAFANO
Senior Fellow for Defense and Homeland Security
The Heritage Foundation

McGraw-Hill

New York / Chicago / San Francisco / Lisbon / London / Madrid / Mexico City
Milan / New Delhi / San Juan / Seoul / Singapore / Sydney / Toronto

The McGraw-Hill Companies

8 9 10   DOC/DOC   0 9

ISBN 0-07-144064-X

This publication is designed to provide accurate and authoritative information in regard to the subject matter covered. It is sold with the understanding that neither the author nor the publisher is engaged in rendering legal, accounting, futures/securities trading, or other professional service. If legal advice or other expert assistance is required, the services of a competent professional person should be sought.

—From a Declaration of Principles jointly adopted by a Committee of the American Bar Association and a Committee of Publishers

McGraw-Hill books are available at special quantity discounts to use as premiums and sales promotions, or for use in corporate training programs. For more information, please write to the Director of Special Sales, McGraw-Hill Professional, Two Penn Plaza, New York, NY 10121-2298. Or contact your local bookstore.

CONTENTS

INTRODUCTION **Every American Has a Role in Homeland Security**   xiii

PART 1

HOW WE GOT HERE FROM THERE: THE EMERGENCE OF MODERN HOMELAND SECURITY

CHAPTER 1   **Homeland Security: The American Tradition**   3

Chapter Overview	3
Chapter Learning Objectives	4
The Earliest Days: Securing Borders and Coasts	4
Threats from Within	5
The New Great Power Faces Foreign Threats	9
World War I: Defense against Sabotage	9
World War II	11
The Cold War	13
The Threat of Shadow War	14
The Emerging Threat to America's Homeland	16
Chapter Summary	18
Chapter Quiz	19
Notes	19

CHAPTER 2   **The Rise of Modern Terrorism: The Road to 9/11**   23

Chapter Overview	23
Chapter Learning Objectives	24

Twenty-First Century Terrorism   24
Global Goals   25
A Sophisticated, Worldwide Organization   26
Effects of Twenty-First Century Terrorism   31
Highly Efficient Attack   35
Threat of Weapons of Mass Destruction   35
Chapter Summary   37
Chapter Quiz   38
Notes   38

CHAPTER 3 **The Birth of Modern Homeland Security: The National Response
to the 9/11 Attacks**   41
Chapter Overview   41
Chapter Learning Objectives   42
The Response to Twenty-First Century Terrorism   42
Taking the Offensive   42
International Cooperation   46
Defensive Efforts   48
Chapter Summary   57
Chapter Quiz   57
Notes   57

PART 2

UNDERSTANDING TERRORISM

CHAPTER 4 **The Mind of the Terrorist: Why They Hate Us**   63
Chapter Overview   63
Chapter Learning Objectives   63
Defining Terrorism   64
Why Terrorism   66
Types of Terrorist Groups   73
Suicide Terrorism   78
The Drive for Mass Destruction   80
Chapter Summary   81
Chapter Quiz   81
Notes   82

CHAPTER 5 **Al-Qaida and Other Islamic Extremist Groups: Understanding
Fanaticism in the Name of Religion**   85
Chapter Overview   85
Chapter Learning Objectives   86

The Muslim World   86
Ideology of Terrorism   89
Common Front against the West   97
Islamic Terrorist Groups   100
Chapter Summary   100
Chapter Quiz   100
Notes   100

CHAPTER 6   **The Transnational Dimensions of Terrorism: The Unique Dangers
            of the Twenty-First Century**   103

Chapter Overview   103
Chapter Learning Objectives   104
America in a Globalized World   104
Defining Transnational Terrorism   105
Current Threat   112
Profiles of Significant International Terrorist Groups   114
Chapter Summary   114
Chapter Quiz   114
Notes   114

CHAPTER 7   **Domestic Terrorist Groups: The Forgotten Threat**   117

Chapter Overview   117
Chapter Learning Objectives   118
The Enemy Within   118
Defining Domestic Terrorism   118
The Incidence of Domestic Terrorism   119
Prevalence of Domestic Terrorism   121
Profiles of Significant Domestic Terrorist Groups and Extremist Movements 123
Evolving Threat   129
Chapter Summary   131
Chapter Quiz   131
Notes   131

CHAPTER 8   **Terrorist Operations and Tactics: How Attacks Are Planned
            and Executed**   133

Chapter Overview   133
Chapter Learning Objectives   134
Terrorist Planning   134
The Terrorist Organization   136
Terrorist Support Operations   139
Phases of a Terrorist Attack   140
Terrorist Operations   142
Chapter Summary   151
Chapter Quiz   151
Notes   152

CHAPTER 9 **Weapons of Mass Destruction: Understanding the Great Terrorist Threats and Getting beyond the Hype**   153

Chapter Overview   153
Chapter Learning Objectives   154
Weapons to Worry About   154
Chemical   155
Biological   161
Radiological   168
Nuclear   172
High-Yield Explosives   176
Chapter Summary   178
Chapter Quiz   179
Notes   179

CHAPTER 10 **The Digital Battlefield: Cyberterrorism and Cybersecurity**   187

Chapter Overview   187
Chapter Learning Objectives   187
The Threat   188
Insider Attacks   188
Outsider Attacks   189
Cyberattacks   190
Terrorist Use of Cyberspace   192
The Current State of Defenses   193
Protecting Your Business   199
Prospects for the Future   202
Chapter Summary   203
Chapter Quiz   203
Notes   203

PART 3

HOMELAND SECURITY: ORGANIZATION, STRATEGIES, PROGRAMS, AND PRINCIPLES

CHAPTER 11 **Homeland Security Roles, Responsibilities, and Jurisdictions: Federal, State, and Local Government Responsibilities**   209

Chapter Overview   209
Chapter Learning Objectives   210
The New Normalcy   210
The National Concept of Protecting the Homeland   210
Organizing for Domestic Security   211
Federal   212

The Role of the Congress   230
State and Local Governments   231
Chapter Summary   233
Chapter Quiz   234
Notes   234

CHAPTER 12 **America's National Strategies: The Plans Driving the War on Global Terrorism and What They Mean**   237

Chapter Overview   237
Chapter Learning Objectives   238
What Is a Strategy?   238
National Security Strategy   240
National Strategy for Combating Terrorism   241
National Strategy to Combat Weapons of Mass Destruction   243
National Military Strategy   244
National Strategy for Homeland Security   245
National Strategy for the Physical Protection of Critical Infrastructures and
  Key Assets   248
National Strategy to Secure Cyberspace   249
National Money Laundering Strategy   250
National Drug Control Strategy   250
Assessing the National Strategies   251
Chapter Summary   258
Chapter Quiz   259
Notes   259

CHAPTER 13 **Domestic Antiterrorism and Counterterrorism: The New Role for States and Localities and Supporting Law Enforcement Agencies**   261

Chapter Overview   261
Chapter Learning Objectives   262
The Front Lines of Terrorism   262
Jurisdictions and Responsibilities   263
State and Local Planning   263
Response   278
Chapter Summary   280
Chapter Quiz   281
Notes   281

CHAPTER 14 **Critical Infrastructure Protection and Key Assets: Protecting America's Most Important Targets**   283

Chapter Overview   283
Chapter Learning Objectives   283
Lifeblood of the U.S. Economy   284
Means for Protecting Critical Infrastructure   286

Types of Critical Infrastructure   290
Chapter Summary   304
Chapter Quiz   304
Notes   304

CHAPTER 15   **Incident Management and Emergency Management: Preparing for
             When Prevention Fails**   307

Chapter Overview   307
Chapter Learning Objectives   307
Thinking . . . and Experiencing the Unthinkable   308
The Emergency Response Challenge   308
Management of Domestic Incidents   310
The All-Hazards Approach   314
Principles and Components of Emergency Management   315
Emergency Management Systems and Operations   316
The Future of National Domestic Incident Management   321
Challenges for State and Local Government Emergency Operations Planning   325
Chapter Summary   328
Chapter Quiz   328
Notes   329

CHAPTER 16   **Business Preparedness, Continuity, and Recovery: Private-Sector
             Responses to Terrorism**   331

Chapter Overview   331
Chapter Learning Objectives   331
New World of Disorder   332
Definitions and Standards   333
Changing Business Environment: The Usama Effect   334
Legal Issues   334
Planning for the Worst   336
Supply Chain Security   345
Physical Security   346
Information Technology Continuity and Recovery   347
Chapter Summary   348
Chapter Quiz   348
Notes   348

CHAPTER 17   **Public Awareness and Personal and Family Preparedness:
             Simple Solutions, Serious Challenges**   351

Chapter Overview   351
Chapter Learning Objectives   352

The Preparedness Challenge   352
Risk Communications   353
Individual, Family, and Community Antiterrorism Measures   360
Principles of Emergency Preparedness Planning   362
Indications of a Terrorist Attack   370
Chapter Summary   371
Chapter Quiz   371
Notes   371

CHAPTER 18 **The Future of Homeland Security: Adapting and Responding to the
Evolving Terrorist Threat While Balancing Safety and Civil Liberties**   373

Chapter Overview   373
Chapter Learning Objectives   374
The Future of Terrorism   374
The Future of Technology   380
The Future of Homeland Security Structures   384
Chapter Summary   386
Notes   386

APPENDIX 1 **Profile of Significant Islamic Extremist and International Terrorist
Groups and State Sponsors**   391

Profiles of Significant Islamic Extremist Terrorist Groups   391
Profiles of Significant International Terrorist Groups   412
Notes   439

APPENDIX 2 **Volunteer Services**   441

Volunteers Are "First Responders" Too   441
The Citizenry Organized—Volunteers   442
Notes   444

APPENDIX 3 **The Media and Issues for Homeland Security**   445

The Media   445
Notes   450

APPENDIX 4 **Medical and Public Health Services Emergency and Disaster
Planning and Response: Public Health and Medical Organizations
Have Unique and Demanding Responsibilities for Preparing and
Responding to Terrorist Attacks**   453

Federal Support for Medical Responses   453
Organizing State and Local Activities   455

APPENDIX 5 **Preparing and Responding to Threats against the Agriculture Sector**   461

Federal Agricultural Security and Response Resources   461
Protection of Critical Agriculture Infrastructure   464
Preparedness and Response   466

INDEX   469

EVERY AMERICAN HAS A ROLE IN HOMELAND SECURITY

"Are you guys ready? Let's roll."

Todd Beamer, passenger of United Airlines Flight 93, September 11, 2001

On September 11, 2001, United Airlines Flight 93 left Newark International Airport in New Jersey bound for San Francisco, California. Shortly after takeoff, a team of four terrorists seized control of the plane. From cell phone conversations the passengers and crew learned that other planes had been hijacked as well and crashed into the Twin Towers at the World Trade Center in New York and the Pentagon in Washington, DC. Passenger Tom Burnett called his wife and reassured her, "Don't worry. We're going to do something." Burnett, fellow passenger Todd Beamer, and others rushed the terrorists. While Burnett and Beamer tried to retake control of the cockpit, the plane crashed into a field in rural Pennsylvania killing all aboard.

The courage of the passengers and crew of Flight 93 prevented an even greater tragedy. In the wake of the terrible 9/11 attacks, however, Americans realized that determination and sacrifice alone were not enough to meet the threat of transnational terrorism. In the years following, the nation undertook an unprecedented effort to provide for domestic security. Our purpose is to describe the nature of the threat to the United States and how America is responding to the danger of terrorism—the policies, principles, strategies, organizations, and programs that are responsible for protecting the homeland, incorporating the efforts of the federal government, state and local officials, business, nongovernmental organizations, and private citizens.

Many of the challenges presented by the tasks of homeland security are ubiquitous. They affect the personal safety of every American and impact every aspect of the nation's political, financial, transportation, health, and legal systems. By some estimates, $100 billion is spent every year protecting Americans from harm.[1] There are few issues more important for each and every citizen to understand. All of us need a foundation in homeland security.

This text provides the three core elements of knowledge required for understanding the challenge of protecting the homeland. Part 1 covers how we got here from there, outlining America's traditional approach to domestic security, the evolution of an unprecedented terrorist threat that led to the September 11 attacks, and the nation's response to the events of 9/11. Part 2 offers an overview of contemporary terrorists—who they are, what they want, and how they operate. This knowledge is essential to understanding the challenge of homeland security. You must "know your enemy." Part 3 describes all the critical elements of the present homeland security regime. Knowing the enemy is not enough; good security requires "knowing yourself" as well. In respect to homeland security, that means we all must understand the measures being taken by government officials, public servants, businesses, and average citizens. Part 3 elaborates on the following key concepts: the definition of *homeland security*, homeland security objectives, and roles and responsibilities.

THE DEFINITION OF HOMELAND SECURITY

The U.S. government defines homeland security as the domestic effort (as opposed to the overseas war on terrorism) to defend America from terrorists. In practice, homeland security efforts have also come to comprise general preparedness under the all-hazards doctrine, which focuses on common efforts that help prepare for both terrorist attacks and other natural or human-made catastrophes, such as hurricanes and accidental chemical spills.

Homeland Security Objectives

The *National Strategy for Homeland Security*, released by the White House in 2002, has significantly shaped America's homeland security agenda. The strategy set three strategic objectives:

- *Preventing Terrorism:* The top priority in America's strategy, this objective includes improving "intelligence and warning" of terrorist activities; "border and transportation security" to keep terrorists and their weapons out of the country; and "domestic counterterrorism," activities by domestic law enforcement agencies to prevent and interdict terrorist activity.

- *Reducing Vulnerabilities:* This objective entails "protecting critical infrastructure" and "defending against catastrophic terrorism," or preventing terrorists from acquiring and using weapons of mass destruction and reducing the vulnerability of the nation to such attacks.

- *Minimizing Damage and Recovering from Attacks:* The final strategic objective involves improving the nation's capability to respond if an attack does occur. Enhancing "emergency preparedness and response" includes coordinated incident management processes and effective response capabilities, ranging from interoperable communications to stockpiling of vaccines. Training and support to state and local fire, emergency, and law enforcement personnel—often called "first responders"—is a key part of this objective.

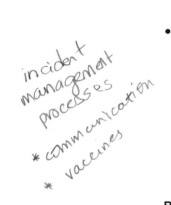

ROLES AND RESPONSIBILITIES

The responsibility for achieving the national homeland security objectives falls upon every segment of American society, starting with federal, state, and local agencies, a vast and overlapping patchwork of more than 87,000 organizations.[2]

Virtually all public servants—police officers, firefighters, emergency medical technicians, municipal workers, public health officials, prosecuting attorneys, councilpersons, mayors, governors, congresspersons, and employees at every federal agency—take part in protecting America from the threat of terrorism.

They all must cooperate with the corporate sector to protect what is called America's "critical infrastructure." As defined by Congress, critical infrastructure means "systems and assets, whether physical or virtual, so vital to the United States that the incapacity or destruction of such systems and assets would have a debilitating impact on security, national economic security, national public health or safety, or any combination of those matters."[3] In short, these are the physical assets that serve as the foundation of the American way of life—our governance, economic vitality, and free civil society.

Critical infrastructure sectors include agriculture, food, water, public health, emergency services, government, the defense industrial base, information and telecommunications, energy, transportation, banking and finance, chemicals and hazardous materials, and postal and shipping. Homeland security policy also focuses on protecting cyberspace (the use of information technologies such as computers and the Internet) and "key assets" such as national monuments (like the Washington Monument in Washington, DC), nuclear power plants, dams, government buildings, and commercial facilities such as skyscrapers.

Because an estimated 85 percent of critical infrastructure is owned by the private sector, American corporations and other commercial organizations play a central role in protecting the homeland. National homeland security efforts aim to coordinate and focus all these public and private organizations, along with the citizenry, by providing common priorities and principles, and coordinating national activities.

A BOOK FOR PROFESSIONALS AND CITIZENS

It is no longer an option, but a civic obligation, for Americans to understand the issues that confront our nation and do their part to defend both security and civil liberties. Every American has a role to play in the war against terrorism. Whether they are a government official coordinating a response to a terrorist act, an emergency responder rolling on a call, a citizen reporting a suspicious incident, a business leader deciding how to best protect employees, or a voter struggling with a controversial issue, all will benefit from a deeper understanding of homeland security issues. *Homeland Security: A Complete Guide to*

Understanding, Preventing, and Surviving Terrorism provides essential information for

- Government leaders and managers
- Emergency responders
- Security personnel
- Business executives
- Concerned citizens
- Volunteers
- Students
- Voters

PRACTICAL INFORMATION

While the book explores both the theoretical and historical underpinnings of its topics, it is not primarily a work of theory or history. *Homeland Security* is a practical textbook and reference source to help its readers understand real-life situations, existing programs, and current policies. The chapters of the book include essential information on

- The most dangerous enemy groups facing our nation
- The tactics and weapons terrorists plan to use against us, including cyberterrorism and other modern threats
- The truth behind the hype about weapons of mass destruction
- Key national strategies for securing the homeland and combating terrorism, plus their implications for first responders, corporate America, and average citizens
- The most important government and private-sector organizations involved in homeland security—what they do and how they work, and sometimes don't work, together
- Practical resources to help readers protect themselves from disasters and assist in the prevention of terrorism

LEARNING OBJECTIVES, ORGANIZATION, AND STYLE USAGE

Homeland Security is designed as a text for both academic and training courses in homeland security and terrorism. It supports the learning objectives established by the programs and guidelines of the Department of Homeland Security and the United States Citizen Corps.

Chapters are presented in the order necessary to build a full conceptual foundation for understanding and responding to the threat of terrorism. Each chapter, however, stands alone. Each provides key learning objectives and a chapter quiz. The material in each chapter provides sufficient information to both master the learning objectives and answer the questions posed at the end of the chapter. Appendices provide additional information on niche areas of homeland security that may be of interest to professional emergency responders.

Chapters also contain From the Source and Issues features. From the Source features provide excerpts from actual documents that influence homeland security policies. Issues features frame key controversial questions regarding various aspects of homeland security that remain subjects of ongoing debate. Both are provided as means to stimulate additional discussion on the learning objectives set up in each chapter.

Significant attention has been given to maintaining consistent style, word usage, and definitions throughout the text. Readers will learn about many international terrorist organizations and key terms associated with them. In general, the book follows the foreign language guidelines of *The Chicago Manual of Style* and in specific adopts the style of the U.S. State Department's style for common usages such as *al-Qaida*, *Usama bin Ladin*, and *Hizballah*. Where source documents are quoted, their original spellings are maintained. Additionally, terms and definitions regarding U.S. homeland security measures are consistent with those currently used by the Department of Homeland Security.

A LASTING CHALLENGE

The global war on terrorism will be a protracted conflict. We will need homeland security for a long time. In the years ahead, many Americans may find themselves playing roles they never expected. Most will meet their obligations in quiet ways. Some will be called upon to display conspicuous heroism as shown by the emergency responders at the World Trade Center and Pentagon, the passengers aboard Flight 93, and the U.S. forces now battling terrorism around the world. All will need as much knowledge as possible to be successful. Knowledge is the first and most important shield in the war against terror. It is in that spirit that *Homeland Security* is presented.

Mark A. Sauter and James Jay Carafano, Ph.D

Washington, DC

NOTES

1. While the *National Strategy for Homeland Security* (September 2002), p. xiii, reports the "United States spends roughly $100 billion per year on homeland security," the actual amount is open to debate. The cited estimate includes DHS agencies and federal, state, and local first responders and emergency services, but excludes most military spending. Private-sector estimates of total homeland security spending, which sometimes include international purchases of technology, range up to $138 billion a year. However, some far lower estimates focus on the increased spending due to the terrorist threat and exclude "normal" spending on law enforcement, fire fighting, and emergency services.

2. Ibid, p. vii.

3. USA PATRIOT Act, Public Law 107-56 (October 26, 2001).

HOW WE GOT HERE FROM THERE

The Emergence of Modern Homeland Security

1

HOMELAND SECURITY

The American Tradition

Those who expect to reap the blessings of freedom must, like men, undergo the fatigues of supporting it.

Thomas Paine

CHAPTER OVERVIEW

Many Americans assume the 9/11 attacks represented an entirely new and unprecedented danger—that in decades past the isolation provided by two oceans had kept the homeland secure. This assumption is largely wrong. Tens of thousands of miles of border and coastline, wealth and resources, vast territory, a diverse population, and open civil society have long made the civilian population of the United States a tempting target. To some degree, every generation of Americans has experienced the anxiety that they might be attacked in their own homes. Each has held public debate over the sufficient means necessary to protect the nation—the right balance of security; economic growth; cooperation among federal, state, and local government; and protection of civil liberties. Over time, American national security policy became increasingly focused on offensive capabilities while the balance between domestic security and civil liberties tilted toward the latter. These traditions proved unable to protect America from the attackers of 9/11 and the modern terrorist threat.

CHAPTER LEARNING OBJECTIVES

After reading this chapter, you should be able to

1. Identify principles that have guided domestic security efforts since colonial times.

2. Explain the traditional level of cooperation between federal, state, and local agencies for domestic security and national preparedness.

3. Gauge the general level of economic resources the United States has dedicated to homeland security during its history and what factors affected expenditures.

4. Describe the role that the protection of civil liberties has played in determining the federal role in homeland security.

5. List some factors that limited the nation's capability to protect the American homeland immediately prior to 9/11.

THE EARLIEST DAYS: SECURING BORDERS AND COASTS

[handwritten margin note: originally, protecting the homeland meant defending towns, borders, and coastline from external attackers]

During America's first century, protecting the homeland remained mostly a matter of defending towns, borders, and coastline from external attackers. Conflicts between colonists and Indians played a principal role in the formulation of an American conception of national security. Communities were largely responsible for protecting their citizens, usually through local militias.[1] Nor did the federal government play a large role in civil preparedness or responding to disasters. The earliest case of congressionally approved domestic assistance followed a devastating fire in Portsmouth, New Hampshire, in 1803. To ease the burden, Congress granted an extra year to pay off bonds owed at the local customhouse. Such measures were an exception rather than the rule.

In the early years of the Republic, invasion by Great Britain—which razed Washington, DC, during the War of 1812—and the security of the border with Canada were also national preoccupations. These fears declined by 1823, but a series of midcentury border crises

intensely disliked

led to renovation of existing forts and harbor defenses. Still, investments in defense were modest, accounting for only a small percentage of the gross domestic product (GDP). The notion of large peacetime security budgets was (anathema) to most Americans. This tradition was abandoned only in wartime or other moments of national crisis.[2] By 1870 trepidation over threats to the northern border and eastern coastline had mostly disappeared, with the exception of a short-lived flap during the Spanish-American War that stirred unfounded fears of a Spanish armada threatening the coast. In the South, episodic apprehension about foreign incursions culminated with the punitive expedition into Mexico in 1916–1917 and patrols on the border through 1929.[3]

apprehension

THREATS FROM WITHIN

Through most of the nation's history threats from within the borders of the United States were less central to American concepts of homeland security. Internal threats have been transient and often regional in focus. The federal government's role in providing defense against domestic threats has always been suspect. During the nineteenth century, drawing on longstanding antiarmy ideology and the colonial experience, Americans generally opposed using federal forces for internal security.[4] Intervention was considered acceptable only in cases of insurrection, widespread public disorder, or extreme domestic terrorism. Before the Civil War, state consent or requests for assistance by state authorities always accompanied the domestic use of federal force.[5]

Federal Power versus Civil Liberties

The Civil War placed enormous strains on the proposition that the federal government could ensure domestic security without abrogating the constitutional rights of its citizens. The Union home front faced not only major military attack, but raids, draft riots, espionage, and sabotage—in one case Confederate spies tried to burn down New York City. Federal authorities responded with an unprecedented test of the limits of their power; they suspended the right of habeas corpus, which requires the government to provide justification before a judge in order to hold a prisoner, and prosecuted U.S. civilians (including conspirators in Lincoln's assassination) in military tribunals.[6]

Habeas Corpus during Civil War

ISSUES:

CIVIL LIBERTIES AND SECURITY—HABEAS CORPUS DURING THE CIVIL WAR

Among the civil liberties guaranteed by the U.S. Constitution is that "The privilege of the Writ of Habeas Corpus shall not be suspended, unless when in Cases of Rebellion or Invasion the public Safety may require it." A writ of habeas corpus is a judicial mandate to a prison official ordering that an inmate be brought to the court so it can be determined whether or not that person is imprisoned lawfully. In 1862, President Lincoln suspended habeas corpus. Among the 13,000 people arrested under martial law was a Maryland Secessionist, John Merryman. Supreme Court Justice Roger B. Taney, ruled in the case of *Ex parte Merryman*, that suspension of habeas corpus was unconstitutional. Lincoln ignored the ruling. After the war, the Supreme Court officially restored habeas corpus in *Ex parte Milligan*, ruling that military trials where the civil courts were capable of functioning were illegal.

Excerpts from Ex Parte Milligan, 71 U.S. 2 (1866)

On the 10th day of May, 1865, Lambdin P. Milligan presented a petition to the Circuit Court of the United States for the District of Indiana to be discharged from an alleged unlawful imprisonment. The case made by the petition is this: Milligan is a citizen of the United States; has lived for twenty years in Indiana, and, at the time of the grievances complained of, was not, and never had been, in the military or naval service of the United States. On the 5th day of October, 1864, while at home, he was arrested by order of General Alvin P. Hovey, commanding the military district of Indiana, and has ever since been kept in close confinement.

During the late wicked Rebellion, the temper of the times did not allow that calmness in deliberation and discussion so necessary to a correct conclusion of a purely judicial question. Then, considerations of safety were mingled with the exercise of power, and feelings and interests prevailed which are happily terminated. Now that the public safety is assured, this question, as well as all others, can be discussed and decided without passion or the admixture of any element not required to form a legal judgment.

No graver question was ever considered by this court, nor one which more nearly concerns the rights of the whole people, for it is the birthright of every American citizen when charged with crime to be tried and punished according to law.

It is essential to the safety of every government that, in a great crisis like the one we have just passed through, there should be a power somewhere of suspending the writ of habeas corpus.

[but] It is difficult to see how the safety for the country required martial law in Indiana. If any of her citizens were plotting treason, the power of arrest could secure them until the government was prepared for their trial, when the courts were open and ready to try them . . . Milligan's trial and conviction by a military commission was illegal.

1. Was the Supreme Court's decision in *Ex parte Milligan* correct? What constitutional issues were at stake, and how do they relate to homeland security?
2. How should society strike a balance between security and civil liberties?
3. What were the implications of *Ex parte Milligan* for providing domestic security?
4. Is the precedent of *Ex parte Milligan* applicable to the challenges of combating terrorism today?

An even more significant departure from the traditions of U.S. security, however, was the use of soldiers as federal marshals during Reconstruction. After the presidential election of 1876, the president dispatched troops to polling stations in South Carolina, Louisiana, and Florida where electoral votes remained in dispute. In a reflection

*Posse Comitatus Act of 1878 — Prohibited Federal troops From enforcing state or congressional approval.

of the ongoing national debate between security and government power, this measure precipitated calls for the passage of the Posse Comitatus Act of 1878, which prohibited federal troops from enforcing state or federal laws without congressional approval.[7]

The Emergence of Federal Roles

- Ku Klux Klan
- Pres. William McKinley

American history from the Civil War to the turn of the century also saw dramatic episodes of labor unrest and domestic terrorism, including Ku Klux Klan activity in the South and Midwest and the assassination of President William McKinley. These incidents were initially treated more as criminal acts than serious national threats. There was strong resistance to strengthening internal security based on longstanding traditions of distrust of government power. Americans looked for cheap, short-term solutions to domestic threats. Despite Posse Comitatus, military forces were often relied on as an expedient. Between 1875 and 1918, state militia or federal troops responded over 1,000 times to labor unrest, viewed by many as instigated by foreign influences.[8]

wise

Fear over the threat of anarchists and communists, called the Red Scare, grew in 1919 after an attempted bomb attack against the U.S. attorney general. Congress rushed through $500,000 in funding for a new antiradical unit in the Department of Justice's Bureau of Investigation, led by a young official named J. Edgar Hoover. In early 1920, federal agents conducted raids across the nation, taking thousands of suspected radicals, many of them immigrants, into custody and prompting an outcry from civil libertarians.[9]

The violence peaked in September 1920, when a bomb pulled by a horse cart tore through Wall Street in lower Manhattan, ripping apart pedestrians and pelting occupants of nearby offices with waves of broken glass that one witness likened to a snowstorm. "What happened came without warning," said John Markle, a Pennsylvania mining executive on a business trip to the financial district, "(t)here was no time to duck . . ." As the smoke cleared, victims of the terrorist attack could be seen strewn across the pavement like "lifeless lumps of clay." The crime was never solved.

The role of federal domestic security forces grew, although sometimes haltingly, throughout this period. Americans expected counties, cities, and states to fulfill most of their governmental needs. But the nation lacked the means to deal with interstate crimes, a growing con-

[handwritten margin notes: "new technologies created interstate crimes. -Prohibition and organized crime."]

cern in a society that saw new technologies emerge that could move people, goods, and services across state borders with increasing speed and frequency. The need for a national bureau of investigation became particularly apparent during the years of Prohibition, which saw an unprecedented increase in organized crime.

The government's role in national preparedness also grew in fits and starts. Traditionally, federal agencies did not have a prominent role in responding to disasters, though the Congress did periodically provide assistance. Over the course of the century, ad hoc legislation was passed more than 100 times in response to hurricanes, earthquakes, floods, and other natural disasters. As the size of the federal government grew, a myriad of agencies and programs emerged that offered some assistance to state and local governments in preparing for, responding to, or mitigating natural disasters, but little thought was given to how to respond to terrorist acts.

THE NEW GREAT POWER FACES FOREIGN THREATS

By the dawn of the twentieth century, as the nation grew in power and stature, it was increasingly eyed as a potential economic and military competitor by European and Asian powers. Soon foreign threats once again became the focus of security concerns. For example, Americans feared, and some of the Kaiser's military strategists actually proposed, German amphibious operations against the United States. The American occupation of Haiti from 1915 to 1934 was justified in part to secure avenues of approach to the United States through the Caribbean.[10] Operations such as this and persistent public calls for improving U.S. defenses against foreign invasion were perennial features of national security debates throughout the first half of the 1900s.

WORLD WAR I: DEFENSE AGAINST SABOTAGE

As the prospects for the United States being drawn into World War I loomed, and the Red Scare peaked, Americans were greatly concerned that foreign provocateurs would fan dissent on the home front. Concerns over espionage and sabotage were also acute. The Espionage

Act of 1917 was followed by the Sedition Act of 1918. Created to prevent interference with the recruitment of troops or exposure of national security information, the Sedition Act made it a federal crime to criticize the government or Constitution. Both acts were repealed in 1921.

To secure the homeland, authorities created an ad hoc security system that included Army and Navy Intelligence and the Department of Justice, as well as quasi-private, volunteer organizations like the Minnesota Commission for Public Safety. This makeshift network largely succeeded in thwarting Imperial German intelligence agents, though it was inefficient and prone to abuse, as some security agencies were used for partisan politics, to dispense vigilante justice, and as part of the crackdowns involved in the Red Scare. The system was abandoned after the war, and most of the volunteer organizations were quickly abolished.[11]

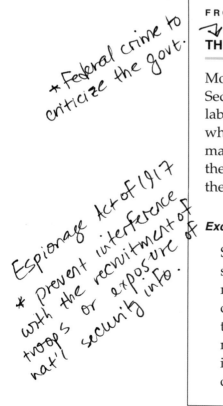

*(handwritten margin notes: * Federal crime to criticize the govt. Espionage Act of 1917 * prevent interference with the recruitment of troops or exposure of nat'l security info.)*

FROM THE SOURCE:

THE SEDITION ACT OF 1918

More than 2,000 prosecutions occurred under the Espionage and Sedition Acts. The most famous of which was that of American labor leader and Socialist presidential candidate Eugene V. Debs, who was sentenced to 10 years in prison for an antiwar speech he made in Canton, Ohio, on June 16, 1918. Among the provisions of the Sedition Act were restrictions against free speech and use of the postal service.

Excerpt from the Act

SECTION 3. Whoever, when the United States is at war, shall willfully make or convey false reports or false statements with intent to interfere with the operation or success of the military or naval forces of the United States, or to promote the success of its enemies, or shall willfully make or convey false reports, or false statements, . . . or incite insubordination, disloyalty, mutiny, or refusal of duty, in the military or naval forces of the United States, or shall willfully obstruct . . . the recruiting or enlistment service of the United States, or . . . shall willfully utter, print, write, or publish any disloyal, profane, scurrilous, or abusive language about the form of government of the United States, or the Constitution of the United States, or the military or naval forces of the United States . . . or shall willfully display the flag of any foreign enemy, or shall willfully . . . urge, incite, or advocate any curtailment of production . . . or advocate, teach, defend, or suggest the doing of any of the acts or things in this section enumerated and whoever shall by word or act support or favor the cause of any country with which the United States is at war or by word or act oppose the cause of the United States therein, shall be punished by a fine of not more than $10,000 or imprisonment for not more than twenty years, or both . . .

SECTION 4. When the United States is at war, the Postmaster General may, upon evidence satisfactory to him that any person or concern is using the mails in violation of any of the provisions of this Act, instruct the postmaster at any post office at which mail is received addressed to such person or concern to return to the postmaster at the office at which they were originally mailed all letters or other matter so addressed, with the words "Mail to this address undeliverable under Espionage Act" plainly written or stamped upon the outside thereof, and all such letters or other matter so returned to such postmasters shall be by them returned to the senders thereof under such regulations as the Postmaster General may prescribe.

WORLD WAR II

The period immediately leading up to World War II proved a watershed in the evolution of American concerns over protecting the homeland. Pressure grew to shift efforts to a more offensive-oriented posture. Army and Navy planners argued over whether the United States should adopt a "continental" defense, focused on securing the borders, or a "hemispheric" defense, a more offensive stance, centered on protecting the homeland from strategic points in the Atlantic, South America, and the Pacific. Political leaders, however, issued scant policy guidance and invested few resources. The public was largely apathetic toward security debates until the war's eve.[12]

Defending the Home Front

unusual

Once war broke out, the federal government moved to protect America's home front. Though untested by a major threat, wartime efforts to protect ports and other key infrastructure were prodigious, including the fielding of more than 200,000 auxiliary military police to guard over 16,000 facilities. Millions more citizens signed up for civilian defense units that provided surveillance and emergency response capabilities—including programs designed to prepare for a Nazi chemical attack.[13]

Civilian Defense

The enemy provided relatively few targets for those patriotic volunteers. During World War II there were only a handful of ineffectual attacks on the continental United States. In June 1942, German submarines landed eight trained saboteurs on Long Island, New York, and near Jacksonville, Florida, as part of a plan called Operation Pastorius. The German infiltrators had spent years in the United States—at least two held U.S. citizenship—and they carried enough cash and sophisticated explosives equipment to destroy key infrastructure across the nation. On the West Coast, a seaplane launched from a Japanese submarine dropped an incendiary bomb near Brookings, Oregon, in September 1942. But the threat of attack in the homeland turned out to have greater legal than strategic implications.

Major Impacts on Civil Liberties

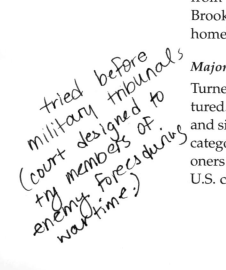

tried before military tribunals (court designed to try members of enemy forces during wartime.)

Turned in by one of their own, the German saboteurs were quickly captured. The legal process following their capture—all were convicted and six were put to death—established the executive branch's power to categorize certain individuals as "enemy combatants," instead of "prisoners of war," and try them before military tribunals, even if they held U.S. citizenship. Meanwhile, the War Relocation Authority was directing the evacuation of over 100,000 persons of Japanese ancestry, purportedly to preclude acts of sabotage and spying. Both decisions sparked debate decades later when they were cited as precedents in debates over the appropriate response to the 9/11 attacks.

THE COLD WAR

For a brief period following World War II, Americans were largely unconcerned about external threats. Then in 1949 the Soviet Union tested its first nuclear weapon, followed less than a year later by the outbreak of the Korean War. These events brought the Cold War home to Main Street America. As the conflict grew more intense, a high level of sustained investment in national security marked a departure from past policies. Between 1948 and 1989, the United States spent an average of 7.5 percent of its GDP each year on defense, compared to the 1 or 2 percent spent annually on the military for most of the nation's history.[14]

Communist Infiltration During the early years of the Cold War, fear of communist agitation and sabotage ran high. Extensive countermeasures included a massive security and personnel screening program for port facilities. Though concern over Soviet espionage was evident before World War II and was an enduring feature of the Cold War, it was only during the first half of the 1950s that the problem monopolized public attention as a homeland security issue.[15]

At the outset of the Cold War, the United States experimented with a defense-in-depth approach, employing everything from coastal antiaircraft posts and civil defense patrols to atomic diplomacy. The United States did not begin to build a deterrent force until 1948. As late as 1957, a highly publicized and controversial presidential blue-ribbon panel study, popularly known as the Gaither Report, argued that deterrence was inadequate and called for a massive bomb shelter building program.[16] Still, by the middle of the decade offensive measures had become the preferred means for protecting the nation, to the point that some argued for launching a preemptive strike against the Soviet Union. Close-in defensive measures, like air and civil defenses, withered.[17] During this period, Americans worried about threats ranging from radiological attacks by secret agents to the poisoning of water reservoirs, but the dominant concern was the Soviet nuclear arsenal. The United States considered and then discarded plans to build a limited antiballistic missile system as both impractical and too expensive, a pattern to be repeated in the 1980s.

Focus on Offensive Measures

1979 – FEMA

Overwhelming reliance on deterrence was an unprecedented feature of Cold War competition. Rather than defending the homeland on U.S. shores, the United States decided to rely on threats of preemption or massive nuclear retaliation to a Soviet attack. This approach squelched demand for increased civil defense and preparedness, both for natural and human-caused disasters. It was not until 1979, in response to the complaints of state and local governments over the plethora of federal agencies that had to be coordinated with following hurricanes, floods, and earthquakes, that the Federal Emergency Management Agency (FEMA) was established to coordinate all federal support to state and local governments. Ironically, as the Cold War dragged on—and anxiety over attacks on U.S. soil gradually eased and overall defense spending as a percentage of GDP declined—the size of the Soviet arsenal actually increased.

THE THREAT OF SHADOW WAR

In contrast to the dominant place of the Soviet Union in American threat perceptions, concern over terrorism waxed and waned over the twentieth century, even as a range of groups carried out attacks against the United States.

Domestic Terrorists

- Independence of Puerto Rico
- KKK
- Vietnam War

September 11 was far from the first time terrorists set their sights on Washington, DC. Puerto Rican extremists shot up the Capitol and tried to kill President Truman in separate incidents during the 1950s. Terrorists seeking the independence of Puerto Rico would launch many more attacks in the following decades. Right-wing radical Klansmen bombed a Birmingham, Alabama, church in 1963, murdering four teenagers. Klan beatings, whippings, and floggings continued through much of the 1960s. At the same time, the seeds of domestic ideological terrorism were being sown in the movement against the Vietnam War, which spawned left-wing terrorist groups, including one that bombed the U.S. Capitol in 1971. By 1975 the number of terrorist groups active in America was so large that when a bomb exploded in New York's LaGuardia Airport, killing 11 people, the police faced a dizzying array of suspects. Although left-wing extremists, Puerto Rican liberationists, the Jewish Defense League, the Palestinian Liberation Organization (PLO), and Croatian nationalists came under suspicion—among others—the crime was never solved.

The FBI, CIA, and other government agencies employed aggressive intelligence gathering and covert tactics to crack down on terrorist groups. But in the 1970s, the American public learned many of these same strategies had been used against lawful dissidents and civil rights groups. Such abuses prompted congressional hearings and led to dramatic restrictions on domestic intelligence operations, including the creation of a bureaucratic "wall" between intelligence gathering and law enforcement.[18] Decades later, the wall would hamper investigations of al-Qaida terrorists preparing to attack the United States. Still, by the 1980s, most nationalist and left-wing ideological terrorist groups in the United States had collapsed.

International Terrorism

The rise of spectacular Palestinian and European terrorism during the 1960s and '70s, often sponsored by the Soviet bloc, failed to prompt substantial U.S. action. But the mid-1980s saw increasing concerns about the terrorist threat to the United States. These included fears that small nuclear devices might be used to strike the 1984 Olympiad in Los Angeles.[19] The Soviet role in terrorism was hotly debated, although the actual threat to the United States may have been far greater than was commonly assumed.[20]

Still, the focus remained on threats to Americans abroad. Amid attacks on U.S. airliners, embassies, and military bases during the 1980s—and a Libyan attempt to pay a Chicago street gang to conduct terrorist attacks in America—the United States moved against so-called state-sponsored terrorist groups backed by nations such as Iran, Syria, and Libya.

By 1986, the United States had launched military strikes against Libya and placed sanctions on it, Iran, and Syria. "History is likely to record that 1986 was the year when the world, at long last, came to grips with the plague of terrorism," commented President Ronald

Reagan in May 1986. In reality, the policies had not ended terrorism supported by state sponsors. In April 1988, Japanese citizen Yu Kikumura was arrested at a New Jersey rest stop. In his car police found three powerful antipersonnel bombs built into fire extinguishers. According to prosecutors, Kikumura was working for Libya on a mission to strike New York City. The Libyan campaign peaked on December 21, 1988, when Pan Am Flight 183 exploded over Lockerbie, Scotland, killing 270 passengers and people on the ground. Iran too continued its backing of terrorist groups such as Hizballah.

late 1980's — threat was primarily for Americans abroad

Still, by the later 1980s, U.S. policy makers perceived the terrorism threat as reduced and primarily of risk to Americans abroad; the White House was far more focused on the breakup of the Soviet Union. Ironically, as will be seen later, the decline of the Soviets—one of the very factors that weakened traditional state-sponsored terrorist groups and reduced American attention to the issue—inspired Usama bin Ladin and helped pave the road to 9/11.

THE EMERGING THREAT TO AMERICA'S HOMELAND

After the Cold War, the nation's approach to combating threats to the homeland assumed a more traditional pattern. Defense spending was reduced to under 3 percent of GDP.[21] But a new threat was growing— Islamic extremists with ideological and often direct links to bin Ladin and al-Qaida. Following attacks on U.S. forces in Yemen and Somalia, foreign terrorists struck the American homeland on February 26, 1993, setting off a bomb in the underground parking lot at New York City's World Trade Center. The plotters failed in their plan to bring the twin towers crashing down, but did kill 6 and wounded more than 1,000. Just months later in June, authorities picked up eight extremists in the Day of Terror plot to blow up landmarks in New York City. But at the time, law enforcement officials failed to grasp the full significance of these events.

1993 – struck America's homeland

Funding for some activities related to homeland security did rise in the mid-1990s, spurred by the 1995 bombing of the Alfred P. Murrah Federal Building in Oklahoma City, Oklahoma, and the sarin gas attack on the Tokyo subway by members of the Japanese Aum Shinrikyo cult, who also hated the United States and had considered gasing the Pentagon and White House. Federal expenditures for domestic preparedness against weapons of mass destruction (WMD) from 1995 to 2000 accelerated from almost nothing to $1.5 billion.[22] Presidential Decision Directive 39, released on June 21, 1995, called for giving "the highest priority to developing effective capabilities to detect, prevent, defeat and manage the consequences of nuclear, biological or chemical (NBC) materials or weapons use by terrorists."[23] In 1996 Congress passed the Nunn-Lugar-Domenici Domestic Preparedness Initiative, which enhanced the capabilities of first responders to deal with WMD. Reflecting a growing concern over terrorism and WMD, Congress held over 80 hearings on related issues between 1998 and 2000.[24]

During this period, al-Qaida and its supporters continued their attacks abroad, hitting U.S. military facilities and embassies. In 1998, bin Ladin pledged to escalate his campaign to drive America from the Middle East. While the Clinton administration ultimately launched diplomatic initiatives, financial crackdowns, prosecutions, covert operations, and even a missile attack against bin Ladin and his followers, U.S. policy responses never reflected the enormity of the threat. Built to combat state-sponsored terrorist groups, U.S. government strategies in both the Clinton and early Bush administrations were marked by a focus on the threat abroad rather than at home, treatment of terrorism as primarily a law enforcement issue, toleration of terrorist sanctuaries, competing priorities and limited resources, poor information sharing and analysis, and inadequate domestic preparedness. Military responses were rare and limited, reflecting narrow congressional and public support for aggressive and sustained international action. Because of this, a highly refined form of political violence received room to metastasize largely unchecked.

In December 1999, Ahmed Ressam was arrested at the U.S.-Canadian border with the materials for a bomb he intended to use against Los Angeles Airport as part of the al-Qaida-linked global millennium terrorist plot. Despite this near miss, there was still little appetite for a broad national agenda to address homeland security.

A Broken System   In 2000 and 2001, despite a variety of leads and warnings, America's homeland security system failed to detect plans for a massive strike against the homeland. While the blame for the attack rests squarely with the criminals who conducted it, and their plot was well crafted and executed, evidence suggests a more effective system could have uncovered and disrupted it. The failure to do so stemmed from a variety of systemic problems, including disjointed government strategies, *divided* balkanized agency responsibilities, an FBI mindset focused on investigating rather than preventing terrorism, grossly inadequate resources, poor technology, a refusal to share information, and just plain sloppy work. Civil liberty safeguards put in place decades before had become *hardened* ossified bureaucratic barriers. When a New York FBI agent asked for help from criminal agents to track down two al-Qaida operatives (who later participated in the 9/11 attacks), he was turned down because of the "wall" between intelligence and criminal cases.

On the morning of September 11, 19 suicide hijackers approached their flights. The existing homeland security system still had a chance to stop them. In 1996 and '97, the White House Commission on Aviation Safety and Security, headed by Vice President Al Gore and known as the "Gore Commission," had sent recommendations for preventing aviation terrorism to the White House. But years later—despite repeated government and media investigations documenting gaps in aviation security—many of the safeguards recommended by the Gore Commission and other experts were still not in place. On this morning, nine of the hijackers were selected for special security screening, according to a federal spokesperson, but all made it through to their flights anyway.

CHAPTER SUMMARY

The distinguishing feature of homeland security initiatives that were undertaken before September 11 was that investments in homeland security were far outpaced by identified requirements and that even those identified requirements underestimated the threat. Those investments that were made closely adhered to traditional organizational responsibilities and missions with only a modicum of innovation, interagency integration, or synchronization of federal, state, local, and private-sector efforts. In many respects, these modest, fragmented efforts followed the traditional American approach of dedicating only limited resources to domestic security.

small portion

In short, despite repeated attacks by al-Qaida against Americans abroad, threats by bin Ladin against the homeland, at least two major attempts by his followers to attack U.S. targets, a successful poison gas attack in Japan by a group with an established hatred of the United States, the Oklahoma bombing, and numerous warnings at all levels of government, the United States failed to understand and respond to the threat of a massive terrorist attack against its territory.

CHAPTER QUIZ

1. Why did a significant federal role for domestic security, except during periods of war, not emerge until the twentieth century?
2. Identify two historical conflicts in which the U.S. government used military tribunals to try civilians arrested in the United States and why these powers were employed.
3. Explain the relationship between civil liberties and domestic security in the American tradition.
4. What was the traditional level of national spending on domestic security? What were the exceptions? Why?
5. List factors that may have helped prevent the U.S. government from detecting the 9/11 plot.

NOTES

1. See, for example, Jill Lepore, *Name of War: King Philip's War and the Origins of American Identity* (New York: Random House, 1999).
2. Mark Grimsely, "Surviving Military Revolution: The U.S. Civil War," McGregor Knox and Williamson Murray, eds., *The Dynamics of Military Revolution, 1300-2050* (Cambridge: Cambridge University Press, 2001).
3. Andrew J. Birtle, *U.S. Army Counterinsurgency and Contingency Operations Doctrine, 1860-1941* (Washington DC: Center of Military History, 1998); Charles P. Stacey, "The Myth of the Unguarded Frontier, 1815-1871," *American Historical Review* 56 (October 1950): 1–18; John S. D. Eisenhower, *Intervention! The United States and the Mexican Revolution, 1913-1917* (New York: Norton, 1993).
4. Lois G. Schwoerer, "No Standing Armies!" *The Antiarmy Ideology in Seventeenth-Century England* (Baltimore: Johns Hopkins University Press, 1974).
5. Robert W. Coakley, *The Role of Federal Military Forces in Domestic Disorders, 1789-1878* (Washington, DC: Center of Military History, 1988).

6. William H. Rehnquist, *All the Laws but One: Civil Liberties in Wartime* (New York: Alfred A. Knopf, 1998), pp. 138–143.

7. Mathew Carlton Hammond, "The Posse Comitatus Act: A Principle in Need of Renewal," *Washington University Law Quarterly* 2/75 (Summer 1997): 3, www.wulaw.wuslt.edu/75-2/752-10.html.

8. For a detailed discussion of the period, see Clayton D. Laurie and Ronald H. Cole, *The Role of Federal Military Forces in Domestic Disorders, 1877-1945* (Washington, DC: Center of Military History, 1997).

9. Nathan Miller, *Spying for America* (New York, Dell Publishing, 1989), pp. 232–34.

10. Hans Schmidt, *The United States Occupation of Haiti, 1915-1934* (New Brunswick: Rutgers University Press, 1995).

11. Carl H. Chrislock, *Watchdog of Loyalty: The Minnesota Commission for Public Safety during World War I* (St. Paul, MN: Minnesota Historical Society Press, 1991).

12. Mark A. Stoler, *Allies and Adversaries: The Joint Chiefs of Staff, the Grand Alliance, and U.S. Strategy in World War II* (Chapel Hill, NC: University of North Carolina Press, 2000), pp. 3–15.

13. For an overview of the defense of the United States during World War II, see Stetson Conn, Rose C. Engelman, and Byron Fairchild, *Guarding the United States and Its Outposts* (Washington, DC: Center of Military History, United States Army, 2000).

14. Defense spending, for example, was 2 percent of GDP in 1940. During the Cold War, spending varied considerably from a low of 3.6 percent of GDP in 1948 to a high of 13 percent in 1954. Office of Management and Budget, *Historical Table, Budget of the United States Government*, Table 3.1: Outlays by Superfunction and Function: 1940-2006, w3.access.gpo.gov/usbudget/fy2002/sheets/hist03z1.xls. For the varieties in Cold War defense spending, see Dennis S. Ippolito, *Blunting the Sword: Budget Policy and the Future of Defense Spending* (Washington, DC: National Defense University Press, 1994), pp. 3–33. The exact percentages of defense spending that can be attributed directly to protecting the homeland or securing other national security interests is difficult to quantify. Some investments served dual functions. America's nuclear arsenal, for example, was intended to protect the nation and discourage Soviet aggression in Western Europe. Homeland security spending by nondefense agencies is even more difficult to measure.

15. Lisle Abbott Rose, *The Cold War Comes to Main Street: America in 1950* (Lawrence, KS: The University Press of Kansas, 1999).

16. Paul Dickson, *Sputnik: The Shock of the Century* (New York: Walker, 2001), p. 161.

17. In 1950 the United States established a civil defense program, and the military organized its first postwar continental air defense commands to protect nearly 100 cities, industrial centers, and military bases. At its height these defenses included constant combat air patrols by the Air National Guard and 240 missile sites operated by almost 45,000 active Army National Guard soldiers. Robert L. Kelly, *Army Antiaircraft in Air Defense, 1946-54*, Historical Study No. 4 (Colorado Springs, CO: Air Defense Command, June 1954); Kenneth Schaffel, *The Emerging Shield: The Air Force and the Evolution of Continental Air Defense, 1945-1960* (Washington, DC: Office of Air Force History, 1991). There were brief spurts of activity. After the Cuban Missile Crisis in 1962, the national civil defense effort received renewed attention when the government initiated a nationwide, nuclear-fallout shelter system. Some homeland defense systems lingered as well. As late as the early 1970s, the Defense Department still maintained nuclear-tipped air defense missiles in the United States. Thomas J. Kerr, *Civil Defense in the US: Bandaid for a Holocaust?* (Boulder, CO: Westview Press, 1983).

18. United States Senate, *Final Report of Select Committee to Study Governmental Operations with Respect to Intelligence Activities*, Book II (Washington, DC: U.S. Government Printing Office, 1976).

19. *Department of the Army Historical Summary, Fiscal Year 1984* (Washington, DC: U.S. Army Center of Military History).

20. The most controversial claims were made in Claire Starling, *The Terror Network: The Secret War of International Terrorism* (New York: Holt, Reinhart, and Winston, 1981). See also Jillian Becker, *The Soviet Connection: State Sponsorship of Terrorism* (London: Alliance for the Institute for European Defence and Strategic Studies), 1985. Bob Woodward, *Veil: The Secret Wars of the CIA, 1981-1987* (New York: Simon & Schuster, 1987) p. 127, concludes that Sterling's research drew heavily on CIA disinformation efforts to inflate the threat of Soviet state-sponsored terrorism. Nevertheless, in the early 1990s Russian officials, including deputy minister Sergei Shakhari and information minister Mikhail Poltoranin, suggested that there was credible archival material substantiating the role of terrorism sponsorship by the Soviet Union and its client states. Many of the relevant archives continued to be closed to Western researchers. See, for example, Mark Kramer, "Archival Research in Moscow: Progress and Pitfalls," Cold War International History Project, wwics.si.edu/index.cfm?fuseaction=library.document&topic_id=1409&id=516, and Gary Bruce, "Update on the Stasi Archives," Cold War International History Project, wwics.si.edu/index.cfm?fuseaction=library.document&topic_id=1409&id=15618.

21. Steven M. Kosiak, *Analysis of the FY 2003 Defense Budget Request* (Washington, DC: CSBA, March 2002), graph 4.

22. Richard A. Falkenrath, "The Problems of Preparedness: Challenges Facing the U.S. Domestic Preparedness Program," Executive Session on Domestic Preparedness, Discussion Paper, John F. Kennedy School of Government (2000), p. 1.

23. Presidential Decision Directive 39, U.S. Policy on Counterterrorism, June 21, 1995.

24. Laura K. Donohue, "In the Name of National Security: U.S. Counterterrorist Measures, 1960-2000," BCIA Discussion Paper 20001-6, John F. Kennedy School of Government, Harvard University, August 2001.

2

THE RISE OF MODERN TERRORISM

The Road to 9/11

*While terrorism is not new, today's terrorist threat is different from that
of the past . . . The new global environment, with its resultant terrorist
interconnectivity, and WMD are changing the nature of terrorism.*

The (U.S.) National Strategy for Combating Terrorism

CHAPTER OVERVIEW

Unprecedented in its destructiveness, the 9/11 attacks heralded the
arrival of a new type of terrorism. The potential of this menace had been
foreshadowed by several plots during the previous decade, including
the 1993 World Trade Center attack, the millennium bombing scheme
against Los Angeles, and Aum Shinrikyo's gas attack in Tokyo, as well
as the cult's intent toward the United States. While these attacks failed
to achieve their full objectives and left American complacency essen-
tially unshaken, they heralded the rise of new terrorist strategies with
global reach bent on not just influencing political events, but also inflicting death and destruction on a grand scale. This chapter describes how
international terrorism evolved and the nature of the threat faced by the
United States in the wake of the September 11 attacks.

After the 9/11 strikes, analysts recognized several characteristics of
this new threat—characteristics that differed dramatically from the
state-sponsored terrorism that had concerned the United States during the waning years of the Cold War. America now had to plan for
adversaries that could build well-funded, sophisticated, transnational organizations free from the strictures of a state sponsorship;

able to exploit conditions created by globalization and related political, social, cultural, and economic dislocation; and savvy in the twenty-first century technologies that allow terrorists to span the globe and threaten mass destruction.

Along with the devastation wreaked on life and property wrought by the September 11 attacks, came a new realization of the serious threat posed by the specter of twenty-first century terrorism.

CHAPTER LEARNING OBJECTIVES

After reading this chapter, you should be able to

1. **Identify the key characteristics of the twenty-first century terrorist organization as represented by al-Qaida.**
2. **List major elements of modern technology and commerce used by twenty-first century terrorists.**
3. **Describe the human and financial costs of the 9/11 attacks.**
4. **Discuss the implications of weapons of mass destruction (WMD) and mass casualties in twenty-first century terrorism.**

TWENTY-FIRST CENTURY TERRORISM

Postwar Japan was one of America's greatest success stories. A successful occupation after World War II led to the rise of a wealthy, democratic nation and a staunch ally for the United States. Few in the United States paid attention to an obscure Japanese religious cult led by a charismatic 40-year-old mystic named Ashara Shoko, even though he preached hatred of America and the coming end of the world. That changed on March 20, 1995, when members of Shoko's Aum Shinrikyo cult released enough sarin gas into the Tokyo subway system to kill 12 commuters and sicken 5,000. The cult failed to murder large numbers only because of the poor quality of the chemical agent employed and mistakes in its dispersal. In the wake of the attack, a crackdown by the authorities led to the arrest and conviction of Ashara and other members of the cult's leadership, as well as the breakup of their extensive financial network and weapons laboratories. The official investigation also revealed details of their activities, including discussion of chemical attacks in the United States, shattering many of the existing preconceptions concerning the nature of modern terrorism. Aum Shinrikyo was not sponsored by a state. The terrorists did not come from the tents of a third-world refugee camp, but from fine, middle-class homes. They did not have specific political aims, but a broad, global vision for the future. They understood how modern technology could serve as the means for achieving their goals. Their ways were not targeted acts of violence, but bold attempts at mass death. They were the harbingers of twenty-first century terrorism.   *precursors*

GLOBAL GOALS

Among earlier generations of terrorists, many groups pursued national goals by launching tactical operations to achieve specific objectives. For example, Palestinian terrorists of the 1960s and '70s demanded the elimination of Israel and used hostage exchanges to gain tactical advantages. Communist organizations such as the Baader-Meinhof gang, while espousing an international ideology, limited most of their actions geographically. They were focused on "liberating" their individual nations from capitalism and assisting their Palestinian allies in the fight against Israel.

In contrast, the al-Qaida organization that evolved over the course of half a decade before 9/11 reflected many of the characteristics of the contemporary global terrorist threat. Al-Qaida portrayed itself as the leader in a worldwide battle, promising to attack "infidel" governments wherever they opposed the development of Islamic theocracies. As will be seen later, the group dedicated itself to establishing a global pan-Islamic caliphate, or Muslim theocracy. Its goals included expelling U.S. influence and friendly governments from Saudi Arabia, Egypt, and other Arab states, along with destroying the state of Israel. As part of this strategy, al-Qaida sought to crush the will and capability of America and its Western allies to resist the emergence of extremist governments. Al-Qaida did not claim to represent one breakaway province, country, region, or even economic class. Instead, the group aimed its appeal at the world's more than 1 billion Muslims. While composed primarily of Sunni Muslims, al-Qaida also sought to transcend traditional religious rivalries by gaining the support of Shiite extremists from groups such as Hizballah.

While earlier groups appealed to such broad motivating forces as communism, racism, and pan-Arabism, no traditional terrorist group succeeded in creating the unifying call to arms demonstrated by al-Qaida.

A SOPHISTICATED, WORLDWIDE ORGANIZATION

Unlike many other groups whose international rhetoric far exceeded their actual membership, al-Qaida proved able to motivate a diverse constituency and mold them into an organizationally and technologically advanced force.

International Membership

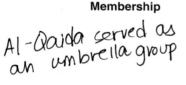
Al-Qaida served as an umbrella group

As part of its broad strategy, al-Qaida formed relationships with a variety of groups, including Egypt's Islamic Group and al-Jihad; Algeria's Armed Islamic Group; Pakistan's Harakat ul-Mujahidin; the Islamic Movement of Uzbekistan; Philippine's Abu Sayyaf; and other groups in nations such as Saudi Arabia, Yemen, and Bangladesh. In effect, al-Qaida served as an umbrella group or "organization of organizations" with affiliated operations in more than 60 countries.[1]

The 9/11 hijackers themselves came from Saudi Arabia, the United Arab Emirates (UAE), Lebanon, and Egypt. Plotters connected to the operation included French, German, Kuwaiti, and Yemeni citizens. Other al-Qaida operations have been linked to citizens or groups from the United States, the Sudan, Somalia, Eritrea, Kenya, Pakistan, Bosnia, Croatia, Algeria, Tunisia, Lebanon, the Philippines, Tajikistan, Turkey, Chechnya, Bangladesh, Kashmir, Azerbaijan, and Indonesia, among others. At one point, the U.S. prison at Guantanamo Bay, Cuba, held prisoners linked to al-Qaida from 38 countries.[2] The movement succeeded in uniting individuals from vastly different backgrounds, including citizens of states hostile to one another.

Large Cadre

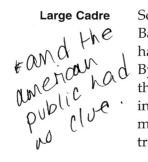

and the american public had no clue.

Some of the most infamous modern terrorist groups, such as the Baader Meinhoff gang and Italian Red Brigades, numbered their hard-core operatives in the dozens and supporters in the hundreds. By some estimates, even the Irish Republican Army fielded fewer than 500 gunmen at its peak. Al-Qaida trained up to 20,000 personnel in its Afghan camps between 1996 and 2001.[3] Its hard-core operatives most likely numbered in the hundreds on 9/11, with thousands of trained supporters spread across the globe.

Decentralized Structure

Al-Qaida decision-making structures were highly developed, as was the organization's tactical execution. The group's decentralized, "flat" administration gave it the capability of planning and executing complex operations despite resistance and setbacks. This sort of networked organization, composed largely of autonomous cells, made the organization resistant to "decapitation" by targeted strikes on its leadership. Al-Qaida leadership could prompt terrorist violence through several types of organizational systems, including centrally controlled operations such as 9/11; al-Qaida supported and/or financed operations carried out by affiliate groups; and "spontaneous" action by small groups or individuals inspired by the cause and often trained at al-Qaida facilities. The last two strategies dramatically increased the number and type of potential attackers, posing special difficulties for counterterrorism officials.

Use of Modern Technology and Exploitation of Social Trends

Much as modern multinational corporations dispersed decision making through the use of technology, al-Qaida exploited emerging trends and tools. The end of the Cold War dramatically increased the ease of international communication, commerce, and travel. As the twenty-first century began, more than 140 million people lived outside their country of origins; millions of people crossed international borders every day.[4] Among them were numerous al-Qaida supporters, conversant in the languages and cloaked in the citizenships of the very societies they hated.

Moving freely through this ever more open and integrated international structure, al-Qaida operatives maintained communication via new technologies such as cell and satellite phones, encrypted e-mail, chat rooms, videotape, and CD-ROMs.[5] This allowed them to disperse their leadership, training, and logistics not just across a region, but around the globe. Operating from safety in Afghanistan, the group's leaders were able to support operations in dozens of nations.

Funded through Sophisticated and Multiple Channels

Al-Qaida established an international network of businesses, criminal enterprises, and charities to support its operations. From heroin smuggling to leather tanning, al-Qaida ventures generated significant revenue and supported an estimated $30 million annual budget which was distributed via formal and informal transfer systems.[6]

Not Reliant on State Sponsors

While al-Qaida prospered during in its Sudanese and Afghan sanctuaries, it was not dependent on those states in the same manner as many terrorist groups during the 1970s and '80s. Indeed, the Taliban government of Afghanistan relied on al-Qaida for capital and military power, discouraging it from cracking down on the group as demanded by the United States. It has been said the Taliban government was in some ways a "terrorist-sponsored state."

Al-Qaida and other groups also sought out operational bases in other countries in the Americas, Africa, Asia, the Middle East, and Europe. In some cases, these countries could not stop them because of weak central governments or war. In others, such as Europe and even the United States, lax security measures and respect for civil liberties combined to provide the terrorists with operational latitude.

*lax security measures and respect for civil liberties

Sophisticated Planning

Whether concocted in Sudanese safe houses, Afghan training camps, or even American apartment buildings, al-Qaida operations have been marked by careful and expert planning and execution. In addition, these terrorists not only understood the culture of their enemies, but were able to employ America's technology against itself.

Al-Qaida attacks have involved years of planning. The 1998 bombings of U.S. embassies in Africa were being plotted as early as 1993.[7] The 9/11 attacks began taking shape in the mid-1990s. At heart, the plot reflected a disturbing ingenuity, sharply contrasting with the standard terrorist tactics of earlier decades. The ability of the group to envision and plan the details of such an intricate operation, with its extensive recruiting and operational support requirements, demonstrated a new level of terrorist capability.

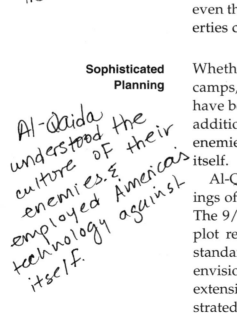
Al-Qaida understood the culture of their enemies & employed America's technology against itself.

THE LAX BOMBER—THE SHAPE OF THINGS TO COME?

On a chilly December afternoon shortly before the year 2000 millennium celebrations, a green Chrysler sedan rolled off the ferry sailing from Canada's Vancouver Island to Port Angeles, Washington, in the United States. When the customs agent Diana Dean handed the driver a customs declaration form, she noticed the driver seemed nervous and fidgety.

Text of Interview by Customs Inspector Diana Dean

"Where are you going?"
"Sattal."
"Why are you going to Seattle?"
"Visit."
"Where do you live?"
"Montreal."
"Who are you going to see in Seattle?"
"No, hotel."

After further questioning, the car was searched; its trunk was packed with about 40 kilograms of explosives and detonators. The name on the driver's license was Benni Antoine Noris, but his real name was Ahmed Ressam a young, middle-class Algerian with a passion for soccer and experience in Afghan terrorist camps. Ressam confessed to U.S. authorities that the explosives were for a terrorist operation against Los Angeles International Airport (LAX), an operation he had been planning in Canada for several months. He said he chose LAX "because an airport is sensitive politically and economically" and the United States was "the biggest enemy" of Islam. Ressam said he had conceived the idea himself, and that while al-Qaida knew about the plot and supplied some support, it was his operation. Little more than $3,000 Canadian dollars and a fake driver's license had been required to prepare his attack.

While an alert customs agent foiled the millennium bomb plot, all the elements required to replicate this form of attack are achievable by any individual or terrorist group.

1. Does the LAX bomber fit the profile of twenty-first century terrorism?
2. How were the LAX bomber operations different from the 9/11 attacks? How were the operations similar?
3. Will future attacks be more like that of the LAX bomber or the 9/11 hijackers?
4. What lessons should have been drawn from the millenium bomb plot?

Strategic Goals

While obscure to many Westerners, al-Qaida's strategy was based upon a complex historical, cultural, geopolitical, and religious framework. Strongly influenced by the successful battle against the Soviet occupation of Afghanistan; al-Qaida strategy depicted the United States as a weaker adversary than the ruthless Soviet Union. Bin Ladin himself described the strategic results of the 9/11 attacks as demoralizing the United States, causing the U.S. government to restrict civil liberties, and—perhaps most importantly—galvanizing Muslims around the world and forcing them to choose sides. "Our goal is for our (world Islamic) nation to unite in the face of the Christian crusade," bin Ladin said after the attacks.[8]

Tight Operational Security

Contrary to some claims, the infiltration of the 9/11 hijackers into the United States and their operations in America were not perfect. For example, most of the conspirators made obvious errors in their visa applications and once in America some of them associated with individuals under scrutiny by the FBI. But in general the plot reflected strong security and no doubt factored in the U.S. government's limited domestic intelligence capabilities.

9/11 terrorists

Most of the hijackers did not have terrorist records, helping them escape the attention of U.S. intelligence.[9] Fifteen of the men were from Saudi Arabia, whose citizens faced relatively little scrutiny from the U.S. visa officials. They got passports and visas under their real names, and then entered the United States from different locations at different times. In accordance with the al-Qaida manual, the men shunned the facial hair and garb of traditional Muslims. They were familiar with Western culture and able to navigate American society. They clearly attempted to keep a low profile, shopping at Wal-Mart and eating at places such as Pizza Hut. According to the CIA, the hijackers avoided laptops in favor of public Internet connections and used at least 133 different prepaid calling cards on a variety of phones.

Based on statements by bin Ladin and other information, while the hijackers knew they were participating in a "martyrdom"—or suicide—operation, many did not know details of the mission or its targets until it was well under way.[10] In the vocabulary of intelligence, the plot was "tightly compartmented" and difficult to penetrate.

Effective Execution

Al-Qaida also proved skilled at managing operations. When Flight 77 hijackers Nawaf al-Hazmi and Khalid al-Mihdhar proved to be terrible flight students, Hani Hanjur arrived back in the United States. Suspected plotters Ramzi bin al-Shibh and Zakaria Essabar couldn't get into the United States, but the plot went on. Muhammad Atta, who piloted the first plane into the World Trade Center, had visa problems when trying to reenter the United States in January 2001 and was caught driving without a license, but managed to avoid drawing the attention of authorities. Other hijackers escaped detection during traffic stops. Even when Zacarias Moussaoui was arrested in August 2001 by FBI agents who considered him a possible suicide hijacker, the plan was not derailed. Days after the arrest, the plotters began buying their tickets. And on the morning of 9/11, many of their plotters and their weapons made it through last-minute security screenings. The ability of the terrorists to seize four aircraft and successfully guide three of them into their targets reflected superb planning, significant skill, and superior tactical execution.

EFFECTS OF TWENTY-FIRST CENTURY TERRORISM

The 2001 attacks certainly qualify as one of the worst crimes in human history. Even considered in military terms, the human and financial destruction of 9/11 mark them as among the world's most devastating attacks. While other uses of force have claimed more lives, few have combined such terrible human losses with the massive economic damage of 9/11, impacts that were magnified by the anthrax attacks that occurred later in 2001.

Human Costs

The human cost of 9/11 can be measured in both physical and psychological terms. By either calculation, the attacks exacted a terrible price on the United States.

Life and Limb

Nearly 3,000 people were killed by the attack, many dying after excruciating physical and psychological ordeals. For those without personal connection to these losses, the scope of the suffering can only be grasped fleetingly, perhaps in the awful images of people choosing to leap hundreds of feet to their deaths from the World Trade Center rather than face the conflagration, or the haunting final phone calls from passengers on the hijacked aircraft. The physical pain of 9/11 will continue for decades among those hurt in the attacks. An untold number of victims, estimated in the thousands, suffered injuries that day and in the ensuing rescue and cleanup operations, some sustaining burns or other wounds that damaged them for life. In a reflection of the same trends exploited by the terrorists, many of those harmed on 9/11 were born abroad; the attack killed people from some 80 nations, including a significant number from predominantly Muslim countries.[11]

Psychological

As discussed earlier, terrorism involves attacks on one set of victims to instill fear in another. Judged this way, the 9/11 attacks set a terrible new standard. Up to 10 million U.S. adults knew someone who had been killed or injured in the attacks. Almost every American, and vast numbers of other people around the globe, experienced the attacks through a suffocating flow of media reports. Research indicated that many millions of Americans outside New York City and Washington, DC, experienced negative psychological symptoms such as nightmares, flashbacks, and other anxiety symptoms linked to posttraumatic stress disorder (PTSD) from September 11.[12] A study showing increased use of cigarettes, alcohol, and marijuana by Manhattan residents after 9/11 raised concerns about yet another type of damage to public health from the attack.[13]

The September 11 Fund, a charity, reported providing cash and services to 100,000 victims, including relatives of those killed, people wounded in the attack, and those who lost employment or housing because of 9/11. By one estimate, 6,000 New Yorkers were displaced from their residences in lower Manhattan. While most were able to return home in the weeks after the attacks, their neighborhood had been transformed from a bustling economic center to a devastated graveyard smothered in the acrid dust of crushed concrete and incinerated human remains.

Financial   The 9/11 attacks were intended to damage America's government, military, and economy. They achieved their greatest success with the last. "Those that were there (in the World Trade Center) are men that supported the biggest economic power in the world," said bin Ladin after the attacks.[14] He later exhorted his followers: "Never be afraid of their (the U.S.) multitudes, for their hearts are empty while their strength has begun to weaken—militarily and economically. This was particularly true after the blessed day of New York, by the grace of Allah, when their losses reached more than one trillion dollars, following the attack and its aftermath . . . Praise be to Allah."[15] Bin Ladin grossly exaggerated the impact of his work. But while the economic damage caused by 9/11 was not enough to cause fundamental harm to the U.S. economy, it did significant financial injury to many locations, sectors, corporations, and individuals.

Short-Term Costs

The most obvious financial costs of the attacks were in the people killed and injured and the buildings, infrastructure, airplanes, and other assets destroyed and damaged on 9/11. Those costs have been estimated at $25 to $60 billion in life and property losses, with immediate insurance costs in the $36 billion to $54 billion range.[16] These immediate, direct losses combined with short-term lost economic output and other damage in the hours and days after the attack. Economic aftershocks rippled through the economy as buildings were evacuated, flights were cancelled, and stock trading halted.

Consumers reduced their spending, and investors decreased their tolerance for risk. Companies in the airline, aerospace, travel, tourism, insurance, lodging, restaurant, and recreation sectors reported drops in demand. During 2001 and 2002, more than 145,000 workers in 34 states lost their jobs for reasons directly or indirectly linked to 9/11, according to a report by the U.S. Bureau of Labor Statistics. Many were from the airline and hotel industries. Because the report counted only certain types of layoffs, the actual number of job losses was almost certainly higher.[17]

Long-Term Costs and the "Terrorism Tax"

The long-term costs of the attack include everything from the impact of loans granted to airlines by the U.S. government to the so-called terrorism tax, which describes increased costs for security. These expenditures include government spending on increased national defense, new homeland security programs, corporate security expenses, travel delays, higher insurance costs, increased red tape, higher shipping costs, increased expenses from immigration restrictions, slower mail, disaster planning, and backup sites for business and government organizations. For example, additional airline security has cost $11 billion by one estimate.[18]

Other costs, while harder to calculate, are clearly significant—a group of U.S. business organizations estimated that problems with the visa system for foreign business travelers coming to the United States cost more than $30 billion from 2002 to 2004 in lost sales, extra expenses, relocation costs, and other losses.[19] The total terrorism tax is certainly many billions of dollars a year on an ongoing basis. Economists assume that such spending diverts investment from more financially productive areas, depressing growth. On the other hand, it can also be argued that good counterterrorism measures can promote growth, protecting activities from disruptions and instilling consumer and customer confidence. Additionally, some security measures may have economic benefits such as improving the efficiency and management of supply chains. In short, while there is a general consensus that security has a significant influence on the economy, the long-term positive and negative impacts of the terrorist tax remain to be seen.

The impact of the 9/11 attacks on the U.S. economy are a case in point. While estimates vary widely, in total the economy of New York

City alone lost $83 billion due to the attacks, while total damage to the United States easily exceeded $100 billion.[20] Strictly speaking, and as evaluated by such measures as percentage of gross domestic product, this loss did not produce a fundamental impact on the U.S. economy, which began recovering from a recession not long after the attacks. However, it did create a substantial hardship for many Americans.

HIGHLY EFFICIENT ATTACK

In the terrible calculus of combat, opponents must weigh the costs of their campaigns against the damage they will inflict on the enemy. Viewed in this way, al-Qaida proved highly efficient, at least when considered solely in relation to the direct impact of 9/11 on the attackers and victims. Al-Qaida's direct expenditures on the 9/11 attacks were between $400,000 to $500,000.[21] For that amount, plus the loss of 19 trained operatives, the terrorists killed some 3,000 Americans and caused more than $100 billion in economic damages.

THREAT OF WEAPONS OF MASS DESTRUCTION

Perhaps the most fundamental lesson of 9/11 was that America's enemies had both the motive and means to cause mass casualties in the United States. While this seems obvious in retrospect, preventing such an attack was never a driving priority of the U.S. government prior to 2001.

While the 9/11 attacks involved the instruments of the everyday world, the interest of terrorists in wrecking widespread havoc prompted greater concerns over the potential use of weapons of mass destruction (WMD). These are nuclear, chemical, biological, radiological, and highly explosive weapons capable of inflicting mass casualties and destruction.

Certainly al-Qaida leaders have not hidden their desire to obtain nuclear, biological, or chemical weapons. "Acquiring weapons for the defense of Muslims is a religious duty," according to Usama bin Ladin. "If I have indeed acquired these weapons, then I thank God for enabling me to do so. And if I seek to acquire these weapons, I am carrying out a duty. It would be a sin for Muslims not to try to possess the weapons that would prevent the infidels from inflicting harm on Muslims."[22]

FROM THE SOURCE:

THE ANTHRAX LETTERS—A SIGN OF THE TIMES?

A week after the airplane strikes of 9/11, another threat few expected shocked Americans. Letters containing anthrax bacteria were mailed from Trenton, New Jersey, to the offices of NBC and The Post in New York City, and probably the National Enquirer in Miami, Florida, on September 18, 2001. On October 9, 2001, letters were mailed to Senate offices in Washington, DC. In addition to people being exposed where the letters were opened, postal workers in Trenton and Washington, as well as a woman in Connecticut, contracted inhalation anthrax from spores that leaked from the letters.

Text of Letter Sent to Senator Tom Daschle on October 9, 2001

> 09-11-01
> YOU CAN NOT STOP US.
> WE HAVE THIS ANTHRAX.
> YOU DIE NOW.
> ARE YOU AFRAID?
> DEATH TO AMERICA.
> DEATH TO ISRAEL.
> ALLAH IS GREAT.

Overall, infections from the anthrax letters killed 5 and sickened 13 others and focused attention on a class of weapons that represent a dangerous and growing threat.

While the letters caused death and injury to only a handful of Americans, they disrupted the lives of millions. Perhaps more troubling than the attacks themselves were the miscues, faulty assumptions, poorly coordinated response, and media frenzy following in their wake, as well as a halting law enforcement investigation that three years after the act had still failed to identify the culprit behind the anthrax letters. The attack served as an object lesson in why mass destruction may have a strong appeal to the practitioners of twenty-first century terrorism.

In part, U.S. policy had accounted for these threats by focusing on preventing the spread of WMD. But just as global trends had facilitated the 9/11 attack, they also increased the risk that terrorists could acquire WMD. Among other factors were an increased availability of critical technologies and experts; the greater ease of international transportation; and the spread of knowledge through the Internet and other media. Ironically, U.S. assistance to Pakistan and the Mujahadeen during the Soviet occupation of Afghanistan, and the Soviet collapse that was hastened by that assistance, may have indirectly facilitated the flow of WMD technology and expertise. Scientists and stockpiles from the former Soviet Union were opened to exploitation. At the same time Pakistan was cooperating with the United States against the Soviets, its experts were developing and proliferating nuclear technology. By 2003, the U.S. government warned: "Presently, al Qa'ida and associated groups possess at least a crude capability to use chemical, biological, and radiological agents and devices in their attacks."[23]

CHAPTER SUMMARY

The 9/11 attacks revealed a fundamental truth to America. No longer could reasonable people deny the need to prepare for enemies—whether al-Qaida and other large terrorist organizations, or smaller groups and individuals—capable of devising and executing sophisticated strategies to unleash weapons of mass destruction against the U.S. homeland. As horrendous as 9/11's destruction proved, it was clear that an even more devastating attack was possible in the future. This finally provided the stimulus to overhaul America's homeland security policies, prompting far more aggressive measures to protect its citizens and allies. Literally within hours of the attack, American policy makers began planning sweeping reforms, major investments, and global operations. The private sector and citizenry also began to change their behaviors. The results would produce fundamental changes at all levels of American society.

CHAPTER QUIZ

1. What are three characteristics of al-Qaida's twenty-first century terrorist organization? Why are they significant?

2. Identify two types of modern technology used by twenty-first century terrorists. Explain why they might be important terrorist tools.

3. What were the consequences of the 9/11 attack?

4. Why might terrorists be more likely to employ weapons of mass destruction in the future?

NOTES

1. *The National Strategy for Combating Terrorism* (February 2003), p. 7.

2. John C. K. Daly, "Revealed Nationalities of Guantanamo," UPI (February 4, 2004), www.upi.com/print.cfm?StoryID=20040204-051623-5923.

3. The National Commission on Terrorist Attacks upon the United States, "Overview of the Enemy, Staff Statement No. 15," p. 10, www.9-11commission.gov/hearings/hearing12/staff_statement_15.pdf.

4. *The National Strategy for Combating Terrorism*, p. 8.

5. Gabriel Weimann, "WWWTerror.Net: How Terrorists Use the Internet," Special Report Number 16, U.S. Institute of Peace, www.usip.org/pubs/specialreports/sr116.html.

6. Budget estimated by the CIA as reported in "Overview of the Enemy, Staff Statement No. 15", p. 11.

7. Ibid, p. 8.

8. CNN.Com, "Transcript of Bin Laden Interview" (February 5, 2002), www.cnn.com/2002/WORLD/asiapcf/south/02/05/binladen.transcript/index.html.

9. Testimony of George J. Tenet before the Joint Congressional Inquiry into Terrorist Attacks against the United States (June 18, 2002), 9-11congress.netfirms.com/Tenet_June.html.

10. Department of Defense, "UBL Transcript" (December 13, 2001), www.defenselink.mil/news/Dec2001/d20011213ubl.pdf.

11. George Bush, "Address to a Joint Session of Congress" (September 20, 2001), www.white-house.gov/news/releases/2001/09/20010920-8.html.

12. William E. Schlenger, et al., "Psychological Reactions to Terrorist Attacks: Findings from the National Study of Americans' Reactions to September 11," *Journal of the American Medical Association* (August 2002): 581–588.

13. David Vlahov, et al., "Sustained Increased Consumption of Cigarettes, Alcohol, and Marijuana among Manhattan Residents after September 11, 2001," *American Journal of Public Health,* 94/2 (February 2004): 253–254.

14. CNN.Com, "Transcript of Bin Laden's October Interview" (February 5, 2002), www.cnn.com/2002/WORLD/asiapcf/south/02/05/binladen.transcript/index.html.

15. Aljazeera.Com, "Message to Iraqis" (October 2003), english.aljazeera.net/NR/exeres/ACB47241-D25F-46CB-B673-56FAB1C2837F.htm.

16. General Accounting Office, "Review of Studies of the Economic Impact of the September 11, 2001, Terrorist Attacks on the World Trade Center" (May 29, 2002), www.bls.gov/opub/ted/2003/sept/wk2/art03.htm.

17. Department of Labor, "Extended Mass Layoffs and the 9/11 Attacks" (September 10, 2003), www.bls.gov/opub/ted/2003/sept/wk2/art03.htm.

18. Gregg Easterbrook, "Fear Factor in an Age of Terror," *New York Times* (June 27, 2004): A1, www.nytimes.com/2004/06/27/weekinreview/27east.html.

19. National Foreign Trade Council, "Visa Backlog Costs U.S. Exporters More Than $30 Billion Since 2002, New Study Finds" (June 6, 2004), www.nftc.org.

20. Estimates of the damages wrought by the 9/11 attack vary depending on the criteria used. The Insurance Information Institute set the initial cost at $40 billion [Insurance Information Institute, *Catastrophes:Insurance Issues,* Part 1 of 2 (January 9, 2002). A study by the Federal Reserve Bank of New York put the cost at $33 to $36 billion. The Federal Reserve Bank's estimate included only immediate earning losses, property damage, and cleanup and restoration costs through June 2002 and did not cover long-term productivity and tax revenue losses [Jason Bram, et al., "Measuring the Effects of the September 11 Attack on New York City," *FRBNY Economic Policy Review,* 8/2 (November 2002): 5]. The City of New York Comptroller set the total economic impact on the city at between $82.8 and $94 billion [Comptroller, City of New York, *One Year Later: The Fiscal Impact of 9/11 on New York City* (New York: City of New York, September 4, 2002), p. 1]. The U.S. General Accounting Office reported that it believed the most accurate assessment places the total direct and indirect costs at $83 billion [U.S. General Accounting Office, Impact of Terrorist Attacks on the World Trade Center, GAO-02-7000R (May 29, 2002), p. 2]. In addition, Wilbur Smith Associates estimated the long-term costs of the 9/11 attacks resulting from reduced commercial aviation range from $68.3 to $90.2 billion [Wilbur Smith Associates, "The Economic Impact of Civil Aviation on the U.S. Economy—Update 2000," (2002)].

21. The National Commission on Terrorist Attacks upon the United States, "Outline of the 9/11 Plot, Staff Statement No. 16," p. 11, www.9-11commission.gov/hearings/hearing12/staff_statement_16.pdf.

22. Declan McCullagh, "Does Osama Have a Nuclear Bomb?" *Wired News* (September 28, 2001): 1, www.wired.com/news/conflict/0,2100,47158,00.html.

23. National Infrastructure Protection Center, "Homeland Security Information Update: Al Qa'ida Chemical, Biological, Radiological, and Nuclear Threat and Basic Countermeasures" (February 12, 2003), www.nipc.gov/publications/infobulletins/2003/ib03-003.htm.

3

THE BIRTH OF MODERN HOMELAND SECURITY

The National Response to the 9/11 Attacks

America is no longer protected by vast oceans. We are protected from attack only by vigorous action abroad, and increased vigilance at home.

President George W. Bush, Jan. 29, 2002

CHAPTER OVERVIEW

Every sector of American society was changed by the 9/11 attacks on the United States and the offensive and defensive U.S. government strategies created to meet future threats. Many of the initiatives, in both the public and private sectors, challenged traditional approaches taken by the United States to ensure domestic security. These changes featured aggressive new U.S. foreign and military policies and efforts to cooperate with other countries in the war on terror. On the home front, they included reforming the intelligence community, refocusing the FBI and other federal agencies, enacting sweeping legislation to strengthen law enforcement, and concluding the most far-reaching reorganization of the federal government in more than 50 years. These vast changes also extended to state and local governments and the private sector. In the end, the changes driven by 9/11 have provided the foundation for a modern system of homeland security.

CHAPTER LEARNING OBJECTIVES

1. Describe the Bush Doctrine and its implications for U.S. foreign policy.

2. Explain how the federal government was reorganized to focus on homeland security.

3. Describe the major tenets of the national homeland security strategy.

4. Define the changes in the U.S. approach to domestic counter-terrorism after 9/11.

5. Identify the major homeland security challenges faced by state and local governments and the private sector.

THE RESPONSE TO TWENTY-FIRST CENTURY TERRORISM

As exhausted rescue workers dug through the smoking remains of the World Trade Center and a large American flag billowed over the hole torn in the Pentagon's side, the Bush administration mapped out its response to twenty-first century terrorism.[1] Some of the early steps were defensive: continuing the grounding of civilian aircraft; closing key government offices and monuments; providing fighter jet cover over major cities; and launching a dragnet for "special interest" aliens and others suspected of terrorist links. But the first major strategic change centered on taking the battle to the enemy by invading Afghanistan and crippling foreign terrorist organizations with international ties.

TAKING THE OFFENSIVE

The president announced an unprecedented offensive against global terrorism in a speech to Congress on September 20, 2001. The speech singled out three global threats that required a concerted response: terrorist organizations with global reach, weak states that harbored transnational terrorist groups, and "rogue" states that

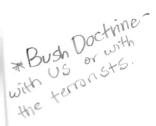

*Bush Doctrine — with US or with the terrorists.

might aid terrorists or undertake terrorist acts themselves. During the speech, President George W. Bush declared, "Every nation in every region now has a decision to make. Either you are with us, or you are with the terrorists." In his speech the president added that, "From this day forward, any nation that continues to harbor or support terrorism will be regarded by the United States as a hostile regime." The declarations in this speech are commonly referred to as the Bush Doctrine.[2]

Preemption

The avowal that nations supporting terrorism were to be considered hostile regimes was significant in light of the U.S. *National Security Strategy* published by the administration the following September. The strategy is a document required by law that outlines the overall ends, ways, and means of ensuring national security. The 2002 strategy reaffirmed the nation's right of preemption, which allows countries to defend themselves against an imminent threat before they are attacked. The strategy broadly interpreted the United States' right to forestall or prevent terrorist acts, particularly where the threat of weapons of mass destruction might be involved.[3]

Opposition to the Bush Doctrine

The Bush Doctrine proved highly controversial, particularly as its tenets were put into practice. There were two main objections to declaring war on terrorism. First, as discussed earlier, there is no universal definition of terrorism, and thus no clear enemy. Second, combating terrorists, whoever they are, is not primarily a military operation, but a matter of law enforcement and social, cultural, and economic conflict. It is not "traditional" war, as one U.S. defense analyst declared, in the sense understood by military professionals. Wars, he argues, are supposed to have "clear beginnings and ends . . . [and] clear standards for measuring success in the form of territory gained and enemy forces destroyed."[4] In short, critics of the Bush Doctrine declared the global war on terrorism was inappropriate because its goals were open-ended, unbounded, and unlikely to achieve decisive results. At the same time, they suggested many around the world would interpret U.S. efforts as "empire building," efforts to expand American power rather than enhance global security.

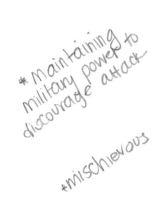

advocate

Maintaining military power to discourage attack

mischievous

Support for the Bush Doctrine

In contrast, proponents of the president's strategy concluded the United States had few practical alternatives. U.S. counterterrorism efforts had been insufficient to stem the growth of transnational terrorist networks and al-Qaida had publicly committed itself to the destruction of the United States.[5] In addition, they argued the means used to defend the nation during the Cold War would be inadequate to deal with the security threats of the twenty-first century. Cold War strategy relied on deterrence (the threat of nuclear war) and containment, the use of military, political, diplomatic, and economic power to limit the spread of communism. It would be difficult to apply deterrence and containment as practiced against the Soviet Union to disparate transnational groups and determined rogue states.[6] The only solution was to go after the terrorists, while remaining prepared to thwart or respond to the attack that would inevitably ensue. This included plans to eliminate the political breeding grounds of terrorists in the Middle East, which President Bush later called the "forward strategy of freedom," a doctrine that would grow to include the liberation of Iraq.

On October 7, 2001, following repeated refusals by the Taliban rulers of Afghanistan to expel bin Ladin, the United States and an antiterrorist coalition of countries began military operations to root out both the Taliban and al-Qaida. Under attack by U.S. airpower and anti-Taliban ground forces, organized opposition disintegrated rapidly, and Kabul, the Afghan capital, fell on November 13, 2001. Many key senior Taliban and al-Qaida leaders, including bin Ladin, escaped capture. Forces from the new Afghanistan government, as well as the U.S. military, and troops in neighboring Pakistan continue to pursue elements of the Taliban and al-Qaida in the region.[7]

ISSUE:

THE BUSH ADMINISTRATION ON PREEMPTION

Excerpt from the 2002 National Security Strategy

While the right of preemption is well-established in international law, the United States has never included a statement in its national security strategy that explicitly addressed the issue before the 9/11 attacks. The 2002 *National Security Strategy*, released in the wake of September 11, contained explicit language on the subject.

> For centuries, international law recognized that nations need not suffer an attack before they can lawfully take action to defend themselves against forces that present an imminent danger of attack. Legal scholars and international jurists often conditioned the legitimacy of preemption on the existence of an imminent threat—most often a visible mobilization of armies, navies, and air forces preparing to attack.
>
> We must adapt the concept of imminent threat to the capabilities and objectives of today's adversaries. Rogue states and terrorists do not seek to attack us using conventional means. They know such attacks would fail. Instead, they rely on acts of terror and, potentially, the use of weapons of mass destruction—weapons that can be easily concealed, delivered covertly, and used without warning.
>
> The targets of these attacks are our military forces and our civilian population, in direct violation of one of the principal norms of the law of warfare. As was demonstrated by the losses on September 11, 2001, mass civilian casualties is the specific objective of terrorists and these losses would be exponentially more severe if terrorists acquired and used weapons of mass destruction.
>
> The United States has long maintained the option of preemptive actions to counter a sufficient threat to our national security. The greater the threat, the greater is the risk of inaction—and the more compelling the case for taking anticipatory action to defend ourselves, even if uncertainty remains as to the time and place of the enemy's attack. To forestall or prevent such hostile acts by our adversaries, the United States will, if necessary, act preemptively.
>
> The United States will not use force in all cases to preempt emerging threats, nor should nations use preemption as a pretext for aggression. Yet in an age where the enemies

of civilization openly and actively seek the world's most destructive technologies, the United States cannot remain idle while dangers gather. We will always proceed deliberately, weighing the consequences of our actions. To support preemptive options, we will:

- build better, more integrated intelligence capabilities to provide timely, accurate information on threats, wherever they may emerge;
- coordinate closely with allies to form a common assessment of the most dangerous threats; and
- continue to transform our military forces to ensure our ability to conduct rapid and precise operations to achieve decisive results.

The purpose of our actions will always be to eliminate a specific threat to the United States or our allies and friends. The reasons for our actions will be clear, the force measured, and the cause just.

1. What are the grounds for preemptive action, and what are the limitations in practicing preemption?
2. Is the concept of preemption expressed in the strategy consistent with how the United States has used force in the past, or is this something new?
3. How do allies and enemies interpret the preemption declaration?
4. Does preemption increase national and homeland security?

INTERNATIONAL COOPERATION

While U.S. military power proved instrumental in dismantling terrorist sanctuaries, American combat operations alone were insufficient to take the offensive in the war on terror. The United States also required international cooperation both to pursue terrorists and enhance homeland security. Effective cooperation also had to expand beyond military means, including areas such as covert operations, intelligence sharing, law enforcement, and trade and travel security. After 9/11, over 100 nations offered the United States some form of assistance or support, perhaps most prominently America's traditional military ally Great Britain. The United States discovered that in the war against global terrorism a class of states that could be termed the "new allies" was also vital. These were states that had ambivalent relations with the United States in the past, but now found themselves in a situation where their internal security concerns and regional objectives coincided with U.S. interests in pursuing global terrorism. They provided basing and overflight rights, intelligence sharing, and counterterrorism support for attacking al-Qaida sanctuaries overseas. In Asia, the rapidly expanding joint effort by the United States and Kazakhstan offered one example of a new alliance at work.[8]

*new alliances are formed

Support also came from organizations such as the North Atlantic Treaty Organization (NATO), originally formed to defend the West against the Soviet Union, and America's only multinational military alliance of major consequence. After the attacks of September 11, the Alliance invoked Article 5 of its charter (the provision for collective self-defense) for the first time in its history. This was a powerful statement of solidarity and a positive sign for future cooperation. NATO also provided assistance in postwar Afghanistan. On September 28, 2001, the United Nations Security Council adopted Resolution 1373 which called for criminalizing terrorist activities, denying funds and safe havens, and establishing a committee to monitor implementation.[9] Other international organizations also had a part to play, including the European Union (EU), Organization for Security and Cooperation in Europe (as the only pan-European body), the Association of Southeast Asian Nations, and the Asia Pacific Economic Cooperation Forum. The United States and the EU, for example, enacted new joint measures to freeze terrorist assets and share intelligence. Additionally, a long list of organizations, such as Interpol, contributed to combating transnational threats. Nongovernmental organizations (NGOs) also assumed important functions in homeland security and counterterrorism. For example, after 9/11 the International Maritime Organization set stricter standards for the security of ports and international shipping. Nevertheless, harmonizing the efforts of these organizations with U.S. security remained a complicated process. In some cases, NGO activities actually proved detrimental and were even accused of being fronts for transnational crime and terrorist activities. The charitable group, the Holy Land Foundation, for example, is alleged to have funneled over $150 million to the terrorist group Hamas.

Cooperation between the United States and other countries, multinational organizations, and nongovernment groups took many forms, from public diplomacy to covert operations. One important avenue of international cooperation was a crackdown on monetary instruments used to finance terrorist attacks, such as the hawala, a short-term, discountable, negotiable promissory note or bill of exchange used widely in the Islamic world. While not limited to Muslim countries, the hawala has come to be identified with Islamic banking. It was alleged that billions of dollars were transferred through these exchanges and that some hawala dealers had ties to terrorists.[10] After 9/11, a concerted effort to combat money laundering, including the use of the hawala, was directed at terrorist financial networks. In the year after 9/11, the White House reported that $113.5 million in terrorist assets had been frozen worldwide: $35.3 million in the United States and $78.2 million overseas.[11]

DEFENSIVE EFFORTS

On the home front, the Bush administration set out to enhance interagency and intergovernmental cooperation, which had been lacking prior to 9/11. These goals were pursued by new legal initiatives; creation of the White House Office of Homeland Security; the drafting of a national homeland security strategy; plans to create a separate regional military command for the defense of North America; and a proposal for a federal Homeland Security Department. Improving airline safety and heightening security awareness for other critical infrastructure systems were also focal points. For example, the government recruited, trained, and deployed 45,000 federal security screeners to airports across the nation. At the same time, the anthrax attacks of fall 2001 galvanized support for increased defensive measures against WMD.

The PATRIOT Act and Other Congressional Initiatives

In response to the September 11 attack, Congress passed a number of significant pieces of legislation. The Aviation and Transportation Security Act established a federal agency to supervise security of commercial aviation. The Maritime Transportation Security Act generated new requirements for the security of ports and shipping. The Enhanced Border Security and Visa Entry Reform Act significantly expanded the information to be collected on visitors to the United States. The Public Health Security and Bioterrorism Preparedness and Response Act mandated additional measures for protecting the food and drug supply.

Perhaps the most significant and controversial of the new laws passed by Congress was the Uniting and Strengthening America by Providing Appropriate Tools Required to Intercept and Obstruct Terrorism (USA PATRIOT) Act. The Act created new crimes, new penalties, and new procedural efficiencies for use against domestic and international terrorists. Although it was not without safeguards, critics contended some of its provisions went too far. Although it granted many of the enhancements sought by the Department of Justice, others are concerned that it did not go far enough.

The PATRIOT Act did serve to improve U.S. counterterrorism in four critical areas. First, it promoted the sharing of information between intelligence and law enforcement investigations—tearing down the "wall" that hampered investigations before 9/11. Second, the Act authorized additional law enforcement tools for pursuing terrorists, tools that were already available for investigating other serious crimes, such as drug smuggling. Third, it facilitated surveillance of terrorists using new technologies like cell phones and the Internet. Fourth, the Act provided for judicial and congressional oversight of the new authorities granted in the legislation.[12]

Reorganization in the White House

One of the first initiatives in the executive branch was the establishment of an Office of Homeland Security within the Executive Office of the President in October 2001. Headed by the Assistant to the President for Homeland Security, former Pennsylvania Governor Tom Ridge, the mission of the office was to develop and coordinate the implementation of a comprehensive national homeland security

FROM THE SOURCE:

EXCERPT FROM THE USA PATRIOT ACT

The USA PATRIOT Act contains over 800 sections, many of which are not controversial and have little to do with civil liberty issues. Among the most important provisions of the law were initiatives to remove the "wall" between law enforcement and intelligence efforts to share information.

Section 203. Authority to Share Criminal Investigative Information

(a) AUTHORITY TO SHARE GRAND JURY INFORMATION-

(1) IN GENERAL- Rule 6(e)(3)(C) of the Federal Rules of Criminal Procedure is amended to read as follows:

`(C)(i) Disclosure otherwise prohibited by this rule of matters occurring before the grand jury may also be made—

`(I) when so directed by a court preliminarily to or in connection with a judicial proceeding;

`(II) when permitted by a court at the request of the defendant, upon a showing that grounds may exist for a motion to dismiss the indictment because of matters occurring before the grand jury;

`(III) when the disclosure is made by an attorney for the government to another Federal grand jury;

`(IV) when permitted by a court at the request of an attorney for the government, upon a showing that such matters may disclose a violation of state criminal law, to an appropriate official of a state or subdivision of a state for the purpose of enforcing such law; or

`(V) when the matters involve foreign intelligence or counterintelligence (as defined in section 3 of the National Security Act of 1947 (50 U.S.C. 401a)), or foreign intelligence information (as defined in clause (iv) of this subparagraph), to any Federal law enforcement, intelligence, protective, immigration, national defense, or national security official in order to assist the official receiving that information in the performance of his official duties.

`(ii) If the court orders disclosure of matters occurring before the grand jury, the disclosure shall be made in such manner, at such time, and under such conditions as the court may direct.

`(iii) Any Federal official to whom information is disclosed pursuant to clause (i)(V) of this subparagraph may use that information only as necessary in the conduct of that person's official duties subject to any limitations on the unauthorized disclosure of such information. Within a reasonable time after such disclosure, an attorney for the government shall file under seal a notice with the court stating the fact that such information was disclosed and the departments, agencies, or entities to which the disclosure was made.

`(iv) In clause (i)(V) of this subparagraph, the term 'foreign intelligence information' means—

`(I) information, whether or not concerning a United States person, that relates to the ability of the United States to protect against—

`(aa) actual or potential attack or other grave hostile acts of a foreign power or an agent of a foreign power;

`(bb) sabotage or international terrorism by a foreign power or an agent of a foreign power; or

`(cc) clandestine intelligence activities by an intelligence service or network of a foreign power or by an agent of foreign power; or

`(II) information, whether or not concerning a United States person, with respect to a foreign power or foreign territory that relates to—

`(aa) the national defense or the security of the United States; or

`(bb) the conduct of the foreign affairs of the United States.

strategy to secure the United States from terrorist threats. The presidential executive order which established the office also created the Homeland Security Council of cabinet- and subcabinet-level officers to coordinate federal activities.

The National Strategy for Homeland Security

The Office of Homeland Security released its national strategy in July 2002, defining homeland security as "a concerted national effort to prevent terrorist attacks within the United States, reduce America's vulnerability to terrorism, and minimize the damage and recover from attacks that do occur."

The strategy established three strategic objectives: (1) preventing attack, (2) reducing vulnerabilities, and (3) minimizing damage. It organized activities into six mission areas: intelligence and warning; border and transportation security; domestic counterterrorism; protecting critical infrastructure and key assets; defending against catastrophic terrorism; and emergency preparedness and response.[13]

The nature of the terrorist threat and its very definition are the source of controversy, but *The National Strategy for Homeland Security* defined it as "(A)ny premeditated, unlawful act dangerous to human life or public welfare that is intended to intimidate or coerce civilian populations or governments."

Changes in the Department of Defense

The first major reorganization of federal agencies after 9/11 was the Department of Defense's establishment of a new military command, U.S. Northern Command (NORTHCOM) on October 1, 2002. Before 9/11 no single military command was responsible for the defense of the United States. NORTHCOM was tasked with the land, aerospace, and maritime defense of the continental United States, Alaska, Canada, Mexico, Puerto Rico, U.S. Virgin Islands, parts of the Caribbean, and the contiguous waters of the Atlantic and Pacific (out to 500 miles). NORTHCOM also offered military assistance to civilian authorities under the lead of other federal agencies.

Establishing the Department of Homeland Security (DHS)

Despite initial misgivings inside and out of the Bush administration about its potential cost in money and potential bureaucratic delays, the administration recommended the creation of a new federal department responsible for homeland security. Passed on November

25, 2002, the Homeland Security Act of 2002 merged over 22 federal entities and 180,000 employees into a single department responsible for immigration enforcement, border and transportation security, information analysis and infrastructure protection, science and technology research and development for homeland security, and emergency preparedness and response. The DHS also assumed control for the Transportation Security Administration, which had been established to screen commercial airline passengers and cargo, as well as oversee security practices for other forms of transportation including rail and public transit systems. However, the Bush administration chose not to fold the FBI—the lead law enforcement agency for combating terrorism—into the DHS; it was a decision that sparked controversy. Other critical homeland security missions also remained outside the DHS, including many activities involving bioterrorism, which came under the Department of Health and Human Services and its subordinate organizations. In addition, the administration rejected calls to create a dedicated domestic intelligence agency. In the months after the creation of the DHS, hopes for major and immediate gains in homeland security from the reorganization sometimes proved unrealistic.[14]

Intelligence and Law Enforcement Reforms

Other significant federal initiatives involved changes in the strategy, resources, priorities, and organizations used to conduct domestic counterterrorism operations. Prior to 9/11, domestic counterterrorism was largely considered a law enforcement matter, with more emphasis on prosecuting terrorists than preemptively destroying terrorist networks. After the attacks, priorities changed. The FBI dedicated itself to preventing terrorism. For example, on May 29, 2002, FBI Director Robert S. Mueller announced a restructuring of the agency including establishing a national network of regional joint interagency terrorism task forces. He also declared that combating terrorism would become the bureau's primary mission.[15]

Among the most significant efforts were initiatives to increase the exchange of information among federal agencies and sharing intelligence with state and local law enforcement. In this regard, the administration created two new organizations for improving the current system. The first was the Terrorism Threat Integration Center (TTIC), created on May 1, 2003. The TTIC was designed to be a central location where all terrorist-related intelligence, both foreign and domestic, could be gathered, coordinated, and assessed. Composed of elements of the FBI, CIA, Department of Defense, Department of Homeland Security, Department of State, and other intelligence agencies, it was placed under the direction of the Director of Central Intelligence.[16]

The second new organization created was the Terrorist Screening Center (TSC) formed as an interagency group under the FBI to consolidate all terrorist watch lists into a single function and provide around-the-clock access to local, state, and federal authorities. The TSC was charged with bringing together databases that included the State Department's TIPOFF database, the FBI's Violent Gang and Terrorist Offender's File, and the Homeland Security Department's many transportation security lists.[17]

State and Local Government

One of the most important lessons of September 11 was the reminder of the critical role state and local governments play in homeland security, brought home by the deaths of hundreds of first responders in New York City and the key role of local agencies in responding to the Pentagon crash site. Americans are governed by a collection of many thousands of state and local jurisdictions. It is these jurisdictions that create and execute most emergency plans and control the police, firefighters, national guard troops, and others on the frontline of homeland security. However, the capabilities among these governments to contribute to homeland security and the initiatives they undertook after 9/11 varied greatly. Before September 11, communities invested most of their efforts toward improving physical security through law enforcement. In addition, there was a spate of focus on information security initiatives, centered primarily on preparations for Y2K, a hugely expensive effort to ensure computer systems would not fail as a result of trying to account for the change of dates in the year 2000.[18]

Consequence management efforts had also long been a concern for local authorities, but the emphasis was on responding to natural disasters and conventional human-made calamities such as arson and accidental chemical spills. After 9/11 there were often halting and tentative movements to create a more holistic and integrated approach to homeland security, but results were mixed. States like New Jersey, for example, created their own counterterrorism offices. The governor of New York proposed expanding the state's investigative services for counterterrorism, amounting to about half the proposed budget of the state police.[19] In total, at least 1,200 state and local legislative acts were passed in the wake of September 11.[20]

Still, response to 9/11 was uneven. Complicating the response was the fact that communities had different needs and priorities. The security requirements for large urban and industrial centers, agricultural regions, and communities surrounding defense installations are all different. Further exacerbating the challenge was a lack of national preparedness standards establishing an expectation of the services and capacity that should be provided by federal, state, and local agencies.[21] In addition, state and local authorities complained that bureaucratic rivalries and security regulations prevented federal officials from sharing critical intelligence with them. Finally, the fiscal burdens of providing homeland security loomed large for many state and local governments. By July 2002, state governments were projecting budget gaps totaling $58 billion. By some estimates additional spending on homeland security by states and major cities after 9/11 topped $6.6 billion.[22] New York City alone reported spending more than $200 million a year on counterterrorism programs.[23] The federal government responded by providing billions of dollars in grants to state and local homeland security agencies, but even this assistance was decried as slow and inadequate.

Private Sector

After the September 11 attacks, there was widespread recognition that the private sector—which controls an estimated 85 percent of America's critical infrastructures—had a central role to play in meeting the challenge of protecting the homeland. There was, however, little consensus on how best to coordinate their efforts, and, in fact, it was difficult to assess the full scope of preparations and vulnerabilities in the private sector. Much of the reported data was accumulated from voluntary surveys, and many companies withhold proprietary information. Still, one estimate concluded that spending on physical and information security by the commercial sector in the United States after the terrorist attacks quickly exceeded $30 billion per year.[24]

Much of this investment was an extension of already existing programs designed to protect assets and ensure continued productivity in the event of natural or human-made calamity. Even before 9/11, commercial disaster recovery and continuity services were a growing business concern. One survey listed over 100 alternative work sites and business recovery and data storage centers in the United States operated by commercial vendors.[25] Events such as the bombing of the Murrah Office building and the run-up to Y2K created a cottage industry of firms specializing in disaster management and offering training, support, and products to federal, state, and local governments. Despite efforts by the federal government to encourage information sharing in the private sector, there remained a great deal of uncertainty over how much additional effort was needed. For example, many industries were unsure how to respond to official terrorist warnings and what liability they might incur if they failed to take additional security measures when the federal government recommended greater precautions. Many executives also failed to see a strong business case for increased investments in security, causing critics to push for stronger government regulations.

The American Public

The 9/11 attacks roused the citizenry of the United States as few events had before. From the volunteers who responded to Ground Zero to the many Americans who donated blood or money to the victims, the American people rushed to contribute after the attack. The public also contributed to homeland security by providing information to the authorities and, in cases such as the apprehension of the Shoe Bomber aboard a commercial flight, directly prevented acts of terrorism. However, the proposed Operation TIPS (Terrorism Information and Prevention System), a plan to encourage everyone from postal workers to truck drivers to report suspicious activity, generated significant opposition from civil libertarians. The Bush administration also moved to mobilize the public in less controversial ways by creating the USA Freedom Corps, which enlisted citizens in various volunteer activities. DHS also sought to enhance preparedness through the Ready Campaign. The government estimated that 113 million Americans saw or read about the campaign and that many responded by stocking emergency supplies or taking other actions. However, certain government recommendations—such as the advice to purchase duct tape as part of a shelter-in-place strategy—became the butt of jokes. Subsequent polling also indicated most Americans remained unaware of preparedness plans for their communities, schools, and workplaces.

CHAPTER SUMMARY

The dramatic changes following the 9/11 attacks created a new concept of homeland security, in many cases reversing regulations, policies, and assumptions that had been in force for decades. The federal government possessed the will, traditions, and money to reorganize itself and change many of its operating procedures. But the process of change was more complex for state and local governments and the private sector, which often lacked resources and clear priorities. These key players would continue to struggle to define their roles and responsibilities for responding to the danger of transnational terrorism.

CHAPTER QUIZ

1. What are the major tenets of the Bush Doctrine?
2. What are the key elements of *The National Strategy for Homeland Security*?
3. Which major organizations with homeland security missions were not included in the new Department of Homeland Security?
4. What obstacles exist to state and local governments playing a greater role in providing homeland security?

NOTES

1. The administration had actually begun to develop a more comprehensive strategy to eliminate the al-Qaida network in the spring and summer of 2001 [Prepared Statement of Condoleezza Rice before the National Commission on Terrorist Attack upon the United States (April 8, 2004), p. 3, www.9-11commission.gov/hearings/hearing9/rice_statement.pdf].

2. For the text of the speech see www.whitehouse.gov/news/releases/2001/09.

3. *The National Security Strategy of the United States*, p. 15.

4. Jeffrey Record, "Bounding the Global War on Terrorism," U.S. Army War College, Strategic Studies Institute (December 2003), 4. See also Michael Vlahos, "Terror's Mask: Insurgency within Islam," Johns Hopkins University, Applied Physics Laboratory (May 2002), p. 2.

5. See, for example, Richard Miniter, *Losing Bin Ladin: How Bill Clinton's Failures Unleashed Global Terror* (Washington, DC: Regnery, 2003); David Frum and Richard Pearle, *An End to Evil: How to Win the War on Terror* (New York: Random House, 2003).

6. For further discussion, see Paul K. Davis and Brian Michael Jenkins, *Deterrence and Influence in Counterterrorism: A Component of the War on al-Qaida* (Santa Monica: RAND, 2002).

7. One of the first published histories of the war was Robin Moore, *The Hunt for Bin Ladin: Task Force Dagger* (New York: Random House, 2003).

8. See, for example, Joint press conference of Secretary of Defense Donald Rumsfeld and Minister of Defense Mukhtar Altynbayev at the Presidential Administration Building, Astana, Kazakhstan (April 28, 2002), news transcript, www.defenselink.mil/news/Apr2002/t04282002_t0428kzk.html.

9. As of January 22, 2002, thirty-two countries reported to the committee on their activities to fight terrorism and cut off support for terrorist groups, www.un.org/Docs/committees/1373/1373/reportsEng.htm.

10. Samir Abid Shiak, "Islamic Banks and Financial Institutions: A Survey," *Journal of Muslim Minority Affairs* 27/1 (1997): pp. 118–119.

11. New initiatives were based on the authority granted by the USA PATRIOT Act, which requires the Secretary of the Treasury to establish a system where banks can identify account holders and match them to a list of suspected terrorists. See the International Money Laundering Abatement and Financial Anti-Terrorism Act of 2001, Title III of the USA PATRIOT Act of 2001, Public Law 107-56, October 26, 2001.

12. Charles Doyle, "The USA Patriot Act: A Sketch," Congressional Research Service (April 18, 2002), pp. 1–5; Rosemary Jenks, "The USA Patriot Act of 2001: A Summary of the Anti-Terrorism Law's Immigration-Related Provisions," Center for Immigration Studies (December 2001), pp. 1–3.

13. *The National Strategy for Homeland Security*, pp. vii–x.

14. James Jay Carafano, "Prospects for the Homeland Security Department: The 1947 Analogy," Center for Strategic and Budgetary Assessment, *Backgrounder* (September 12, 2002): 15.

15. Remarks prepared for delivery by Robert S. Mueller III, Director, Federal Bureau of Investigation at a Press Availability on the FBI's Reorganization Washington, DC (May 29, 2002), www.fbi.gov/pressrel/speeches/speech052902.htm; FBI Strategic Focus (May 29, 2002) www.fbi.gov/page2/52902.htm; U.S. Department of Justice, *Report to the National Commission on Terrorist Attack upon the United States: The FBI's Counterterrorism Program Since September 2001* (April 14, 2004), www.fbi.gov/publications/commission/9-11commissionrep.pdf.

16. U.S. Department of State, International Information Programs, "Fact Sheet: Bush to Create Terrorist Threat Integration Center" (January 28, 2003), usinfo.state.gov/topical/pol/terror/03012806.htm.

17. James Jay Carafano and Ha Nguyen, "Better Intelligence Sharing for Visa Issuance and Monitoring: An Imperative for Homeland Security," *Heritage Backgrounder #1669* (October 27, 2003), www.heritage.org/Research/HomelandDefense/BG1699.cfm#pgfId-1078078.

18. The spending estimate is based on National Communications System, Report 99-62, www.ncs.gov/n5_hp/Customer_Service/XAffairs/NewService/NCS9962.htm. For an overview of Y2K lessons learned, see David Mussington, *Concepts for Enhancing Critical Infrastructure Protection: Relating Y2K to CIP Research and Development* (Santa Monica, CA: Rand, 2002), pp. 11–18.

19. Various state and local initiatives are listed on the National Governors Association, Center for Best Practices Web site, www.nga.org/center.

20. National Conference of State Legislatures, "Protecting Democracy: America's Legislatures Respond," www.ncsl.org/programs/press/responsebook2002. For an overview of state

programs and initiatives, see Office of Homeland Security, State and Local Actions for Homeland Security (July 2002); National Emergency Management Association, State Organizational Structures for Homeland Security (2002), www.nemaweb.org/News/ NEMA_Homeland_Security_Report.pdf.

21. For example, an assessment of the requirements of major cities is provided in The United States Conference of Mayors, "A National Action Plan for Safety and Security in America's Cities" (December 2001), www.usmayors.org/uscm/news/press_releases/doc- uments/ActionPlan_121101.pdf.

22. The National Governors Association estimated that homeland security spending could top $4 billion per year. The National Conference of Mayors estimates that in total the 200 largest cities will spend an additional $2.6 billion.

23. Written testimony of Raymond W. Kelly, Police Commissioner of the City of New York, before the National Commission on Terrorist Attack upon the United States (May 18, 2004).

24. Bill Zalud, "Post-Sept. 11th, Security Re-evaluates; Expects Impact through 2002," *Security*, http://www.secmag.com/CDA/ArticleInformation/features/BNP_Features_Item/0,5411 ,69674,00.html.

25. "Alternative Site Survey," *Disaster Recovery Journal* (Summer 2002): 84–93.

UNDERSTANDING TERRORISM

4

THE MIND OF THE TERRORIST

Why They Hate Us

While nothing is easier than to denounce the evildoer, nothing is more difficult than to understand him.

Attributed to Feodor Mikhailovich Dostoyevsky

CHAPTER OVERVIEW

For many people terrorism is easier to recognize than define, yet its definition carries crucial policy implications. However, perhaps even more important is an understanding of the groups and individuals who carry out terrorism. By studying what groups choose terrorism and why, as well as the factors that cause individuals to become terrorists, it becomes easier to devise and execute strategies to reduce the threat. This chapter reviews the various definitions of terrorism and considers the debate over the origins and goals of transnational terrorist activities.

CHAPTER LEARNING OBJECTIVES

After reading this chapter, you should be able to

1. Define the major elements of terrorism.
2. List significant categories of terrorist groups.
3. Discuss forces that prompt individuals to join terrorist groups.

4. **Clarify the factors behind suicide terrorism.**

5. **Explain factors that have increased the willingness of terrorists to inflict mass casualties.**

DEFINING TERRORISM

Debated for decades by diplomats and scholars, there is still no single, accepted definition of terrorism—not even within the U.S. government. International law also offers little clarity. United Nations treaty negotiations involving the overall definition of terrorism have been stymied by disputes over the Israeli-Palestinian conflict. According to the cliché, "one man's terrorist is another man's freedom fighter." Yet the attempt to define terrorism is important; the meaning of the term impacts legal and policy issues ranging from extradition treaties to insurance regulations. It also influences the critical war of ideas that will shape the level and role of terrorism in future generations.

Historical Definition

The word *terrorism* emerged during the French revolution of the late 1700s to describe efforts by the revolutionary government to impose its will through widespread violence; the *Académie Française* soon defined terrorism as a "system or rule of terror."[1] However, the repression of populations by their own governments is usually not included in the modern definition of terrorism, especially by Western governments.

U.S. Government Definitions

Numerous U.S. government publications, regulations, and laws reference terrorism. America's *National Strategy for Homeland Security* defines it as: "any premeditated, unlawful act dangerous to human life or public welfare that is intended to intimidate or coerce civilian populations or governments."[2] But even here ambiguity arises, such as in the definitions of *unlawful* and *public welfare*.

The State Department's Definition

As part of its mandate to collect and analyze information on terrorism, the State Department uses a special definition from the U.S. legal system. According to this law, terrorism means "premeditated, politically motivated violence perpetrated against noncombatant targets by subnational groups or clandestine agents."[3] Terrorist group means "any group practicing, or which has significant subgroups which practice, international terrorism." International terrorism is described as terrorism involving citizens or the territory of more than one country. In a policy that sparks some disagreement, the department counts noncombatants as not just civilians, but also unarmed and/or off-duty military personnel, plus armed troops who are attacked outside zones of military hostility.

The FBI Definition

The FBI, in accordance with the Federal Code of Regulations, delineates terrorism as "the unlawful use of force or violence against persons or property to intimidate or coerce a Government, the civilian population, or any segment thereof, in furtherance of political or social objectives." The Bureau divides terrorism into two categories: domestic, involving groups operating in and targeting the United States without foreign direction; and international, involving groups that operate across international borders and/or have foreign connections.[4]

As might be expected, the FBI's definition is similar to that used in various U.S. criminal codes it enforces. For example, the United States Code describes international terrorism as violent acts intended to affect civilian populations or governments and occurring mostly outside the United States or transcending international boundaries.[5]

Central Elements of Terrorism

These sometimes conflicting definitions raise a number of questions. For example, under U.S. standards, foreign governments can be "state sponsors" of terrorism, but can countries themselves be considered terrorist groups? Do individual "lone wolves"—such as the Unabomber, a deranged recluse who mailed bombs to ideologically selected victims he had never met, or Baruch Goldstein, a U.S. citizen who machine gunned 29 Muslim worshippers to death in Israel—count as terrorists? A study by the Federal Research Division of the Library of Congress addressed some of these issues by defining a terrorist action as "the calculated use of unexpected, shocking, and unlawful violence against noncombatants (including, in addition to civilians, off-duty military and security personnel in peaceful situations) and other symbolic targets perpetrated by a clandestine member(s) of a subnational group or a clandestine agent(s) for the psychological purpose of publicizing a political or religious cause and/or intimidating or coercing a government(s) or civilian population into accepting demands on behalf of the cause."[6]

When all these definitions are synthesized, *terrorism* usually includes most or all of the following central elements:

- Conducted by subnational groups
- Targeted at random noncombatant victims
- Directed at one set of victims in part to create fear among a larger audience
- Aimed at coercing governments or populations
- Planned to get publicity
- Motivated by political, ideological, or religious beliefs
- Based on criminal actions (actions that would also violate the rules of war)

ISSUE:

WHAT IS TERRORISM?

"Wherever we look, we find the U.S. as the leader of terrorism and crime in the world. The U.S. does not consider it a terrorist act to throw atomic bombs at nations thousands of miles away [Japan during World War II], when those bombs would hit more than just military targets. Those bombs rather were thrown at entire nations, including women, children, and elderly people …" Usama bin Ladin asserted.[7] It's no surprise terrorists and their sympathizers reject America's definitions of terrorism. Yet even many people who strongly oppose terrorism dispute key

---

WHY TERRORISM

Why do groups take up terrorism? Are individual terrorists born or made? These questions have attracted the attention of numerous

components of the American definition. They claim attacks on groups such as military troops and armed settlers should not count as terrorism. They also complain about the United States' focus on subnational groups, saying it relegates the killing of noncombatants by governments—especially killings by American allies such as Israel—to a lower priority. "Denying that states can commit terrorism is generally useful, because it gets the U.S. and its allies off the hook in a variety of situations," opined one British newspaper writer.[8]

One response to this dispute has been to focus on specific tactics rather than general definitions. Despite fierce bickering over the general meaning of terrorism, United Nations delegates have managed to hammer out agreements based on "operational" descriptions of terrorism, condemning specific tactics such as hijackings, bombings, and hostage-taking.

In addition, international legal standards such as the Geneva Conventions offer clear, if often disregarded, guidelines. Under the rules of war, accepted by the United States and many other nations, countries are expected to settle their differences peacefully if possible. Should combat break out, warring parties must not target noncombatants and are expected to do their best to prevent civilian casualties. For example, operations that might kill civilians must be militarily necessary and planned to minimize the risk to innocent victims.

1. When is it appropriate for a nation to take military action, such as bombings in urban areas, which will undoubtedly claim the lives of innocent civilians? What makes this different from terrorism?

2. Are fighters who attacked U.S. troops after the occupation of Iraq considered terrorists, even if their violence was directed at armed soldiers in a combat zone?

3. Why is it important for international bodies to reach an overall definition of terrorism as opposed to focusing on outlawing specific terrorist tactics?

4. What is the best definition of terrorism?

scholars. Their approaches include political, organizational, physiological, psychological, and multicausal explanations and hypotheses focused on causative issues such as frustration-aggression, negative identity, and narcissistic rage.[9] Yet such academic interpretations suffer from a lack of supporting data (due to the difficulty of interviewing and surveying terrorists), the absence of predictive value, and the difficulty of deriving theories capable of explaining extraordinarily diverse cultural, political, and individual motivations.

Terrorism Works—At Least Terrorists Think So

A more utilitarian explanation for why groups and individuals practice terrorism is that the tactics of terrorism often work, though terrorists all too frequently fail to achieve their strategic goals through terrorist acts. To be sure, the actions of some terrorist groups such as Japan's Aum Shinrikyo have been primarily driven by the twisted psyches of key leaders and the dynamics of cultism. But across the globe, groups that harness terror have often been able to obtain publicity, funds and supplies, recruits, and some times social change, political concessions, and even diplomatic clout—along with revenge on their enemies. Often the aim is to prompt an overreaction by authorities, leading to a crackdown that wins sympathy for the terrorists. In certain circumstances—especially those where social and political conditions limit peaceful avenues of social change or where military conditions are unfavorable—armed groups may perceive terrorism as the only viable strategy to achieve these results.

Emergence of Modern Terrorism

While terrorism has been a recognized form of warfare for centuries, modern terrorism dates from the aftermath of World War II. After that conflict, the world witnessed the rise of guerilla (Spanish for "little war," a term originating in resistance to Napoleon's occupation of Spain in the nineteenth century) combat, in which small, unconventional insurgent units challenged colonial governments backed by traditional military forces. These guerilla armies often saw themselves as legitimate military units fighting an enemy army to establish a new political entity. In some cases they may have qualified as such under the Geneva Conventions by carrying their weapons openly, wearing uniforms, maintaining a clear command structure, and following the law of war, along with other practices. But in what is now called "asymmetric warfare," the guerillas did not try to match their better-equipped opponents in pitched engagements on the open battlefield, where they would be handily defeated. Instead they looked for weaknesses to exploit, for example, using their mobility to ambush colonial convoys and then escaping into the jungle or mountains. Eventually terrorism became part of the arsenal for many guerilla groups, used to diminish the will of colonial armies and their supporters at home. Guerillas attacked colonial civilians and assassinated sympathizers. This often prompted brutal responses by the colonists, such as widespread torture and executions, which helped the guerillas by creating more supporters.

Inspired by the success of these anticolonial "freedom fighters," a variety of nationalist and ideological groups took up arms, often with support from the Soviet Union and other sponsors. Their refinement of tactics such as hijackings, bombings, and political sieges—amplified by shrewd use of the powerful new global media network—would come to define the modern age of terrorism.

Palestinian Terrorism Gets Results—To a Degree

The apparent efficacy of terrorism was proven to the world most dramatically by Palestinian groups. In June 1967, Israel inflicted a humiliating defeat on its Arab neighbors during the 6-Day War, occupying the West Bank and Gaza Strip and setting the stage for the era of modern international terrorism. Palestinian guerillas—losing hope that their Arab allies could be counted on to evict the Israelis and reluctant to take on the powerful Israeli military directly—turned to terrorism. One of the first modern terrorist acts took place on July 22, 1968, when gunmen belonging to a faction of the Palestine Liberation Organization (PLO) hijacked an Israeli passenger flight, winning the release of Palestinian prisoners and receiving worldwide publicity. Many other attacks occurred in the following years, perhaps most notably in 1972 when Palestinian "Black September" terrorists seized Israeli hostages at the Munich Olympics. Here the terrorists hijacked not a plane, but an international media event already being covered by an army of international journalists. Images of Palestinian operatives in ski masks guarding their captives, and word of their demands, spread across the globe as the incident ended in a massacre.

Despite—or perhaps because of—his links to such terrorism, PLO leader Yasir Arafat was invited to speak at the United Nations in 1974, where he addressed the delegates while wearing a gun on this belt. This was followed by a series of PLO diplomatic victories facilitated by publicity from the Palestinian terrorist attacks, along with support from oil-rich Arab states. Ultimately, Arafat became an international figure, and the Palestinian issue assumed a central role in the world's diplomatic agenda—events which might never have happened in the same way had the Palestinians focused on conventional military attacks against Israel instead of spectacular terrorist strikes. On the other hand, it's worth noting that the PLO efforts failed to achieve their one-time stated goal of the destruction of Israel or, to date, an even more limited goal of creating an independent Palestinian state.

Iranian-Backed Terror Changes U.S. Policy

During the next decade, terrorism again seemingly proved effective, this time for the Lebanese group Hizballah and its supporters in the Iranian and Syrian governments. U.S. forces were trying to stabilize Lebanon in 1983, and Hizballah, whose members aimed to make Lebanon a Shiite Muslim state, wanted the Americans out of the way. In April, a suicide bomber blew up the U.S. Embassy in Beirut, killing 63 people. The blast was linked to "Islamic Jihad," used as a front name for Hizballah and other Iranian-supported terrorist groups. In October, suicide bombers hit barracks housing U.S. Marines and allied French paratroopers. Two-hundred and forty-two Americans and 58 French troops died in the attack, claimed by Islamic Jihad.[10] After a limited military response, the United States pulled its troops from Lebanon.

Hizballah then moved to another terrorist tactic, seizing and in some cases killing U.S. and other Western hostages. The ensuing crisis ultimately led the Reagan White House to break its policies and make a deal with Iran, the group's principal backer, to trade arms for hostages.

U.S. pledges to bring Hizballah leaders such as Imad Mughniyah to justice for these and other terrorist attacks proved hollow; the group remains a significant player in the region's affairs. Though again, it is worth noting that while Hizballah has achieved notable short-term victories, such as the withdrawal of U.S. forces from Lebanon, its ultimate strategic goal of political and military dominance remains elusive.

Bin Ladin Viewed Terrorism as Successful

Reflecting on a decade of terrorist attacks against the United States bin Ladin mocked U.S. pledges to stand firm in the Middle East, "[I]t shows the fears that have enveloped you all. Where was this courage of yours when the explosion in Beirut took place in 1983 . . . You were transformed into scattered bits and pieces; 241 soldiers were killed, most of them Marines. And where was this courage of yours when two explosions made you to leave Aden [Yemen] in less than twenty-four hours [after a bin Ladin–linked bombing in 1992]! But your most disgraceful case was in Somalia . . . you left the area in disappointment, humiliation, and defeat, carrying your dead with you."[11]

Such perceptions helped set the stage for 9/11. "It is now undeniable that the terrorists declared war on America—and on the civilized world—many years before September 11th . . . Yet until September 11th, the terrorists faced no sustained and systematic and global response. They became emboldened—and the result was more terror and more victims," concluded Condoleezza Rice, the Bush administration's National Security Advisor, in 2003.[12]

FROM THE SOURCE:

LIBRARY OF CONGRESS PROFILE OF VELUPILLAI PRABHAKARAN, LEADER OF THE LIBERATION TIGERS, OF TAMIL EELAM (LTTE)

Velupillai Prabhakaran was born on November 27, 1954 . . . He is the son of a pious and gentle Hindu government official, an agricultural officer, who was famed for being so incorruptible that he would refuse cups of tea from his subordinates. During his childhood, Prabhakaran spent his days killing birds and squirrels with a slingshot. An average student, he preferred historical novels on the glories of ancient Tamil conquerors to his textbooks. As a youth, he became swept up in the growing militancy in the northern peninsula of Jaffna, which is predominately Tamil. After dropping out of school at age 16, he began to associate with Tamil "activist gangs." On one occasion as a gang member, he participated in a political kidnapping. In 1972 he helped form a militant group called the New Tamil Tigers, becoming its co-leader at 21. He imposed a strict code of conduct over his 15 gang members: no smoking, no drinking, and no sex. Only through supreme sacrifice, insisted Prabhakaran, could the Tamils achieve their goal of Eelam, or a separate homeland. In his first terrorist action, which earned him nationwide notoriety, Prabhakaran assassinated Jaffna's newly elected mayor . . . Prabhakaran won considerable power and prestige as a result of the deed, which he announced by putting up posters throughout Jaffna to claim responsibility. He became a wanted man and a disgrace to his pacifist father. In the Sri Lankan underworld, in order to lead a gang one must establish a reputation for sudden and decisive violence and have a prior criminal record . . . Gradually and ruthlessly, he gained control of the Tamil uprising. Prabhakaran married a fiery beauty named Mathivathani Erambu in 1983. Since then, Tigers have been allowed to wed after five years of combat. Prabhakaran's wife, son, and daughter (a third child may also have been born) are reportedly hiding in Australia. The LTTE's charismatic "supremo," Prabhakaran has earned a reputation as a military genius. A portly man with a moustache and glittering eyes, he has also been described as "Asia's new Pol Pot," a "ruthless killer," a "megalomaniac," and an "introvert," who is rarely seen in public except before battles or to host farewell banquets for Tigers setting off on suicide missions. He spends time planning murders of civilians, including politicians, and perceived Tamil rivals. Prabhakaran is an enigma even to his most loyal commanders. Asked who his heroes are, Prabhakaran once named actor Clint Eastwood. He has murdered many of his trusted commanders for suspected treason. Nevertheless, he inspires fanatical devotion among his fighters . . . Prabhakaran has repeatedly warned the Western nations providing military support to Sri Lanka that they are exposing their citizens to possible attacks."[13]

TYPES OF TERRORIST GROUPS

Such lessons from the 1970s and '80s continue to influence the broad range of groups now conducting terrorist operations. Just as the very definition of terrorism is hotly debated, so is the issue of how best to categorize organizations that employ the strategy. Their memberships, motivations, and legal status are often murky and fluid. One way to classify them is through their objectives. While some groups have multiple objectives, most can be placed into one of four main types: ideological (motivated by extreme left- or right-wing political goals), nationalist (driven by desire to achieve autonomy for specific populations), religious (inspired to create political or social transformation in the name of religion), and issue-oriented (efforts to achieve specific policies, e.g., abortion or animal rights laws). In some cases—such as the Revolutionary Armed Forces of Colombia [Fuerzas Armadas Revolucionarias de Colombia (FARC)], which opposes the Colombian government, and the Liberation Tigers of Tamil Eelam (LTTE), which fights the government of Sri Lanka on behalf of the Tamil ethnic minority—the groups may operate as guerilla movements that also use terrorist techniques.

While the factors that spawned these groups vary widely, as do the motives of their personnel, their existence can in part be traced to certain basic dynamics.

Conditions for Terrorism

As discussed, terrorism is by definition a political act carried out by perpetrators with ideological motives. Famed Prussian military theorist Karl von Clausewitz famously declared that, "War is the continuation of policy (politics) by other means." For many radicals, terrorism can be defined similarly. Among guerilla groups, terrorism may be the continuation of war by other means, a strategy used in additional to conventional military tactics. In all these cases, terrorism emerges from the furnace of social, ideological, or religious strife.

Strife Breeds Terrorism

The emergence and survival of terrorist groups are often linked to specific societal conditions. Factors that produce rich soil for the growth of terrorism include political violence, social strife, poverty, dictatorship, and modernization. In many cases, these factors spark guerilla warfare or violent protest movements that midwife terrorist groups. For example, Palestinian guerillas switched from guerilla attacks to hijackings. Extremists involved in the U.S. antiwar and civil rights demonstrations moved from legal dissent to terrorism.

The type of strife capable of engendering terrorism must involve enough energized participants for a terrorist group to recruit and obtain logistical support. In some cases, especially where external state sponsors exist, the necessary level of support may be quite shallow. In other cases, terrorist groups may have widespread backing. Nationalist groups, such as various Palestinian and Irish extremists, have drawn significant popular support from a broad spectrum of society. In the United States and Europe, ideological groups, such as left-wing extremists, and issue-oriented terrorist groups, such as American animal rights zealots and pro-life radicals, have attracted backing from the fringes of legitimate protest movements.

In many but certainly not all cases, terrorist groups address legitimate grievances, but with illegitimate means in the pursuit of extremist solutions. For example, animal rights extremists seek to reduce the suffering of animals, but use bombings and other illegal tactics in the hope of ending all animal testing. Palestinian terrorists demand rights for their people but are willing to target innocent victims and pursue the destruction of Israel.

Poverty and Ignorance

"We fight against poverty because hope is an answer to terror," said President Bush in 2002, echoing the opinions of many that material deprivation promotes political violence.[14] While poverty is often cited as a precursor to terrorism, history shows that relatively affluent countries have often faced terrorism, while many terrorists are from middle- or upper-class backgrounds. For example, most of the 9/11 hijackers were from the relatively affluent nation of Saudi Arabia and followed the orders of a millionaire leader.

Analysis by Princeton economist Alan B. Krueger failed to detect strong correlations between poverty and the existence of international terrorism groups. The data also suggested no link between lack of education and terrorism. "Instead of viewing terrorism as a response—either direct or indirect—to poverty or ignorance, we suggest that it (terrorism) is more accurately viewed as a response to

no link between →
terrorism & money/education
instead: lower levels of freedom

political conditions and longstanding feelings of indignity and frustration that have little to do with economic circumstances," concluded Krueger.[15]

Political Oppression

However, Krueger and others have suggested a link between international terrorism and countries with lower levels of freedom and weak civil societies. In general, nations with high levels of freedom, such as the Western democracies, have managed to channel political conflict into nonviolent avenues. In recent years, domestic ideological and separatist terrorism has appeared to ebb in the United States, Europe, and Japan. Large terrorist campaigns have mostly originated with the citizens of oppressive regimes, such as those in the Middle East. But it is often unclear whether this relationship is one of correlation or causality. Do oppressive conditions cause terrorism, or are they themselves fostered by terrorism? Could underlying social factors that lead a society toward dictatorship also encourage terrorism? Ironically, states with the highest level of political subjugation, such as the former Soviet Union, managed to limit terrorism. Repressive governments may be at their most vulnerable when they are increasing rights; while democracy is often an antidote to widespread terrorism, increasing freedom may relax controls that had inhibited terrorist activity. Certainly Russia has endured a much greater toll of terrorist violence since the fall of communism.

The disputed relationship between terrorism and poverty may be mediated by the issue of freedom. Oppressive regimes can stunt economic growth and exacerbate social and cultural tensions. For example, poverty in Pakistan left many young people unable to afford any education other than that offered by the *madrassas*, Islamic academies that often pushed radical teachings. Perhaps the clearest link between global poverty and terrorism is the existence of failed states and uncontrolled regions, such as those in Afghanistan and Pakistan, where terrorist groups were able to operate with limited opposition. On the other hand, North Korea, an extremely poor yet highly authoritarian state appears to have little terrorism. Thus, it appears that countries with weak civil societies and poor security have the greatest prospects for terrorist recruitment.

→ terrorism has a deeper root in religion than any other condition.

→ there is no other way they are taught.

weak civil societies poor security

Modernization and Cultural Conflict

In the wake of 9/11, enormous attention has been paid to the pains of modernity and cultural change in the Muslim world. For young people facing conflict between their traditional values and the allure of Western culture, the answer that resolves the contradiction may be Islamic extremism. This choice may prove especially attractive to those with specific personality types.

Terrorists: Born and Made

By definition, terrorists are those who dedicate themselves to the murder of innocent victims. Because such behavior is so objectionable to most people, they are tempted to attribute it to individual or group pathology, dismissing the killers as "animals," "crazy people," or "psychopaths."

Yet research and observation shows most terrorists are not mentally ill. Indeed, terrorist organizations often screen out disturbed recruits, whose suitability for training and effectiveness in the field may be limited. Neither is there a specific personality type—a "terrorist type"—common to most terrorists.[16] While there appear to be psychological commonalties among many terrorists, their basic psychological structure is not radically different from certain other groups in society. Their eventual terrorist behavior is also strongly influenced by the ideologies of their groups and common but effective methods of indoctrination, social control, and training.

Terrorist Demographics

Studies show most terrorists have been young, single, fit males.[17] Such a profile would be expected of people required to conduct quasi-military operations and also matches the demographic cohort most associated with criminal violence. Of course, women have also been active in many terrorist organizations, which are often lead by middle-aged men. The socioeconomic and educational backgrounds of terrorists vary widely, both within and between groups, but many observers see a trend of higher educational backgrounds among international terrorists.

*Majority are from Western universities

Individual Psychology

While terrorists are generally not psychotic, they are also not average. After all, they self-select themselves to conduct activities that are considered morally reprehensible and/or excessively risky by many members of their societies. In this regard, terrorist recruits may combine some of the psychological factors that lead people to join high-risk military units and criminal organizations. They are risk takers attracted to the excitement of conflict. Other psychological predispositions may also encourage them to join a terrorist movement, such as a need to belong, prove themselves, or blame their troubles on an external enemy. In some cases, they may be criminals out for personal gain such as money, power, and notoriety.

Selection, Indoctrination, and Control

No matter their precise individual motives, those who join terrorist groups are put through extensive selection, indoctrination, and control procedures to produce the personnel needed by the group. Most human beings are inculcated with an aversion to killing; this is systematically removed by the terrorist group using some of the same techniques employed by military organizations. Recruits begin with some ideological affinity for the cause; often they have moved from the role of sympathizer to active supporter, perhaps after a triggering event seen in the media or experienced in their own lives. Once in the group, they may take an oath of allegiance and are indoctrinated to think of themselves as members of a noble endeavor. While outsiders may see them as criminals, they view themselves as soldiers. Recruits are encouraged to delegate their moral responsibilities to the group's leadership and dehumanize the enemy. The intended victims are stripped of their individual humanity by being referred to in terms such as "infidels," "capitalist pigs," or "mud people."

Complex rationales may be built upon the group's specific ideology. One al-Qaida leader advised the group's followers that it was proper to attack "infidels" (nonbelievers) even if others might be killed because if the bystanders were "innocent" they would go to paradise, and if they weren't, they deserved to die anyway.[18] It is common for the leadership to claim the group has no choice but to engage in terrorism, thereby shifting the blame to the target group. Finally, it is common for terrorists to invoke the "greater good" argument, claiming that the death of innocent victims is justified by the outcome of the conflict. For example, Timothy McVeigh called the children killed in the Oklahoma City bombing "collateral damage," using the U.S. military phrase for unintended damage caused during combat.[19] "We are willing to take the lives of these innocent persons, because a much greater harm will ultimately befall our people if we fail to act now," declares a terrorist leader in *The Turner Diaries*.[20]

SUICIDE TERRORISM

A suicide attack can be defined as a planned strike in which a willing attacker must kill himself or herself in order for the attack to succeed. This contrasts with an operation in which the attacker has a high likelihood of being killed, but could possibly avoid death by escaping or being captured alive. Suicide attacks offer tactical advantages; the bomber can deliver the explosives directly into the heart of the target and set them off without delays caused by timers. There is no need for an escape plan and no risk a captured operative will give up the group's secrets. In the case of the 9/11 attacks and certain truck bombers, the terrorists were able to create a level of destruction unattainable by conventional tactics.

Perhaps more important than the tactical benefits of the suicide attack is its psychological impact, which reinforces the zealotry of the attacker and the vulnerability of the victim in a far more dramatic fashion than would be achieved by delayed explosives or standoff weaponry.

Groups Using Suicide Tactics

Suicide attacks are neither a new nor purely Islamic manifestation of terrorism. The use of suicide attacks during combat became known to the American people in the early 1900s, when American troops in the Philippines battled Islamic Moro rebels (ideological forebears of the modern Abu Sayyaf, or Bearer of the Sword, terrorist group in that country). The rebels believed that killing Christians was a route to paradise; after ritual preparations they would charge the better-armed Americans armed only with a sword or knife known as a "kris": "[A]ccounts abounded of seemingly peaceful Moros suddenly drawing kris and killing multiple American soldiers or civilians before being killed themselves."[21] Then came the kamikaze aerial and seaborne attacks of World War II, during which Japanese crewmembers slammed explosives-filled craft into U.S. Navy ships. In modern times, the Liberation Tigers of Tamil Eelam (LTTE), or Tamil Tigers, have earned the reputation as the most prolific suicide terrorists in the world. Separatists fighting on behalf of the mostly Hindu Tamil minority group in Sri Lanka, the group's Black Tiger suicide squad, and other members have blown up the prime ministers of two countries, various celebrities, a battleship, and a host of other targets. LTTE operatives carry cyanide capsules, and dozens have killed themselves rather than face questioning by the authorities.[22]

A study by Robert A. Pape found incidents of suicide terrorism are on average more deadly than other attacks and have increased dramatically over recent years; most involved terrorists trying to force democratic governments to withdraw from disputed territories seen by the terrorists as their homelands.[23]

Suicide in the Name of Islam

Starting with the bombings of the U.S. Embassy and Marine barracks in Beirut during 1983, through the Palestinian suicide bombings in Israel during the 1990s, the 9/11 attacks and bombings in Iraq, spectacular suicide attacks have become associated with Islamic radicals.

Islamic history and theology record a special place for suicide attacks. *Istishad* is the Arabic religious term meaning to give one's life for Allah. In general terms, this form of suicide is acceptable in the Islamic tradition, as opposed to *intihar*, which describes suicide motivated by personal problems.[24]

As with other terrorists, suicide bombers are generally sane. Those unfamiliar with this tactic may picture a suicide bomber as a deranged or despondent individual, perhaps impoverished and uneducated, taking his or her life on the spur of the moment. In reality, they are often willing cogs in a highly organized weapons system manufactured by an organization. Research indicates Palestinian suicide bombers are no less educated or wealthy than average for their communities.[25] The process of producing a suicide bomber begins with propaganda, carried heavily by local media, praising earlier bombers. Once identified, a potential bomber is often put through a process lasting months that includes recruitment (with the promise of substantial payments to the bomber's family), indoctrination, training, propaganda exploitation, equipping, and targeting. The bomber is then provided with a device built for him or her and delivered to the location with instructions on the target and how to reach it. The results are often a devastating attack that gains international publicity—all for an investment by the terrorist group in materials and transportation estimated at about $150.[26]

THE DRIVE FOR MASS DESTRUCTION

On a seemingly normal September day, highly trained terrorists unleash a complex plot involving the simultaneous hijacking of four jet airliners filled with passengers headed to U.S. destinations. Members of an internationally feared group, the hardened hijackers display fanatical loyalty to a well-known terrorist leader nicknamed the "Master." They end up destroying the airliners in fiery explosions carried across the world by the media, achieving their objectives and sparking international debate about the proper response to terrorism.

But the year is 1970, not 2001. The terrorist group is the Popular Front for the Liberation of Palestine (PFLP), not al-Qaida. And before blowing up the jets, the terrorists evacuated all the prisoners. Rather than seeking to kill large numbers of victims, the plot was designed to force the release of imprisoned terrorists and gain publicity, both of which it succeeded in doing.

The separatist and ideological terrorists of the 1970s and '80s may have shocked the world with many of their attacks, but their agenda was in many ways conventional. They focused on specific goals and were open to negotiated political settlements. To appeal to wider constituencies, control the escalation of their conflicts, and prevent reprisals against their state sponsors, these terrorists often limited the violence of their attacks. In 1970, the terrorists blew up the planes; three decades later, the hijackers blew up not only the aircraft, but all their passengers, victims on the ground, and themselves.

In recent decades, the rise of religious terrorist groups has been followed by an increasing escalation in the level of destruction sought, from the nerve gas attack of Aum Shinrikyo to the 9/11 attacks. While the yearly number of international terrorist attacks dropped dramatically from 1983 to 2003, as measured by the U.S. State Department, the average lethality of the attacks in recent years, at least on U.S. citizens, appears to have increased.[27] Analysis by the Gilmore

Commission indicated a similar increase in overall casualties per attack.[28] A related trend over the last several years involves attacks on "soft targets" such as hotels, religious facilities, and business area—a trend the U.S. Department of State blames for a dramatic increase in terrorist injuries from 2002 to 2003.[29]

Increasingly, America's enemies have the capability and will to inflict mass casualties. As discussed elsewhere in this text, groups such as al-Qaida and Aum Shinrikyo have recruited operatives with high levels of education and technical sophistication. Combined with the increasing spread of both the knowledge and components required to create WMD, along with techniques for advanced conventional explosives techniques, such groups have an increasing capability to launch mass casualty attacks.

There may be no political settlement that will satisfy modern religious terrorist groups. They are motivated by a black-and-white view of humanity and cannot tolerate the existence of the enemy. They do not depend on the support of state sponsors who can be pressured by the West. Because they are not afraid to die, and often have no fixed territories or populations to protect, they are less subject to traditional strategies of deterrence.

CHAPTER SUMMARY

Terrorism is politically motivated violence carried out in most cases by sane and intelligent operatives. Even the increase in suicide and mass casualty terrorist attacks can best be understood as tactics that reflect reasoned, if immoral, strategic decisions by organized groups.

In order to alter the underlying circumstances that create and enable terrorism, the United States must understand the organizing principles and motivation of the specific groups that intend to do the nation harm.

CHAPTER QUIZ

1. Identify three major elements that define 9/11 as a terrorist attack.

2. Name significant categories of terrorist groups and explain their motivation.

3. Are terrorists born or made?

4. What role does mental illness play in suicide bombings?

5. Explain factors that have increased the propensity of terrorists to inflict mass casualties.

NOTES

1. Adam Roberts, "The Changing Faces of Terrorism," *BBCi*, August 27, 2002, www.bbc.co.uk/history/war/sept_11/changing_faces_01.shtml.

2. *The National Strategy for Homeland Security*, p. 14.

3. 22 USC, Chapter 38, Section 2656f.

4. Federal Bureau of Investigation, *FBI Policy and Guidelines: FBI Denver Division: Counterterrorism*, denver.fbi.gov/inteterr.htm.

5. 18 USC, Chapter 113B, Section 2331.

6. Rex A. Hudson, "The Sociology and Psychology of Terrorism: Who Becomes a Terrorist and Why?" Congressional Research Service (September 1999), p.12.

7. Peter L. Bergen, *Holy War, Inc: Inside the Secret World of Osama Bin Laden* (New York: Touchstone, 2002), pp. 21–22.

8. Brian Whitaker, "The Definition of Terrorism," *The Guardian* (May, 7, 2001), www.guardian.co.uk/elsewhere/journalist/story/0,7792,487098,00.html.

9. Hudson. "The Sociology and Psychology of Terrorism."

10. FoxNews.Com, "Marines Remember 1983 Beirut Bombing" (October 23, 2002), www.foxnews.com/story/0,2933,101035,00.html.

11. PBS NewsHour, "Declaration of War against the Americans Occupying the Land of the Two Holy Places" (August 1996), www.pbs.org/newshour/terrorism/international/fatwa_1996.html.

12. Condoleeza Rice, Remarks to the National Legal Center, New York (October 31, 2003), www.whitehouse.gov/news/releases/2003/10/20031031-5.html.

13. Hudson, "The Sociology and Psychology of Terrorism."

14. George W. Bush, Remarks at United Nations Financing for Development Conference, Monterrey, Mexico (March 22, 2002), www.whitehouse.gov/news/releases/2002/03/20020322-1.html.

15. Alan B. Krueger and Jitka Maleckova, "Seeking the Roots of Terrorism," *The Chronicle of Higher Education; The Chronicle Review* (June 6, 2003), chronicle.com/free/v49/i39/39b01001.htm.

16. Hudson. "The Sociology and Psychology of Terrorism."

17. Ibid.

18. *United States of America v. Usama Bin Laden, et al.*; United States District Court, Southern District of New York (November 4, 1998).

19. CNN.Com, "FBI: McVeigh Knew Children Would Be Killed in OKC Blast" (March 29, 2001), www.cnn.com/2001/US/03/29/mcveigh.book.01.

20. Macdonald, *The Turner Diaries*, p. 98.

21. Graham H. Turbiville, Jr., "Bearers of the Sword Radical Islam, Philippines Insurgency, and Regional Stability," *Military Review*, (March–April 2002), fmso.leavenworth.army.mil/FMSOPUBS/ISSUES/sword.htm#end7.

22. Hudson, "The Sociology and Psychology of Terrorism," p. 33.

23. Robert A. Pape, "Dying to Kill Us," *New York Times* (September 22, 2003): A17.

24. Hudson, "The Sociology and Psychology of Terrorism," p. 34.

25. Scott Atran, "Genesis of Suicide Terrorism," *Science*, 299 (March 7, 2003): 1534–1539.

26. Ibid., 1537.

27. U.S. State Department, *Patterns of Global Terrorism 2003* (Washington, D.C.: Department of State, April 2004), revised June 22, 2004 and reissued, www.state.gov/s/ct/rls/pgtrpt/2003/33771.htm.

28. Advisory Panel to Assess Domestic Response Capabilities for Terrorism Involving Weapons of Mass Destruction, The Gilmore Commission Final Report (Santa Monica: Rand, December 15, 2003), p. J-2.

29. *Patterns of Global Terrorism*, www.state.gov/s/ct/rls/pgtrpt/2003/33771.htm.

5

AL-QAIDA AND OTHER ISLAMIC EXTREMIST GROUPS

Understanding Fanaticism in the Name of Religion

The ruling to kill the Americans and their allies—civilians and military—is an individual duty for every Muslim who can do it in any country in which it is possible to do it, in order . . . for their armies to move out of all the lands of Islam, defeated and unable to threaten any Muslim.

"Jihad against Jews and Crusaders," World Islamic Front Statement, February, 1998

CHAPTER OVERVIEW

Al-Qaida, other radical terrorist groups, and sponsors such as the nation of Iran represent the most potent terrorist threat against the United States. Their record of successful attacks across the globe demonstrates the power of the ideology that sustains them—Islamic extremism, a heretical perversion of religious doctrines. More than one billion people from dozens of nations follow the Islamic faith. Even though only a small fraction of this population appears to support terrorism, it is a fraction that represents a substantial pool of support and recruits for terrorist groups.

While the terrorists have twisted many of Islam's principles, their ideology and motives draw upon its foundations. In order to understand the terrorists, it is critical to grasp their faith and view of history. In the eyes of these terrorists, they are engaged in a historic battle that began many centuries ago and includes inspirational *indiv a* events that most Americans understand vaguely if at all.

While many terrorist groups fight under the flag of religious crusade, and there is cooperation among them, the threat is not monolithic. The groups are separated by factors such as religious sect, nationality, and ideology. Al-Qaida has sought to bring many of these groups together, while the nation of Iran has continued to support terrorism in the name of its own version of Islam. To the extent these efforts succeed, the threat to the American homeland will grow, adding to the menace posed by the supporters of al-Qaida and the Iranian-supported Hizballah terrorist group who have already infiltrated the United States.

CHAPTER LEARNING OBJECTIVES

After reading this chapter, you should be able to

1. **Identify the basic tenets of the Muslim faith and its primary sects.**
2. **Outline important themes in Islamic history.**
3. **Describe the beliefs and motives of radical Islamic groups.**
4. **List the primary Islamic extremist terrorist groups.**

THE MUSLIM WORLD

More than one-fifth of the world population is Muslim. Most are not Arabs, but hail from such nations as Indonesia, Pakistan, and India. Other countries with large Muslim populations include Turkey, Egypt, Iran, Bangladesh, Nigeria, Algeria, and Morocco. Significant numbers of Muslims live in numerous other nations from the United States to China.

The Basic Faith   Islam is a monotheistic religion whose basic belief is, "There is no god but God (Allah), and Muhammad is his Prophet." Islam in Arabic means "submission;" someone who submits to God is a Muslim. Muslims believe Muhammad, a merchant who lived in what is now Saudi Arabia from circa AD 570 to 632, received God's revelations through the angel Gabriel. Words believed to have come directly from

God through Muhammad were compiled into the Qur'an, Islam's holy scripture. *worship as a god*

According to Islam, Muhammad is the final prophet of God. The faith asserts that Abraham, Moses, and Jesus bore revelations from God, but it does not accept the deification of Christ. As in Judaism and Christianity, the religion includes concepts such as the eternal life of the soul, heaven and hell, and the Day of Judgment.

The five pillars of Islamic faith outline the key duties of every Muslim:

1. *Shahada*. Affirming the faith
2. *Salat*. Praying every day, if possible five times, while facing Mecca
3. *Zakat*. Giving alms
4. *Sawm*. Fasting all day during the month of Ramadan
5. *Hajj*. Making a pilgrimage to Mecca

Islamic law, called the *sharia*, and other traditions outline social, ethical, and dietary obligations; for example, Muslims are not supposed to consume pork or alcohol. Religious leaders may also order *fatwas*, or religious edicts, authorizing or requiring certain actions. Finally, the Muslim faith includes the concept of *jihad*. Seen broadly, jihad means "striving" for the victory of God's word, in one's own life or that of the community. Seen narrowly, it refers to holy war against infidels, or nonbelievers, and apostates. Both the concepts of fatwa and jihad have been commandeered by extremists who, despite the disagreement of many Islamic leaders, use them to order and justify terrorism.

Perhaps most importantly, the Islamic tradition is all-encompassing, combining religious and secular life and law. After Muhammad's death, Muslims selected caliphs, or successors. These *caliphates* represented Islamic empires that combined religious and political power and lasted in various forms until 1924. As will be seen, the battles of these caliphates with the West bear an important role in the ideology of al-Qaida and other extremist groups. However, it was early disputes among Muslims over the identities of the rightful caliphs that lead to schisms in Islam.

Sects and Schisms

Less than 30 years after the death of Muhammad, the reigning caliph was murdered. The struggle for succession lead to a civil war that divided Muslims into sects, two of which remain most influential today.

Sunni

The largest denomination of Muslims is the Sunni branch. They make up the majority of most Middle Eastern countries and Indonesia, plus substantial populations in many other nations. Usama bin Ladin and most members of al-Qaida are Sunni. Sunnis believe themselves to be the followers of the sunna(practice) of the prophet Muhammad.

Shiite

The second largest Islamic denomination, estimated to constitute some 10 to 15 percent of Muslims, is the Shiite (or Shi'a) sect. Shiite Muslims believe that Ali, the son-in-law of Muhammad, was the first of the twelve imams appointed by God to succeed the Prophet as leader of Muslims. Iran is almost entirely Shiite and Iraq mostly so, although members of the Sunni minority in effect ruled Iraq under Saddam Hussein's regime. Pakistan and Saudi Arabia have significant Shiite minorities.

Fundamentalism and Radicalism: Wahhabism, Salafiyya, and Beyond

Founded by ibn Abd al Wahhab in the 1700s, Wahhabism has become a powerful strain of the Muslim faith. The faith has been called a "back to basics" purification of Sunni Islam. Its theological power was matched by the economic clout of its best-known adherents, the al-Saud dynasty, which conquered the holy cities of Mecca and Medina, creating Saudi Arabia in 1924. Since then, the Saudi government has used vast amounts of its petro-dollars to spread this variant of Islam, whose most extreme dimensions captured the imagination of Saudi native Usama bin Ladin.

Other important Islamic doctrines are the Takfir and Salafist systems. Salafists demand a return to the type of Islam practiced in its first generation, before what they regard as its corruption. They seek the absolute application of sharia, or religious law. Takfiris are committed to attacking false rulers and apostates. According to Takfir doctrine, members may violate Islamic laws, such as by drinking alcohol or avoiding mosques, in order to blend in with the enemy.

People who view Islam as a model for both religious and political governance, especially those who reject current government models in Islamic nations, are often called "Islamists." "Jihadists" is a word used for those committed to waging holy war against the West and what they consider apostate rules in Muslim-populated nations.

However, critics contend that even using these words provides an undeserved religious legitimacy to the cause of these terrorists and defames the Islamic religion.

Modern Challenges

As discussed earlier, political oppression is linked to terrorism. While poverty is not a proven cause of terrorism, it creates conditions that can allow terrorist groups to operate and recruit. Both circumstances are common in the Islamic world. Countries with a majority of Muslims are far less likely to be free than other nations.[1] They also tend to be poorer.[2] Many Muslim regions are also experiencing a "youth bulge," with a disproportionate number of citizens in the 15- to-29-year-old age range, for whom poor economic and educational prospects may increase the attraction of extremism and the pool of potential terrorists.[3] Finally, large numbers of refugees are found in many Muslim nations, creating social strains and providing sanctuary for extremists.

IDEOLOGY OF TERRORISM

Where leftist and many separatist terrorist groups have focused on producing brand new social structures and governments, in certain ways Islamic extremists fight to re-create the past. In a manner foreign to many Westerners, these terrorists harken back to a sacred and glorious past. They also appeal to what bin Ladin and others refer to as the "Islamic Nation," an idealized vision of a massive and united international Islamic population transcending national, ethnic, and class boundaries.

Glorious Past and Bitter Defeats

Islamic extremists often attempt to cast their actions as a defensive jihad against U.S. and Israeli aggression, placing current conflicts in the context of a war for religious control of the world that began more than 1,000 years ago. Following the birth of Islam, Muslim influence spread rapidly, as did the development of nations that practiced the faith. The faith expanded across the globe, including large parts of Europe such as Spain. During medieval times, the caliphates were militarily powerful, economically vibrant, and scientifically advanced.

House of Islam; House of War

As scholar Bernard Lewis described, the growth of the Islamic world was central to the Muslim philosophy: "In principle, the world was divided into two houses: the House of Islam, in which a Muslim government ruled and Muslim law prevailed, and the House of War, the rest of the world, still inhabited and, more important, ruled by infidels. Between the two, there was to be a perpetual state of war until the entire world either embraced Islam or submitted to the rule of the Muslim state."[4]

The Crusades

During this time, Islam also came into conflict with Christianity. In the Middle Ages, the Catholic Church organized *crusades*, military campaigns initially focused on capturing the holy city of Jerusalem from Muslim control. In the West, *crusade* ultimately became a word that described the fight for a noble cause. But in the Islamic world, the word was understood to mean an invasion by infidels and still resonates today. Bin Ladin repeatedly invoked the name of famous Muslim warriors from the crusades, including Saladin, who defeated the Christians and recaptured Jeruselem during the twelfth century.

Muslim Strength Fades

But the military might of the Muslim nations flagged. By the early 1900s, European powers had conquered most of the Muslim world and carved much of it up into colonies. As the colonialists withdrew in succeeding decades, they left behind a Muslim world divided into countries and ruled by a variety of often secular strong men and dictators.

"After the fall of our orthodox caliphates on March 3, 1924 and after expelling the colonists, our Islamic nation was afflicted with apostate rulers . . . .These rulers turned out to be more infidel and criminal than the colonialists themselves. Moslems have endured all kinds of harm, oppression, and torture at their hands," concludes the al-Qaida manual.

Extremism Rises

The violent Muslim Brotherhood, founded in 1928, fought against colonial governments and secular "apostate" Muslim rulers for a return to Islamic governance. Represented in scores of countries, the Brotherhood became especially active in Egypt after World War II and engaged in bloody battles across the Middle East, battling the influence of secular pan-Arabist and communist ideologies.

ISSUE:

A CLASH OF CIVILIZATIONS?

After 9/11, as Americans struggled to understand why they had been targeted and determine appropriate responses, attention turned to an essay written years before by a Harvard professor. In *The Clash of Civilizations*, published in 1993, Samuel Huntington had predicted that cultural conflict would replace ideological strife in the future. "Civilizations—the highest cultural groupings of people—are differentiated from each other by religion, history, language and tradition . . . the fault lines of civilizations are the battle lines of the future," he suggested.[5] Huntington predicted conflict between the Western and Islamic civilizations could increase.

The enormity of the hatred manifested by the 9/11 attacks, and media reports of jubilation at the attacks among some in the Islamic world, led Americans to wonder if al-Qaida's actions did indeed represent some large conflict between civilizations. Certainly bin Ladin attempted to portray the situation as a cultural war between "Islam and the crusaders." There is also no doubt many residents of Islamic nations disapprove of U.S. foreign policy and culture. Many are angry about American support for Israel and repressive regimes with large Muslim populations. A major 2002 poll of residents in nine Islamic nations revealed most did not have a favorable opinion of America; a parallel poll in the United States revealed similar feelings toward the Muslim world. The poll also indicated that while most Americans did not believe the United States was at war with the Muslim world, they thought Muslims believed it was.[6]

However, that same poll revealed that most Muslims surveyed did not believe the 9/11 attacks were justified. Muslim nations have also provided support to the United States and its allies during the war on terrorism. The United States points to this and its past military defense of Muslim populations in Kuwait, Kosovo, and Somalia as evidence the clash is not between civilizations. As additional proof, the United States points to the millions of Muslims living with equal rights as American citizens.

Rather than a clash *between* civilizations, the U.S. government and some scholars suggest Islamic extremist terrorism represents a *within a* civilization clash. As President Bush put it, "This is not a clash of civilizations. The civilization of Islam, with its humane traditions of learning and tolerance, has no place for this violent sect of killers and aspiring tyrants. This is not a clash of religions. The faith of Islam teaches moral responsibility that enobles men and women, and forbids the shedding of innocent blood. Instead, this is a clash of political visions."[7]

1. Is the war on terrorism more of a battle between cultures or specific political entities?

2. How do al-Qaida and other Islamic extremist terrorist groups use religious themes to pursue their objectives?

3. What do these issues suggest about strategies to reduce terrorism? Would improving relations between the populations of the United States and Muslim nations help decrease terrorist activity?

The Evolution of Religious-Inspired Terrorism

In 1979, Islamic extremists entered battle with the world's two greatest superpowers. These events combined to light the fuse on what would become an explosion of Muslim extremism and a shadow war that would lead to 9/11. That year the U.S.-installed Shah of Iran was toppled by Ayatollah Khomeini, a charismatic Shiite religious leader supported by trained operatives from the PLO camps and many more average Iranian citizens who hated the Shah's regime. Iran's leader promptly declared America the "Great Satan" and allowed his followers to seize the U.S. Embassy and hold 52 hostages. Khomeini's triumph fueled religious fundamentalism across the Middle East, along with disdain for the United States, whose response to the hostage taking was a botched raid that left dead American troops and burned equipment strewn across the Iranian desert.

Even followers of rival Muslim sects such as the Sunnis appeared energized by Khomeini's triumphs over America. Days after the occupation of the U.S. Embassy, Islamic radicals in Mecca, Saudi Arabia, seized the Grand Mosque and hundreds of hostages. Rooted out by a bloody military operation, many of the terrorists were publicly beheaded by Saudi authorities. In Libya, a mob—unchecked by local authorities—burned the U.S. Embassy.

Extremists were further infuriated when the Israel-Egypt Peace Treaty was signed that same year (Egyptian president Anwar Sadat was assassinated two years later). Finally, in December the Soviet Union invaded Afghanistan, starting a war against Islamic guerillas that would contribute to the collapse of communism and the emergence of twenty-first century terrorism.

1980s: Emergence of Shiite Extremist Terrorism

In 1981 Tehran released its American hostages, in part because of Iranian fears of attack from incoming President Ronald Reagan. Embroiled in a debilitating war with neighboring Iraq, the fundamentalist regime increasingly turned to terrorism as a tool. Iranian hit teams targeted opponents around the world. For example, a former Iranian diplomat was murdered in Maryland by an American operative dressed as a postal worker; the accused killer later surfaced in Iran.[8] At the same time, Tehran began sponsoring a variety of terrorist groups. One of them, al-Dawa, or "The Call," was dedicated to attacking Iraqi interests. In December 1981, the group demonstrated a terrorist technique previously unfamiliar to many, dispatching a suicide bomber to demolish Iraq's embassy in Beirut. Lebanon had become a cauldron of religious and political hatred containing Syrian and Israeli invaders, local religious militias, and Iranian Revolutionary Guards. Into that caustic mix dropped the U.S. Marines, dispatched to separate the nation's warring factions in late 1982. In Beirut the Americans would meet Imad Mughniyah, their most lethal foe until the days of bin Ladin, and his Hizballah organization, backed by Iran with support from Syria.

Hizballah, whose members hated the Israelis and aimed to make Lebanon a Shiite Muslim state, wanted the Americans out of the way. On April 18, 1983, a suicide bomber blew up the U.S. Embassy in Beirut, killing 63 people, including 17 Americans among whom were

---

FROM THE SOURCE:

MOST WANTED POSTER, IMAD MUGHNIYAH

The FBI reward for Imad Mughniyah is based on his alleged connection to the murder of Navy diver Robert Stethem, but
Mughniyah has been linked to other terrorist attacks against
Americans, including the bombing of the U.S. Marine barracks
in Beirut. See Figure 5.1.

---

many of the CIA's leading experts on the region. The blast was linked
to Islamic Jihad, used as a front name for Hizballah and other Iranian-
supported terrorist groups.

extremely bad

The marines, hunkered down in strategically execrable emplace-
ments near the Beirut airport, tangled with a complicated assortment
of adversaries struggling for the future of Lebanon. Shortly before

 Signal

reveille on the warm morning of October 23, a yellow Mercedes truck
roared over concertina wire obstacles, passed two guard posts before
sentries could get off a shot, slammed through a sandbagged position
at the entrance to the barracks, and exploded with the force of 12,000
pounds of dynamite.[9] The building, yanked from its foundations by
the blast from the advanced explosive device, imploded, crushing its
inhabitants under tons of broken concrete and jagged steel.
Simultaneously a second suicide bomber hit the Beirut compound
housing French paratroopers. When rescuers finished tearing
through the smoking rubble, while dodging fire from enemy snipers,
they counted 241 Americans and 58 French troops dead. Islamic Jihad
claimed responsibility.[10]

The American public clamored for a response. President Reagan
considered major attacks on the Syrian-controlled Bekaa Valley where
Iranian Revolutionary Guards supported Hizballah. But after disagreements in the administration, Reagan settled for shelling and a
limited air strike on other targets (including Syrian positions)—attacks
that were seen as ineffective by American adversaries and allies
alike.[11] Mughniyah, the suspected mastermind of the attacks, and his
operatives remained unscathed in their terrorist sanctuary. For months

MOST WANTED POSTER FOR IMAD FAYEZ MUGNIYAH. (FEDERAL BUREAU OF INVESTIGATION, WWW.FBI.GOV/MOSTWANT/TERRORISTS/TERMUGNIYAH.HTM.)

CONSPIRACY TO COMMIT AIRCRAFT PIRACY, TO COMMIT HOSTAGE TAKING, TO COMMIT AIR PIRACY RESULTING IN MURDER, TO INTERFERE WITH A FLIGHT CREW, TO PLACE A DESTRUCTIVE DEVICE ABOARD AN AIRCRAFT, TO HAVE EXPLOSIVE DEVICES ABOUT THE PERSON ON AN AIRCRAFT, AND TO ASSAULT PASSENGERS AND CREW; AIR PIRACY RESULTING IN MURDER; AIR PIRACY; HOSTAGE TAKING; INTERFERENCE WITH FLIGHT CREW; AND PLACING EXPLOSIVES ABOARD AIRCRAFT; PLACING DESTRUCTIVE DEVICE ABOARD AIRCRAFT; ASSAULT ABOARD AIRCRAFT WITH INTENT TO HIJACK WITH A DANGEROUS WEAPON AND RESULTING IN SERIOUS BODILY INJURY; AIDING AND ABETTING

IMAD FAYEZ MUGNIYAH

Alias:	Hajj

DESCRIPTION

Date of Birth Used:	1962	Hair:	Brown
Place of Birth:	Lebanon	Eyes:	Unknown
Height:	5'7"	Sex:	Male
Weight:	145 to 150 pounds	Citizenship:	Lebanese
Build:	Unknown		
Language:	Arabic		
Scars and Marks:	None known		
Remarks:	Mugniyah is the alleged head of the security apparatus for the terrorist organization, Lebanese Hizballah. He is thought to be in Lebanon.		

CAUTION

Imad Fayez Mugniyah was indicted for his role in planning and participation in the June 14, 1985, hijacking of a commercial airliner which resulted in the assault on various passengers and crew members, and the murder of one U.S. citizen.

REWARD

The Rewards For Justice Program, United States Department of State, is offering a reward of up to $25 million for information leading directly to the apprehension and/or conviction of Imad Fayez Mugniyah.

Source: http://www.fbi.gov/mostwant/terrorists/termugniyah.htm

the Marines kept up the fight, sustaining numerous casualties. But as the Lebanese security situation continued to disintegrate, the administration pulled the leathernecks from Lebanon in February 1984.

Hizballah continued its attacks, kidnapping numerous Western hostages and murdering a captive American CIA official and a

Marine officer, allegedly with the close cooperation of Tehran (as of 2004, the group had killed more Americans abroad than any other terrorist group, including al-Qaida). By the early 1990s, the organization had emerged as a political movement in Lebanon and expanded from its Middle Eastern base to strongholds in Latin America's tri-border area where Argentina, Brazil, and Paraguay meet. Imad Mughniyah, the purported killer of Americans in Lebanon, and his Iranian sponsors were linked to two huge car bomb attacks on Jewish targets in Argentina that left more than a hundred dead.

1990s: Emergence of Sunni Extremist Terrorism

Unable to afford Afghanistan's price in blood and gold, the Soviets began to withdraw in 1988. The ebbing tides of war left aground thousands of hardened foreigner mujahideen (holy warriors) who had traveled from across the world to fight communism in support of radical Islam. A 6-foot, 6-inch, left-handed Saudi multimillionaire and mujahideen financier decided to help the so-called Afghan Arabs identify their next battle. In 1988, Usama bin Ladin began forming an organization of these militants; he called it al-Qaida ("the base" in English) after a training camp in Afghanistan.[12] (The CIA provided funding and weapons to the mujahideen, but denies having supported bin Ladin directly during the Soviet war.)

As discussed earlier, bin Ladin went on to mold al-Qaida into an Islamic terrorist "organization of organizations" that combined numerous organizations with members from dozens of nations.

The Enemies: The United States and Its Allies

The international fighters turned their attention toward the relatively moderate governments of such Islamic countries as Egypt and Saudi Arabia, which they viewed as apostates, and the United States, Israel, and the United Nations, which they considered infidels and blood enemies. Al-Qaida began developing an ideology based on the eviction of the United States from the Middle East, the overthrow of U.S. allies in the Islamic world, and the destruction of the Israeli state. This call of Islamic extremism exercised renewed magnetism for Muslims angry with PLO compromises, aware of communism's failure as a model, and unmoved by self-proclaimed pan-Arabist leaders such as Libya's Muammar Qadhafi and Iraq's Saddam Hussein, who were attacked as secularists. The collapse of

Soviet communism, for which the mujahideen claimed partial credit, emboldened radicals with a belief they could defeat the remaining superpower.

shock

The U.S.-led war against Hussein in early 1991 fueled the movement; when the United States permanently positioned troops in Saudi Arabia after the war, al-Qaida saw it as a galvanizing issue and promised to drive the "crusaders" from the "land of the two holy mosques (Mecca and Medina.)" Over the coming years, al-Qaida and its supporters would establish a record of delivering on their promises, even returning to targets, such as the World Trade Center and U.S. Navy ships in Yemen, to complete their destruction.

Major operations executed, coordinated, or inspired by al-Qaida include bombings targeted at U.S. troops in Yemen during 1992; assistance to the guerillas who killed numerous U.S. troops in Somalia in 1993; the car bomb killing of five Americans in Saudi Arabia during 1995; bombings of the U.S. embassies in Kenya and Tanzania, that killed some 300 people in 1998; the planned bombing of the LA airport in 1999; the murder of 17 U.S. sailors in a suicide attack on the USS *Cole* in 2000; the 9/11 attacks; and deadly strikes in Saudi Arabia, Turkey, Indonesia, and other locations.

COMMON FRONT AGAINST THE WEST

Long divided by denomination, ethnicity, and other factors, Islamic extremists have found a common cause in their hatred of the United States. Al-Qaida sought to exploit this by rallying extremist organizations to its side. In February, 1998, bin Ladin announced a new terrorist alliance, the "International Islamic Front for Jihad against the Jews and Crusaders." The group issued a fatwa, or Islamic religious ruling: "The ruling to kill the Americans and their allies—civilians and military—is an individual duty for every Muslim who can do it in any country in which it is possible to do it . . . We—with Allah's help—call on every Muslim who believes in Allah and wishes to be rewarded to comply with Allah's order to kill the Americans and plunder their money wherever and whenever they find it. We also call on Muslim ulema [religious figures], leaders, youths, and soldiers to launch the raid on Satan's U.S. troops and the devil's supporters allying with them, and to displace those who are behind them so that they may learn a lesson."[13]

Sunni and Shiite Extremists Cooperate

Although the Islamic Front was composed of Sunni Muslims, there have been signs of cooperation between its members and the Shiite Hizballah and Iranians. An arrested al-Qaida operative testified to ties between that group and Hizballah. The 9/11 Commission found "far greater potential for collaboration between Hezbollah and al Qaeda than many had previously thought."[14] The commission reported that al-Qaida operatives had "traveled to Iran and Hezbollah camps in Lebanon for training in explosives, intelligence and security" and that bin Ladin was interested in Hizballah's tactics in the 1983 bombing of U.S. marines in Lebanon. While these terrorist groups may have different political agendas and even contrasting religious views, these may not prevent them from cooperating when operations are in their mutual interest.

Success in a Common Goal

On June 25, 1996, a sophisticated truck bomb tore apart the Khobar Towers, a U.S. military complex in Dharan, Saudi Arabia, killing 19 Americans and wounding hundreds more. "We thought it was the end of the world. Some were crying; some just sat on the ground and held their ears," said a witness. The attack followed another bombing of Americans a year earlier in Saudi Arabia; an attack the 9/11 Commission reported was supported financially by bin Ladin.

The Khobar Towers attack, which produced images of destruction similar to the 1983 Marine barracks bombing, produced an outcry in the United States. "I am outraged by it," declared President Clinton. As President Reagan before him, Clinton promised, "The cowards who committed this murderous act must not go unpunished."[15] But they did. Later identified in a U.S. indictment as Saudi Shiite extremists backed by Iran and linked to Hizballah, the Khobar bombers remained free after their attack. According to the 9/11 Commission, there is "strong but indirect evidence" that al-Qaida cooperated in the attack.

America responded to the terrorist threat in Saudi Arabia by pulling out of the Khobar Towers and relocating its troops to a remote area of Saudi Arabia; by the summer of 2003, most U.S. troops would be out of Saudi Arabia entirely.

Potential for Ongoing Cooperation

The withdrawal from Saudi Arabia occurred after the U.S. liberation of Iraq; the quick and successful initial stage of that operation lessened the need for a Saudi base. But the operation appeared to energize Hizballah. With agents on four continents, "We see them actively casing and [conducting surveillance on] American facilities," said then-CIA director George Tenet in 2003. Around the same time, Hizballah's leader was reiterating the group's position on the United States. "In the past, when the Marines were in Beirut, we screamed, 'Death to America!'" Hassan Nasrallah declared in 2003. "Today, when the region is being filled with hundreds of thousands of American soldiers, 'Death to America!' was, is and will stay our slogan."[16] While Hizballah had not been known to launch attacks in the United States, U.S. officials stepped up their scrutiny of the group's operatives in the United States.

Iraq as a Magnet

Extended U.S. occupation and insurgent warfare created a destination for Islamic extremists, much as Afghanistan and to a lesser extent Lebanon had in years before. U.S. forces captured hundreds of foreign fighters, many with links to al-Qaida.[17] The Ansar al-Islam group and the linked Jama'at al-Tawhid and Jihad organizations, also called the al-Zarqawi network, lead by Sunni extremist Abu Musab al-Zarqawi, carried out operations against U.S. and other coalition and UN targets. Hizballah and Iranian agents also infiltrated the country.[18] Both Shiite and Sunni extremists opposed U.S. plans to foster a democratic government in Iraq (although historical tensions between the groups remained evident).

Democracy Is a Deviation

The United States aimed to demonstrate the power of democracy in the Middle East. But peaceful democratic change is a "deviant and misleading practice that contradicts Allah's teachings to fight in the name of God," according to bin Ladin. The driving principle of Islamic extremism is summarized in the al-Qaida manual: "an Islamic government would never be established except by the bomb and rifle. Islam does not coincide or make a truce with unbelief, but rather confronts it."[19]

ISLAMIC TERRORIST GROUPS

For detailed information on individual groups see Appendix 1.

CHAPTER SUMMARY

Islamic extremists believe they are fighting a war that has lasted for centuries and will continue until they have prevailed. Comprised of numerous organizations and numbering many thousands of hardened terrorist and active supporters, the Islamic extremist movement is not monolithic but is capable of cooperation. It will harness the most effective weapons it can muster to achieve victory. Democracy and economic reform may lessen the appeal of these groups but will not eliminate their rallying cry or potential for catastrophic violence.

CHAPTER QUIZ

1. Identify three countries outside the Middle East with substantial Muslim populations.
2. Explain two different meanings of *jihad*.
3. Describe the capabilities of Hizballah.
4. Recount two key strategic objectives claimed by Usama bin Ladin.

NOTES

1. Freedom House, "Freedom in the World Survey," www.freedomhouse.org/research/muslimpop2004.pdf.
2. Michael Cosgrove, "International Economics and State-Sponsored Terrorism," *Journal of the Academy of Business and Economics* (February 2003), articles.findarticles.com/p/articles/mi_m0OGT/is_2_1/ai_113563605.
3. John L. Helgerson , "The National Security Implications of Global Demographic Change," Remarks to the Denver World Affairs Council and the Better World Campaign, Denver, Colorado, April 30, 2002, www.cia.gov/nic/speeches_demochange.html.
4. Bernard Lewis, "The Revolt of Islam," *New Yorker* (November 19, 2001), www.newyorker.com/fact/content/?011119fa_FACT2.

5. Samuel P. Huntington, "The Clash of Civilizations?" *Foreign Affairs*, 72/3 (Summer 1993): 22, www.foreignaffairs.org/19930601faessay5188/samuel-p-huntington/the-clash-of-civilizations.html.

6. Richard Benedetto, "Great Divide Splits U.S., Islamic Cultures, Poll Finds," *USA Today* (March 4, 2002), p. 1, www.usatoday.com/news/washington/2002/03/05/poll.htm.

7. George W. Bush's remarks at the United States Air Force Academy Graduation Ceremony, United States Air Force Academy, June 2, 2004, www.whitehouse.gov/news/releases/2004/06/20040602.html.

8. The alleged killer was later reported to have worked for an official newspaper and appeared in an Iranian movie. See BBC, "Kandahar film's murder mystery," (December 30, 2001), news.bbc.co.uk/1/hi/world/south_asia/1734315.stm.

9. CBS.Com, "Beirut Barracks Attack Remembered" (October 23, 2002), www.cbsnews.com/stories/2003/10/23/world/main579638.shtml.

10. Department of Defense, "Report of the Department of Defense Commission on Beirut International Airport Terrorist Act, October 23, 1983."

11. PBS Frontline, "Hostages taken at the U.S. Embassy in Iran," www.pbs.org/wgbh/pages/frontline/shows/target/etc/cron.html.

12. CNN.Com, "Transcript of Bin Laden's October Interview" (February 5, 2003), www.cnn.com/2002/WORLD/asiapcf/south/02/05/binladen.transcript/index.html.

13. World Islamic Front Statement, " Jihad against Jews and Crusaders" (February 23, 1998), www.fas.org/irp/world/para/docs/980223-fatwa.htm.

14. "Overview of the Enemy."

15. Philip Shenon, "23 U.S. Troops Die in Truck Bombing in Saudi Base," *New York Times* (June 26, 1996): A1.

16. Josh Meyer, "Hezbollah Vows Anew to Target Americans. Bush Officials, Fearing Attacks, Debate Whether to Go after the Group and Backers of Iran and Syria," *Los Angles Times* (April 17, 2003), p. 1, www.latimes.com/news/nationworld/iraq/world/la-war-hezbollah17apr17,1,4681007.story?coll=la%2Dhome%2DheadlinesApril 17,2003.

17. Department of State, *Patterns of Global Terrorism*.

18. James Risen, "A Region Inflamed; The Hand of Tehran," *New York Times* (November 24, 2003): A10.

19. "Message to the Iraqis."

6

THE TRANSNATIONAL DIMENSIONS OF TERRORISM

The Unique Dangers of the Twenty-First Century

HAMAS and PIJ in the U.S. warrant equal vigilance due to their ongoing capability to launch terrorist attacks inside the U.S.

FBI Director Robert Mueller III, 2004

CHAPTER OVERVIEW

International and transnational terrorism impacts the United States in several ways. Most important are direct attacks against the U.S. homeland and citizens abroad. But America's homeland security is also affected by terrorist groups that organize and raise funds here in the United States to support violent acts against U.S. allies and innocent civilians around the world. Along with global terrorist networks, transnational criminal organizations pose a threat to U.S. security, especially when they cooperate with terrorist groups that exploit the trade in illegal drugs, a phenomenon known as narco-terrorism. This both increases the supply of drugs in America and destabilizes U.S. allies. The capabilities of international terrorist groups have been enhanced in many past cases by the assistance of foreign governments, known as state sponsors of terrorism.

CHAPTER LEARNING OBJECTIVES

After reading this chapter, you should be able to

1. Define transnational terrorism.
2. Understand modern trends in transnational terrorism involving the United States.
3. Identify major international terrorist groups operating in the United States and their objectives.
4. Explain the concept and dimensions of narco-terrorism.
5. Identify terrorist state sponsors and trends in their support of international terrorism.

AMERICA IN A GLOBALIZED WORLD

When President George Washington urged his young nation to avoid foreign entanglements in his 1796 farewell address, he could hardly have imagined the complexity of America's current relationship with the world. Connected to other countries by technology, economics, travel, news media, diplomacy, security, and vast numbers of immigrants from an array of ethnic and religious backgrounds, the United States has become linked inextricably to virtually every corner of the planet. This phenomenon is often called globalization

Long before 9/11, American security analysts pondered the implications of globalization. Since 1989, the U.S. State Department has provided an annual review of global terrorism. The 1999 report, marking a decade of tracking terrorist trends, included a prominent inset with a picture and brief biography of Usama bin Ladin. The analysis concluded that the al-Qaida leader was a major threat who believed himself capable of directing terrorist strikes worldwide.[1] The assessment could not have been more accurate. The State Department report illustrated that even in advance of these strikes Americans knew a great deal about the potential enemies it might face in the future and their growing capacity to use transnational means to threaten global peace and stability. In fact, long before 9/11, experts had largely reached a common view on three key points.

1. The diversity of possible threats is increasing.
2. There will be more nonstate threats with global reach.
3. States may act in concert with these groups.

They were right on all three counts.[2]

DEFINING TRANSNATIONAL TERRORISM

Under the U.S. legal definition, transnational, or *international*, terrorism occurs primarily outside the territorial jurisdiction of the United States, or transcends national boundaries by its means, the people it intends to terrorize, or the location in which the terrorists operate or seek asylum. International terrorist groups can also be defined as those whose leadership and personnel are primarily foreign and whose motives are primarily nationalist, ideological, or religious.

Modern History of Transnational Terrorism against the United States

As holiday travelers dashed through New York's La Guardia Airport on the evening of December 29, 1975, thoughts of upcoming New Year's Eve celebrations disappeared with an enormous explosion. "A bright blue flash. A blast of air. Deafening noise. Broken glass rained down," described one account.[3] The impact was so strong one survivor thought a plane had crashed into the terminal, but the actual cause was a time bomb placed in a coin-operated storage locker. The device killed 11 people and wounded more than 70 more. Survivors saw bodies, body parts, and blood strewn across the airport, but there was no screaming, reported one observer: "It seemed like everyone was in shock. The whole thing was just a complete wreck, with mobs of people just standing around. You can't believe it until you see something like this."[4]

The blast prompted a massive investigation. But in 1975, there were so many terrorist groups with the capabilities and intent to target the United States that the police faced a daunting task. Domestic groups such as left-wing extremists and the Jewish Defense League came under suspicion. The FALN (Fuerzas Armadas de Liberacion Nacional Puertorriquena), a Cuban-backed Puerto Rican independence group, had detonated a deadly bomb in a New York tavern less than a year before and appeared a potential.[5]

There was also an extensive roster of international terrorists to consider. U.S. citizens abroad had recently been targeted by communist ideological terrorists from Germany and Japan, among others, and a variety of Middle Eastern groups. While not believed likely to attack the United States, Irish Republican Army (IRA) operatives were known for their devastating bombings in Great Britain and support activities in New York and elsewhere in the United States. Investigators considered the Palestine Liberation Organization (PLO), which quickly denied involvement. Then, in September 1976, Croatian nationalist terrorists, seeking independence from Yugoslavia, hijacked a TWA jet leaving La Guardia. They also left a bomb in a coin-operated locker at New York's Grand Central Station. It went off while being dismantled, killing one police officer and badly wounding another. Despite differences in the airport and train station bombs, and denials from the captured hijackers, officials continued to suspect the Croatians of involvement in the La Guardia blast. The crime was never solved.

One lesson, however, was clear. U.S. citizens at home and abroad were at risk from international terrorist groups with a vast range of ideologies but one common belief—that attacking American targets could further their causes.

Attacking US citizens can further their cause.

Ideological Groups

As the leader of the capitalist world and military ally of many nations, the United States found itself the target of numerous ideologically motivated terrorist groups. Left-wing organizations, such as the German Red Army Faction (also known as the Baader-Meinhof group), Japanese Red Army, Greek left-wing terrorists, and Philippine communist terrorists, attacked Americans abroad. Many of these groups received support from communist nations and Palestinian groups. Neo-fascist terrorists, some believed to have Middle Eastern backing and connections to right-wing extremists in the United States, also posed a potential threat to Americans in Europe, with their bombs targeted at public gatherings killing almost 100 people in 1980 alone.

Nationalist and Palestinian-Israeli Conflict

Many terrorists have opposed the United States because of its actual or perceived role in their separatist or nationalist conflicts. U.S. citizens, while not directly targeted in most cases, have been put at risk by the attacks of organizations such as the Irish Republican Army, the Basque separatist organization ETA, and Liberation Tigers of Tamil Eelam (LTTE). However, the most significant of nationalist conflicts for the United States has been the consequences of the struggle between the Palestinians and Israelis.

During the 1970s and '80s, PLO and other Palestinian terrorists from secular and leftist factions killed numerous Americans during their operations abroad, which were sometimes coordinated with European and Japanese leftist terrorists. The Palestinian terrorist strategy and some of its major strikes are detailed earlier in this book. However, the extensive list of Palestinian terrorism includes numerous other attacks on Americans. During a 1973 raid on a U.S. Pan American jetliner in Rome, terrorists slaughtered many of the passengers with machine gun fire and grenades; a statement claimed the attack was in retaliation for U.S. arms shipments to Israel. In October 1985, Palestinian commandos seized the Italian cruise liner *Achille Lauro* and killed wheelchair-bound American Leon Kinghoffer and threw him into the sea. On March 30, 1986, a bomb made of Soviet-Bloc Semtex plastic explosive blew up aboard TWA Flight 840 heading from Rome to Athens. The blast tore open a hole in the fuselage; four victims, including eight-month-old Demetra Klug, were sucked out and plummeted thousands of feet to their deaths. A Palestinian terrorist group called the attack revenge for a recent naval battle between the United States and Libya, an ally of Palestinian extremists and a state sponsor of terrorism.

State Sponsorship

Much of the world's terrorism during the 1980s was supported by state sponsors—nations that supported terrorist groups as part of their international security policies. Aside from the Soviet Bloc, which provided varying levels of patronage to a number of terrorist organizations before its demise, the United States traditionally counted Iran, North Korea, Cuba, Syria, Libya, Sudan, and Iraq as state sponsors.

Of those, Libya was considered one of the most flagrant; its flamboyant dictator Muammar Qadhafi tangled with the United States for years, often using Palestinian and other terrorist groups to pursue his objectives. This even included offering $2.5 million to a Chicago street gang called the El Rukns in return for terrorist attacks in the U.S. homeland—a scheme later broken up by American law enforcement. After a Libyan-sponsored bombing killed two U.S. servicemen in Germany, United States war planes struck Libya in 1986. But Qadhafi continued his attacks, often using Japanese Red Army (JRA) terrorists. They targeted U.S. facilities abroad, and in April 1988, alleged JRA terrorist Yu Kikumura was arrested for a plot to set off bombs in New York City.

The Libyan campaign peaked on December 21, 1988, when Pan Am Flight 103 exploded over Lockerbie, Scotland, killing 270 passengers and people on the ground.

However, over the last decade Libya and most other state sponsors have reduced their support of terrorism in the face of U.S. and international pressure. Qadhafi eventually renounced terrorism, agreed to compensate the families of Pan Am Flight 103 victims, and arranged to dismantle his WMD program. Sudan has expanded its cooperation with the West, and Iraq's terrorist sponsors—who provided undisputed support to certain terrorist groups and had less clear connections to al-Qaida—were removed by the U.S. invasion. Cuba, North Korea, and Syria—which has continued to support Hizballah and Palestinian terrorist groups and is suspected of assisting anti-American insurgents in Iraq—remain as sponsors, although none is as active now as in the past.

Transnational Crime and Narco-Terrorism

Besides global terrorist networks, there are other nonstate actors, with goals geared toward personal gain rather than public objectives, whose actions nevertheless have significant consequences for homeland security. International criminal organizations participate in drug and arms trafficking, money laundering, cigarette smuggling, piracy, counterfeiting, illegal technology transfers, identity theft, public corruption, and illegal immigration. Assessments of the international crime threat are that it is pervasive, substantial, and growing. For example, organized alien smuggling networks bring over 500,000 illegal immigrants into the United States annually and move four million people worldwide, generating revenues of over $7 billion. Worldwide money laundering is estimated at $1 trillion. Individuals engaged in these criminal activities are also increasingly employing sophisticated methods and advanced technologies.[6]

There is no single global crime cartel, but there is evidence that groups have cooperated in joint operations. Though virtually no country is free of organized crime, the eight largest crime organizations are centered in China (including Hong Kong and Taiwan), Colombia, Italy, Japan, Mexico, Russia, the United States, and Canada. Each group has extensive international links and cuts across regions of strategic concern to the United States. In recent years Albanian, Burmese, Filipino, Israeli, Jamaican, Korean, Thai, Nigerian, and Pakistani groups have also drawn the concern of international law

ISSUE:

ARE INTERNATIONAL CRIMINAL ORGANIZATIONS A THREAT TO HOMELAND SECURITY?

Some observers maintain that criminal organizations are not a direct threat to the security of the United States since they seek to exploit and manipulate rather than coerce or compel the state to take specific acts. Nor do they directly threaten the stability of the nation.[8] Transnational criminal organizations, however, can impact on homeland security threats in several distinct and important ways. Organized crime and corruption can undermine political, economic, and social stability of weak states thus increasing the potential for governments to be co-opted by authoritarian regimes or terrorist groups. This threat is particularly evident in central Asia, central and southeast Europe, and South America. Criminal groups can also facilitate, fund, supply goods and services to, or even act on behalf of terrorist groups. There are reports the Camorra crime organization and other criminal groups based around Naples, Italy, supplied heavy weapons to the ETA terrorist group in exchange for cocaine and hashish. Arms smuggling groups have also been linked to terrorist groups.[9] The line between these groups can become vague. In some instances, including a major U.S. and Canadian methamphetamine ring, money gained from drug trafficking has been sent to terrorist groups.[10] Also, other transnational groups mimic criminal activities, using the same methods and techniques to evade law enforcement and exploit the gaps in U.S. domestic security. Finally, the toll of international crime in social costs, lost revenue, and the demand for intelligence and law enforcement resources complicates and exacerbates the challenge of responding to terrorist groups.

1. Should major criminal organizations be considered threats to America's homeland security?
2. What priority should be placed on investigating transnational criminal organizations?

3. Are any of the tools used in the war on terrorism appropriate for use against criminal groups? If so, which ones?

4. Are there reasons these groups should *not* receive substantial focus?

enforcement. The organizations also appear to be evolving, employing looser, more adaptive, and innovational command structures.[7]

Narco-Terrorism

In the area of drug smuggling the nexus between terrorism and criminal activity is particularly troubling. According to the U.S. Drug Enforcement Administration (DEA), a narco-terrorist organization is a "group that is complicit in the activities of drug trafficking to further or fund premeditated, politically motivated violence to influence a government or group of people." Almost half of the groups designated by the State Department as "foreign terrorist organizations" may be tied to the drug trade, the DEA estimates. Because "drugs and terror frequently share a common ground of geography, money, and violence," keeping drug money from financing terror is an important part of the nation's counterterrorism strategy.[11]

The international market in drugs can provide several benefits to terrorist groups. They can acquire operating funds from producing drugs and/or protecting those who do. They also benefit from the instability produced by drug trafficking and may also see value in encouraging the use of drugs by the United States and other enemy populations. For example, the Taliban government of Afghanistan earned huge amounts of money from the opium trade during the time it was sheltering al-Qaida, and the DEA has claimed there is "multi-source information" that bin Ladin has been involved in the financing and facilitation of heroin trafficking.[12] The Afghan heroin trade continued after the U.S. invasion, although the public evidence tying it to remnant Taliban and al-Qaida forces is not conclusive.

The link between drugs and terror is most evident among the terrorist groups active in Colombia such as the Revolutionary Armed Forces of Colombia (FARC). These groups are responsible for a substantial amount of the cocaine and heroin sold in America. They also target U.S. citizens and property in Colombia, often using their trademark strategy of kidnapping for ransom. According to public records, more than 70 Americans have been kidnapped by terrorist and criminal groups in Colombia; at least 13 have died.[13] U.S. security assistance to the Colombian government has also put Americans in harm's way. The FARC has reportedly described such assistance as an "act of war."[14] A U.S. pilot was killed by FARC guerillas in 2003 after his

---

FROM THE SOURCE:

U.S. DEPARTMENT OF JUSTICE ANNOUNCEMENT OF INDICTMENT OF FARC LEADERS (NOVEMBER 2002)

The first indictment, returned in October (2002) and unsealed today, charges three defendants with conspiring in 1997 to take U.S. nationals Jerel Shaffer and Earl Goen hostage while they were working in Venezuela in the import/export and oil industries. The indictment names as defendants: Jorge Briceno Suarez, a/k/a "Mono Jojoy" and "Carlos," the overall military commander of the FARC and, at the time of the events described in the indictment, the commander of the Eastern Bloc of the FARC; Thomas Molina Caracas, a/k/a Tomas Medina Caracas and "El Patron" and "El Negro Acacio," who at the time was the commander of the 16th Front of the FARC; and a FARC member known as "El Loco" and "Fernando."

The indictment charges that Briceno Suarez and Molina Caracas, along with FARC members and others, worked together in targeting and taking the U.S. nationals hostage in Venezuela, detaining the victims against their will and transporting Shaffer to the jungles of Colombia, where he was bound, beaten and held hostage at gunpoint for nine months until about $1 million was paid for his release. While Shaffer was being transported, his FARC captors murdered two local residents. As a result, the maximum legal punishment for the hostage taking charge is the death penalty.

. . . A third indictment, also unsealed today in the District of Columbia, charges FARC senior commander Henry Castellanos Garzon, a/k/a "Comandante Romana," with hostage taking and conspiracy to commit hostage taking for the March 1998 kidnaping of four Americans. The indictment, originally filed under seal in December 1998, charges Romana with kidnaping Louise Augustine, Todd Mark, Thomas Fiore and Peter Shen—all Americans—and a foreign national. The indictment states that Romana personally interrogated the hostages about their assets and the financial state of their families, in an effort to determine whether to demand ransom and how much. The hostages were released one month after their kidnaping without the payment of any ransom.[15]

plane crashed into the jungle. Three U.S. citizens flying with him were captured and held hostage by the group.

CURRENT THREAT

The collapse of communism and negotiations to settle major nationalist disputes, such as those in Ireland and Israel, have reduced or eliminated the power of many traditional ideological and nationalist international terrorist groups. However, the threat of international terrorism remains real. For example, while PLO-affiliated groups reduced their international attacks after accepting the concept of coexistence with Israel, the al-Aqsa Martyrs Brigades has launched suicide strikes within Israel, killing U.S. citizens and many Israeli noncombatants. An even greater threat is posed by the Palestinian terrorist groups HAMAS and the Palestine Islamic Jihad (PIJ). Dedicated to the destruction of Israel and hostile toward the United States, these radical Islamic groups have mounted major suicide bomb attacks against Israel, claiming numerous American lives. In 2004 the FBI confirmed their "ongoing capability to launch terrorist attacks inside the U.S." Historically, however, these groups have limited their militant activities to Israeli targets and have reserved the United States for fundraising, recruitment, and procurement. Criminal investigations of these groups and Hizballah supporters have revealed extensive fundraising and support efforts in the United States, where the groups can count on the assistance of numerous sympathizers.[16]

Other groups such as the Tamil separatists of the LTTE, which has a large Canadian support network, possess operatives in or with easy access to the United States. The remnants of the Aum Shinrikyo group, while not reported to have a presence in the United States, are capable of attacking U.S. citizens in Japan and Russia. The United States must remain vigilant about such groups that currently exhibit the capability, if not intent, to attack the American homeland or U.S. citizens abroad. A change in U.S. policy or an internal strategic decision could provide these groups with a new intent to attack suddenly and without warning.

But the monitoring of intents and capabilities is made more challenging by the evolving terrorist threat. As in the 1970s and '80s, when terrorist groups with disparate ideologies cooperated in training and operations, and mirroring the cooperation of Islamic extremist groups, modern international groups appear to be sharing resources. For example, the Colombian government has asserted that at least seven members of the IRA have provided training to members of the FARC in areas such as advanced explosives and mortar techniques (three men with IRA links were arrested in Colombia; although these men were later acquitted, improvements in FARC tactics and other factors strongly suggest IRA assistance).[17] Information flow on effective techniques may occur even without direct contact between groups. There are claims that al-Qaida sympathizers have received instruction in maritime terrorist techniques perfected by the Tamil separatists of the LTTE.[18]

Certain areas of the world have become petri dishes for terrorism, including the remote triborder region of Paraguay, Argentina, and Brazil. The U.S. military has reported this area serves as a support base for HAMAS, as well as the Islamic extremist groups Hizballah and Islamaya al Gama'at. "These organizations generate revenue in the triborder area through illicit activities that include drug and arms trafficking, counterfeiting, money laundering, forged travel documents, and even software and music piracy. Additionally, these organizations provide safe havens and assistance to other terrorists that transit the region," claimed one report to Congress.[19]

PROFILES OF SIGNIFICANT
INTERNATIONAL TERRORIST GROUPS

For detailed information on significant terrorist groups see Appendix 1.

CHAPTER SUMMARY

Over the last three decades, the primary terrorist threat to the U.S. homeland from international terrorists has shifted from traditional groups motivated by ideological, nationalist, and state-sponsor goals to Islamic extremists. However, several nationalist and ideological groups, along with the remnants of the Aum Shinrikyo cult, maintain both a capability to strike U.S. citizens and a hostility toward U.S. policies. History also indicates the likelihood that additional international terrorist threats will emerge against the United States.

CHAPTER QUIZ

1. What is international terrorism?
2. List two major international terrorist groups, other than al-Qaida, that have conducted support operations in the United States during recent years.
3. Identify a major international terrorist group, other than al-Qaida, with the capability to attack U.S. citizens.
4. What is narco-terrorism?
5. Name a terrorist state sponsor that has dramatically reduced its support for terrorism in recent years and another that has not.

NOTES

1. U.S. State Department, *Patterns of Global Terrorism 1999* (2000), p. 32.
2. Sam J. Tangredi, "The Future Security Environment, 2001-2025: Toward a Consensus View." In *QDR 2001 Strategy-Driven Choices for America's Security*, edited by Michèle A. Flournoy (Washington, DC: National Defense University, 2001), p. 28. Tangredi's assessment was reached by comparing 35 major assessments of the future security environment conducted in the decade after the end of the Cold War.

3. John Springer, "LaGuardia Christmas Bombing; 27 Years Later, Case Still Unsolved," Court TV (December 2002), www.courttv.com/news/hiddentraces/laguardia/page1.html.

4. Leslie Maitland, "Witnesses Tell of Horror," *New York Times* (December 30, 1975): 75.

5. On Cuban support for the FALN, see, for example, Edmund Mahoney, "A Man and a Movement in Cuba's Grip," *The Hartford Courant* (November 7, 1999): A1.

6. *UN Global Report on Crime and Justice* (1999); *Global Trends 2015: A Dialogue about the Future with Nongovernment Experts,* National Intelligence Council (December 2000), p. 41; *International Crime Control,* Government Accounting Office (August 2001), GAO-01-629.

7. Phil Williams, "Transnational Criminal Networks." In *Networks and Netwars,* edited by John Arquilla and David Ronfeldt (Santa Monica: RAND, 2001), pp. 63–64.

8. Phil Williams, "Combating Transnational Organized Crime." In *Transnational Threats: Blending Law Enforcement and Military Strategies,* edited by Carolyn W. Pumphrey (Carlisle, PA: Strategic Studies Institute, 2000), pp. 190–191; Thomas V. Fuentes, "Phil Williams' View of Criminal Organizations and Drug Trafficking: Another Perspective." In *Transnational Threats,* p. 204.

9. Glenn E. Curtis and Tara Karacan., "The Nexus among Terrorists, Narcotics Traffickers, Weapons Proliferators, and Organized Crime Networks in Western Europe," Congressional Research Service (2002).

10. Statement for the Record of Louis J. Freeh, Director, Federal Bureau of Investigation, on International Crime before Subcommittee on Foreign Operations, Senate Committee on Appropriations (April 21, 1998), www.usdoj.gov/criminal/cybercrime/freeh328.htm.

11. Statement of Karen P. Tandy, Administrator, Drug Enforcement Administration, before the House Committee on International Relations (February 12, 2004), www.dea.gov/pubs/cngrtest/ct021204.htm.

12. Statement of Asa Hutchinson, Administrator, Drug Enforcement Administration, before the Senate Judiciary Committee Subcommittee on Technology, Terrorism, and Government Information (March 13, 2002), www.dea.gov/pubs/cngrtest/ct031302.html.

13. U.S. House of Representatives, Committee on International Relations, "Summary of Investigation of IRA Links to FARC Narco-Terrorists in Columbia" (April 24 2002), www.house.gov/international_relations/findings.htm.

14. Ibid.

15. Department of Justice, "Attorney General Ashcroft Announces Indictments of FARC Members on Drug Trafficking, Hostage Taking Charges" (November 13, 2002), www.usdoj.gov/opa/pr/2002/November/02_crm_667.htm.

16. Department of Justice, "PIJ Support" (February 3, 2003), www.usdoj.gov/opa/pr/2003/February/03_crm_099.htm.

17. House International Relations Committee, Summary of Investigation of IRA Links to FARC Narco-Terrorists in Columbia." U.S. House of Representatives (April 24, 2002), wwwc.house.gov/international_relations/107/findings.htm.

18. Reuters, "Expert Says Islamic Militants Trained for Sea Attacks" (January 21, 2003), www.haaretzdaily.com/hasen/pages/ShArt.jhtml?itemNo=254625&contrassID=1&subContrassID=8&sbSubContrassID=0&listSrc=Y.

19. Gary D. Speer, "Posture Statement Before the 107th Congress" (March 5, 2002), www.defenselink.mil/dodgc/lrs/docs/test02-03-05Speer.rtf.

7

DOMESTIC TERRORIST GROUPS

The Forgotten Threat

This is the endgame for the animal killers and if you choose to stand with them you will be dealt with accordingly. There will be no quarter given, no half measures taken.

Eco-Terrorist Statement Claiming Responsibility for a 2003 Bombing

CHAPTER OVERVIEW

Political protest is both a right and tradition of the American people. However, for certain groups protest has led to extremism, which has led, in some cases, to terrorism. Homegrown terrorists have fought for a wide range of right-wing, left-wing, nationalist, and special-interest causes. United by their disdain for the democratic system and choice of political violence as a tactic, they have made domestic terrorism by far the most frequent form of terrorist activity in modern U.S. history.

Recent trends in domestic terrorism suggest a continuing level of violence employing sophisticated tactics that make detection and arrest more difficult. With a proven interest in WMD, domestic terrorists pose a significant threat to the U.S. homeland.

CHAPTER LEARNING OBJECTIVES

After reading this chapter, you should be able to

1. Define domestic terrorism.
2. Describe modern historical trends in domestic terrorism.
3. Identify major extremist movements linked to modern domestic terrorism.
4. Explain the threat raised by evolving characteristics of domestic terrorism.

THE ENEMY WITHIN

George Metesky was a quiet man. None of his neighbors suspected that he was responsible for a string of bombings that terrorized New Yorkers for 16 years. In January 1952, Metesky confessed to being the "Mad Bomber" and planting 32 bombs in New York, which injured 16 people. Metesky was hardly an aberration. America has never been immune from the threat of political violence emanating from domestic sources, be they individuals like Metesky, or large organized groups. It is the kind of threat that will likely present itself again in the future.

DEFINING DOMESTIC TERRORISM

In contrast with Islamic extremist and international terrorism, which often occurs abroad under the direction of foreign leaders, domestic terrorism is usually conducted by U.S. citizens operating in their own country. The FBI defines *domestic terrorism* as "acts of violence that are a violation of the criminal laws of the United States or any state, committed by individuals or groups without any foreign direction, and appear to be intended to intimidate or coerce a civilian population, or influence the policy of a government by intimidation or coercion, and occur primarily within the territorial jurisdiction of the United States."[1]

THE INCIDENCE OF DOMESTIC TERRORISM

Domestic terrorism has been the most common form of terrorism in the United States and until 9/11 was the most deadly. The FBI recorded 353 incidents or suspected incidents of terrorism in this country between 1980 and 2001; 264 of these incidents were attributed to domestic terrorists.[2] Domestic terrorism cases nearly doubled from 1999 to 2003 according to the Bureau.[3] Between 1999 and 2001 alone the FBI prevented 10 possible domestic terrorist incidents, including two potentially large-scale, high-casualty attacks by right-wing groups.[4]

ISSUE:

WHAT IS THE LINE BETWEEN EXTREMISM AND TERRORISM?

In July 1999, Benjamin Smith, a follower of the white supremacist World Church of the Creator (now known as The Creativity Movement) and its doctrine of racial holy war, launched a shooting spree across Indiana and Illinois. His targets were Asians, Jews, and blacks; he killed two people and wounded nine more before committing suicide.[5] The next month Buford O. Furrow, a mentally disturbed racist with links to the Aryan Nations, walked into a Los Angeles–area Jewish community center and opened fire with an AR-15 rifle, wounding five people, including three children from the facility's day-care center. After stealing a car, Furrow gunned down a Filipino-American postal worker, whom he considered a "target of opportunity" because he was a minority who worked for the federal government. Once arrested, Furrow reportedly announced he had wanted to send "a wake-up call to America to kill Jews."[6]

In both cases, the killers had longstanding ties to known extremist groups. But in neither case was there proof they had been acting as part of a plot. Such cases pose a serious challenge for those tasked with preventing domestic terrorism. It is a rare person who wakes up one morning and suddenly abandons a

° Holocaust Museum shooting

mainstream life, picks up a gun, and begins killing for a political cause. In most cases, the killer has been associated with a political or ideological movement and moved, sometimes with others or the group as a whole, to the fringes of legal dissent, before making the leap from protest to terror. It is this connection between legitimate protest, extremism, and terrorism that has often challenged America's response to domestic terrorism. As discussed earlier, during the 1960s and '70s, the FBI and U.S. intelligence community gathered vast amounts of information on demonstrators, extremists, and terrorists alike. Abuses by these agencies led to severe restrictions on domestic intelligence gathering. When those restrictions were linked to lapses in the investigation of al-Qaida before 9/11, domestic intelligence gathering capabilities were increased.

Still, the American people are sensitive to law enforcement agencies investigating people "before the crime." Yet evidence shows that both deranged individuals and terrorist cells sometimes rely on legal extremist groups for inspiration and support, in some cases given unwittingly, in such areas as fundraising, recruiting, communications, and intelligence. Christian Identify and other white supremacist groups are often accused of using their propaganda to incite violence. In a similar way, environmental extremist groups list suggested targets and methods for "direct action" information on their Internet sites. Pro-life extremists go so far as to post online detailed instructions on how to create an explosive device that can foil the fire suppression systems at abortion clinics. Yet these groups often ensure their activities do not cross the line into conspiracy or other criminal areas.

The Southern Poverty Law Center decided to take its own steps to stop what it considers dangerous racist groups. It has filed multimillion dollar lawsuits against them. One example involved a group called the White Aryan Resistance (WAR). In 1988 WAR assigned a follower to help organize a group of neo-Nazi skinheads in Portland. After being trained, the group killed an Ethiopian student, gaining praise from WAR's leader for doing their "civic duty." A jury decided WAR's leader bore partial responsibility for the killing and awarded millions of dollars in damages to the victim's family. The center also won a major negligence suit in 2000 against the Aryan Nations, whose current and former members and supporters, such as Buford Furrow, have been involved in numerous terrorism and hate crime cases.

1. Where is the line between free speech and supporting a terrorist group? *When a crime is committed.*

2. What are appropriate ways for the government to prevent extremist organizations from crossing the line and providing assistance to terrorist groups? How far should the government be able to go in collecting intelligence on extremists with no documented connection to terrorist activity?

3. What are suitable roles for citizens and private organizations in taking action against extremist groups?

PREVALENCE OF DOMESTIC TERRORISM

Social and political changes after World War II fermented domestic terrorism across the ideological spectrum. The notorious Ku Klux Klan (KKK) was reinvigorated by adherents determined to halt the progress of the civil rights movement. The racist Klan terrorized activists throughout the South, spreading fear by the glow of their flaming crosses. In 1963, Klansmen bombed a Birmingham, Alabama, church, murdering four teenagers. Klan beatings and floggings continued throughout much of the 1960s. At the same time, more seeds of domestic ideological terrorism were being sown in the movement against the Vietnam War. The left-wing Weather Underground Organization (WUO) emerged in 1970 from the fringes of the peaceful antiwar movement. In the next few years the group set off blasts at often empty locations from Harvard University to the U.S. Capitol. A murderous WUO plan to bomb a dance at Fort Dix, New Jersey, derailed when several terrorists blew themselves up by accident. In the aftermath of that blast, many members dropped political violence, while others went on to support terrorist activity by new communist and black "liberation" extremist groups.

Nationalist groups also terrorized the United States. Puerto Rican extremists, acting in the tradition of their radical forebears who had attacked the Congress and tried to kill President Truman in separate incidents during the 1950s, took up arms. The FALN, a Spanish acronym for the Armed Forces of National Liberation, and Los Macheteros demanded independence for the U.S. Commonwealth. They blasted and robbed their way through the 1970s and '80s, claiming responsibility for such attacks as the January 1975 bombing of the historic Fraunces Tavern in downtown New York, which cost four lives. (Many of their members were eventually arrested and later given clemency by President Bill Clinton in 1999; a number of the 1950s Puerto Rican terrorists had been freed by President Jimmy Carter some 20 years before.)

The FBI, CIA, and other government agencies employed aggressive intelligence gathering and covert tactics to crack down on domestic terrorist groups. By the 1980s, with the collapse of the leftist United Freedom Front (UFF), most nationalist and left-wing ideological terrorist groups in the United States were finished. Their place was taken by right-wing extremism. The Order, a faction of the Aryan Nations, seized national attention during the 1980s. The tightly organized racist and anti-Semitic group opposed the federal government, calling it the "ZOG," or Zionist Occupation Government. Taking a page from *The Turner Diaries*, which inspired the group, Order terrorists engaged in bombings, counterfeiting, robberies, and murder. Their attempt to inspire a race war failed, and the group's leader was killed in a 1984 shoot-out with authorities.

Crimes of The Order brought attention to a loose network of right-wing extremists across the United States. United by a hatred of the U.S. government and minority groups, these groups continued to grow into the 1990s. Bloody government standoffs at the Ruby Ridge, Idaho, home of a suspected right-wing extremist in 1992 and the Waco, Texas, compound of a religious cult in 1993 became defining events and rallying cries for extremists and antigovernment "militia movements." A series of attacks followed. In 1995, Timothy McVeigh, a decorated Army veteran of the Gulf War with extremist views, used a truck bomb to kill 168 victims at the Alfred P. Murrah Federal Building

Timothy McVeigh

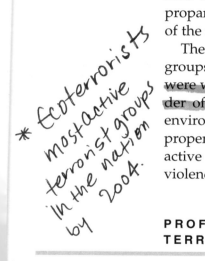

Atlanta Olympic Games

in Oklahoma City. The next year a bomb exploded during the Atlanta Olympics; federal authorities accused extremist Eric Rudolph with that and other crimes, including a deadly attack on an abortion clinic. Rudolph managed to escape arrest for years and served as an inspiration for many extremists. Followers of the paramilitary militia planned to attack Fort Hood, Texas, on July 4, 1997, before they were arrested. In 1999 law enforcement officials arrested right-wing extremists who planned to use an ammonium nitrate fuel oil (ANFO) bomb to detonate a facility in California that held millions of gallons of liquid propane. Provoking a government crackdown, civil war, and the end of the federal government was their alleged movement.[7]

The 1990s also saw significant activity by special-interest terrorist groups. The fringes of the pro-life movement produced terrorists who were willing to kill in order to stop what they believed to be the murder of unborn children during abortions. Ecoterrorists, fighting for environment preservation and animal rights, caused huge amounts of property damage. By 2004 these groups had become among the most active terrorist groups in the nation and showed signs of turning to violence.

Ecoterrorists most active terrorist groups in the nation by 2004.

PROFILES OF SIGNIFICANT DOMESTIC TERRORIST GROUPS AND EXTREMIST MOVEMENTS

Many terrorist groups have drawn psychological sustenance, recruits, funds, and operational support from the fringes of legitimate protest groups. The following profiles include some references to certain hate groups or other organizations that, while they may have been linked to terrorists, are themselves legal enterprises.

Left-Wing Extremists

As a significant force, communist terrorist groups have disappeared in the United States. Some of their anticapitalist principles have been picked up by anarchists, such as those who rampaged during the 1999 World Trade Organization (WTO) meeting in Seattle. In contrast with the large numbers of peaceful protestors at the WTO and subsequent gatherings, and often in opposition even to those practicing peaceful civil disobedience, "black bloc" anarchists, named for their black garb, engage in rioting, property destruction, and fighting with police. The FBI asserts these groups "represent a potential threat in the United States."[8]

Separatist: Black

The New Black Panther Party for Self-Defense, linked to former members of the Nation of Islam, advocates a radical black nationalist agenda with racist and anti-Semitic elements. While the group has threatened violence, it cannot be considered a terrorist group. The earlier "black liberation" movement, allied with leftist terrorist groups during the 1970s, suffered a similar demise. Former Black Liberation Army member Joanne Chesimard, aka Assata Shakur, remains a fugitive in Cuba after escaping from prison, where she was serving a sentence for her part in the murder of a New Jersey police officer in 1973. Also reported in Cuba are Michael Robert Finney and Charles Hill, members of the black militant group Republic of New Africa, who allegedly hijacked a plane after murdering a New Mexico state police officer. (See Chapter 6 for information on Cuba's support of leftist and Puerto Rican terrorists in the United States.)

Separatist: Puerto Rican

Los Macheteros and the FALN also reduced their activities in recent years, especially against targets in the United States. However, law enforcement officials have linked separatist terrorists to several bombings in Puerto Rico during recent years.

Right-Wing Terrorists and Hate Groups

A widespread and overlapping set of beliefs, groups, and individuals, the extreme right wing in the United States is estimated at up to 25,000 extremists and 250,000 sympathizers, although the exact number is impossible to determine.[9] Their precise ideological perspectives vary, although many agree with al-Qaida that the U.S. government is corrupt, its people morally weak, and its agenda set by Jewish Americans and Israel. Several major movements make up this population, which is divided into hundreds of groups and splinter organizations.

Christian Identity

The Christian Identity movement is the significant ideological force among the extreme right wing. Based on a decades-old idea imported from Britain, the faith asserts that Aryans (non-Jewish people of

[handwritten margin note: National Alliance—America's most powerful hate organization]

European descent) are a lost tribe of Israel and God's chosen people. Believers are united in a hatred of Jews, blacks, and other minorities—often described as soulless "mud people." Many Christian Identity adherents, estimated to number 25,000 or slightly more, anticipate the imminent arrival of Armageddon and a major race war.[10] A relatively new splinter ideology called the Phineas Priesthood represents those who assume the mission of attacking abortionists, homosexuals, and race mixers.

The Christian Identity philosophy unites a number of groups and also informs the belief system of groups such as the Neo-Nazi National Alliance, started by the late William Pierce, author of *The Turner Diaries*. The National Alliance, with international ties and sophisticated recruitment techniques, is regarded as America's most powerful hate organization. The group's members and sympathizers have been linked to numerous violent acts.

Militia Movement

Known for their belief in "black helicopters" and other conspiracy theories, militia members gained widespread publicity in the 1990s after the Waco and Ruby Ridge incidents. The militia movement believes the federal government is attempting to repeal constitutional rights, especially those involving the right to own guns. Organized into paramilitary groups, many militia followers are convinced that UN and foreign troops are being introduced into the United States as part of the "New World Order." These beliefs have lead to a number of terrorist plots.

Ku Klux Klan (KKK)

Once a powerful force in post–Civil War America, and again a feared movement during the civil rights era, the KKK has become a fragmented set of competing organizations united by their hatred of blacks, Jews, and assorted other enemies. They still maintain the capability for violence. In early 2003, an Imperial Wizard of the White Knights of the Ku Klux Klan was arrested on weapons charges.[11]

Sovereign Citizens

Groups such as the Montana Freeman and Republic of Texas have adopted what one observer called a "right-wing anarchist" philosophy. They reject the legitimacy of federal, state, and local government institutions based on convoluted interpretations of the Constitution, legal system, and American history. These extremists are known for harassing local government officials and have resorted to violence.

Other Right-Wing Extremist Groups

Groups that follow one or more right-wing extremist movements include the Nazi Low Riders, originally linked to the racist Aryan Brotherhood prison gang; the Creativity Movement, active under a different name in the 1990s; the Aryan Nations; and racist skinheads such as the Hammerskin Nation. The far right also includes Neo-Confederates, who seek a return to the social norms of the Confederacy; Orthodox Christians, who promote biblical standards and punishments as the law.

Religious Extremists

Along with those who claim Christianity condones terrorism and American Islamic extremists who have supported foreign terrorist groups, the Jewish Defense League (JDL) has a long history of attacking those it believes are opposed to its faith, the State of Israel, and the Jewish people. In 2003, a member of the JDL pleaded guilty in a plot to bomb a California mosque and the field office of a U.S. congressional representative.[12]

Issue-Oriented

Issue-oriented groups occupy the extreme fringes of legitimate political movements pursuing pro-life, environmental, animal rights, and other causes.

Pro-Life

Army of God

In their desire to stop abortion, some extremists have moved beyond protest, past civil disobedience, and into murder and terrorism. A number of them have operated in the name of the Army of God. The organization maintains a Web site; its overt supporters praise violence but stop short of illegal threats. In addition, supporters have created an Army of God manual with instructions for sabotaging and blowing up abortion clinics.

One pro-life terrorist was Clayton Waagner, a convicted felon with a fondness for casinos, cigarettes, and Crown Royal bourbon.[13] Waagner escaped from jail in 2001 and set out to terrorize abortion providers. In June 2001, Waagner began threatening specific abortion clinic staffers and posted a message on the the Army of God Web site announcing, "I am going to kill as many of them as I can." He also sent hundreds of letters to abortion clinics. On many of the envelopes was typed the phrase: "Time Sensitive Security Information, Open Immediately"; inside was white powder purported to be anthrax. Sent soon after the real anthrax attacks of fall 2001, these hoax letters spread fear across the nation.[14] Waagner was later captured and sent to prison. Antiabortion extremists have also assassinated abortion providers.

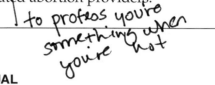
to profess you're something when you're hot

FROM THE SOURCE:

THE ARMY OF GOD MANUAL

The follow excerpts are from a manual used by this extremist pro-life group.

> [C]overt applications of disguises is [*sic*] also important. Street Man Recon is dressing up as a street person, with really scruffy clothes, empty beer cans in paper bags sticking out of the pockets of a filthy trench coat, etc. Such people not only are eminently forgettable, they tend to drive the attention of a casual observer away from them. This is what you want. You can stagger your way through a strip mall or medical complex in the middle of the night and be ignored or forgotten by anyone who sees you. Then, having done recon to ensure no witnesses, empty building, access to target roof, etc., you can either return another night or strike quickly, only to leave again, not running, but slowly staggering away . . .
>
> These days, the typical death camp [abortion clinic] is often a veritable fortress, complete with lots of brick, bars, reinforced glass, surveillance cameras, etc. etc. ad nauseum. This description is particularly true of many of the Hoods (Planned Parenthoods, that is). The main reason for this is that they are self-insured.
>
> By far the most important security device in the arsenal of these hoodlums is their Halon Fire Prevention System. In order to properly terminate a product of construction of this

> type, high explosives are not needed. However, introducing a flammable and igniting it is not sufficient since the Halon System is designed to deplete oxygen from the inside of the building . . . Remember for those not using time delay devices, fuses are not all created equal, so pre-test whichever variety you use. Defenders of life with easy access to quality fusing should spread the wealth around since it is not contraband.

Eco-Terrorism

While many Americans support environment protection and oppose cruelty to animals, a significant number of extremists believe society has not gone nearly far enough in these areas. The FBI estimates such radicals have committed more than 1,100 criminal acts in the United States since 1976, causing at least $110 million in damages.[15]

For example, the Earth Liberation Front (ELF) demands an end to environment damage. The group became known for "monkey-wrenching," or sabotage of organizations seen to be damaging nature. Monkeywrenching started with tree spiking and destruction of logging equipment, but arson has now become a key tactic for ELF-related terrorists. Targets have included auto dealerships selling sport utility vehicles, construction sites, and even fast-food restaurants. The August 1, 2003, arson of a La Jolla, California, condominium complex cost an estimated $50 million in property damages, according to the FBI.[16] A Colorado arson attack in 1998, which caused $12 million of damage at the Vail ski resort, was in retaliation for an expansion that destroyed habitat for the lynx.[17]

Founded in Great Britain, the Animal Liberation Front (ALF) aims to stop what it considers the exploitation of animals, which includes medical testing involving animals and the fur trade. While it claims to repudiate acts that could harm "any animal, human and nonhuman," the group encourages its members to take "direct action," which might involve attacks on targets such as fur companies, mink farms, restaurants, and animal research laboratories. However, there are significant concerns the eco-terrorist movement is slipping toward violence.

A group linked to ALF is ~~Great Britain's Stop Huntingdon Animal Cruelty (SHAC)~~ organization, which is dedicated to stopping animal testing by a company called Huntingdon Life Sciences (HLS). According to the FBI, "Investigation of SHAC-related criminal activity has revealed a pattern of vandalism, arsons, animal releases, harassing telephone calls, threats and attempts to disrupt business activities of not only HLS, but of all companies doing business with HLS." In 2003, terrorists exploded bombs at two California companies linked to HLS. The second blast was followed by a claim of responsibility from the Revolutionary Cells of the Animal Liberation Brigade. The claim stated, "Now you will all reap what you have sown. All customers and their families are considered legitimate targets . . . You never know when your house, your car even, might go boom . . . Or maybe it will be a shot in the dark . . . We will now be doubling the size of every device we make. Today it is 10 pounds, tomorrow 20 . . . until your buildings are nothing more than rubble. It is time for this war to truly have two sides. No more will all the killing be done by the oppressors, now the oppressed will strike back."[18]

Recently an intellectual leader of the eco-terrorist movement has called for a gradual shift to violent tactics in order to achieve their goals. Were these extremists to adopt violence, they would be especially difficult to stop. Eco-terrorists share a highly decentralized operating system that includes high levels of focus on operational security and knowledge of law enforcement techniques. Their attacks are well planned, and they share their tactics via the Internet.

EVOLVING THREAT

to convert someone

In contrast with its early days, when dogmatic Marxist groups proselytized via pamphlets and Klansmen recruited under flaming crosses, the modern domestic terrorist threat has adopted advanced organizational and operational techniques that make it increasingly insidious.

Loose Affiliations, "Leaderless Resistance," and Lone Wolves

Domestic terrorists from various groups have demonstrated an ability to work by themselves or in small groups. In right-wing extremist vernacular, they can operate as "leaderless resistance," operating from general instructions or directives, perhaps spread via Web sites.

Such small cells are difficult to detect and stop. In some cases, hateful ideologies may inspire action from disturbed individuals. For example, a 35-year-old member of the National Alliance was arrested in 2002 as he sat outside a Jewish preschool in Nashville holding an AR-15 rifle. In his car officials found a semiautomatic handgun with 27 rounds of armor-piercing ammunition, binoculars, laser range finder, retractable steel baton, and latex gloves. A search of his residence, a storage facility, and a buried supply cache turned up explosive devices, time fuses, ammo, smoke grenades, blasting caps, military training manuals, and a copy of the *The Turner Diaries*. The man, who had cheered when 9/11 occurred, had written an e-mail stating, "I no longer feel like I belong to the cesspool of multicultural filth known as the 'United States,' " investigators reported. Authorities found evidence the extremist had searched the Internet for information on Buford Furrow and feared he planned to gun down Jewish children in an attack similar to Furrow's 1999 rampage. The extremist, who defenders claimed was mentally ill, provided information that led to the arrest of another white supremacist and had allegedly been in contact with a National Alliance official.[19]

WMD Because of their religious views, some right-wing extremists—like al-Qaida—appear to lack constraints against the use of WMD. They may view such attacks as likely to kill unbelievers and minorities and an effective way to provoke a theologically sanctioned civil war. Domestic terrorists have a record of obtaining WMD elements. During the 1990s, law enforcement officials arrested extremists with the poison ricin on at least two occasions. In 2003, officials found the materials for a cyanide bomb, along with half a million rounds of ammunition, pipe bombs, machine guns, silencers, and extremist literature, in the storage unit of William Krar in Noonday, Texas. Although Krar was known for his antigovernment views and one of his accomplices in a fake ID scheme was a militia member, he denied being part of a terrorist plot, saying, "For the record, I'm neither nor a terrorist or a separatist. I've never desired to hurt anyone or the country that I love."[20] However, some observers recalled the 1985 raid on a right-wing extremist group called The Covenant, the Sword, and the Arm of the Lord (CSA). Inside the group's Arkansas compound, officials discovered a 30-gallon drum of cyanide, which the members planned to place in the water supplies of major cities as part of a Christian Identity–inspired plot.[21]

CHAPTER SUMMARY

American extremist movements provide the foundation for terrorist groups representing a broad range of motives. These terrorists, especially those representing right-wing extremist and eco-terrorist causes, will continue to pose a substantial threat to the homeland. Because of the decentralized organizational structure of these groups, and the desire of some of them to obtain WMD, law enforcement officials must maintain a high level of vigilance.

CHAPTER QUIZ

1. What is domestic terrorism?
2. How did domestic terrorism evolve from the 1970s to present?
3. What are three major extremist movements linked to modern domestic terrorism?
4. List the evolving threats posed by modern domestic terrorism.

NOTES

1. Statement of John E. Lewis, Deputy Assistant Director, Counterterrorism Division, Federal Bureau of Investigation before the Senate Judiciary Committee (May 18, 2004), www.fbi.gov/congress/congress04/lewis051804.htm.
2. Ibid.
3. Federal Bureau of Investigation, "Preventing Terrorist Attacks on U.S. Soil: The Case of the Wrong Package Falling into the Right Hands" (March 9, 2003), www.fbi.gov/page2/april04/040904krar.htm.
4. Testimony of Robert S. Mueller, III, Director, FBI, before the Senate Select Committee on Intelligence (February 11, 2003), www.fbi.gov/congress/congress03/mueller021103.htm.
5. CNN.Com, "Alleged Racist Killer Smith Kept Hate-Filled Journal" (July 9, 1999), www.cnn.com/US/9907/09/illinois.shootings.
6. CNN.Com, "L.A. Shooting Suspect Charged with Hate Crimes, (Aug. 12, 1999), www.cnn.com/US/9908/12/california.shooting.03.

7. Denny Walsh, "Jury Finds Pair Guilty in Propane Tank Plot. They Face Life in Prison for Conspiring to Blow Up an Elk Grove Facility," *The Sacramento Bee* (May 22, 2002), www.homelandsecurity.org/NewsletterArchives/24052002.htm.

8. Testimony of Dale L. Watson, Executive Assistant Director, Counterterrorism/Counterintelligence Division, FBI before the Senate Select Committee on Intelligence (February 6, 2002), www.fbi.gov/congress/congress02/watson020602.htm.

9. Kris Axtman, "The Terror Threat at Home, Often Overlooked," *Christian Science Monitor* (December 29, 2003): 1.

10. Anti-Defamation League, "Extremism in America: Christian Identity," www.adl.org.

11. Statement of John S. Pistole, Executive Assistant Director, Counterterrorism/Counterintelligence, FBI, before the National Commission on Terrorist Attacks upon the United States (April 14, 2004), www.fbi.gov/congress/congress04/pistole041404.htm.

12. Department of Justice, "Jewish Defense League Member Pleads Guilty in Plots to Bomb Mosque, Offices of Congressman Issa" (February 4, 2003), www.usdoj.gov/usao/cac/pr2003/019.html.

13. Bureau of Alcohol, Tobacco, Firearms and Explosives, "Wanted" www.atf.gov/wanted/pages/17waagner.htm.

14. Department of Justice, "Clayton Lee Waagner Found Guilty of Making Anthrax and Death Threats—Faces Maximum Possible Sentence of Life Imprisonment," www.usdoj.gov/opa/pr/2003/December/03_crt_661.htm.

15. Statement of John E. Lewis, Deputy Assistant Director, Counterterrorism Division, Federal Bureau of Investigation before the Senate Judiciary Committee (May 18, 2004), www.fbi.gov/congress/congress04/lewis051804.htm.

16. Ibid.

17. Testimony of Louis J. Freeh, Director, FBI before the Senate, Committees on Appropriations, Armed Services, and Select Committee on Intelligence (May 10, 2001), www.fbi.gov/congress/congress01/freeh051001.htm.

18. Statement of John E. Lewis.

19. Department of Justice, "National Alliance Member Michael Edward Smith Sentenced to 121 Months for Hate Crime" (March 17, 2004), www.usdoj.gov/usao/tnm/press_release/3_17_04.htm.

20. CNN.Com, "Man with Huge Weapons Cache Sentenced to 11 Years" (May 4, 2004), www.cnn.com/2004/LAW/05/04/cyanide.sentencing.ap.

21. Jessica Stern, "The Prospect of Domestic Bioterrorism," Council on Foreign Relations, www.cdc.gov/ncidod/EID/vol5no4/stern.htm.

8

TERRORIST OPERATIONS AND TACTICS

How Attacks Are Planned and Executed

. . . the dialogue of bullets, the ideals of assassination, bombing, and destruction, and the diplomacy of the cannon and machine-gun.

"Military Studies in the Jihad against the Tyrants"
(The al-Qaida Manual)

CHAPTER OVERVIEW

While the ideologies of terrorist groups may vary, they often employ many common tactics and weapons. This chapter outlines the most common ways terrorists organize themselves and conduct their operations. Organizational structures significantly affect the conduct of modern terrorist activities. While the range of potential terrorist activities is vast, certain common organizational principles are used to prepare and conduct most operations, whether they target government buildings with plastic explosives or key computer systems with cyberattacks. Understanding these basic principles, tactics, and weapons is a key step toward preventing and responding to terrorist attacks.

Technology also plays an important role in understanding the nature of the modern terrorist threat. The instruments used by terrorists have evolved with emerging technologies. In ancient times, terrorists struck with daggers, stabbing their victims in public markets to spread fear. The development of modern explosives allowed extremists to attack with far greater impact, a trend being accelerated by the increasing sophistication and availability of automatic weapons, plastic explosives, missiles, and WMD. Technology has also created entirely new venues for terrorism: jet airliners opened the way for hijackings, and the Internet created a new battleground in cyberspace. Other new technologies such as advanced communications systems enabled terrorists to disperse their operations while still maintaining command and control. Technological forces, exacerbated by the rise of extremist groups bent on achieving significant casualties, are combining to make terrorist attacks increasingly lethal.

CHAPTER LEARNING OBJECTIVES

After reading this chapter, you should be able to

1. **Identify common organizational features of terrorist groups.**
2. **Explain the major tactical phases of a terrorist operation.**
3. **Describe considerations used by terrorists in selecting targets.**
4. **List common terrorist tactics.**

TERRORIST PLANNING

Terrorist groups typically function based on a hierarchy of planning levels. Each group has a driving *ideology*—a top-level orientation, such as religious or racial extremism, from which the organization generates strategic objectives. These objectives have ranged from forcing the withdrawal of the United States from the Middle East to sparking a race war in America. To pursue its goal, the group develops a plan, which focuses resources to achieve specific results. Plans are driven by *doctrine*, or the basic principles that guide operations. On the level of specific missions, terrorist units use *tactics*, or practiced actions relating to the group and its adversary, which are built upon the individual skills possessed by members of the group.

Terrorism by the Book

In the 1980s, state sponsors such as the Soviets, Cubans, and Palestinians, who trained large numbers of terrorists during the Cold War, and the Iranians, who influenced terrorist groups in later years, refined the concepts for adopting terrorism to the realities of a globalizing world. Their students performed on an international stage; interested parties could study the attributes of successful attacks, and learn the lessons of failed ones, from the nearest television or newsstand. Behind the scenes, counterterrorism officials could also trace the dissemination of sophisticated techniques, such as advanced bomb-making skills, from one group to another.

Soviet and Western military doctrine, detailed in widely available manuals, provided many of these groups with a fundamental understanding of military tactics and skills that could be used for terrorism. From these and other sources, specific terrorist texts evolved. *Minimanual of the Urban Guerilla*, written by a South American revolutionary, detailed tactics for communist guerillas attacking U.S.-supported nations. These tactics were emulated by terrorists in the Americas and Europe, among other locations.

At home, *The Anarchist's Cookbook*—with its detailed instructions on topics such as explosives, lock picking, and document fraud—has been associated with numerous extremists. Right-wing radicals have closely studied *The Turner Diaries*, a novel in which racists take over the United States. The book, with detailed descriptions of terrorist operations, was cited as an inspiration by Timothy McVeigh, who bombed Oklahoma City's Murrah Federal Building in 1995, and other domestic terrorists.[1]

One of the most important terrorist documents today is "Military Studies in the Jihad against the Tyrants," also known as the al-Qaida manual. Found in the British residence of a suspect in al-Qaida's 1998 bombing of the U.S. embassies in Africa, it was translated and introduced into evidence at a federal court. Reflecting lessons from decades of jihadist combat in the Middle East, it probably also represents the influence of a burly al-Qaida terrorist named Ali Mohamed. Trained by the U.S. military in Special Forces tactics while an Egyptian military officer, Mohamed served as a sergeant in the U.S. Army during the late 1980s, teaching troops at Fort Bragg, North Carolina, about the Middle East. During this time Mohamed was also an al-Qaida operative, and before his eventual capture, he translated U.S. military manuals and provided advanced special operations–type training to the group.[2]

Terrorist Skills and Weapons

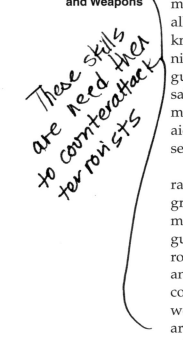

These skills are need then to counterattack terrorists

Successful terrorist operations require a broad range of talents. Most members of a terrorist group have only limited capabilities; none has all the skills needed. These competencies include ideology/religious knowledge; weapons; explosives; small unit tactics; intelligence techniques or tradecraft such as clandestine communication and disguises; counterintelligence; codes and ciphers; map reading; sabotage; surveillance and countersurveillance; photography; document falsification; foreign languages; propaganda; medicine/first aid; the operation of aircraft, automobiles, and watercraft; target selection and assessment; and hand-to-hand combat.

Modern terrorist groups include personnel capable of using a range of weapons. In the case of domestic and international terrorist groups that threaten the United States, this arsenal includes automatic weapons such as the M-16, M-60, AK-47, G-3, and Uzi; handguns; shotguns; man portable air defense systems (MANPADS) rocket-propelled grenades (RPGs); explosives such as dynamite, C-4 and other plastic explosives, improvised explosives, and detonation cord and various detonators; grenades; knives and other edged weapons; explosive suicide belts and vests; clubs; garrotes; martial arts weapons; mace; fire bombs; and improvised poisons and chemical agents.

THE TERRORIST ORGANIZATION

Dramatic offensive operations are what get the terrorists the publicity they desire. But it is secrecy that allows them to survive. Because they usually operate in hostile environments against far more powerful conventional forces, terrorist groups must focus on maintaining security. For a terrorist, detection usually means defeat.

Leadership

Security often begins with a command-and-control organization and a group leader located far from the field of operations. Modern technology such as satellite phones and the Internet have made it easier for commanders in a relatively secure area to direct operations in a more dangerous one. Often led by a charismatic individual with extensive training, the group may also use committees and subcommands to coordinate action.

In some cases, terrorist movements may even forgo centralized leadership. Operatives in related groups, or even individual free-lancers, may initiate attacks on behalf of the larger group. Individual radicals may adopt the practice of "leaderless resistance," forming tiny independent cells and conducting their own attacks in response to inspirational messages and strategic guidance conveyed via Web sites, e-mail, and books.

Types of Followers

Participants in the organization may fall into several categories as depicted in Figure 8.1. Hardened operatives known as *cadre* carry out terrorist operations and attacks and train others. Those who can be termed active supporters may not participate in attacks, but do know-ingly provide intelligence and logistical support to operations. Passive supporters are sympathizers to the cause, but restrict their support, perhaps by joining and contributing to legal front groups. *The Turner Diaries* divides terrorists into "illegals," who are known to the authori-ties as operatives and operate underground with the mission of con-ducting direct attacks, and "legals," who may portray themselves as law-abiding activists while at the same time supporting a terrorist group by providing propaganda, legal defense, funding, intelligence, and the initial screening of potential recruits. Terrorists often move through these categories, starting by joining legal extremist groups and gradually becoming more radical until they are selected for member-ship in the terrorist organization. The overlap between the far fringes of legal extremist groups and terrorist groups can create special chal-lenges for law enforcement officers, who must monitor and prevent ter-rorist activity without violating the civil liberties of legitimate protestors.

Cell Structure

In order to maintain security, the groups often organize themselves into cells, small units of several individuals with specific missions. The members of one cell may never meet those in another. This pre-vents a single individual from knowing the identities or operations of the larger group, limiting the damage if the individual is cap-tured.

Cells can be divided into a number of categories:

- *Operational.* Carries out missions

FIGURE 8.1

CLASSIC CATEGORIES OF TERRORIST GROUP AND SUPPORT MEMBERSHIP. IN MODERN TERRORISM, LOOSELY AFFILIATED SUPPORTERS MAY TAKE DIRECT ACTION AS PART OF "LEADERLESS RESISTANCE."

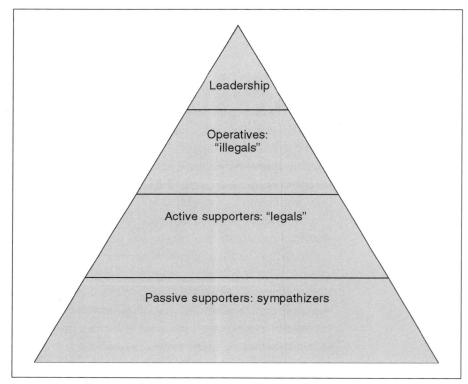

- *Intelligence.* Collects information through surveillance and other methods
- *Logistics/auxiliary.* Supports operations with funds, supplies, weapons, housing, and other needs
- *Sleeper.* A common term most often used to describe cells of trained operatives waiting underground for orders to carry out a mission

Operational Security   One essential tool for terrorists is preventing intelligence and law enforcement from uncovering information about their organization and operations. "Married brothers should observe the following," instructs the al-Qaida manual, "not talking to their wives about

Jihad work . . ." The manual also includes detailed instructions on the use of countersurveillance, codes, and cover stories to avoid detection. Iyman Faris followed many of these precepts of operational security. While his wife and neighbors in Ohio knew him as a family man and truck driver, the naturalized U.S. citizen with the gleaming smile was actually an al-Qaida operative. Born Mohammad Rauf in Kashmir in 1969, Faris—who reportedly held a license to transport hazardous materials—drove his rig across the country delivering cargo to businesses and airports. He also found time to visit Pakistan and Afghanistan, where he met Usama bin Ladin, joined the jihad against America, and began working with al-Qaida's top operational leaders, according to court documents filed by U.S. authorities.

Along with a scheme to bring down the Brooklyn Bridge and an alleged role in supporting a plot to bomb an Ohio shopping mall, Faris was asked to obtain tools to derail trains. These tools were code-named "mechanics shops" in e-mail messages between Faris and al-Qaida, according to court documents. The plans hit a roadblock during a 2003 reconnaissance operation in New York, when Faris spotted the tight security surrounding the Brooklyn Bridge. He e-mailed his leaders that "The weather is too hot," indicating the plot could not succeed because of the bridge's security and structure. But in this case, al-Qaida security procedures were not strong enough. Before he could launch an attack, Faris was arrested, reportedly tripped up when his e-mail messages to al-Qaida were found in the computer of a captured terrorist. He ultimately pled guilty to terrorism-related charges.[3]

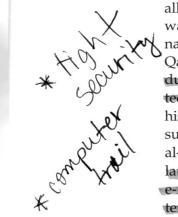

* tight security

* computer trail

TERRORIST SUPPORT OPERATIONS

A horrific explosion is over in seconds. A hostage situation usually lasts days at most. But the activities needed to generate and support such terrorist operations require months or years of effort. These activities include recruitment and indoctrination; network building; training; logistics, supply, and communication; and propaganda and psychological operations. They are what make the group an ongoing enterprise and provide the foundations for actual attacks.

PHASES OF A TERRORIST ATTACK

Most terrorist attacks involve common phases that take an operation from the first steps of target selection to the final phases of reviewing an attack and determining lessons learned for future operations.

Target Selection   Terrorist groups have thousands of potential targets. Based on their strategy, they identify and strike specific ones. While each attack is unique, common factors inform the target selection process of many terrorist organizations. Because their general aim is to attack one group of people in order to influence others, their objectives are often selected for their symbolism or other factors that make them *high-value targets*.

The principle of symbolic value accounts for the disproportionate number of attacks on American citizens, who represent a system hated by a wide range of terrorists; on embassies, which symbolize the nations whose diplomats they house; and against national airlines, which bear flags, crews, and passengers of target nations. Among domestic terrorists, government offices—such as the Oklahoma City building that represented the federal government Timothy McVeigh so detested—are often on target lists. In the 9/11 attacks, al-Qaida believed the World Trade Center represented the U.S. economy; the Pentagon, the U.S. military; and the Capitol, U.S. support for Israel.

Once terrorists have identified potential high-value targets, they assess their vulnerabilities, such as the lack of defensive measures, and tactical characteristics, such as the ease of escape offered by nearby roads. Locations with limited defenses are called *soft targets*. Some locations are both high-value and soft targets. For example, in 2003, terrorists, apparently acting independently, attacked McDonald's restaurants across the globe. Assailants from various different groups but with a common aversion to this American icon threw a hand grenade at a Greek restaurant; tossed a Molotov cocktail into a Norwegian outlet; left a time bomb under the table in one Turkish McDonald's and bombed two others; hurled a fire bomb at a Saudi restaurant; used TNT to blow up the men's room in a Lebanese restaurant; set fires outside restaurants in Germany and France; and exploded a bomb near an Argentine restaurant.[4]

Many other factors impact target selection, such as timing. The periods before elections, or during important holidays and anniversaries, may add psychological value. The previous history of a target may be important: terrorists failed to destroy the World Trade Center on their first try in 1993 and so returned to finish the job in 2001. In other cases, the symbolic value of a target may be combined with its functional value, as when attackers seek to inflict not just psychological but economic or military damage as part of their strategy.

Operational Phases

Once the target is selected, the attack is planned and conducted through a series of phases. First, the group gathers intelligence and conducts reconnaissance activities. This is followed by operational planning of the attack; recruitment of specialized personnel; surveillance on the target; countersurveillance to ensure the plotters have not been detected; rehearsals and dry runs; training for specific elements of the attack; movement to the attack; the attack itself; escape and/or exfiltration from the site; exploitation of the attack through propaganda or intelligence techniques; and after-action reviews (for example, the al-Qaida manual includes numerous detailed critiques of botched attacks).

FROM THE SOURCE:

THE AL-QAIDA MANUAL ON SURVEILLANCE OF A FIXED TARGET

Surveillance, Intelligence, and Observation (Information about the enemy places)

The Organization's command needs detailed information about the enemy's vital establishments, whether civilian or military, in order to make safe plans, reach firm decisions, and avoid surprises. Thus, the individual who gathers information about a desired location should, in addition to drawing a diagram, describe it and all its details.

The Drawing: The brother [*brother* is how the terrorists refer to one another] should draw a diagram of the area, the street, and the location which is the target of the information gathering. He should describe its shape and characteristics. The drawing should be realistic so that someone who never saw the location could visualize it. It is preferable to also put on the drawing the directions of traffic, police stations, and security centers.

The Description: It is necessary to gather as much information about the location as possible. For instance:

Traffic directions and how wide the streets are
Transportation leading to the location
The area, appearance, and setting of the place
Traffic signals and pedestrian areas
Security personnel centers and government agencies
Embassies and consulates
The economic characteristics of the area and traffic congestion times
Public parks
Amount and location of lighting

It is preferable to photograph the area as a whole first, then the street of the location. If possible, panoramic pictures should be taken . . . The photographer should be experienced with and proficient in film processing and developing. It is risky to use an outside film processing service . . .

TERRORIST OPERATIONS

The variety of terrorist operations is limited only by the imagination and resources of terrorists. Al-Qaida operatives' brainstorming for the 9/11 attacks included hijacking up to 10 planes and crashing some of them into nuclear reactors.[5] But certain operations have become especially frequent and successful components of the terrorist repertoire.

Ambushes The ambush, a surprise attack from a concealed position on a moving or temporarily halted target, is a common military tactic that has often been used by terrorists abroad. In early 2003, a Kuwaiti civil servant ambushed a vehicle carrying U.S. civilian contractors outside Camp Doha, Kuwait. The attacker, who claimed inspiration from al-Qaida, killed one American and wounded another.[6] The al-Qaida manual includes instruction on ambushes and suggests blocking the victim's car in traffic and then opening fire.

Sabotage By disrupting normal activities to inflict damage, terrorists can spread fear in uniquely insidious and effective ways. Attacks on infrastructure such as power lines can foster widespread feelings of vulnerability. The terrorists may also see value in subverting their adversary's technology. For example, monkeywrenching, a tactic used by environmental extremists, includes placing spikes in trees that saboteurs do not want cut down. Loggers who accidentally hit the hidden spikes with their chain saws can be badly injured. A far more destructive example is the derailment of trains, plotted by al-Qaida after 9/11 and employed by other groups in years past. In October 1995, one person died and dozens more sustained injuries after a group calling itself the Sons of the Gestapo used sophisticated techniques to derail a 12-car Amtrak passenger train in Arizona. In 1986, someone removed a 39-foot-long section of rail along tracks used to transport spent nuclear fuel through Minnesota. A train carrying lumber hit the sabotaged section and derailed before the train with the nuclear waste arrived. Near the site, authorities found a sign reading, "Stop Rad-Waste Shipments."

A related type of attack seeks to create environmental damage. For example, an al-Qaida prisoner claimed the group had planned to use timed devices to ignite wildfires across western American.[7]

Kidnappings Kidnappings require extensive planning and logistical capabilities, but they have proven to be an effective fundraising and propaganda tactic for terrorists across the globe. The Revolutionary Armed Forces of Colombia (FARC) and the Colombian National Liberation Army (ELN) have abducted numerous Americans for money. The Abu Sayyaf group in the Philippines, an al-Qaida ally, has also specialized in this technique, in one case demanding $10 million and the release of prisoners in exchange for a kidnapped American. The captive managed to escape. Another of their American victims, Guellermo Sobero, was beheaded that year. In some cases, the planned profits of a kidnapping may be counted purely in propaganda. In 2002, terrorists abducted *Wall Street Journal* reporter Daniel Pearl in Pakistan and then beheaded him and released a video of the crime. A similar fate befell Americans Nicholas Berg and Paul Johnson during 2004. Other spectacular kidnappings have included those of Italian Premier Aldo Moro, captured by the communist Red Brigade and murdered in 1978, and U.S. Marine Corps Lieutenant Colonel William "Rich" Higgins and CIA Officer William Buckley, kidnapped and killed in separate incidents during the 1980s, allegedly by Hizballah, the Iranian-backed group that abducted numerous Americans and other Westerners in Lebanon.

Hostage Taking

A term sometimes used synonymously with kidnapping, *hostage taking* more commonly refers to the seizure of a group of victims in order to gain publicity or concessions. Often conducted as part of a siege or hijacking, hostage taking is highly risky for the terrorist, whose chances of escape are limited. Perhaps the most widely known hostage incident occurred during the Munich Olympics in 1972, when Palestinian terrorists captured Israeli athletes at the games, creating a running standoff that ended in the deaths of the hostages. Another spectacular hostage incident occurred in 2002, when Chechen terrorists occupied a Moscow theater, seizing more than 800 hostages from numerous countries. Russian security forces ended the episode by pumping anesthetic gas through the facility's ventilation system, allowing them to kill the terrorists, but also poisoning many of the hostages.

Antiaircraft Missiles

Weighing just 40 pounds, these missiles—also known as MANPADS or SAMs (surface-to-air missiles)—can bring down a 100-ton passenger jet from a mile away. While U.S. forces seized large numbers of these systems from al-Qaida and Taliban fighters in Afghanistan, thousands more are in circulation around the world. In recent decades, MANPADS are estimated to have downed around two dozen large and small civilian aircraft, killing hundreds of people. As of 2004, at least five large jet airliners had been attacked. Two attacks killed all on board; two caused significant damage but no deaths. In the third incident, two missiles believed fired by al-Qaida followers missed an Israeli Boeing 757 leaving Kenya. This attack reinvigorated efforts to find ways to protect U.S. jetliners from attack.[8]

ISSUE:

PROTECTING COMMERCIAL JETS FROM MISSILES: COSTS AND BENEFITS

Everyone agrees it's possible for a terrorist hiding outside a major U.S. airport to fire a missile or MANPADS at a commercial passenger jet, downing the aircraft, potentially killing hundreds of people in the air and on the ground, and causing a huge psychological and financial blow to the aviation industry.

The challenge is what to do about it. Following the attempted shoot-down of the Israeli 757 in 2002, Department of Homeland Security (DHS) stepped up its research efforts, allocating $100 million to study possible solutions. But critics have attacked the program, saying it moved far too slowly.

There are a number of ways to reduce the risk of a MANPADS attack. One is proliferation control, or reducing the number of weapons that could fall into terrorist hands. There are a number of such programs, including bounties for missiles turned in by citizens in Iraq and Afghanistan. But many terrorist groups already have missiles, and there are far too many more for any program to eliminate entirely. Securing the areas around airports is another tactic; but the flight paths of commercial aircraft make them vulnerable to attackers far outside airport perimeters. Takeoff and landing patterns could be changed, encouraging pilots to make extremely steep takeoffs and spiraling descents. But these techniques pose safety risks of their own and are of limited utility, as are reactive maneuvers by large commercial aircraft. There are even suggestions that airplanes could be hardened to withstand missile strikes more effectively. Even if possible, such engineering solutions would require years of design and production, plus great expense.

Advocates of more aggressive MANPADS defenses urge the implementation of some of those systems plus "technical countermeasures," or technological defense systems. One form of countermeasure is called *expendables*, objects such as flares and heat-emitting disks that are expelled from the aircraft to confuse a missile's heat-seeking devices. However, they do not work well against more advanced MANPAD systems. Detractors also say the American public might be unwilling to put up with flares dropping from the skies around crowded airports. Laser-based systems, known as infrared countermeasures (IRCM), are more effective; they use energy to jam the missile's homing system. Their downside is cost, which can run more than $1 million per unit, plus operational, maintenance, training, and support costs. It has been suggested they could be mounted on towers to protect airports, but a more common strategy is to place them on the aircrafts themselves, as the military does. Even outfitting half the nation's passengers jets with such sophisticated infrared countermeasures could take several billion dollars and six years to complete. By some estimates, protecting the entire fleet could run $5 billion to $10 billion per year. Even if the cost can be brought down significantly, an aggressive MANPADS defense will almost certainly cost many billions of dollars.[9]

1. How serious of a threat do MANPADS pose to the American flying public?

2. How much emphasis should the U.S. government place on proliferation control?

3. Should airports and the jurisdictions around them be required to increase security against missile attacks? Should the aviation system make changes in flight patterns to make attack more difficult, even if it adds risk in other ways and inconveniences passengers?

4. Given the many other competing homeland security priorities, should the U.S. government push for technical countermeasures on passenger jets? How much should be spent on defending against this threat, considering other terrorist threats that also need to be countered?

Maybe → don't allow people to park vehicles along roads surrounding airports. Roaming patrol in those areas.

Hijackings
In the 1970s, hijacking became a staple of terrorist activity. Some significant hijackings include the Entebbe (airport) Incident, the 1976 diversion of a passenger plane to Uganda, where the passengers were later rescued by Israeli commandos; and the 1985 hijacking of a TWA Boeing 727 headed from Athens to Rome, during which U.S. sailor Robert Stethem was tortured, killed, and tossed from the plane. U.S. authorities indicted Hizballah leader Imad Mughniyah in connection with the crime and offered a $5 million reward for his capture.

Bombings
Over the ages, many terrorists have agreed with a philosophy expressed in the al-Qaida's manual: "Explosives are believed to be the safest weapon . . . Using explosives allows them to get away from enemy personnel and to avoid being arrested . . . In addition, explosives strike the enemy with sheer terror and fright." Bombings may involve elaborate weapons from the crude to the sophisticated and strategies of varying complexity. For example, an attack may involve two bombs, one to breach outer defenses and the other to attack the location within. An initial bombing may be followed by a second, or "secondary device," timed to hit rescue workers. In recent decades, the development of suicide bombing has added a grim new dimension to this terrorist tactic.

Leave-Behind Bombs

One of the simplest and most effective terrorist tactics is the time bomb. Left behind by an operative, the hidden bomb escapes detection until it explodes. In early 1975, Puerto Rican nationalists killed four people with a bomb left outside a Wall Street bar. Less than a year later, a time bomb in a locker blasted holiday travelers at New York's LaGuardia Airport, killing 11 people. Despite a massive investigation of numerous terrorist groups, the case was never solved.

In more recent years, cell phone technology has provided an effective way to detonate bombs remotely, such as the device that killed five U.S. citizens at Jerusalem's Hebrew University in 2002. In 2002, a terrorist bombing at a Bali nightclub claimed 202 lives. In 2004, terrorists killed almost 200 people during a coordinated set of bombings aboard Spanish commuter trains.

Letter Bombs

From the American Unabomber to suspected Islamic extremists, terrorists have long used the mail system to deliver death to the doorsteps of their enemies. The mail has also been used to deliver WMD and toxic elements such as anthrax mailed to U.S. targets in 2001 and the toxic agent adamsite sent to U.S. and foreign embassies in Europe during 2003.

Booby Traps and Improvised Explosives

Booby traps may serve as the primary tool of operations, such as in assassinations, or to support other objectives. For example, they may protect weapons caches or be left behind at the scenes of kidnappings or other operations to impede investigators. The al-Qaida manual includes detailed instructions on creating booby traps, including one devised to blow up a victim's television set. "However," the manual cautions, "a brother [terrorist] should not be allowed the opportunity to work with setting booby traps until after he has mastered the use of explosives . . . because the first mistake a brother makes could be his last mistake."

Terrorists may also create improvised explosive devices. According to U.S. authorities, al-Qaida planned to blow up U.S. high-rise complexes by sealing apartments located in them, filling the apartments with natural gas, and detonating them with timers.

Grenade Attacks

Deadly, preassembled, and requiring little skill to use, grenades are an effective weapon, especially for poorly skilled or supported operatives. A 2002 grenade attack by suspected Islamic militants against a Protestant church in Pakistan killed two Americans and wounded many more.

Aircraft Bombings

Midair bombings have killed hundreds of passengers in recent years. Major attacks include an Air India Boeing 747 downed in 1985 with more than 300 people aboard; a TWA plane ripped open by a 1986 bomb that sucked four victims, including an eight-month-old baby, to their deaths thousands of feet below; a (South) Korean Airlines plane bombed by North Korean agents in 1987; and a French UTA flight destroyed in 1989. The 1988 destruction of Pan Am Flight 103 with a bomb planted by Libyan agents remains one of the most deadly terrorist attacks against American interests, claiming 270 passengers and victims on the ground.

The terrorists keep developing technology in the hopes of evading bomb detection procedures and equipment. A terrorist with a bomb in his shoe failed to destroy a 2001 flight when his fellow passengers subdued him. The U.S. government warned of far more advanced "teddy bear bombs," or explosive-impregnated fabrics such as coats or pillows that could be smuggled aboard aircraft without being detected by X-ray machines.[10]

Car Bombs

The lethality of a conventional bomb is linked to its size. The use of cars or trucks allows terrorists to deliver larger payloads to their targets. Islamic terrorists linked to al-Qaida killed 6 and injured more than 1,000 with a bomb left in the World Trade Center parking garage in 1993. A huge truck bomb destroyed the Oklahoma City federal building in 1995. The next year, an explosives-laden fuel truck detonated outside a U.S. military facility in Saudi Arabia; the attack—supported by Iran according to U.S. officials—killed 19 Americans.

Suicide Attacks Starting in the 1980s, car bombers increasingly added a new component to their attacks—suicide. With no need for escape, the bombers could deliver their explosives directly into the heart of the target. Eventually suicide attacks grew to include strikes by individuals and even boats loaded with bombs. Finally, the terrorists mastered the use of airplanes as suicide weapons.

Suicide Bombing by Car and Truck

The United States was introduced to suicide bombings on April 18, 1983, when a blast tore through the U.S. Embassy in Beirut, killing 63 people. Al-Qaida and its sympathizers have been linked to numerous suicide car and truck attacks, including the deadly bombings of two U.S. embassies in Africa in August 1998; the detonation of a truck loaded with propane gas outside a Tunisian synagogue in 2002; and explosions at a residence for Americans and other foreigners in Saudi Arabia in 2003.

Suicide Bombing by Boat

Al-Qaida members piloting a small boat crammed with explosives blew up the USS *Cole* in 2000, killing 17 sailors berthed with the ship in Yemen (the group had failed in an earlier attempt against a U.S.

Navy ship when the suicide boat sank under the weight of the explosives). Two years later, an explosive-filled boat rammed a French oil tanker off the coast of the same country.

Suicide Bombing by Individual

While individual terrorists have undertaken suicide bombing missions in several areas of the world, Israel has become identified as the chief target of such attacks. Numerous U.S. citizens have died in suicide attacks by Palestinian terrorists, including during major attacks in 2003, 2002, and 1995. Palestinian extremists have pioneered suicide bombing techniques, including the indoctrination of bombers and the production of suicide belts filled with explosives and engineered to allow easy detonation by the bomber. Other groups have also focused on suicide attacks, most notably the Liberation Tigers of Tamil Eelam (LTTE), or Tamil Tigers.

Suicide Bombing by Aircraft

A natural evolution in the progression of suicide terrorist techniques, the use of airplanes for suicide bombings had already been developed by Japan's kamikaze pilots, who rammed their explosives-packed aircraft (and suicide torpedoes and boats) into U.S. ships during the waning days of World War II. (*The Turner Diaries*, the novel that served to inspire a number of domestic terrorists, includes a suicide flight into the Pentagon by the protagonist.)

In 1994, an emotionally disturbed American crashed a small plane onto the White House grounds. That same year, Algerian hijackers planned to ram a French airliner into the Eiffel Tower or explode it over Paris but were thwarted when commandos seized the aircraft on the ground. Intelligence reports indicated other terrorists had also considered this tactic before it was employed to such devastating effect on 9/11.

Hoaxes   Just the threat of attack can achieve terrorist goals, from creating fear to generating intelligence. Bomb threats can disrupt airline flights and, when repeated, engender complacency among security personnel and the public. Terrorists may also stage hoaxes in order to study the response of authorities in order to plan more effective attacks. In some cases, such as the 2001 anthrax attacks, a terrorist tactic can spawn hundreds or even thousands of imitation hoaxes. After the anthrax attacks, authorities wasted untold amounts of time and money responding to suspicious powders sent via the mail by a pro-life terrorist, other hoaxers, and even unthinking practical jokers.

Other Common Tactics

Among other terrorist actions are assassinations; sieges, which involve the seizure of a building or other location with symbolic value and/or occupants; raids, which may target specific individuals such as tourists or critical infrastructures; drive-by shootings, sometimes conducted by motorcyclists; sniping; rocket or mortar attacks; robberies; and fire bombings.

CHAPTER SUMMARY

Terrorists have a huge number of potential targets and a range of capabilities with which to hit them. While those responsible for securing the homeland must consider all possible terrorist attacks, certain tactics have proven especially common. More than a thousand years ago, knife attacks inspired fear; in the modern world, terrorists have used videotaped beheadings to achieve the same effect.

When new types of attacks occur, they have often been foreshadowed by earlier incidents. Yet even new tactics involve traditional operational phases, which offer opportunities to disrupt the terrorists. Stopping terrorists before they strike again has gained a new urgency in the modern era, where the next major component of the terrorist arsenal is WMD.

CHAPTER QUIZ

1. What organizational features do terrorist groups use to maintain their security?
2. What makes an attractive target for a terrorist?
3. Name two major tactical phases of a terrorist operation.
4. Identify three terrorist tactics that have claimed large numbers of victims.

NOTES

1. Andrew Macdonald, *The Turner Diaries* (Fort Lee, NJ: Barricade Books, 1996), p. 98.

2. Alan Feuer and Benjamin Weiser, "Translation: The How-to Book of Terrorism," *New York Times* (April 5, 200): A1.

3. "Iyman Faris Sentenced for Providing Material Support to Al Qaeda" (October 28, 2003), www.usdoj.gov/opa/pr/2003/October/03_crm_589.htm. For wife's lack of knowledge see Pierre Thomas, Mary Walsh, and Jason Ryan, "The Terrorist Next Door," ABCnews.com (September 8, 2003), www.abcnews.go.com/sections/wnt/US/sept11_faris030907.html.

4. U.S. Department of State, *Patterns of Global* Terrorism 2003 (Washington, DC: Department of State, April 2004), pp. 23, 65.

5. National Commission on Terrorist Attacks Upon the United States "Outline of the 9/11 Plot." Staff Statement No. 16, Twelfth Public hearing, www.9-11commission.gov/staff_statements/staff_statement_16.pdf, p. 13.

6. Unless otherwise noted, details on terrorist attacks noted in this chapter are from *Patterns of Global Terrorism* and the State Departments "Significant Terrorist Incidents, 1961-2003: A Brief Chronology," http://www.state.gov/r/pa/ho/pubs/fs/5902.htm.

7. USATODAY.Com, "FBI: Al-Qaeda Detainee Spoke of Fire Plot" (July 11, 2003), www.usatoday.com/news/washington/2003-07-11-alqaeda-fire_x.htm.

8. The Federation of American Scientists, "MANPADS Proliferation," www.fas.org/asmp/campaigns/MANPADS/MANPADS.html; Congressional Research Service "Homeland Security: Protecting Airliners from Terrorist Missiles" (November 3, 2003).

9. "MANPADS Proliferation."

10. John Mintz and Sara Kehaulani Goo, "Pillow Bombs Feared on Planes: U.S. Says Al Qaeda Explosives Could Also Be Stuffed into Coats, Toys," *Washington Post* (October 14, 2004): A5.

9

WEAPONS OF MASS DESTRUCTION

Understanding the Great Terrorist Threats and Getting beyond the Hype

A direct attack against American citizens on American soil is likely over the next quarter century. The risk is not only death and destruction but also a demoralization that could undermine US global leadership.

The Hart-Rudman Commission Report, April 2001

CHAPTER OVERVIEW

It would be a dangerous folly to confuse the unfamiliar with the improbable. There are terrorist weapons that can inflict catastrophic destruction, inflicting tens of thousands of casualties and hundreds of billions of dollars in physical destruction. There are terrorist groups that want these weapons, and there are ways for them to get them. On the other hand, Americans are not powerless in the face of these dangers. Understanding them and separating hype from reality is the first step to effectively responding to the threat of weapons of mass destruction, often referred to as chemical, biological, radiological, nuclear, and high-yield explosives (CBRNE). This chapter reviews how each of the CBRNE threats might be obtained and employed, as well as how effective they might be.

CHAPTER LEARNING OBJECTIVES

After reading this chapter, you should be able to

1. Understand how CBRNE weapons can be manufactured, obtained, and employed by terrorists.

2. Describe the difficulties of employing chemical weapons in a terrorist attack.

3. Describe the steps required to manufacture biological weapons and the challenges a terrorist might face in each step.

4. Understand the nature of casualties and damages that might be produced by a radiological dispersal device and how the effects of a "dirty bomb" might be mitigated.

5. Discuss the difficulties terrorists face in obtaining nuclear weapons and material.

6. Discuss why the use of improvised high-explosive devices are among the most likely to be used in a terrorist attack.

WEAPONS TO WORRY ABOUT

It was something no one expected. In 1974, an extortionist threatened to explode a nuclear weapon in the center of Boston. He wanted $200,000. Federal agents and scientists from the Atomic Energy Commission scrambled to the scene. No one was really sure what to do. The money was delivered to a prearranged spot, but never picked up. It was a hoax. The next year, a blackmailer threatened to blow up New York's water supply with a nuclear weapon unless he received $30 million. It was another fraud. In 1984, authorities worried that small nuclear devices would be smuggled into the Olympiad in Los Angeles. This fear also proved unfounded. A month after the 9/11 attacks, intelligence reports warned of the possibility that a stolen Russian nuclear weapon might be bound for New York City. Nothing occurred. Because these threats did not happen, it does not mean that they could not happen.

CHEMICAL

Before the Aum Shinrikyo sarin nerve gas attack on a Tokyo subway station in 1995, chemical munitions were thought of primarily as battlefield weapons. On March 20, 1995, members of the cult released enough gas into the subway system to kill 12 commuters and sicken 5,000. The cult failed to murder large numbers because of the poor quality of the chemical agent employed in the attack. But, Aum Shinrikyo did demonstrate to the world that modest chemical strikes might be an effective terrorist weapon, with the potential to cause mass casualties.[1] Equally troubling, the strike illustrated how even unsuccessful attacks can cause extensive disruption and fear.

Scope of the Chemical Threat

Depending on the type of agent, concentration, and dose received, chemical weapons can inflict a variety of casualties from discomfort to permanent injuries or death. A light dose of sulfur mustard gas, for example, will result in an individual developing painful skin blistering and eye and lung irritation over a period of a few hours. On the other hand, a person who inhaled 100 milligrams of sarin, a deadly nerve gas, for one minute would have a 50 percent chance of dying within 15 minutes. Chemical weapons are usually employed in aerosol form to be either inhaled through the lungs (particles in the 1 to 7 micron range) or absorbed through the skin (70 microns or less), sizes that are a fraction of the size of a human hair.

The Chemical Weapons Convention prohibits signatories from manufacturing, stockpiling, or using chemical weapons.[2] The convention, however, has not prevented states from developing and even employing chemical arms. The technology and expertise required to produce viable chemical weapons is within reach of many potential enemies. Also of concern are leftover stocks from Cold War chemical arsenals that are still awaiting destruction. They could be sold, stolen, or sabotaged. The safety and security of the vast Russian stockpiles might be considered the most serious, present problem.[3]

States are not the only threat. Even terrorist groups with modest means could produce small amounts of an effective chemical weapon. Compromising on purity, shelf-life, and safety could make agents even easier to manufacture. Two obstacles have to be overcome. First, an enemy must obtain precursors, the component chemicals required to produce a lethal chemical compound. These can be stolen, purchased, or manufactured. Most precursors are commercially available since they also have industrial uses. The major obstacles to obtaining these materials is the Australia Group, a cooperative of countries working to manage the export of precursor chemicals, and the associated national export controls that track the production and use of precursor chemicals.[4] These controls provide some security, but determined terrorists might overcome these impediments by buying precursors in small amounts, employing substitute chemicals, manufacturing precursors from simpler compounds, or obtaining chemicals from suppliers not covered by the nonproliferation regime.

Making Chemical Weapons

Production of large quantities of chemical weapons requires industrial facilities. A manufacturing capability sufficient to produce thousands of kilograms of sarin gas would cost approximately $30 million. Special facilities can be constructed or commercial plants could be converted to the manufacture of chemical agents. Some 100 countries already have the capacity for large-scale production.

The ability to produce chemical weapons, however, is not beyond the means of any determined terrorist. An adequately financed organization could field a fairly significant threat. The Aum Shinrikyo group, for example, had a substantial manufacturing capacity. A reasonable expectation is that 20 to 30 kilograms of sarin gas could be manufactured at the cost of several million dollars. An even more modest capability, sufficient to manufacture a few kilograms of low-quality chemical weapons might be assembled for tens of thousands of dollars using readily available commercial laboratory equipment in a facility under 1,000 square feet.

Clandestine labs can be hidden anywhere. The illegal methamphetamine production in the United States offers an illustration of the problem. Meth labs use highly toxic and explosive chemicals. Labs have been found in farms, garages, apartments, and basements. Los Angeles law enforcement estimated that in 2000, labs dispersed throughout two counties in California had the capacity to manufacture 44.6 metric tons of methamphetamine a year. Federal authorities during that period seized only 3.87 tons. These figures suggest both the potential scope of illegal, small-scale chemical production and the difficulty of finding clandestine facilities, even when they leave prominent signatures like noxious odors and large amounts of obviously contaminated trash discolored by chemicals.

Delivering Chemical Weapons

Manufacturing deadly agents is only part of the process of fielding a credible threat. Effectively delivering chemical munitions is a significant obstacle. Large-scale chemical attacks require a significant volume of material both to achieve coverage of the target area and to compensate for wind, temperature, and humidity, which can disperse or diminish an agent's effectiveness. The population density of the target area for the attack is also an important factor. For example, under moderate weather conditions 300 kilograms of sarin gas dispensed by air would kill about 60 to 200 people in a .22 square kilometer area (based on a population density of 3,000 to 10,000 people per square kilometer).[5]

Dispensing chemicals is also a challenge. The best method for mass dispersal is employing sprayers such as crop dusters. Sprayers force liquids through a specially designed nozzle to create a suspension of fine particles that can drift over a large area. Even with a reliable dispenser, however, the challenge of transporting and delivering high volumes of chemical weapons under the right environmental conditions for a lethal attack against a large open-area target are difficult. In high temperatures the chemicals will evaporate. In the cold, they will condense and fall to the ground. High winds will disperse chemicals rapidly. The best conditions for a chemical attack may be a temperature inversion where air is trapped over a target area. Complex urban terrain can also significantly alter the dispersal pattern of chemical agents. Some experimentation suggests that the shape and array of buildings in a cityscape will prevent the uniform distribution of the agent over a target area.

On the other hand, smuggling into or manufacturing small quantities of chemical agents within the United States and employing them in confined spaces such as buildings or subways using some kind of simple release mechanism or a ventilation system would be relatively easy and, depending upon the type of agent, the number of people exposed could be in the thousands. Buildings with mechanical ventilation, for example, introduce outdoor air at the rate of about 15 to 20 cubic feet per minute. As a result, there is a constant potential for contaminants to be quickly funneled throughout the building. The chimney effect of air rising through stairwells and elevator shafts can also disperse air and chemical agents rapidly.

Industrial Chemical Threat

Perhaps of greater concern, however, should be the many toxic chemicals used for industrial and commercial purposes that might be exploited by terrorists. Tanker trucks, railcars, ships, pipelines, and trucks carrying barrels of poisons or other hazardous materials, and chemical manufacturing and storage facilities are all prospective weapons. In 2001, the Environmental Protection Agency reported that at least 123 U.S. chemical plants contain enough chemicals that, if a major release occurred, each could result in a million or more casualties. In one agency survey of 15,000 chemical facilities, the mean population that might be potentially affected by a toxic chemical release in a worst-case scenario was 40,247.[6]

Indeed, chemical accidents, fires, and spills, many causing death and significant property damage, are not an unknown occurrence. Many of these incidents occurred near densely populated areas. For instance, a study of chemical releases in New York over a five-year period found that more than half the releases were near residences. Seventy-five percent of the events occurred within one-quarter mile of a household.[7] Chemical accidents throughout the United States have resulted in significant damage. For example, from 1986 to 1999 releases from pipelines caused, on average, 23 fatalities, 113 injuries, and $68 million in damage per year.

The most likely dangerous agents that could be released by a deliberate terrorist attack would be either toxic chemicals or flammable substances. Of the two, toxic chemicals could be potentially the more dangerous since they tend to represent a greater downwind hazard. Anhydrous ammonia and chlorine are the mostly widely used industrial chemicals that might be the target of a sabotage effort. Both can represent substantial vapor hazards. For instance, most chlorine in the United States is transported in 90-ton railcars. The downwind hazard for a release from a railcar in an urban setting is 22.5 kilometers. The gas plume could kill outright any exposed individual up to six kilometers away and inflict permanent lung damage on those farther downwind.

On the other hand, while flammable substances present less of a vapor hazard, they can still represent a substantial danger. For example, in 1989, a massive release of isobutene, ethylene, hexane, and hydrogen from a Phillips 66 chemical plant in Houston ignited in a fireball that exploded with a force of 2.3 kilotons. The disaster killed 23 and injured 130, leaving $750 million in damage at the plant and hurling debris 9.5 kilometers into neighboring communities.

ISSUES:

BHOPAL—REAL-LIFE CHEMICAL DISASTER

The 1984 release of methyl isocyanate from a Union Carbide pesticide factory in a suburb of Bhopal, India, sickened 200,000 and killed 2,500. Although it was not known at the time, the gas was formed when a disgruntled plant employee, apparently bent on spoiling a batch of methyl isocyanate, added water to a storage tank. The water caused a reaction that built up heat and pressure in the tank, quickly transforming the chemical compound into a lethal gas that escaped into the cool night air. This industrial disaster illustrated the potential casualties that might result from a catastrophic release of deadly chemicals as a result of sabotage.

Excerpt from the Union Carbide Lessons Learned Report

Emergency Response. Union Carbide had a contingency plan for emergencies. This plan provided a basic framework and some guidelines. In Bhopal, however, the "unthinkable" had happened and the terrible facts of the tragedy were overwhelming. However, the versatility of our staff, their stamina in the face of long, grueling hours, and a systematic approach to communications that had been in place for some time were significant assets.

Press Coverage. In the first days, scheduled news conferences helped us deal with the hundreds of inquiries that poured in from around the world. There was no way we could respond to every individual call. But many of the frequently asked questions were considered when we prepared for daily briefings. There was another benefit to the news conferences. They were public forums on which many key constituents, such as employees, shareholders, and customers, relied for information. They also demonstrated how the company would deal with the crisis as well as the demands of its ongoing businesses. We understood that above all we would have to demonstrate, as best we could, our integrity and competence. Additionally, I'm persuaded that the exceptional performance of Union Carbide employees throughout the world confirmed what we said. It also reassured all of us and our constituents that we would not hide or crumble in the face of adversity.

New Safety Procedures. The impact of Bhopal went well beyond Union Carbide. It changed views and practices among the entire U.S. chemical industry. It provided impetus to the development and enactment of federal laws requiring companies to notify government and the public about toxic substances they make or use. The EPA's Federal Superfund Reauthorization, spurred by the Bhopal tragedy, helped bring about a network of local emergency planning councils, in which corporate specialists work with their neighboring communities to safely deal with unthinkable environmental disasters.[8]

1. What caused the Bhopal disaster? Could similar tragedies happen in the United States?
2. How could terrorists exploit such events?
3. What should be done to limit such terrorist threats?

In addition to striking industrial facilities, small-scale attacks could also be made with an arsenal of contaminants and toxins that are available to virtually anyone or are stored in areas that have little or no security to prevent tampering or sabotage. Fuels, pesticides, and solvents, for example, can all be used as poisons and contaminants that might cause some casualties and inflict psychological harm and economic disruption. One analyst calls these attacks "toxic warfare" and notes a growing tendency of terrorist groups overseas to conduct strikes using readily available materials.[9] These practices could be adopted for attacks in the United States.

Product or Commodity Tampering

Chemical attacks could also be made through product tampering or poisoning of food and water supplies or disrupting agricultural production. Because of the volume of material required for widespread contamination, large-scale attacks that might inflict catastrophic damage would be extremely difficult. For example, a water source would have to be contaminated with significant amounts of cyanide to produce a lethal drink of water.[10]

By comparison, product tampering and small-scale, and potentially very deadly, attacks are eminently achievable. In 1982, for example, seven people in the Chicago area died as a result of ingesting Tylenol laced with cyanide. In addition to the actual attack, the public was bewildered by a wave of 270 incidents of suspected product tampering reported to the Food and Drug Administration in the wake of the incident. Many of these were outright hoaxes. Still, the affair demonstrated the widespread concern and confusion that could be generated by a product-tampering campaign.

BIOLOGICAL

Biological weapons use living microorganisms including bacteria, rickettsias, fungi, or viruses to cause infections that incapacitate or kill. A gram or less of many biological weapons can inflict high lethality. Weight for weight, they can be hundreds to thousands of times more lethal than the most deadly chemical agents and can, in some cases, be produced at much less cost. Some weapons are communicable and can be spread easily beyond the initial target.

Toxins are chemicals produced by bacteria, fungi, plants, or animals that act as poisons. Usually they are classified as either chemical or biological weapons, though in fact they have some characteristics of both. While they are derived from organic sources, unlike biological weapons they are not living organisms, do not reproduce, and are not communicable. As with with biological weapons pound for pound they can be hundreds to thousands of times more lethal than an equivalent amount of chemical nerve agent. However, like chemical weapons the effects of some toxins can appear in seconds to minutes rather than requiring hours or weeks for symptoms to appear, as is often true in the case of biological infections. Unlike chemical weapons, toxins can often be difficult to detect and diagnose. For scientific research and development or nonproliferation issues it may be useful to group toxins with biological weapons, but medical considerations and casualty response, assessment, and treatment emergency personnel should distinguish toxin weapons as a separate category.[11]

Scope of Biological Weapons Threat

Terrorist groups are capable of performing some form of biological or toxin warfare. Individuals with some graduate-level science education or medical training could produce bioweapons, though the skills required for creating very small and stable agents does require some sophistication. In some cases, biological attacks can be mounted without any scientific skills or medical knowledge. (See Figure 9.1.)

Developing Biological Weapons

There are four essential tasks involved in producing a biological agent: obtaining seed stocks, production, stabilization, and preparation for distribution. First, a seed stock of the pathogen or toxin-producing organism must be obtained. Not all biological agents and toxins are sufficiently lethal or stable to be used as weapons. To preclude biological materials that can be readily weaponized from being readily available, there are restrictions on the most dangerous pathogens, based on the Biological and Toxin Weapons Convention.[12] Even without an implementing protocol for the convention many countries, principally operating under the cooperation of the

Australia Group, have worked to prevent the acquisition of seed stocks by terrorist groups or states attempting to mount weapons programs. Each state is responsible for implementing its own measures. Enforcement, however, is inconsistent.

In addition, there are means to overcome the restrictions imposed by the Australia Group. Stocks can be purchased under the guise of conducting legitimate scientific research. In 1984 and 1985, for example, the Rajneeshee cult in Oregon set up its own medical corporation and obtained pathogens from the American Type Culture Collection, a nonprofit organization that serves as a repository of biological materials for scientific and medical research. The cult later used some of these materials to conduct terrorist attacks.[13] In 1996, and again in 2002, the U.S. government moved to tighten restrictions on pathogen transfers, but the possibility that an enemy could obtain seed materials from a source in the United States or other countries remains a concern.[14]

Seed stocks can also be stolen or extracted from a natural source. In some instances, as in the case of smallpox, this could be very difficult.[15] In other cases, sources are more readily available. Some toxins, for example, can be extracted from plants or animals, though they are difficult to produce in large quantities. Thus, the second task in fielding a bioweapon is to produce the biological or toxin agent in bulk. Protein toxins, for example, are produced from bacteria by batch fermentation. Much of the technology required for this task can be employed in both industrial biotechnology and commercial fermentation.

The technical procedures for weapons production are available in open-source, scientific literature. Over 100 states have the capacity to manufacture biological weapons on a large scale. A basic facility can be constructed and operated for less than $10 million. However, any terrorist group, given a competent team of graduate students and a facility no larger than a few hundred square feet, could field a small-scale program for a few hundred thousand dollars or less. The Biological and Toxin Weapons Convention limits the proliferation of some technologies. The challenge of implementing controls for dual-use science and technology is one major obstacle to enforcing the convention.

The third task is stabilizing the biological or toxin agents for storage and dissemination. Freeze-drying, introducing chemical additives, or microencapsulation (coating droplets of pathogens with a

FIGURE 9.1

BIOTERRORISM AGENTS AND DISEASES

Category	Agents/Diseases	Definition
A	Anthrax (*Bacillus anthracis*) Botulism (*Clostridium botulinum toxin*) Plague (*Yersinia pestis*) Smallpox (variola major) Tularemia (*Francisella tularensis*) Viral hemorrhagic fevers (filoviruses [e.g., Ebola, Marburg] and arenaviruses [e.g., Lassa, Machupo])	The U.S. public health system and primary healthcare providers must be prepared to address various biological agents, including pathogens that are rarely seen in the United States. High-priority agents include organisms that pose a risk to national security because they • Can be easily disseminated or transmitted from person to person • Result in high mortality rates and have the potential for major public health impact • Might cause public panic and social disruption • Require special action for public health preparedness
B	Brucellosis (*Brucella* species) Epsilon toxin of *Clostridium perfringens* Food safety threats (e.g., *Salmonella* species, *Escherichia coli* O157:H7, *Shigella*) Glanders (*Burkholderia mallei*) Melioidosis (*Burkholderia pseudomallei*) Psittacosis (*Chlamydia psittaci*) Q fever (*Coxiella burnetii*) Ricin toxin from *Ricinus communis* (castor beans) Staphylococcal enterotoxin B Typhus fever (*Rickettsia prowazekii*) Viral encephalitis (alphaviruses [e.g., Venezuelan eastern and western equine encephalitides) Water safety threats (e.g., *Vibrio cholerae*, *Cryptosporidium parvum*)	Second highest priority agents include those that • Are moderately easy to disseminate • Result in moderate morbidity rates and low mortality rates • Require specific enhancements of the CDC's diagnostic capacity and enhanced disease surveillance
C	Emerging infectious diseases such as Nipah virus and hantavirus	Third highest priority agents include emerging pathogens that could be engineered for mass dissemination in the future because of • Availability • Ease of production and dissemination • Potential for high morbidity and mortality rates and major health impact

Source: Information in this table provided by the Centers for Disease Control and Prevention at www.bt.cdc.gov/agent/agentlist-category.asp.

protective material) are all proven methods, and the equipment needed to perform them is not difficult to obtain. Commercial freeze dryers, for example, are widely used in the food and beverage industry. Small-scale dryers, used to produce market samples, can also be used in biotechnology applications.

The fourth task is preparing agents for dispersal. Biological and toxin weapons usually take the form of liquid slurries (a mixture of water and fine particles) or a powder. Liquid slurries are easiest to prepare, but less effective and heavier. Powders are created through a milling process, a technically challenging component of weapons production, but again one that mirrors commercial processes.

Obtaining the means to manufacture ultrafine particles is central to producing potentially highly lethal agents. The lethality of many pathogens rises considerably when they are inhaled. Particles between one to five microns in diameter are ideal. They remain in the air longer and can be inhaled deep into the lungs where the membranes are thinner and small particles can pass more easily into the body and initiate respiratory infections. In addition, coatings can also be used to prevent clumping and ensure particles remain small.

Producing ultrasmall particles that are both clump-free and highly stable is a trademark of programs that reflect a greater degree of technical skill and higher costs, requiring tools such as sophisticated spray dryers,[16] electron microscopes (which alone cost $50,000 to $250,000 or more), and hazard containment facilities.

Delivering Biological Attacks

The means available to deliver biological and toxin weapons range from very difficult to easy. The most lethal means for delivering biological agents is in an aerosol form. This can be done effectively by sprayers and, far less efficiently, by explosive devices such as self-dispensing cluster bombs, which destroy part of the agent when they detonate. Cruise missiles, unmanned aerial vehicles (UAVs), or aircraft could perform sprayer attacks, but only effectively if specialized spraying equipment was employed that ensured proper dispersal and prevented particle clumping. Clumping of agents can degrade the effectiveness of an attack. Large particles quickly drop to the ground or, if inhaled, do not easily pass into lung tissue, significantly lessening the potential for infection. Conventional sprayers on crop dusters or air tankers that are used to fight forest fires, for example, would probably not be very effective at dispensing agents in the one- to five-micron range. Mechanical stresses in the spraying system might also kill or inactivate a large percentage of particles, by some estimates up to 99 percent. However, if a terrorist had a large supply, say 50 kilograms of a virulent bioweapon, or was not terribly concerned about achieving maximum effects, crude dispensers might be adequate.

Any method of delivering biological agents, from dropping a liquid slurry out of helicopters to sprinkling agents on the sidewalk, might achieve some success, but weather conditions and complex urban terrain will affect dispersal and the life span of the microbes (many are sensitive to ultraviolet light and temperature extremes), and thus high casualties and even widespread contamination are not assured. When Aum Shinrikyo flung anthrax off a tall building; the agent was so dispersed or of such poor quality that there were no casualties.[17]

Environmental Considerations

Attackers wanting to ensure high lethality or widespread contamination would probably seek means that would limit the environmental stresses on the agent and vector it directly onto the intended target. Ventilation systems and air conditioners might prove useful means for injecting agents into confined spaces. For example, the 1976 outbreak of pneumonia that sickened and killed American Legionnaires attending a convention in Philadelphia was caused by the bacterium *Legionella,* which spread through the hotel by the air-conditioning system.[18] An inventive enemy might be able to adapt such a method for a deliberate attack. Alternatively, agents released in a subway system would be widely dispersed by the movement of trains, which act like huge pistons forcing air to move rapidly through subway tunnels. Portable atomizers might be employed to contaminate subway cars, airport terminals, or campus recreation rooms.

Intentional contamination of food and water is another possible form of biological attack. Natural outbreaks of waterborne contamination are already an enduring concern. A protozoan infestation in the Milwaukee water supply in 1993 killed 50 and sickened 400,000.

Intentionally fouling water supplies, however, is difficult. Though there are over 55,000 community water systems, the opportunities for an effective attack are less of a risk than generally assumed. Municipal waterworks are already designed to filter out or kill impurities and pathogens. A combination of filtration and disinfection technologies can address most risks, if properly applied. Contaminants, for example, can be removed by inexpensive and widely available carbon filters. Additionally, agents would be disbursed and diluted requiring huge volumes of contaminant to have any effect. In short, waterborne attacks are feasible, but difficult.[19]

Product Tampering

On the other hand, product tampering or contamination of food supplies is an ever-present danger. Contaminated food is already a serious problem. Food-borne disease causes an average of 76 million illnesses each year, 325,000 hospitalizations, and 5,000 deaths, creating an economic cost that by some estimates ranges up to $32 billion.[20] Humans can also be exposed to a range of deadly or debilitating toxins by ingesting contaminated plant and animal products, or less frequently by contact or inhalation. Beans, peppers, carrots, and corn, for example, are ideal vehicles for carrying botulinum. Biological or toxin agents could be introduced effectively through a wide variety of commodities from cookies to cosmetics. Improper storage, poor sanitation, and cross-contamination during the production, transportation, processing, or storage of medicine, food supplies, or other consumables can further spread toxins or biological agents.

Infectious Disease

Finally, another means of bioattack is to spread infectious diseases through humans, animals, or insects. Infectious diseases are already the third leading cause of death in the United States and battling them is an ongoing health issue. For example, a recent outbreak of mosquito-borne dengue fever in Hawaii, a disease not endemic to the United States, sickened 119 people. Responding to the outbreak cost over $1.5 million. An enemy might attempt to introduce diseases not common in the United States such as cholera, dengue, dengue hemorrhagic fever, and dengue shock syndrome. The threat of an epidemic varies with the type of agent employed; the nature of the attack; the method of transmission; the medical countermeasures required and available to prevent or treat the disease; and the size of the target population.

RADIOLOGICAL

Radiological weapons rely on radiation, rather than blast, to cause death and casualties. They can also disrupt, damage, and deny access to areas, systems, and facilities. Radiation inflicts casualties by destroying or damaging human cells. High-dose radiation can kill or incapacitate individuals. Lower doses can create both short-term (such as lowering the body's immune response and making individuals more susceptible to illness and disease) and long-term (including causing various forms of cancer) health problems. In addition, some radioactive isotopes, such as cesium-137, bond easily with common materials like concrete and soil, and could represent long-term health and contamination risks in an affected area.[21]

Scope of the Radiological Threat

The distance from the radioactive source, the manner of dispersal, weather conditions (which will affect how far contaminated particles mixed in a debris cloud or aerosol attack will disperse), the degree of protection (e.g., buildings, overhead cover), and the type of radiation will significantly affect the manner of the threat. Alpha particles, for example, travel a short distance and most will not penetrate beyond the dead layer of epidermal skin. They are harmful, however, if inhaled or swallowed. Beta particles can penetrate the skin and inflict cellular damage, but they can be blocked by common materials like plastic, concrete, and aluminum. In contrast, gamma rays and neutrons are far more powerful and do not lose energy as quickly as alpha and beta particles when they pass through an absorber like clothing or walls. Heavy lead shielding, great amounts of other shielding with absorbent or scattering material (e.g., several feet of earth or concrete), or significant distance (perhaps in kilometers) may be required to avoid high-dose exposure.[22] In an urban attack, buildings might absorb or shield significant amounts of radiation, significantly reducing the initial prospects for casualties, though the cleanup of contaminated buildings would have substantial economic consequences.

Types of Threats

Radiological weapons can take two forms: radiological dispersal devices, or spreading contamination through attacks on critical infrastructure including systems that supply food and other commodities, or by striking nuclear facilities.

A dirty bomb attack could take many forms. Relatively large weapons with highly radioactive material would likely be required to kill or sicken great numbers of people. A truck bomb, for example, with 220 kilograms of explosive and 50 kilograms of one-year-old spent fuel rods would produce a lethal dosage zone with a radius of about one kilometer. The explosion of such a device employed in an urban area against a large, unsheltered population might contaminate thousands or more.[23]

Although producing a radiological weapon is far easier than building a nuclear bomb, a highly effective radiological dispersal device that can be easily transported to its target could be difficult to fabricate. Iraq, for example, attempted and failed to develop a practical weapon.[24]

Among the problems in building a large device is that significant amounts of very highly radioactive material must be heavily shielded or the material will melt carrying containers and sicken or kill anyone attempting to assemble or transport the weapon. Because of shielding requirements and the heat generated by some highly radioactive nuclear material (such as fuel rods for nuclear reactors), weight can be a significant factor in determining the size and potency of a weapon. For example, one assessment concluded that sufficient radioactive material to contaminate 230 square kilometers would require about 140 kilograms of lead shielding. Other means of distribution can also face technical and material challenges. If an enemy wanted to distribute radiological material as a fine aerosol (with the ideal size being about one to five microns), it would require a degree of specialized knowledge, as well as specialized handling and processing equipment to mill the radioactive agent and blend it with some inert material to facilitate dispersion and increase the risk of inhalation.

Obtaining Radiological Material

Unlike nuclear weapons, a radiological dispersal device does not require plutonium or enriched uranium. All that is needed is some form of radioactive material. Any nuclear reactor is capable of producing material for a radiological weapon. Worldwide, the International Atomic Energy Association (IAEA) lists 438 nuclear power reactors, 651 research reactors (284 in operation), and 250 fuel cycle plants. Highly radioactive material, such as spent fuel rods or other waste material is subject to export controls. It is, however, far more easily bought or stolen than weapons-grade material. Security worldwide is uneven, and trafficking in these materials is not unprecedented. Since 1993, the IAEA has recorded 531 cases of illegal transactions in radioactive material.

Additionally, there are tens of thousands of radiation sources in medical, industrial, agricultural, and research facilities. Illicitly obtaining these materials is well within the realm of the possible. According to the IAEA over 100 countries have inadequate regulatory systems for controlling radioactive material. Even the United States has significant gaps in its export rules covering highly radioactive substances. Current regulations permit virtually unlimited export of high-risk materials.[25]

Weapons Effects

The impact of the weapon on those who did not receive an immediately lethal, incapacitating dose of radiation is hard to predict. Even the largest radiological dispersal device is only likely to inflict catastrophic casualties if long-term cancer risks are considered. But whether contamination on that scale can be achieved with a dirty bomb is debatable.[26] The effects of a radiological weapon would have a latency period between exposure and the onset of symptoms from hours to weeks, or even years in the case of some cancers. Thus, a weapon might have considerable psychological impact, though the immediate physical damage and disruption might not be great or, in some cases, even apparent.

Prompt modern medical treatment can dramatically improve survivability after radiation injury for individuals who do not receive an initial lethal high dose of radiation. In particular, dramatic medical advances have been made in caring for individuals with suppressed immune systems, a common by-product of radiation attack. In addition, the danger of low-dose exposure from a radiological weapon may be far less than is commonly assumed. The long-term effect of low-dose radiation is determined by the capacity of irradiated tissue to repair DNA damage within individual cells. This is governed by a number of exposure, health, and genetic factors. There is some scientific evidence that current models may overestimate risks.[27]

On the other hand, due to public fears of radiation, the psychological effects of an attack might be out of proportion to the physical threat. Posttraumatic stress and major depression disorders, for example, could be major problems.[28] The economic impact of a radiological strike should also not be underestimated. If contamination is extensive, just removing irradiated material could have significant consequences. For comparison, eliminating low-level radioactive waste from biomedical research facilities represents substantial cost. Shipping these materials to an appropriate storage facility can cost up to $300 or more per cubic foot. The economic consequences of an attack would also have to include the cost of evacuating contaminated areas and housing, feeding, and caring for displaced persons, as well as lost worker productivity.

Radiological Threats from Nuclear Infrastructure

For achieving catastrophic damage through a radiological attack, strikes on nuclear power infrastructure or other nuclear facilities offer a far better option than exploding dirty bombs. At its worst, a major release of radiation from a reactor or spent fuel storage site caused by sabotage or a direct attack could kill tens of thousands. Many of the 103 operational nuclear plants, 16 decommissioned plants that contain spent fuel, and 37 nonpower licensed reactors in the United States are sufficiently close to major population centers that an attack on one of these facilities would cause large numbers of people to evacuate and severe economic disruption in addition to threatening lives and property. The cleanup effort of a major radiological release from a nuclear facility would be substantial, well into the billions of dollars.[29]

The vulnerability of nuclear facilities to ground, sea, and air attack is a subject of some controversy. It is unclear whether the crash of a large, fully fueled, commercial aircraft could inflict sufficient damage to create a significant release of nuclear material or that damaging other facilities such as spent fuel storage facilities or containment cooling systems could cause catastrophic damage. The potential for successful ground- or sea-borne attacks against nuclear material or radioactive waste material in transit are also issues.[30] Still, they are clearly not easy marks. Even if an attack was successfully launched, it is not a given that the strike would reap catastrophic effects.

NUCLEAR

The effects of a nuclear weapon are blast, heat, and nuclear radiation. Their relative importance varies with the yield of the bomb. With an explosion of about 2.5 kilotons (equivalent to the explosive energy of 2,500 tons of TNT), they are all devastating and about equal in killing power, with immediately fatal injuries at a range of 1 kilometer. As the yield increases, the volume of blast and heat grow rapidly, outpacing the immediate effects of radiation.[31]

Scope of Nuclear Threat

Several nations possess nuclear weapons (see From the Source box). There are also prospects for states such as Iran and North Korea to field nuclear arsenals. The commercial or research nuclear infrastructure of any country, however, can be used as the foundation for a weapons program. Some of the technologies and know-how required for production are dual-use, well-known, and, considering that devices can be built with equipment available in the 1940s, not even state-of-the-art. On the other hand, some of these tasks, such as refining highly enriched uranium or constructing the explosive lens used to construct the core of a plutonium implosion device, can be technically difficult and expensive to master. In addition, claims that nuclear weapons can be fashioned through simpler means or by employing low-enriched nuclear materials seem questionable.[32]

Producing Nuclear Weapons

The most significant obstacle to fielding a nuclear device is obtaining the nuclear material that is necessary to produce a chain reaction that unleashes an atomic explosion. Acquiring highly enriched uranium or plutonium through industrial production would consume considerable technical, industrial, and financial resources and thus is an activity largely limited to states.[33] A weapon using a design no more sophisticated than the U.S. bombs dropped on Japan could produce a kiloton yield with as little as 25 kilograms of highly enriched uranium or 8 kilograms of plutonium.[34] Some argue, however, that more modern weapon designs can result in a kiloton yield with as little as one kilogram of nuclear material.[35] A program capable of manufacturing six weapons (yielding in the range of 10 to 25 kilotons) might cost about $4 billion.[36]

Weapons are easier to produce if developers are willing to accept trade-offs in testing, safety, size, weight, shelf life, and yield predictability. Foreign assistance by nuclear-capable states can greatly speed the progress of nuclear weapons development. On the other hand, these cost assessments also assume that a program would proceed smoothly without false starts, accidents, or organizational problems in addition to security concerns, economic constraints, foreign intervention, or political decisions that could significantly lengthen development and production times. In over a decade, for example, Iraq is estimated to have spent 20 times the cost of a minimal program and did not produce a workable bomb.

So far, nuclear weapons have been produced only through indigenous state-run programs. A nuclear shortcut might be to purchase or steal weapons or weapons-grade material. This is a credible threat, not only from enemy states, but also from well-financed nonstate groups. There is little reliable data on black-market prices for weapons-grade nuclear material, but one study suggests nominal prices for these commodities could be $1 million per kilogram or more.[37] There are groups capable and willing to make such investments. For example, Aum Shinrikyo had $1 billion in resources at its disposal. Documents seized from the cult reveal it had an interest in buying nuclear weapons, though its efforts never came to fruition.[38] Nor was the cult's efforts an aberration. Worldwide, in the last decade 10 percent of the almost 400 documented cases of attempted nuclear materials smuggling involved plutonium or highly enriched uranium.

Nuclear Smuggling

There are great unknowns concerning the nuclear black market. Publicly available information suggests most cases of attempted smuggling involve scam artists or amateur criminals rather than well-organized conspiracies. But these activities do not preclude the existence of a more serious threat that may be largely hidden from either public scrutiny or Western intelligence. Such efforts might

FROM THE SOURCE:

THE *N*TH COUNTRY EXPERIMENT

Designing a nuclear weapon is not the most difficult task in creating a terrorist weapon. In the 1960s, for example, in an experiment, the U.S. government commissioned three physicists to design a nuclear weapon without access to classified information. After a year-long effort, the team produced a design for a workable bomb using only open-source material.[39]

The following set of rules was given to the experimenters in memorandum form at the beginning of the Nth Country Experiment.

*From the **N**th Country Project Report*

*The Operating Rules for the **N**th Country Project*

A. J. HUDGINS

1. The purpose of the so-called "Nth Country Experiment" is to find out if a credible nuclear explosive can be designed, with a modest effort by a few well trained people without contact with classified information. The goal of the participants should be to design an explosive with a militarily significant yield. A working context for the experiment might be that the participants have been asked to design a nuclear explosive which, if built in small numbers, would give a small nation a significant effect on their foreign relations.

2. An informal committee has been chosen to monitor this experiment. In order to provide maximum assurance that the committee does not, in fact, perturb the experiment in a casual or unrecorded manner, all communications regarding the substance of the experiment will be in writing. The men doing the experiment are expected to avoid conscientiously any contact

with classified information in order to maintain the integrity of the primary assumption. They may request further guidance or specific information from the committee through A. J. Hudgins.

3. The experimenters are expected to use any means available to obtain as much unclassified information as they believe to be pertinent. The experiment will have to be conducted in such a way that all sources of unclassified information can be explicitly identified. It is important that as much as possible of the progress of the experiment be put in writing. Secretarial help will be available.

4. It is not expected that the experimenters do all of the routine work involved in the design themselves. Help in computation or in other mechanics such as information search should be requested only through the committee. In each case there must be a specific request detailing the result desired. In other words, the experimenters must state the problem and their boundary conditions for its solution. The committee will see to it that the best response possible is obtained in a timely fashion.

5. Even though this experiment will be based upon the use of information from unclassified sources, the Atomic Energy Act and AEC regulations require that any design efforts related to nuclear explosives be given proper security protection. This requires that the work books and any elaboration or deduction from unclassified information be classified properly and that all such information be protected in accord with the Laboratory Security Manual.

6. For the purposes of this experiment it should be assumed explicitly that any material may be fabricated in any shape. The purpose of this assumption is to remove fabrication and procurement problems from the area of the experiment.

involve state or nonstate groups. Obtaining weapons-grade material from states such as India, Iran, North Korea, or Pakistan is possible. Recent revelations concerning the activities of Pakistani scientist A. Q. Khan show that commerce involving covert transfers of materials and technologies relating to nuclear weapons technologies and materials have become substantial in recent years.[40] Another likely source would be siphoning material from an established, legitimate program with excess material. But export controls and security measures are a significant impediment. There are, however, gaps that can be exploited. Every nuclear country, including the United States, has some issues over the security of its materials. Some stockpiles around the world are particularly vulnerable. Of greatest concern, is the safekeeping of Russian nuclear weapons and material, which represents 95 percent of the world total outside America. It is known, for example, that at least 4.5 kilograms of weapons-grade uranium has been stolen from Russian institutes in the last 10 years.

Overall, the enforcement of the Nuclear Nonproliferation Treaty and the effectiveness of U.S. initiatives have had a mixed record of success.[41] As far as is known no group has successfully bought or stolen weapons or has the capability to build a weapon. This is cold comfort. These weapons are highly sought after.

Delivering Nuclear Weapons

Nuclear weapons can be delivered by ballistic missiles or cruise missiles or smuggled to the continent by ships or aircraft. Britain, China, France, and Russia all have nuclear-tipped ballistic missiles that can reach targets in the United States. For enemies of the United States, the state of their technical skills and resources may determine the choice of delivery means. Building nuclear warheads in the 500-kilogram or smaller range is a significant technical challenge. Terrorists would likely be limited to attempting to smuggle a nuclear weapon or its components into the United States.

HIGH-YIELD EXPLOSIVES

Before September 11, 2001, the two most notable terrorist attacks on the United States in recent memory were the bombing of the Murrah office building in Oklahoma City and the February 26, 1993, bombing of the World Trade Center. While little discussed of late, the use of large explosive devices are a formidable threat and will remain so in the years ahead.

Scope of Explosive Threat

Bombs kill by blast effects, flying debris, and ensuing fires, toxic releases, or other damage wrought by the explosion. In a conventional explosive, energy is derived from a sudden, violent chemical reaction. High explosives are materials that have a very fast rate of explosive reaction, emitting a detonating wave that can move up to 9,000 meters per second. Large, or high-yield, conventional explosive devices can either be manufactured bombs or improvised explosive devices.

Delivery of Weapons

Weapons can be delivered by a wide variety of means including missiles, UAVs, and bombs covertly transported by air, land, and sea vehicles. The delivery system will largely determine the scale of the attack. Virtually any size group could undertake a large-bomb attack employing some form of covert delivery means. For example, the strike on the Murrah office building in Oklahoma City, executed by two individuals with limited means, consisted of a truck bomb carrying 4,800 pounds of explosives. It caused tens of millions of dollars in damage and killed 168 people.[42]

While a wide range of groups could undertake high-yield explosive attacks, it is unlikely that any one strike could achieve catastrophic destruction. For example, by one analysis, the resources required to respond to the detonation of a very large high-yield explosive weapon would be less than one-third the response force required in the wake of a 10-kiloton nuclear blast.[43] The reduced response size gives some indication of how conventional explosives compare with nuclear arms. It should be noted, however, that high-yield explosive devices employed against some critical infrastructure, such as dams, nuclear plants, and chemical factories, might have the potential to trigger a near-catastrophic event.

Obtaining High-Yield Explosive Weapons

High-yield explosive devices can be obtained in a number of ways. Military bombs, submunitions, and explosives can be illicitly bought or stolen. Submunitions, for example, are manufactured by 33 countries. Fifty-six nations stockpile submunitions, and 18 of these are not members of the Convention on Certain Conventional Weapons, which is designed to limit the spread of some types of military hardware.[44] The Wassenaar Arrangement lists submunitions as a controlled munition, but participation in the arrangement is voluntary and can be circumvented.[45]

Weapons can also be fashioned from commercial explosives and other chemicals using information from books, magazines, and the Internet. In fact, a 1997 Department of Justice report concluded that anyone interested in manufacturing a bomb could easily obtain detailed instructions from readily available sources. Al-Qaida produced its own bomb-making instructions in books, CD-ROMs, and videos.

Bomb-making materials are not difficult to obtain. Commercial explosives are readily available. For example, in 2001, 2.38 million metric tons of explosives, used for a wide variety of industrial and commercial purposes, were manufactured within the United States.[46] Bombs can also be synthesized from a variety of readily available chemical precursors, all with legitimate commercial uses, such as ammonium nitrate, sodium nitrate, potassium nitrate, nitromethane, concentrated nitric acid, concentrated hydrogen peroxide, sodium chlorate, potassium chlorate, potassium perchlorate, urea, and acetone. For example, the bomb employed in the 1993 World Trade Center attack consisted of approximately 500 to 700 kilograms of a fertilizer-based explosive and three large metal cylinders (about 60 kilograms) of compressed hydrogen gas.[47]

CHAPTER SUMMARY

Weapons of mass destruction (WMD) are often referred to as chemical, biological, radiological, nuclear, or high-yield explosive (CBRNE) arms. Despite the WMD moniker not all CBRNE weapons are capable of inflicting catastrophic harm, resulting in tens of thousands of casualties and hundreds of billions of dollars in damage. Nuclear arms are the most dangerous, but they are difficult to obtain or manufacture. Biological or chemical arms can be produced more easily, but delivering them in ways that cause significant casualties is far from easy. On the other hand, producing biological, chemical, and radiological weapons that can inflict some casualties, as well as significant psychological and economic disruption, are eminently achievable, even by terrorist groups with limited assets.

CHAPTER QUIZ

1. Why is the size of chemical, biological, or radiological particles an important factor in determining the risk of casualties?

2. Why are nonproliferation treaties an inadequate guarantee that CBRNE weapons can be kept out of the hands of terrorists?

3. What means might be used to reduce casualties from a dirty bomb?

4. What are precursors, and why are they important for determining the potential of terrorists to produce biological and chemical weapons?

5. What is the most likely CBRNE weapon to be employed by a terrorist group?

6. What emergency response measures might be applicable to all CBRNE threats?

7. How might weather and terrain affect chemical or biological weapon attacks?

8. What CBRNE threats are limited to enemies with substantial resources and industrial capacity?

9. What attacks on critical infrastructure might create CBRNE-like affects, and how likely are they?

10. What are the likely means of delivering CBRNE weapons?

NOTES

1. The scope of the cult's chemical weapons program is described in Robert Jay Lifton, *Destroying the World to Save It: Aum Shinrikyo, Apocalyptic Violence, and the New Global Terrorism* (New York: Henry Holt, 2000), passim.

2. Bureau of Arms Control, "Chemical Weapons Convention Signatories/Ratifiers" (November 12, 2001), www.state.gov/t/ac/rls/fs/2001/956.htm. More information on the Chemical Weapons Convention is available on the convention Web site, www.opcw.org/html/glance/index.html. The text of the Chemical Weapons Convention is at www.cwc.gov/treaty.

3. In 1999, Russia still had some 40,000 metric tons of chemical weapons. Igor Khripunov and George W. Parshall, "U.S. Assistance to Russian Chemical Weapons Destruction: Identifying the Next Step," *The Nonproliferation Review* (Fall 1999): 1. U.S. efforts to provide funds and assistance for the destruction of these stocks have been ongoing since 1996, but progress has been intermittent. A signatory to the Chemical Weapons Convention, Russia is obliged to destroy its chemical weapons stocks. In June 2001, it declared it could not meet its commitment to eliminate its chemical arsenal by 2007 and required a five-year extension. The Organization for the Prohibition of Chemical Weapons recently stated its doubts that the country has the means to achieve this goal. The United States also has chemical weapons stored and waiting destruction at eight sites across the country and at Johnston Atoll in the Pacific. Department of Defense, "U.S. Chemical Weapons Stockpile Information Declassified" (January 22, 1996), www.defenselink.mil/news/Jan1996/b012496_bt024-96.html.

4. The Australia Group meets annually to discuss export licensing measures of its 34 participant nations. Members in the Australia Group do not undertake any legally binding obligations; rather they rely on nations to establish and supervise controls. For more information see the group's Web site, www.australiagroup.net/index_en.htm.

5. Office of Technology Assessment, *Proliferation of Weapons of Mass Destruction: Assessing the Risks* (August 1993), p. 53, www.wws.princeton.edu/cgi-bin/byteserv.prl/~ota/disk1/1993/9341/934101.PDF.

6. For more on chemical risks see Environmental Protection Agency, *The Chemical Safety Audit Report FY 1997* (October 1998), passim, www.epa.gov/swercepp/pubs/97report.pdf. See also Testimony of Paul Orum before the Subcommittee on Superfund, Toxics, Risk, and Waste Management, Senate Environment and Public Works Committee (November 14, 2001); James C. Belke, "Chemical Accident Risks in U.S. Industry—A Preliminary Analysis of Accident Risk Data from U.S. Hazardous Chemical Facilities," (Environmental Protection Agency, September 25, 2000). The EPA defines a worst-case scenario as the release of the largest quantity of a regulated substance from a single vessel or process line failure that results in the greatest distance to the endpoint.

7. *Hazardous Substance Emergency Events Surveillance, Cumulative Report 1993-1997* (New York State Department of Health, September 1999), p. 4.

8. Union Carbide, *Bhopal, India, Lessons Learned: Ammonium Nitrate and Nitric Acid Hazard and Response.*

9. See Theodore Karasik, *Toxic Warfare* (Santa Monica, CA: Rand, 2002), passim.

10. For example, to generate a dose of 25 milligrams in the first quarter liter (about a cup) that a person might drink from a 200,000 gallon clear well would require 188 kilograms of cyanide. See Donald C. Hickman, "A Chemical and Biological Warfare Threat: USAF Water Systems at Risk" (USAF Counterproliferation Center, US Air War College, September 1999), fn 53, www.au.af.mil/au/awc/awcgate/cpc-pubs/hickman.htm.

11. J. M. Madsen, "Toxins Are Weapons of Mass Destruction: A Comparison and Contrast with Biological-Warfare and Chemical-Warfare Agents," *Clinical Laboratory Medicine* 3 (2001): 593–605.

12. Current efforts to strengthen the convention have stalled on developing a legally binding protocol to increase confidence in compliance. There are strong technical and political disagreements on the goals and means of verification. Countries with large commercial and

defense sectors in biological research have expressed a number of concerns. As of May 2004, 31 countries had not signed the Biological and Toxin Weapons Convention. For a list, see projects.sipri.se/cbw/docs/bw-btwc-nonsig.html. In addition, absent formal protocols for preventing the spread of biological arms, the Australia Group is working to minimize the risks of biological weapon proliferation through transshipment or export. The text of the convention is given at www.brad.ac.uk/acad/sbtwc/btwc/convention/documents/btwctext.pdf.

13. Judith Miller, et al., *Germs: Biological Weapons and America's Secret War* (New York: Simon & Schuster, 2001), pp. 26–27.

14. For more about the American Type Culture Collection, see the Web site at www.atcc.org/About/AboutATCC.cfm. In addition to the American Type Culture Collection, there are about 200 laboratories in the United States that maintain germ collections. The Department of Health and Human Services' Select Agent Registration Enforcement Program is responsible for tracking the transfer of pathogens for scientific and medical research. Distributing materials in the United States and internationally is also subject to regulation by the Departments of Agriculture, Commerce, Energy, Interior, Justice, Labor, State, Transportation, Treasury, Homeland Security, International Air Transport Association, and Environmental Protection Agency.

15. The smallpox disease has been eradicated. The only known stocks of smallpox, for example, are secured in the Institute of Virus Preparations in Russia, and the Centers for Disease Control and Prevention in the United States. There is widespread concern that seed stocks of smallpox may still exist outside the two official repositories. This fear is principally due to the vast biological weapons program run by the Soviet Union, which included weaponizing smallpox. The Russian government claims that all the stocks used in this program have been accounted for, but some analysts, including Ken Alibek, a former deputy director in the Soviet bioweapons program, believe that unregistered stocks may still exist. There are rumors, for example, that North Korea may have obtained smallpox stocks from Russian sources. There is also some fear that smallpox could be extracted from the remains of victims. The Soviets conducted research expeditions to recover remains buried in the permafrost in Siberia and extract genetic materials. It is unlikely that a living organism or viral DNA was extracted from the material. See Kenneth Alibek, "Biological Weapons in the Former Soviet Union: An Interview with Dr. Kenneth Alibek," *The Nonproliferation Review* (Spring/Summer 1999): 9. On the other hand, scientists have recovered and revived frozen microbes from the Antarctic that were thousands of years old. This research indicates that the DNA for some bacteria can remain viable up to a million years, suggesting that the recovery of exterminated diseases, given the right environmental conditions, is not impossible.

16. Spray drying is the most widely used industrial process for forming and drying solid particles. Spray drying involves atomizing a liquid feedstock into a spray of droplets that are dried with hot air.

17. Statement of W. Seth Carus before a Joint Hearing of the Senate Select Intelligence Committee and the Senate Judiciary Committee (March 4, 1998), judiciary.senate.gov/oldsite/carus.htm.

18. The bacteria thrived in the water of the hotel cooling tower. As water was lost into the air by evaporation, clouds of droplets containing legionellas were drawn into the air intakes of the building or may have fallen on passersby. "Legionnaires' Disease," OSHA Technical Manual, Section III, Chapter 7, www.osha-slc.gov/dts/osta/otm/otm_iii/otm_iii_7.html; D.W. Keller, et al., "Community Outbreak of Legionnaires' Disease: An Investigation Confirming the Potential for Cooling Towers to Transmit Legionella Species," *Clinical Infectious Diseases* 22(1996):257–261.

19. Timothy E. Ford and William R. Mackenzie, "How Safe Is Our Drinking Water?" *Postgraduate Medicine* 108/4 (September 15, 2000): 11

20. For an overview of the threat of biological agroterrorism see Anne Kohnen, "Responding to the Threat of Agroterrorism: Specific Recommendations for the United States Department of Agriculture," BCSIA Discussion Paper 2000-29, ESDP Discussion Paper ESDP-2000-04, John F. Kennedy School of Government, Harvard University (October 2000). Estimates for the cost of food-borne illness vary considerably based on what criteria are used. See Jean C. Buzby, et al., "Bacterial Foodborne Disease: Medical Costs and Productivity Losses," *Agricultural Economics* 741(August 1996), www.ers.usda.gov/publications/Aer741/index.htm.

21. "Cesium," Summary Fact Sheets for Selected Environmental Contaminants to Support Health Risk Analyses, edited by John Peterson, et al. (Chicago: Argonne National Laboratory and US Department of Energy, Richland Operations Office, July 2002).

22. David G. Jarret, *Medical Management of Radiological Casualties* (Bethesda, MD: Armed Forces Radiological Research Institute, 1999), pp. 4–9; "Shielding Use and Analysis," Hanford ALARA Reference Center, pp. 1–4, www.hanford.gov/alara/PDF/analysis.pdf.

23. In one proposed scenario it was estimated that a device consisting of 100 kilograms of C-4, 50 grams of cesium-137, and 2 kilograms of plutonium detonated in a convention center in San Diego would kill 31 and possibly result in up to 1,969 additional fatalities and sicken 6,569. *NBC Scenarios: 2002-2010 Center for Counterproliferation and the Defense Threat Reduction Agency*, (Washington, DC: Center for Counterproliferation, April 2000), pp. 14, 19.

24. United Nations, Tenth Report of the Executive Chairman of the Special Commission established by the Secretary General pursuant to paragraph 9(b)(i) of Security Council Resolution 687 (1991), and paragraph 3 of resolution 699 (1991) on the Activities of the Special Commission, S/1995/1038 (17 December 1995), part VII.

25. Charles D. Ferguson, et al., "Commercial Radioactive Sources: Surveying the Security Risks," Monteray Institute of International Studies, Occasional Paper, 11 (January 2003), pp. 45, 64.

26. For example, one scenario of a radiological dispersal device attack on New York City suggests residents in a 1,000 square kilometer area could suffer death rates from cancer ranging from 1 in 10 within a kilometer of the attack, to a 1 in 100 risk for all those living in Manhattan, and a 1 in 10,000 for those living up to 15 kilometers downwind of the attack. See Testimony of Henry Kelly. These figures, however, are not for immediate casualties, but for long-term cancer risks. They do not include accounting for factors such as the protective effects of buildings, medical treatment, or cleanup. In addition, this analysis was based on radiation-exposure standards derived from Environmental Protection Agency and Nuclear Regulatory Commission guidelines and does not address the fact that these standards are somewhat controversial and may overstate long-term threats. The modeling used for this scenario draws on linear no-threshold theory (LNT). See Michael Levi and Henry Kelly, "Dirty Bombs Continued," *FAS Public Interest Report* 55 (May 2002), LNT holds that any amount of radiation dose, even those close to zero, is harmful. Therefore, low-dose exposure is assumed to have similar effects to high-dose exposure, but with lower incidence (i.e., less casualties per the number exposed). There is no scientific consensus over whether LNT is appropriate for accurately predicting casualties. For contrasting views on the debate see Myron Pollycove, "The Rise and Fall of the Linear No-Threshold (LNT) Theory of Radiation Carciogenesis," Presentation to the Institute of Physics (1997), cnts.wpi.edu/RSH/Docs/PollycovePhysics.html; Richard Wakeford, "Low Dose Irradiation—A Threshold Assumption Is Inappropriate," Paper presented to the Southport Conference, 1999, www.srp-uk.org/srpcdrom/p7-3.doc.

27. The Health Physics Society, "Radiation Risk in Perspective: Position Statement of the Health Physics Society," (March 2001), www.Hps.Org/Documents/Radiationrisk.pdf; National Radiological Protection Board, "Risk of Radiation-Induced Cancer at Low Doses and Low Dose Rates for Radiation Protection Purposes," Documents of the NRPB, 6/11 (1995), pp. 1–7; Animal Studies of Residual Hematopoietic and Immune System Injury from Low Dose/Low Dose Rate Radiation and Heavy Metals, *Armed Forces Radiobiology Research Institute Contract Report 98-3*, (1998), p. 1. See also *Medical Management of Radiological Casualties Handbook* (Military Medical Operations Office, Armed Forces Radiobiology Research Institute, December 1999), pp. 34–39; Health Risks Associated with Low Doses of Radiation, Electronic Power Research Institute, EPRI TR-104070 (Palo Alto, CA: Electronic Research Institute, 2002), passim.

28. Defense Threat Reduction Agency, et al., *Human Behavior and WMD Crisis: Risk Communication Workshop: Final Report* (March 2001), www.bt.usf.edu/Reports/AHA-report-hospital-mass-casualties-2000.PDF.

29. For details see *Cleanup of Large Areas Contaminated as a Result of a Nuclear Accident*, International Atomic Energy Agency, Technical Reports Series No. 300 (Vienna, International Atomic Energy Agency, 1996), passim; United States House of Representatives, Committee on Interior and Insular Affairs, Subcommittee on Oversight and Investigation, "Calculation of Reactor Accident Consequences (CRAC2) for U.S. Nuclear Power Plants (Health Effects and Costs) Conditional on AN SST1 Release" (November 1, 1982).

30. Project on Government Oversight, *Nuclear Power Plant Security: Voices from Inside the Fences* (Washington, DC: Project on Government Oversight, September 12, 2002); Douglas M. Chapin, et al., "Nuclear Power Plants and Their Fuel as Terrorist Targets," *Science* 297 (September 20, 2002): 1997–1999.

31. For, example, by one analysis, a 12.5-kiloton nuclear explosion in the port area of New York City would kill 52,000 people outright and another 10,000 from injuries. There could also be several hundred thousand cases of radiation sickness. See Ira Helfand, et al. "Nuclear Terrorism," *British Medical Journal* 324 (February 9, 2002): 356. For a discussion on the factors that affect the level of casualties and destruction in the wake of a nuclear detonation see Office of Technology Assessment, *The Effects of Nuclear War* (Washington, DC: Congress of the United States, May 1979), pp. 3–12.

32. Gururaj Mutalik, et al., *Crude Nuclear Weapons: Proliferation and the Terrorist Threat* (Cambridge, MA: International Physicians for the Prevention of Nuclear War, 1996), p. 10. A report in *USA Today* stated that U.S. scientists have secretly demonstrated in experiments that bombs could be built with low-enriched material, though it is unclear how practical such devices would be as weapons or whether the results of a detonation would approximate the explosive power of a nuclear weapon. Peter Eisler, "Fuel for Nuclear Weapons Is More Widely Available," *USA Today* (February 27, 2002): 1.

33. The most common and commercially viable methods for enriching uranium (i.e., separating out uranium 235 molecules from natural uranium) are gaseous diffusion (accounts for about 57 percent of world capacity) or centrifuge enrichment (about 30 percent of world capacity). Gaseous diffusion involves forcing uranium hexafluoride through a series of porous membranes, separating out the lighter uranium 235 molecules. The centrifuge process feeds uranium hexafluoride though a series of vacuum tubes and spins them to separate out the lighter molecules. These processes require special equipment such as special aluminum alloy, maraging steel, fiber composites, and equipment for the production of uranium hexafluoride. Plutonium production is carried out in two stages. First, uranium fuels are irradiated in a nuclear reactor, and then the plutonium is chemically separated from the uranium.

34. These estimates are made by the International Atomic Energy Agency. See *IAEA Safeguards Glossary*, 1987 Edition, IAEA Safeguards Information Series No. 1 (Vienna: International Atomic Energy Commission, 1987), pp. 23–24.

35. Thomas B. Cochran and Christopher B. Paine argue that current estimates are based on building a first-generation, low-technology bomb and that with more sophisticated designs far less amounts of bomb-making material might be required. They conclude 3 kilograms of highly enriched uranium or 1 kilogram of plutonium could be sufficient to achieve a yield in the kiloton range. Thomas B. Cochran and Christopher B. Paine, *The Amount of Plutonium and Highly-Enriched Uranium Needed for Pure Fission Nuclear Weapons* (Washington, DC: Natural Resources Defense Council, 1994), passim.

36. This estimate is based on the South African nuclear weapons program employing a gun-type weapon. The gun type is the simplest form of nuclear device. Critical mass is achieved by firing one slug of highly enriched uranium into another in the presence of a high neutron source such as tritium. Alternatively, 60 kilograms of plutonium would be needed for six implosion-type devices. The advantage of requiring less material is offset by the difficulties of building and testing an implosion device. It might well be possible for a program to cost less than the South African effort, which opted to "overdesign" its weapons rather than rely on actual nuclear testing to ensure predictable yields. Again, a program that was willing to accept compromises in the safety, shelf life, and accuracy of weapon systems might develop a capability for less money. For more details on the South African program see David Albright, "South Africa's Secret Nuclear Weapons Program, Institute for Science and International Security" (May 1994), passim, www.isis-online.org/publications/southafrica/ir0594.html; Thomas B. Cochran, "Highly Enriched Uranium Production for South African Nuclear Weapons," *Science & Global Security* 4 (1994): 161–176. Costs are converted to current dollars using a conversion factor of .362.

37. Rensselaer W. Lee, III, *Smuggling Armageddon: The Nuclear Black Market in the Former Soviet Union and Europe* (New York: St. Martin's Press, 1998), p. 43.

38. *Global Proliferation of Weapons of Mass Destruction: A Case Study on the Aum Shinriky*, Senate Government Affairs Permanent Subcommittee on Investigations (October 31, 1995) Staff Statement, Part VI: Overseas Operations.

39. Dan Stober, "No Experience Necessary," *Bulletin of the Atomic Scientists* 59/2 (March/April 2003): 56–63. For a summary of the project report see W. J. Frank, ed., *Summary Report of the Nth Country Experiment*, Lawrence Radiation Laboratory, UCRL 50249 (March 1967), www.gwu.edu/%7ensarchiv/nsa/NC/nuchis.html.

40. Douglas Frantz and Josh Meyer, "For Sale: Nuclear Expertise," *Los Angeles Times* (February 22, 2004), p. A1; and "The Nuclear Network: Khanfessions of a Proliferator," *Jane's Defence Weekly* (March 3, 2004), http://www.janes.com/security/international_security/news/jdw/jdw040226_1_n.shtml..

41. The capacity to circumvent the treaty was amply demonstrated by Iraq. After the Gulf War, it was discovered the country had violated its safeguard agreements. In response, the IAEA developed new safeguard techniques to detect undeclared nuclear activities, known as the Programme 93+2. This resulted in the Model Protocol that countries may add to their existing safeguard agreements with the agency. Even if these are adopted world-wide, however, loopholes will remain. John Simpson, "Redressing Deficiencies in the Nuclear Nonproliferation Treaty." In *Controlling Weapons of Mass Destruction: Findings from USIP-Sponsored Projects*, edited by Deepa M. Ollapally (Washington, DC: United States Institute of Peace, September 2001), pp. 10–14.

42. *Oklahoma City—Seven Years Later* (Oklahoma City, OK: Oklahoma City National Memorial Institute for the Prevention of Terrorism, 2002), p. i.

43. Antulio J. Echevarria, *The Army and Homeland Security: A Strategic Perspective* (Carlisle Barracks, PA: U.S. Army War College, Strategic Studies Institute, March 2001), p. 11.

44. Human Rights Watch, *A Global Overview of Explosive Submunitions* (May 2002), pp. 1, 6, 7, hrw.org/backgrounder/arms/submunitions.pdf. The Convention on Certain Conventional Weapons and its protocols direct limits on weapons that indiscriminate or cause unnecessary suffering or superfluous injury. The text and protocols can be found at www.un.org/millennium/law/xxvi-18-19.htm.

45. Wassenaar Arrangement, List of Dual-Use Goods, Technologies, & Munitions List, Munitions List, (July 5, 2002) p. 142, www.wassenaar.org/list/wa-list_01_3ml.pdf.

46. Deborah A. Kramer, "Explosives." In *Explosives-2001* (Reston, VA: U.S. Geological Survey, 2001), p. 25.1.

47. Dave Williams, "The Bombing of the World Trade Center in New York City," *International Criminal Police Review* (1998), www.interpol.int/Public/Publications/ICPR/ICPR469_3.asp.

10

THE DIGITAL BATTLEFIELD

Cyberterrorism and Cybersecurity

The whole system is going to crash—a digital Pearl Harbor of sorts.

Scott Berinato, CIO *Magazine*

CHAPTER OVERVIEW

Cyberterrorism is a poorly understood threat. This chapter describes forms of terrorist attack and discusses the potential effects of a terrorist cyberattack and means to protect against these dangers. It addresses protecting both the government and commercial sector against terrorist threats. In addition, this chapter highlights other ways that terrorists use the Internet and information technology to prepare for, support, and conduct attacks.

CHAPTER LEARNING OBJECTIVES

After reading this chapter, you should be able to

1. Describe the most likely sources of a digital attack.
2. Describe the ways that cyberattacks might be conducted.
3. List the principles and steps to preventing and preparing for a terrorist attack against information systems.
4. Identify the various ways that terrorists use information technology.

THE THREAT

Robert Hanssen was a model FBI agent. Hanssen was in charge of counterintelligence operations, finding out people who were spying on the United States. It was the most secret and sensitive work in the agency. Hanssen was considered an expert in the field. The only problem was that he was working for the other side. Arrested in February 2001, Hanssen had spied for the Soviet Union for well over a decade. As an authorized user of highly classified computer systems, Hanssen was able to employ various means for stealing sensitive data including encrypted floppy disks, removable storage devices, and a Palm handheld device.

While many fear terrorists may attempt a digital "Pearl Harbor" to cripple the Internet, the range of possible concerns is far broader. Cyberwarfare can take many forms. The Hanssen case is a reminder that the infinite benefits of digital technology bring infinite concerns as well.

Definition Digital attacks include a range of activities: stealing information and services, corrupting data, covertly monitoring or taking remote control of computers, and shutting down entire systems. Attacks may be against defined entities such as individual computers, or against the Internet itself, attempting to deny or degrade access to a large number of users.

INSIDER ATTACKS

Surveys continue to suggest that the highest percentage of illicit computer activity is from "insiders," in other words, actions by current or former employees, either malicious acts or crimes intended for personal profit.[1] The continued prevalence of internal threats is understandable. Employees have the greatest access to computers and business records and thus are often in a position for the unauthorized viewing, use, entry, or alteration of data to produce false transactions and tamper with information or sabotage systems. In some cases, these acts can be extreme. In one case, a law enforcement agent obtained information from the National Crime Information Center (NCIC) to track and down and murder his girlfriend.[2]

Insiders could also be instruments for conducting terrorist attacks, but coordinating a deliberate act of terrorism through an insider operative requires either recruiting or placing agents with the appropriate skills and knowledge in positions where they can gain access to the system to be struck. Such tactics are not inconceivable. In 1997, a disgruntled Coast Guard employee used her programming skills to crash the service's nationwide computer system.[3] A terrorist act might evolve in a similar way.

OUTSIDER ATTACKS

Although less in number, some security analysts consider the threat of outside attacks a potentially even more significant security risk. The overwhelming majority of these attacks occur through the Internet, which could originate from anywhere in the world and attack any system accessed through the World Wide Web.

Accurate, unclassified intelligence on the source of attacks and the capabilities of various states and transnational organizations is limited. Information on individual illicit activity against the commercial sector is more widely available. According to one study, attacks against commercial industries worldwide are undertaken mostly by individuals, with 70 percent of these intrusions originating from 10 countries.[4] The most frequent attacks are directed against high-tech companies, financial services, media/entertainment services, and power and energy companies.

Virtually any state or nonstate group can launch a digital attack. An offensive cyberweapon can be fashioned with a single, individual computer and a modem. Mastering the skills to plan and conduct a rudimentary digital strike is not difficult. There is a vast amount of material available in open-source literature that explains how to attack computer systems.[5] In fact, cybercrime, attacking computer systems for personal gain, is already a real and growing problem. Cost estimates of illicit computer activity vary considerably, but certainly the economic damage is in the range of billions of dollars a year.[6] Enemies can adopt many of the methods of cybercrime to digital attacks or employ cybercrimes to supplement other activities.

CYBERATTACKS

Cyberattacks consist of packets of information sent to specifically targeted computers or distributed randomly via the Internet. These inbound packets consist of external and internal components. The external component is routing information that gives the source and destination of the packet, much like an address on a letter. The internal component is the content of networked information, such as the body of an e-mail, computer programs, or graphic, audio, or video files. Some attacks rely on external components to create "packet flooding," sending so many packets that it exceeds the capacity of bandwidth, processing power, or storage capacity at a transit or end point in the system. Alternatively, the internal components of a packet might be instructions, which could perform various digital attacks like ordering a system to simply shut down.

Malicious Codes

Malicious codes can strike computers in a number of ways. Programs might include a "trap door" or "back door" instructions to allow an attacker to gain access to a computer whenever the intruder wishes. A malicious code could be a "Trojan horse" (a code hidden in a legitimate program that directs unauthorized functions), a virus (a self-replicating code that attacks single computers), a worm (which infects multiuser systems), or a logic bomb (a time-delayed virus that strikes some time after it enters a computer system). Packet instructions can also direct propagation, having an infected system replicate attack instructions and forward them to other systems. Some analysts forecast the development of intelligent superworms that prescreen systems to identify vulnerabilities and direct their agents to attack specific computers, control certain functions, and coordinate the activities of controlled computers across the Internet.[7] (See Figure 10.1.)

Purpose of Attacks

Digital attacks could be used for everything from disrupting communications to causing physical destruction. For example, an enemy might attempt to create a catastrophic failure in the Supervisory Control and Data Acquisition (SCADA) systems of the national energy network. Such systems monitor and control the flow of oil and gas through pipelines and the transfer of electricity across transmis-

F I G U R E   1 0 . 1

AN EXAMPLE OF A TYPICAL INFORMATION NETWORK.

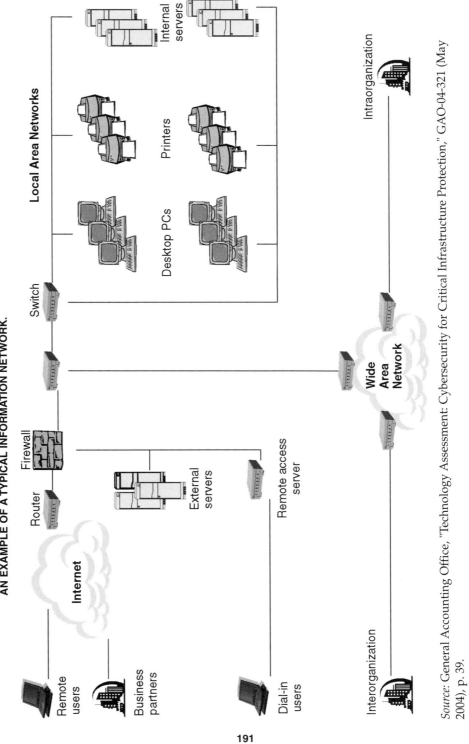

Source: General Accounting Office, "Technology Assessment: Cybersecurity for Critical Infrastructure Protection," GAO-04-321 (May 2004), p. 39.

sion lines. An attack might cause power outages, spark explosions, and unleash fuel spills.[8]

Potential Effects of Cyberattack

Even modest digital strikes can inflict costly damage. The I Love You virus, unleashed in May 2000 by a single hacker, infected over one million computers worldwide in less than five hours, eventually creating an estimated $10 billion in damages and lost productivity.[9] On the other hand, as with many other threats, scale matters. Enemies with advanced technical skills, robust intelligence systems, access to substantial computer and telecommunications assets, and ample funds will represent a significantly greater threat than individual hackers or terrorists using commonly available intrusion software. For example, an exercise sponsored by the U.S. Naval War College determined that a large-scale strike required an effort of about $200 million, access to a state intelligence network, and five years to plan.[10]

TERRORIST USE OF CYBERSPACE

The Internet is normally thought of as a target for terrorists, though it is used far more frequently as an instrument to support their activities. Today, all active terrorist groups have an established presence on the Internet using hundreds of Web sites. These sites are used to serve terrorists and their support groups, communicate with potential supporters, and influence the international press.[11]

One use of the Internet is to conduct psychological warfare, an attempt to spread rumors, disinformation, and threats that will undercut public confidence and morale. For example, since the September 11 attacks, al-Qaida has produced Web sites with frequent warnings of even larger impending attacks against the United States. The content of the sites are often reported by the Western media, which in turn generates concern over terrorist threats.

The Internet is also used by terrorists for publicity and propaganda purposes. Web sites are used to explain and justify activities. They can be used to recruit new members, solicit funds, or communicate information to the international media. The Basque separatist organization ETA, for example, maintains Web sites in several languages.

Terrorists also view the Internet as a vast library for obtaining and sharing information. The Internet has been used to gather intelligence from public sources on potential targets. Web sites are also used to share information from tutorials on how to spread computer viruses to how to manufacture bombs and poisons. Many terrorist Web sites post *The Terrorist's Handbook* and *The Anarchist Cookbook*, two well-known manuals that describe a variety of bombmaking techniques.

Finally, terrorists use the Internet to plan and coordinate operations. Chat rooms, e-mail, and information posted both overtly and covertly on Web sites are all employed to send and receive instructions. For example, federal officials found thousands of encrypted messages from the password-protected area of a Web site on the computer of Abu Zubaydah, the reported mastermind behind the September 11 attacks.

THE CURRENT STATE OF DEFENSES

Since a digital strike may cross several countries, Internet service providers, and telecommunications linkages, all subject to varying legal requirements, reporting standards, and capabilities to monitor Internet traffic, tracing the source of an attack may be problematic, if not impossible. There is no international regime or convention governing digital attacks equivalent to prohibitions against other means such as chemical or biological weapons. Further complicating the challenge of attributing digital attacks is a recent trend in illicit computer activity to initiate actions from multiple points through automated means, rather than individual manual entries. The automated, multiple-point attacks are more difficult to block, and the origins problematic to identify. Even if illicit intrusions are recognized, it may be hard to distinguish digital attacks from other activities such as recreational hacking or cybercrime.

Consequences of an Attack

While there are opportunities for dramatic incidents, computer attacks may have difficulty achieving desired objectives. As the pace of illicit computer activities has risen so have countermeasures designed to block them. Estimates of spending on security vary considerably, but it is clear that the commercial and government sectors are investing billions of dollars in Internet security software including firewalls, intrusion-detection and anti-worm/virus programs, digital certificates, and authentication and authorization programs, as well as billions more on disaster recovery initiatives designed to retrieve data or capabilities in the wake of a debilitating digital or physical attack. According to one recent study, spending could increase to $6.7 billion by 2004.[12]

Developing Countermeasures and Their Impact on Threats

Defeating systems that employ sophisticated encryption software can be especially time-consuming and expensive. The computing power available to the average individual at reasonable cost will no doubt grow in the near future. Price performance for computer power has been dropping by 20 to 30 percent a year, but this is an advantage available to both sides. Security standards are continually evolving to match emerging threats. The United States, for example, is moving toward an advanced encryption standard of 128-bit key size in order to outpace the ability of decryption programs to defeat security safeguards. Public key infrastructure (PKI), a system designed to ensure the capability to conduct secure transactions online, is also being implemented by both the government and commercial sectors.[13]

Indeed, attention to the challenges of protecting information infrastructure has grown steadily in recent years. In 1998, the Department of Defense conducted exercise Eligible Receiver, during which a team of 35 experts from the National Security Agency was given three months to plan and execute an attack on defense security systems using commonly available hardware and software. The team claimed if it had actually conducted the attack, it would have brought down the Department of Defense command and control systems, as well as major portions of the national electric power grid, and 911 systems. Some doubted these claims, and the Department of Defense did not provide public reports that could be used to verify them.[14] Yet, this exercise served as a clarion call for increased investments in information security technology. Y2K preparations further spurred new management initiatives.[15] Over the years, government, business, and voluntary international organizations have also become more adept at identifying computer attacks on the Internet and distributing warnings and countermeasures against future threats.[16]

**Government
Efforts**

The government, in particular, is making more deliberate efforts to counter intentional digital attacks than it was just a few years ago. Recently, for example, the National Institute of Standards and Technology issued a draft of the first comprehensive guidelines for federal agencies to evaluate and certify the safety of their computer systems against cyberattacks.[17]

Government efforts may be having some impact. One study finds that while the number of illegal intrusions continues to grow, the number of attacks on U.S government systems has declined since its peak in 2001. The study recorded 2,031 overt attacks on government systems in 2001 and projected 1,400 attacks would be made in 2002, perhaps suggesting that government systems are less seen as a source of "low-hanging fruit" for digital attacks.[18]

Government Vulnerabilities

For all this effort, there is still much vulnerability in public information systems. Even in the areas that are supposed to be protected there are a number of important concerns. The Department of Defense, for example, relies largely on commercial off-the-shelf systems (COTS) for most of its computer needs.[19] The department also depends on leased commercial telecommunications support. Thus, key elements of "secure" systems can be largely dependent on less secure public infrastructure, software, and equipment.

The operational practices of some government organizations are also a problem. Even self-assessments by the Department of Defense and other federal agencies acknowledge significant management issues and poor security practices.[20] The condition of state and local efforts is also an issue. Preparedness varies greatly from region to region. Many state and local law enforcement agencies lack the high-end computer forensics training and capabilities needed to deal with computer attacks or other forms of electronic crimes, though effective systems are widely available.[21]

Cyberspace Security Response

One of the first priorities of the federal government is the creation of a national cyberspace security response system. To oversee this effort the DHS created the National Cyber Security Division (NCSD) under its Information Analysis and Infrastructure Protection Directorate.

The NCSD was built upon capabilities transferred to the DHS from the former Critical Infrastructure Assurance Office, the National Infrastructure Protection Center, the Federal Computer Incident Response Center, and the National Communications System. The missions of the NCSD include conducting cyberspace analysis, issuing alerts and warnings, improving information sharing, responding to major incidents, and aiding in national-level recovery efforts. The NCSD also operates the department's Science and Technology Directorate to provide requirements for research and development efforts.

FROM THE SOURCE:

GUIDELINE FOR THE SECURITY OF INFORMATION SYSTEMS

In 1996, the Department of Commerce's National Institute of Standards developed a set of principles to guide information security programs.

Accountability. The responsibilities and accountabilities of owners, providers, and users of information should be explicit.

Awareness. Owners, providers, users, and other parties should readily be able, consistent with maintaining security, to gain appropriate knowledge and be informed about measures for the security of information systems.

Ethics. The information systems and the security of information should be provided and used in such a manner that the rights and legitimate interests of others are respected.

Multidisciplinary. Measures, practices, and procedures for the security of information systems should address all relevant considerations.

Proportionality. Security level, costs, measures, practices, and procedures should be appropriate and proportionate to the risks and vulnerabilities and the value and degree of reliance on the information system.

Integration. Measures, practices, and procedures should be coordinated and integrated with other security and business practices to create a coherent security system.

Timeliness. Public and private parties should act in a timely coordinated manner to prevent and respond to security breaches.

Reassessment. The security of information systems should be reassessed periodically.

Democracy. The security of information systems should be compatible with the legitimate use and flow of data and information in a democratic society.[22]

The public-private architecture that supports the national response system consists of several components. The US-CERT is a partnership between the DHS and the private sector. The US-CERT relies on collaborative partnerships with computer security incident response teams (CSIRTs). The CSIRTs are individual teams that work together voluntarily as a network to deal with computer security problems and their prevention. These security and computer responses have been established in government, commercial, and academic organizations. Each CSIRT has a constituency, a group of users or organizations that are served by the team; these may be members of a specific agency such as a company or university; a computer network; or representatives of certain operating systems. The functions, size, capabilities, and staff for these organizations can vary a great deal. CSIRTs are funded through a variety of means.

Information is also shared through the private sector with Information Sharing and Analysis Centers (ISACs). ISACs are industry groups formed to give companies that own and operate elements of national critical infrastructure a place to exchange information about security threats and vulnerabilities.

In addition to these organizations the NCSD coordinates with Internet service providers (ISPs), security product and service providers, and other organizations participating in cyberattack watch, warning, and response functions. The organizations include industry trade groups such as the Electronics Industry Association and private entities like Carnegie Mellon University's CERT Coordination Center.

TAKING THE OFFENSIVE—WHAT TO DO?

The nation's capacity to preempt, deter, and respond to cyberassaults is problematic. Countering digital threats with foreign policy, legal, and economic instruments is difficult because of the problems in attributing responsibility for attacks and the lack of international consensus and frameworks for dealing with cyber issues.[23] Many attacks are likely to take place through the illegal use of commercial systems. Enemy states might attempt to escape the prospect of large-scale digital warfare with the United States by conducting small, discrete strikes that place a premium on avoiding attribution of the attacker's identity. Nonstate groups (particularly if they can avoid attribution) may be undeterred by any threat posed by U.S. offensive capabilities. In fact, many governments, including that of the United States, have little control over the actions of individual groups of computer users. In December 1998, a group of anonymous hackers known only as the Legion of the Underground (LoU) declared war on Iraq and China for "human rights abuses," calling for an assault on all computer systems in the two countries. Many of the details of this incident are unconfirmed, but it appears the group declared its effort was inspired by hackers in China known as the Hong Kong Blondes, which as it later turned out may have never existed. After worldwide protests by other hacker groups, LoU withdrew its declaration. While it seems that no cyberattacks were ever actually conducted, the incident demonstrates the kind of convoluted and murky battles that may emerge on the Internet in the future.[24] Even if the United States identifies the country of origin for a major attack, it may be difficult to tell if the act is state-sponsored or a rogue individual act.

Not only may America not know who it is combating, it may be impossible to evaluate the real nature of current threats and what they portend for the future. There is, for example, little unclassified information on the nature of state threats. In addition, statistical information on illicit computer activity is extremely soft. Data on the commercial sector are obtained from surveys of corporations and security experts, often drawing sweeping results from the very few surveys returned and assuming corporate responses are completely honest and accurate in describing their own vulnerabilities. Statistics on the level of both government and commercial intrusions are also suspect. Most are based on estimates, since many systems cannot determine with any accuracy all illicit activity. Finally, the level of damage and disruption caused by worst-case digital attacks is unclear. There are no consistent criteria for accounting for lost productivity. In short, there is little useful historical data with which to evaluate threat trends and predict future requirements.[25]

1. Why is it difficult to go after those responsible for terrorist cyberthreats?
2. What can the United States do to proactively reduce terrorist cyberthreats?
3. Is this a problem the federal government should worry about? Who should be responsible?

PROTECTING YOUR BUSINESS

Private-sector institutions such as businesses, schools, hospitals, and nonprofit organizations of all sizes can and should take precautions against cyberattacks. According to one survey one out of every three businesses in the United States was affected by MyDoom, a computer virus spread through the Internet in January 2004 that exploited Microsoft software. Security experts generally agree on the basic principles of a sound information technology security program. In addition, best practices suggest commonsense measures that even small companies can take to protect themselves against digital attacks.

Principles of Cyberdefense

A key consideration in establishing cyberdefenses is that security solutions must be consistently applied across the organization. Gaps in security measures from either inadequate technologies or lax security practices will leave an entire information system vulnerable to intrusion.

The best way to validate and maintain security is by establishing a risk management program, a structured sequence of activities designed to produce a plan that makes sense for the organization based on its needs and the technology available. A risk management program would include implementing security awareness and training; establishing organization policies and regulations; instituting cooperative security management (cooperative arrangements with partners, Internet service providers, and contractors); implementing appropriate physical security measures (such as locks and guards); and adopting risk mitigation measures (such as insurance and contingency planning) to ensure the continuity of operations and disaster recovery. In addition to these key principles for establishing cybersecurity, The National Institute of Standards and Technology lists additional guidelines for securing information technology systems.[26]

Steps for Protecting against Cyberthreats

The Internet Security Alliance, a collaborative effort between the Electronics Industry Association and private entities like Carnegie Mellon University's CERT Coordination Center, recommends a series of steps for protecting small businesses. These steps represent an easy-to-follow plan with precautions that are achievable within the means available to small companies.[27]

Password Protection

Passwords are the basic form of computer security for preventing unauthorized access and exploitation of information systems. Without limiting access, information can be read, changed, or destroyed by anyone who gains entry to the network. Passwords need to be complicated so that they cannot be easily found out.

Businesses should establish an electronic environment that requires strong passwords by mandating their length, structure, complexity, and how frequently they should be changed. Employees need to be educated on password policies.

Software

Using software that protects against computer viruses is a relatively inexpensive means to protect against computer attacks. Antivirus software should be installed on every machine and updated weekly.

Security Practices

The most common methods for transmitting computer viruses are though e-mail attachments (such as word files, pictures, music, and spreadsheets) and through files downloaded from a Web site. Preventative steps can be taken to avoid introducing a malicious code into information systems. These include not using the "preview" function for e-mail contents, not opening attachments identified as malicious, and deleting suspect e-mails, such as chain e-mails, e-mails from unknown individuals, or those with suspicious subjects such as "OPEN THIS!"

Security Hardware

Firewalls are computer programs that act similarly to gate guards. They examine communications coming into an information system from the Internet or other external systems, as well as information being sent out. Without firewalls, hackers will likely be able to gain access to computer systems and determine what information is available as well as the network's vulnerabilities. Some technical assistance is usually required to install, establish, and maintain firewalls.

Remove Unused Software and User Accounts

Unused software and user accounts (such as the accounts of terminated employees) can be exploited by attackers as a means to gain entry into computer systems. As equipment is upgraded, old or deleted files, programs, and user account information may remain. A process should be established to remove or destroy data on all computer hard drives when the equipment is used for other purposes, discarded, donated, or sold.

Physical Security

Even with password protection, antiviral software, and firewalls, an attacker that gains physical access to a computer will likely be able to bypass security measures and exploit or sabotage an information system. Thus, companies need to provide physical security for electronic devices including desktop computers, laptops, handheld devices, and servers.

Back Up Important Information

Copying files, folders, and software onto some other media, such as a CD-ROM or Zip disk, will offer some protection against the loss or corruption of data from a cyberattack. Backup copies should be made on a routine schedule and stored in a secure, remote location.

Update Software

Software vendors routinely update their products to fix problems or improve their software. These efforts include applying software "patches" to upgrade security components within the software or remove vulnerabilities, such as code defects that can be exploited by malicious programs. It is important to know how vendors provide updates and establish procedures for ensuring they are applied.

Limit Access to Sensitive and Classified Data

Access to data stored in computer systems can be limited to specific users. Technical assistance may be required to establish authorized access controls. In addition, employees can be educated to not share inappropriately sensitive information (such as privacy data like social security numbers and financial records such as credit card numbers) in unsecured e-mails and databases.

PROSPECTS FOR THE FUTURE

Because of the rapid rate of computer technology development the future scope of the threat may be hard to quantify. To keep pace with new dangers, new defensive technologies will no doubt be needed. For example, more advanced systems could be required to meet the operational requirements of the law enforcement, military, and intelligence communities. These needs will include solutions for retrieving, storing, and analyzing very large media storage devices, tools to automate the collection of data files, and means for both circumventing and protecting encryption systems.[28]

CHAPTER SUMMARY

Cyberthreats are real. The potential for catastrophic attacks that might cause billions of dollars in damage and risk millions of lives is debatable. There is no question, however, that terrorists are already using the Internet and other information technologies to serve their purposes. While both the public and private sectors have undertaken initiatives to improve cybersecurity, much remains to be done. There are a number of commonsense steps that can be taken to improve cybersecurity.

CHAPTER QUIZ

1. What are the various ways that terrorists might use the Internet and other information technologies?
2. What is a cyberattack?
3. What is the most likely cyberthreat?
4. Why are cyberattacks difficult to defend against?
5. What is the best means to deal with cyberthreats?

NOTES

1. Robert Richardson, *CSI/FBI Computer Crime and Security Survey* (San Francisco: Computer Security Institute, 2003), p. 4.
2. Department of Defense, "The Insider Threat to U.S. Government Information Systems," NSTISSAM INFOSEC/1-99 (July 1999), p. 2, www.nstissc.gov/Assets/pdf/NSTISSAM_INFOSEC1-99.pdf.
3. Ibid., p. 3.
4. The countries are the United States (30 percent), South Korea (9 percent), and China (8 percent), with the remaining 47 percent coming from Germany, France, Canada, Taiwan, Italy, Great Britain, and Japan. See Riptech, *Internet Security Threat Report* (January 2002), pp. 15, 21, www.riptech.com.

5. For example, a posting on the public Web site BugTraq detailed computer code that could be embedded in a Web site capable of reformatting a visitor's hard drive and deleting files. See Michelle Delio, "How Much Hack Info Is Enough?" *Wired News* (November 19, 2002), www.wired.com/news/infostructure/0,1377,56463,00.html.

6. One estimate, for example, concluded that the damage caused by electronic viruses in the first half of 1999 was over $7 billion. Statement of Michael A. Vatis before the Subcommittee on Technology and Terrorism, Senate Judiciary Committee (October 6, 1999), www.fib.gov/congress/congress99/nipc10-6.htm. See also Richard Power, "Estimating the Cost of Cyber Crime," Paper presented to the Conference on International Cooperation to Combat Cybercrime and Terrorism, Stanford University, Stanford, CA (December 6–7, 1999), www.oas.org/juridico/english/Power.Conf.PPT.FINAL.PPT. The British firm Mig2 collects information from a variety of open sources and measures the economic value of attacks worldwide. According to its analysis worldwide economic damage from digital attacks for 2002 is estimated at $36 to $44 billion. Mig2, "Hacker Attacks on Government Systems Declining Year-on-Year" (November 13, 2002), www.mi2g.com.

7. Brandon Wiley, "Curious Yellow: The First Coordinated Worm-Design," blanu.net/curious_yellow.html.

8. For an assessment of this threat see Alexander E. Farrell, et al., "Bolstering the Security of the Electrical Power System," *Issues in Science and Technology*, 3 (Spring 2002): 53.

9. This estimate was made by Computer Economics, an independent research firm, www.computereconomics.com/index.cfm.

10. The exercise found the financial sector the most vulnerable to attack. Even this attack, the exercise concluded, would fail to achieve a digital "Pearl Harbor." French Caldwell, et al., "Digital 'Pearl Harbor' Wargame Explores Cyberterrorism," Gartner, E-17-6580 (August 7, 2002), passim.

11. Gabriel Weimann, "WWW.Terror.Net: How Terrorism Uses the Internet," United States Institute of Peace, Special Report Number 116 (March 2004), www.usip.org/pubs/special-reports/sr116.pdf.

12. Lori Enos, "Report: Security Software Sales to Surge," *E-Commerce Times* (October 4, 2000), www.ecommercetimes.com/perl/story/4460.html. The report was prepared by Gartner Group Division Dataquest.

13. PKI uses a public key cryptographic system where two mathematically related keys are used. One key is used to encipher or decipher the information, and the other key is used to perform the reverse operation. One of the keys must be kept secret and is known as the private key, while the other key may be distributed to anyone and is called the public key. Within a PKI, a data structure called a certificate is used to bind a specific identity to a specific public key. For more information see William T. Polk and Nelson E. Hastings, "Bridge Certification Authorities: Connecting B2B Public Key Infrastructures," Paper for the National Institute of Standards and Technology, p. 2, csrc.nist.gov/pki/documents/B2B-article.pdf.

14. DoD News Briefing with Kenneth H. Bacon (April 16, 1998), www.defenselink.mil/news/Apr1998/t04161998_t0416asd.html.

15. David Mussington, *Concepts for Enhancing Critical Infrastructure Protection: Relating Y2K to CIP Research and Development* (Santa Monica, CA: Rand 2002), pp. 11–18. The use of two digits to represent a four-digit year, and the inherent fault of "00" being interpreted as 1900 instead of 2000, was a standard computer programming practice. The Y2K effort involved ensuring systems were capable of correctly processing the year 2000 date or were replaced before errors caused widespread problems. See *The Journey to Y2K: Final Report of the President's Council on Year 2000 Conversion* (March 29, 2000), www.y2k.gov/docs/LASTREP3.htmnp.

16. These centers are referred to as Computer Emergency Response Teams (CERT). One of the most well known is at Carnegie Mellon University, www.cert.org. Another well-established CERT is at the Department of Defense, www.cert.mil.

17. Ron Ross and Marianne Swanson, *Guidelines for the Security Certification and Accreditation of Federal Information Systems* (Initial Public Draft), NIST Special Publication 800-37 (Gaithersburg, VA: National Institute of Standards and Technology, October 2002), p. viii. The most significant shortfall of the NIST guidelines is that they are not compulsory though the department has the authority under the Computer Security Act of 1987 to impose mandatory standards.

18. Mi2g, "Hacker Attacks." Some, however, question whether the study, which relies solely on open-source reporting by U.S. federal agencies, accurately captures the full scope of illegal intrusions. Attacks may go undiscovered or be unreported for security or legal reasons. Mark Shachtman, "Study Makes Less of Hack Threat," *Wired News* (November 14, 2002), www.wired.com/news/politics/0,128383,00.html.

19. For example, a recent survey by the MITRE corporation suggests the Defense Department draws heavily on computer applications that employ open-source software, where any user has access to the source code of a program. The use of commercial open-source software could allow for the exposure of system vulnerabilities or the introduction of malicious codes into computer applications. MITRE, *Use of Free and Open-Source Software* (Washington, DC: Defense Systems Information Agency, November 6, 2002).

20. Office of Management and Budget, *FY 2001 Report to Congress on Federal Government Information Security Reform,* www.ncs.gov/nstac/ConvergenceReport-Final.htm. This finding was confirmed by U.S. General Accounting Office, *Computer Security: Progress Made, but Critical Federal Operations and Assets Remain at Risk,* GAO-03-303T (November 19, 2002), p. 2.

21. Hollis Stambaugh, et al., *Electronic Crime Needs Assessment for State and Local Law Enforcement,* National Institute of Justice Research Report (March 2001), p. xi. Among the systems capable of recovering data from hard drives and programs, even after the data are deleted, is the widely used Forensic Recovery of Evidence Device. See www.digitalintel.com/fred.htm.

22. Marianne Swanson and Barbara Guttman, *Generally Accepted Principles and Practices for Securing Information Technology Systems,* U.S. Department of Commerce, National Institute of Standards and Technology (September 1996), p .4.

23. For an introduction to transnational prohibitions to cyberthreats see Richard W. Aldrich, *Cyberterrorism and Computer Crimes: Issues Surrounding the Establishment of an International Regime* (U.S. Air Force Academy, CO: Institute for National Strategic Studies, April 2000); Abraham D. Sofaer, "Toward an International Convention on Cybercrime," *The Transnational Dimension of Cybercrime and Terrorism,* edited by Abraham D. Sofaer and Seymour E. Goodman (Stanford, CA: Hoover Institute Press, 2001), pp. 221–248. Both conclude concurrent prohibition and enforcement regimes are inadequate, though improving measures will be difficult. Added restrictions face a host of legal, diplomatic, and economic issues and enforcement would be problematic.

24. Neil Taylor, "The Hacker Hoax," *IT Daily* (August 18, 1999), www.computeruser.com/newstoday/99/08/18/news3.html.

25. George Smith, "How Vulnerable Is Our Interlinked Infrastructure?" *Issues in Science and Technology* (Fall 1998): 1–10.

26. Swanson and Guttman, *Principles and Practices for Securing Information Technology Systems.*

27. "Common Sense Guide to Cyber Security for Small Businesses," (Washington, DC: Internet Security Alliance, March 2004).

28. *Law Enforcement Tools and Technologies for Investigating Cyber Attacks,* (Hanover, NH: Institute for Security Technology Studies, June 2002), pp. 3–5.

HOMELAND SECURITY

Organization, Strategies, Programs, and Principles

11

HOMELAND SECURITY ROLES, RESPONSIBILITIES, AND JURISDICTIONS

Federal, State, and Local Government Responsibilities

Americans should find comfort in knowing that millions of their fellow citizens are working every day to ensure our security at every level— federal, state, county, municipal. These are dedicated professionals who are good at what they do.

Governor Tom Ridge at his swearing-in ceremony as Director, Office of Homeland Security, October 8, 2001

CHAPTER OVERVIEW

The national homeland security framework established in the wake of the September 11 attacks is still a work in progress. This chapter outlines the progress and the current organizations, programs, and principles governing domestic security activities in the United States after three years of concerted effort. Included here is a review of the concepts driving national initiatives, a summary of the roles and responsibilities assigned to various federal agencies, and a discussion of the role of state and local governments. This is a foundational chapter for the remaining topics discussed in Part 3. It lays the groundwork for the discussions about the government, the private sector, volunteer efforts, and personnel protection that are covered in the remaining chapters of the text.

CHAPTER LEARNING OBJECTIVES

After reading this chapter, you should be able to

1. Define homeland security and the overarching principles guiding domestic security activities.
2. Describe how the president oversees and influences homeland security.
3. Describe the organization and mission of the Department of Homeland Security.
4. Understand the roles of the Department of Defense and the Congress.
5. Describe the relationship between the federal, state, and local governments.

THE NEW NORMALCY

On a crisp October morning less than a month after the 9/11 tragedies, President Bush signed an order establishing the Office of Homeland Security and introduced its director, Tom Ridge. The office was established to provide initial coordination of federal efforts for improving homeland security. Ridge would bear much of the responsibility for the effort. Twice elected governor of Pennsylvania, he quickly became immersed in the most significant reorganization of the federal government since the restructuring of the Pentagon in 1947. Within two years Ridge became the secretary of a new Department of Homeland Security. The creation of the department and other federal initiatives has significantly reshaped how the United States provides for domestic security.

THE NATIONAL CONCEPT OF PROTECTING THE HOMELAND

The term *national security* denotes the full scope of activities involved in protecting the country's domestic and foreign interests. National security activities range from fighting wars and conducting counter-terrorism operations overseas to securing U.S. borders and fighting terrorism within the United States.

Protecting the homeland (U.S. states and territories) is a matter for two components of national security—*homeland defense* and *homeland security*. Homeland defense is the traditional responsibility of protecting U.S. territory from armed invasion and external acts of aggression.[1] For example, a ballistic missile fired by North Korea at the United States would clearly be an act of war and a threat to the nation. Defending against this danger would be a homeland defense mission, as would certain activities such as combat air patrols flown by the military over U.S. metropolitan areas.

Homeland security is the second subset of national security primarily concerned with protecting U.S. territory. It is defined by the *National Strategy for Homeland Security* as "a concerted national effort to prevent terrorist attacks *within* the United States, reduce America's vulnerability to terrorism, and minimize the damage and recover from attacks that do occur."[2] In short, homeland security is focused on terrorism in the United States. These terrorist acts could include kidnappings; bombings; shootings; attacks involving chemical, biological, radiological, or nuclear weapons; cyberattacks; or other forms of malicious violence, whether perpetrated by U.S. citizens or foreigners.

The definition of homeland security does not include countering terrorist attacks against U.S. interests overseas, such as attacks on U.S. military bases or embassies. Similarly, counterterrorism operations abroad, whether they are military, intelligence, or diplomatic measures are generally not considered part of homeland security, though they may contribute to providing information or support for homeland security activities. Alternatively, there are some overseas activities, such as certain law enforcement activities, visa issuance, and transportation security, that are considered extensions of domestic homeland security programs.

ORGANIZING FOR DOMESTIC SECURITY

The structure of American governance plays a significant role in determining the manner in which the United States addresses the homeland defense and security missions. Under the U.S. federalist system, power is shared between federal and state governments. The division of responsibilities is largely defined by the U.S. Constitution. In turn, these divisions prescribe duties for protecting the homeland. The federal government, for example, is charged by the Constitution with "providing for the common defense." Thus, homeland defense is principally a federal mission and the responsibility of the Department of Defense and the armed forces of the United States. In contrast, the Tenth Amendment to the Constitution reserves to the states and the people all power not specifically delegated to the federal government. As a result, responsibilities for homeland security, which include a broad range of activities undertaken by federal and state governments, local municipalities, the private sector (such as businesses and nongovernmental organizations), and individual citizens, are far more diverse.

FEDERAL

The federal government is comprised of the executive branch, the Congress, and the judiciary. The executive branch fulfills its homeland security responsibilities by executing and enforcing federal laws, such as the Homeland Security Act of 2002. Congress's role in homeland security includes not only its legislative powers, but its oversight responsibilities for the activities of the executive branch. The judiciary also has a key role in protecting the homeland. It has responsibility for interpreting the laws of the United States and how they are applied by federal, state, and local governments.

The Executive Office of the President

The president's two principal instruments for directing the policies governing the protection of the homeland are the National Security Council and the Homeland Security Council.

The National Security Council

The National Security Council (NSC) was established by the National Security Act of 1947.[3] Its mission is to develop national security strategy and policy. The membership of the NCS includes the president, vice president, the secretary of state, the secretary of the treasury, the secretary of defense, and the assistant to the president for national security affairs. The chairman of the joint chiefs of staff is the statutory military advisor to the council, and the director of central intelligence is the intelligence advisor. The heads of other executive departments and agencies and other senior U.S. officials may also be invited to attend as needed.

Strategy and policy are largely formulated by the president's national security advisor and NSC staff that vet and coordinate recommendations with the secretaries and staffs of the departments. The formal procedures governing the policy-making process are dictated by presidential decision directives. These procedures are generally consistent from one administration to the next. While the NSC sets overall policies, operations and activities to implement these policies are undertaken by the various departments and other agencies. Coordination between the NSC staff and the departments is made through committees consisting of members of the departments. Depending on the significance of the issue and the seniority of the staff required to effect coordination, matters are referred to the Principals Committee, the Deputies Committee, or policy coordinating committees.

The NSC's activities cover the full scope of national security matters, although its deliberations primarily focus on issues of foreign affairs. The council directly manages policies and strategies related to counterterrorism operations overseas, and it is the final arbitrator on issues related to homeland defense. This was in fact the case after the September 11 attacks when the NSC directed policies regarding the employment of combat air patrols over metropolitan areas.

The Homeland Security Council

Policies and strategies related to homeland security on the other hand are a matter for the Homeland Security Council (HSC). Initially established by executive order by President Bush, the HSC was later formally established by the Homeland Security Act of 2002. The statutory members of the HSC are the president, the vice president, the secretary of homeland security, the attorney general, and the secretary of defense. Other members attend as directed by the president. Policy coordination is done through a series of committees much as in the NSC. For example, the assistant secretary of homeland defense is the department's representative to the HSC staff and normally represents the Department of Defense at HSC principals and deputies committee meetings and provides representatives to interagency policy coordination committee meetings.

Like the NSC, the HSC has a senior advisor and a council staff, albeit on a much smaller scale. Initially, the HSC staff was divided into 11 policy coordinating committees. The number of divisions in the policy staff was later reduced to six, roughly mirroring the structure of the critical mission areas of homeland security and the organization of the Department of Homeland Security. The major divisions of the staff are domestic counterterrorism, border and transportation security, critical infrastructure, emergency response and recovery, and bioterrorism preparedness.

Like the NSC, the HSC is also responsible for developing national strategies and policies. However, while the HSC structurally functions in a manner similar to the NSC, in practice the focus of the two staffs is quite different. Many of the federal government's national security practices and policies are well developed, honed over nearly a half century of addressing foreign policy issues during the Cold War. Therefore, the NSC focuses more on developing policies than evaluating how they are executed by the departments. In contrast, many homeland security programs are still being formulated. Therefore, rather than just vetting and coordinating policies and strategy, the HSC often becomes involved in creating and developing new initiatives. Thus, its role tends to be more operational than the NSC. For example, the council staff took a lead role in developing Project BioShield, a multiyear research program to develop medical responses to bioterrorist threats. In addition, unlike the NSC, the HSC engages in extensive coordination with state and local governments and the private sector since they also play a significant role in homeland security.

The president can issue directives developed by the HSC. These are called homeland security presidential directives (HSPD). The HSPDs serve to direct federal agencies to undertake policies and programs that support homeland security.

Common HSC/NSC Responsibilities

While the two councils deal with different issues, in some cases their concerns and responsibilities overlap. Both, for example, may be engaged in issues with regard to foreign policy toward Canada and

Mexico. As a result, there is often coordination between the two staffs. The Homeland Security Act also authorizes the president to conduct joint meetings of the two councils. Eventually, as the processes and procedures for homeland security become well established, it may be possible to combine the two councils into a single staff whose tasks mirror the more traditional functions of the NSC. In the near term, however, the NSC and HSC will likely remain separate, with their staffs operating under different statutory authorities.

Office of Management and Budget

Another organization within the Executive Office of the President that plays a significant role in homeland security and homeland defense is the Office of Management and Budget (OMB). Neither the NSC nor the HSC have budgetary oversight concerning the programs and activities under their purview. The OMB reviews the budget submissions of the departments for compliance with administration policies and directives. As a result, while the HSC is responsible for providing strategic direction to the Department of Homeland Security and other federal agencies with respect to the challenges of domestic security, it is the task of OMB to ensure that the appropriate level of resources is requested in the president's annual budget request to Congress to perform the tasks called for by administration policies and strategy.

FROM THE SOURCE:

THE HOMELAND SECURITY COUNCIL

Excerpt from Executive Order Establishing the Office of Homeland Security and the Homeland Security Council, October 8, 2001

Sec. 5. Establishment of Homeland Security Council

a) I hereby establish a Homeland Security Council (the "Council"), which shall be responsible for advising and assisting the President with respect to all aspects of homeland security. The Council shall serve as the mech-

---

anism for ensuring coordination of homeland security-related activities of executive departments and agencies and effective development and implementation of homeland security policies.

(b) The Council shall have as its members the President, the Vice President, the Secretary of the Treasury, the Secretary of Defense, the Attorney General, the Secretary of Health and Human Services, the Secretary of Transportation, the Director of the Federal Emergency Management Agency, the Director of the Federal Bureau of Investigation, the Director of Central Intelligence, the Assistant to the President for Homeland Security, and such other officers of the executive branch as the President may from time to time designate. The Chief of Staff, the Chief of Staff to the Vice President, the Assistant to the President for National Security Affairs, the Counsel to the President, and the Director of the Office of Management and Budget also are invited to attend any Council meeting. The Secretary of State, the Secretary of Agriculture, the Secretary of the Interior, the Secretary of Energy, the Secretary of Labor, the Secretary of Commerce, the Secretary of Veterans Affairs, the Administrator of the Environmental Protection Agency, the Assistant to the President for Economic Policy, and the Assistant to the President for Domestic Policy shall be invited to attend meetings pertaining to their responsibilities. The heads of other executive departments and agencies and other senior officials shall be invited to attend Council meetings when appropriate.

(c) The Council shall meet at the President's direction. When the President is absent from a meeting of the Council, at the President's direction the Vice President may preside. The Assistant to the President for Homeland Security shall be responsible, at the

President's direction, for determining the agenda, ensuring that necessary papers are prepared, and recording Council actions and Presidential decisions.

Subsequently, the Homeland Security Act of 2002 established a National Homeland Security Council by law. The statutory members are the president, vice-president, secretary of homeland security, secretary of defense, the attorney general, and others as designated by the President.

The Department of Homeland Security

A common misconception held by many Americans is that the Department of Homeland Security (DHS) is responsible for all homeland security activities. This is far from accurate. Even at the federal level virtually every federal agency has some responsibilities. In addition, the DHS has many non–homeland security responsibilities from collecting tariffs and duties to providing immigration services and protecting U.S. fisheries. In fact, more than one-third of the department's budget is for its service missions and regulatory functions. The DHS, however, does have the lion's share of federal responsibilities for protecting the homeland, accounting for over 60 percent of the annual federal spending on domestic security.

The department has four major directorates: Border and Transportation Security; Emergency Preparedness and Response; Science and Technology; and Information Analysis and Infrastructure Protection.

Border and Transportation Security

The Border and Transportation Security (BTS) Directorate is responsible for maintaining the security of the nation's borders and transportation systems. Its principal homeland security mission is to prevent the entry of terrorists or terrorist assets (such as smuggled weapons or illicit financial instruments) while ensuring the efficient flow of lawful traffic and commerce. Within the directorate, the Transportation Security Administration (TSA) has statutory responsibility for security of airports and commercial aviation and the authority to establish regulatory security requirements on other modes of public transportation. Other homeland security activities are conducted by the Bureau of Customs and Border Protection (CBP), which oversees security at U.S. land borders and ports of entry, and the Bureau of Immigration and Customs Enforcement (ICE), which provides interior immigration and customs law enforcement.

In addition to its other responsibilities, the BTS is responsible for providing oversight of the visa issuance and monitoring process. All foreign visitors, with the exception of citizens participating in the Visa Waiver Program, must obtain a visa before entering the United States. The Homeland Security Act of 2002 assigned the DHS responsibility for establishing visa policies, setting training requirements, and effecting coordination for the implementation of security measures.[4]

Emergency Preparedness and Response

The Emergency Preparedness and Response (EPR) Directorate oversees federal preparedness, response, and mitigation efforts for both natural and technological disasters, including terrorist acts. The EPR is responsible for coordinating the National Response Plan (NRP). The NRP is in reality a family of plans that direct how the federal government will respond to all kinds of disasters. The EPR would also coordinate all federal support to state and local governments in the event federal resources are required. The directorate also focuses on risk mitigation in advance of emergencies by promoting the concept of disaster-resistant communities, including providing federal support for local governments that promote structures and communities that reduce the chances of being hit by disasters. It coordinates with private industry, the insurance sector, mortgage lenders, the real estate industry, homebuilding associations, citizens, and others to create model communities in high-risk areas.

The principal component of the ERP is the Federal Emergency Management Agency (FEMA). FEMA's authorities are derived from the Robert T. Stafford Disaster Relief and Assistance Act of 1984, which authorizes the president to supplement the resources of overwhelmed states and localities. The president can declare a major disaster upon the request of the governor of the affected state.[5]

Science and Technology

The Science and Technology (S&T) Directorate is the primary research and development arm of the Department of Homeland Security. It conducts research on homeland security technologies both for the department and to support the technology needs of state and local governments. The vast majority of research performed by the directorate is "extramural," performed under contract by existing academic and commercial research facilities. For example, in 2004 the directorate let a contract to establish a Homeland Security Research Institute. The S&T Directorate is authorized by Congress to maintain the institute for three years as a federally funded research development center.

Most of the S&T Directorate's research is managed by the Homeland Security Advanced Research Projects Agency (HSARPA). Another common misperception is that HSARPA, like the Department of Defense's Defense Advanced Research Projects Agency (DARPA) engages in high-risk ventures that might produce extraordinary benefits, much like the research that resulted in the creation of the Internet. The HSARPA's research agenda is quite different. The primary focus is on near-term capabilities, off-the-shelf technologies that can be ready for use in six months to two years. A large part of the research program involves "systems engineering," ensuring that technologies are adopted to meet the specific needs of the intended users.

Information Analysis and Infrastructure Protection

The Information Analysis and Infrastructure Protection (IAIP) Directorate provides the DHS with the capability to assess a broad range of intelligence information concerning threats to the homeland and to issue timely warnings. The IAIP has three primary components: the Office of Information Analysis (IA), the Office of Infrastructure Protection (IP), and the Homeland Security Operations Center (HSOC). This directorate is not an intelligence collecting activity. IAIP does not have field agents, satellites, or other intelligence collection assets. Rather, IAIP analyzes information collected by other agencies to develop sector-specific warnings for various components of the department, the private sector, or state and local municipalities. Conducting this analysis and disseminating appropriate warnings are tasks primarily performed by the directorate's IA and IP offices.

The HSOC monitors conditions throughout the United States and administers and makes recommendations on establishing alert levels for the Homeland Security Advisory System (HSAS), an important component of the intelligence and early warning mission area. The HSAS employs a series of color codes to designate various levels of national preparedness in anticipation of a terrorist attack. Associated with each threat condition are a range of suggested protective measures (such as implementing various contingency plans), with federal, state, and local agencies responsible for developing and implementing their own specific response activities.[6]

ISSUES:

WARNING THE NATION

Homeland Security Presidential Directive 3 (HSPD-3), published in March 2002, established the color-coded Homeland Security Advisory System. Since its inception, the system has been controversial. Local and state governments have complained about the cost of implementing additional security and that alerts are insufficiently specific. The citizenry is equally perplexed. On the other hand, the system has provided clearer guidance for organizing federal activities.

Excerpt from the Homeland Security Presidential Directive 3 (HSPD-3)

Guidance for Federal Departments and Agencies

The following Threat Conditions each represent an increasing risk of terrorist attacks. Beneath each Threat Condition are some suggested Protective Measures, recognizing that the heads of Federal departments and agencies are responsible for developing and implementing appropriate agency-specific Protective Measures:

Low Condition (Green). This condition is declared when there is a low risk of terrorist attacks. Federal departments and agencies should consider the following general measures in addition to the agency-specific Protective Measures they develop and implement:

Refining and exercising as appropriate preplanned Protective Measures;

Ensuring personnel receive proper training on the Homeland Security Advisory System and specific preplanned department or agency Protective Measures; and

Institutionalizing a process to assure that all facilities and regulated sectors are regularly assessed for vulnerabilities to terrorist attacks, and all reasonable measures are taken to mitigate these vulnerabilities.

Guarded Condition (Blue). This condition is declared when there is a general risk of terrorist attacks. In addition to the Protective Measures taken in the previous Threat Condition, Federal departments and agencies should consider the following general measures in addition to the agency-specific Protective Measures that they will develop and implement:

Checking communications with designated emergency response or command locations;

Reviewing and updating emergency response procedures; and

Providing the public with any information that would strengthen its ability to act appropriately.

Elevated Condition (Yellow). An Elevated Condition is declared when there is a significant risk of terrorist attacks. In addition to the Protective Measures taken in the previous Threat Conditions, Federal departments and agencies should consider the following general measures in addition to the Protective Measures that they will develop and implement:

Increasing surveillance of critical locations;

Coordinating emergency plans as appropriate with nearby jurisdictions;

Assessing whether the precise characteristics of the threat require the further refinement of preplanned Protective Measures; and

Implementing, as appropriate, contingency and emergency response plans.

High Condition (Orange). A High Condition is declared when there is a high risk of terrorist attacks. In addition to the Protective Measures taken in the previous Threat Conditions, Federal departments and agencies should consider the following general measures in addition to the agency-specific Protective Measures that they will develop and implement:

Coordinating necessary security efforts with Federal, State, and local law enforcement agencies or any National Guard or other appropriate armed forces organizations;

Taking additional precautions at public events and possibly considering alternative venues or even cancellation;

Preparing to execute contingency procedures, such as moving to an alternate site or dispersing their workforce; and

Restricting threatened facility access to essential personnel only.

Severe Condition (Red). A Severe Condition reflects a severe risk of terrorist attacks. Under most circumstances, the Protective Measures for a Severe Condition are not intended to be sustained for substantial periods of time. In addition to the Protective Measures in the previous Threat Conditions, Federal departments and agencies also should consider the following general measures in addition to the agency-specific Protective Measures that they will develop and implement:

Increasing or redirecting personnel to address critical emergency needs;

> Assigning emergency response personnel and pre-positioning and mobilizing specially trained teams or resources;
>
> Monitoring, redirecting, or constraining transportation systems; and
>
> Closing public and government facilities.
>
> 1. Should the United States have a national alert system? Why? What are the likely benefits and limitations of having a national alert system?
>
> 2. How do you think the HSAS could be improved?
>
> 3. Who should pay for increased security as a result of changing alert levels? Why?

In addition, to its monitoring activities, the HSOC also serves as a national emergency operations center for coordinating the federal response to homeland security emergencies. The HSOC also maintains the Homeland Security Information Network (HSIN). The HSIN will provide a collaborative tool for sharing information with states, territories, and major urban areas through the Joint Regional Information Exchange System (JRIES). Initially, the system will be limited to sensitive, but unclassified, information, but in the future it is intended to carry secret information to the state level. Finally, IAIP has responsibility for coordination of planning and provision of National Security and Emergency Preparedness (NS/EP) communications for the federal government.

Coast Guard and Secret Service

In addition to the department's major directorates, the U.S. Coast Guard and Secret Service are independent agencies within the DHS that have significant homeland security responsibility. The Coast Guard serves as the lead national agency for maritime security. Homeland security roles include protecting the flow of commerce and the marine transportation system from terrorism; maintaining maritime border security against illicit drugs, illegal aliens, firearms, and weapons of mass destruction; preventing and responding to hazardous material spills; and coordinating efforts and intelligence with federal, state, and local agencies. Many of its homeland security duties are conducted in conjunction with its other missions. For example, by law the Coast Guard provides captains of the port (COTP) who have responsibility for enforcing regulations for the protection and security of vessels, harbors, and waterfront facilities; anchorages; bridges; safety and security zones; and ports and waterways under their jurisdiction. As part of their responsibilities they review and approve the port security plans and chair local port security committees.

The Coast Guard enjoys a unique legal status that makes the service an effective homeland security instrument. The Coast Guard is considered one of the uniformed military services and routinely works with the other armed forces, though it is not part of the Department of Defense and not subject to the limitations of Posse Comitatus. The Coast Guard also has status as a law enforcement, intelligence, and regulatory agency. The service, for example, has the authority to inspect shipping containers for safety and hazardous materials, authorities that it can use to ensure that containerized shipping is not used as a terrorist weapon.

The Secret Service provides protection to the president and other senior personnel in the U.S government. In addition, the Secret Service is responsible for coordinating security for specially designated national security events such as the Super Bowl and presidential nominating conventions. Finally, from the time when the Secret Service served as part of the U.S. Treasury Department, the Secret Service retains responsibilities for investigating certain financial crimes.

In addition to the major organizations within the department, several offices within the secretariat of the DHS have significant responsibilities. The Office of State and Local Government Coordination and Preparedness is responsible for coordinating DHS activities with state and local governments, managing homeland security grants, and coordinating a range of education and training activities. Other offices of note include the department's Office of International Affairs, which assists in coordinating activities and programs with foreign countries, and the Office of the Chief Information Officer, which is responsible for developing and integrating the department's many information technology programs.

The Intelligence Community

Intelligence support for all matters of national security, including homeland security and homeland defense, is provided by the U.S. Intelligence Community. The Central Intelligence Agency (CIA) and 14 other agencies, including the DHS and the Coast Guard, comprise the national Intelligence Community.[7] Before the passage of the Intelligence Reform and Terrorism Prevention Act of 2004, the director of Central Intelligence (DCI), who also served as the director of the CIA, was responsible by law for coordinating the activities of the community including establishing priorities for intelligence collection and to some degree analysis of critical issues. In practice, the DCI had little authority over members of the community, particularly the substantial intelligence resources in the Department of Defense. The DCI, for example, did not have oversight of the budgets of intelligence agencies outside the CIA. Much of the coordination was performed through interagency activities such as the DCI Nonproliferation Center and the National Intelligence Council.[8] The Intelligence Reform and Terrorism Prevention Act of 2004 created a director of National Intelligence (DNI) to replace the DCI. The DNI will serve as the head of the Intelligence Community, but not the CIA director. In addition, the DNI will have broad oversight responsibilities to manage national intelligence operations, particularly with regard to setting budget and intelligence collection priorities. The DNI will also be the president's principal intelligence advisor.

Terrorist Threat Information and Screening Centers

To enhance intelligence support for homeland security in 2003 President Bush created two information fusion centers, the Terrorist Threat Information Center (TTIC) and the Terrorist Screening Center (TSC). The TTIC is designed to be a central location where all terrorist-related intelligence, both foreign and domestic, is gathered, coordinated, and assessed. It is composed of elements of the FBI, CIA, Department of Defense, Department of Homeland Security, Department of State, and other intelligence agencies. The TTIC mission is to optimize the use of terrorist threat-related information, expertise, and capabilities to conduct threat analysis and inform collection strategies; ensure information sharing across agency lines; integrate terrorist-related information collected domestically and abroad in order to form the most comprehensive threat picture possible. The TTIC is also responsible for developing terrorist threat assessments for the national leadership and provides the president's daily terrorist threat report.

While the TTIC is primarily responsible for threat assessments with regard to domestic terrorist threats, it coordinates its activities with intelligence integration activities. The TTIC is collocated with the DCI and FBI counterterrorism centers and the FBI's National Joint Terrorism Task Force, and it works closely with the DHS IAIP. In 2004, the president ordered that the TTIC be integrated into a new organization, the National Counterterrorism Center (NCTC), which would have responsibility for coordinating counterterrorism operations federal-wide.

The TTIC also maintains a secure Web site to provide access to top-secret information to government officials from all agencies involved in the war against terrorism. Plans are that eventually TTIC online will give access to a much broader community of analysts, including allowing more information sharing with state and local officials and the private sector. Currently, the director of the TTIC reports directly to the DCI.[9]

A second presidential initiative was the creation of the TSC under the FBI to consolidate all terrorist watch lists into a single function and give around-the-clock access to local, state, and federal authorities. The TSC will bring together databases that include the State Department's TIPOFF,[10] the FBI's Violent Gang and Terrorist Offender's File, and the DHS's many transportation security lists. The TSC will make it easier for consular officers to determine whether a visa applicant is a potential terrorist. The main source of the TSC's information will be the TTIC.

The Intelligence Reform and Terrorism Prevention Act of 2004 created a NCTC under the DNI. The law also made the TTIC part of the NCTC.

The Federal Bureau of Investigation

Primary domestic intelligence support for counterterrorism is provided by the Federal Bureau of Investigation, a component of the Department of Justice.[11] As part of an announced restructuring of the

FBI on May 29, 2002, the FBI director declared that combating terrorism would become the Bureau's primary mission.[12]

Several components of the FBI are primarily organized to respond to the threat of terrorism. The FBI has established a network of 84 Joint Terrorism Task Forces (JTTFs) to put federal, state, and local law enforcement together to investigate threats and share information. The National Joint Terrorism Task Force (NJTTF) in Washington, DC, includes representatives from 30 agencies, spanning the fields of intelligence, public safety, and federal, state, and local law enforcement. The NJTTF collects terrorism information and funnels it to the regional JTTFs, other terrorism units within the FBI, and intelligence and law enforcement agencies. The Foreign Terrorist Tracking Task Force (FTTTF) works to prevent terrorists from entering the country and tracks down suspects within the United States.

The Bureau's Counterterrorism Watch (CT Watch) is the FBI's center for terrorism prevention operations. Incoming threats are given an initial review by CT Watch staff; those deemed credible are passed on to FBI investigators for urgent action. CT Watch also produces daily terrorism threat briefing materials and intelligence reports for national security policy makers and members of the intelligence and law enforcement communities.

The USA PATRIOT Act

The USA PATRIOT Act, a law passed with overwhelming support in Congress immediately following the September 11 terrorist attacks, plays an important role in facilitating law enforcement and intelligence activities in support of domestic counterterrorism operations.[13] Several provisions of the act are key for promoting appropriate sharing of information between intelligence and law enforcement investigators and providing counterterrorism investigators tools that law enforcement agents already had available to investigate other serious crimes.

Prior to passage of the PATRIOT Act, law enforcement officials were generally restricted from sharing information provided to a grand jury with members of the intelligence community. The act permitted the sharing of matters involving foreign intelligence uncovered during a grand jury with counterterrorism law enforcement investigators. Another section of the PATRIOT Act amends the National Security Act to permit the Justice Department to disclose to the CIA foreign intelligence acquired in the course of a criminal investigation. The PATRIOT Act also modified the Foreign Intelligence Surveillance Act of 1978, which established special groups of judges to supervise law enforcement investigations involving classified subjects and material.[14] While the passage of the PATRIOT Act has engendered much controversy and concern over potential abuses of civil liberties, virtually all the investigatory tools provided by the act have already been used for many years to prosecute other criminal acts and have been upheld as legitimate by the courts. In addition, there are no recorded abuses of the powers granted under this act.[15]

Department of Defense

The Pentagon conducts homeland defense and can also provide assistance for homeland security in support of other federal civilian agencies. The assistant secretary for homeland defense is responsible for policy matters and providing oversight of military support to civil authorities.

Assistant Secretary of Homeland Defense

The assistant secretary of homeland defense's primary responsibilities focus on setting department polices regarding homeland security–related issues. The secretary also oversees coordination of research and development activities with the S&T Directorate of the DHS. Much of the DOD's support for developing homeland security technologies is done through the Technical Support Working Group (TSWG), an interagency activity that works to adopt existing technologies to meet new mission requirements.

Another mission managed by the assistant secretary is the DOD's critical infrastructure protection program, which includes the security of military installations and facilities. These activities are managed by the newly established Defense Program Office for Mission Assurance. Most of the DOD's budget for homeland security activities supports critical infrastructure protection programs.

Within the military services, each has adopted a different method for organizing and addressing domestic security issues. The Joint Staff established a Homeland Security Directorate within its Strategy and Policy Directorate (J5). The Air Force formed a Homeland Security Directorate under the Deputy Chief of Staff for Air and Space Operations, but also maintains a separate Air Staff section for civil support. The Army created a homeland security integrated concept team, led not by the Army staff but by a director of homeland security at the Army Training and Doctrine Command at Fort Monroe, Virginia. In addition, the Army has a Consequence Management Integration Office serving under its director of military support on the Army staff. The Marine Corps also created an integrated concept team and established a homeland security section at its Warfighting Lab at Quantico, Virginia. It is not clear that the Navy has created any unique command structure to deal with domestic security issues.

U.S. Northern Command

The military defense of most of the United States is the responsibility of the U.S. Northern Command (NORTHCOM) headquartered in Colorado Springs, Colorado. NORTHCOM's area of responsibility includes the continental United States, Alaska, Canada, Mexico, and the surrounding water out to approximately 500 nautical miles. The defense of Hawaii and U.S. territories and possessions in the Pacific remains the responsibility of U.S. Pacific Command. The commander of NORTHCOM is also the commander of the binational U.S.-Canada North American Aerospace Defense Command (NORAD).

Military support to civil authorities is governed by a number of federal statutes. The Insurrection Act allows the president to dispatch forces at the request of a governor or state legislature to suppress insurrections or allows the president to use troops to enforce federal law in the event of a rebellion.[16] Other laws permit using military forces in emergency situations dealing with nuclear material or weapons of mass destruction.[17] Finally, DOD can provide support to civilian agencies according to the provisions of the Stafford Act. The Pentagon is limited, however, by the Posse Comitatus law, which prohibits federal forces from performing law enforcement activities without the permission of Congress. The act, however, does not preclude the military from providing logistical support, loaning equipment, and offering technical advice, facilities, and training to civil authorities.[18]

In addition, Army and Air National Guard forces can also be used to provide military support to civil authorities. The National Guard of each state or territory is commanded by its governor. Governors can assign state missions as allowed by state constitutions and statutes. Individuals or units are called into federal service under either Title 32 or Title 10 of the U.S. Code. Title 32 covers federally funded, nonfederal duty status, which includes periodic training and participation in congressionally directed domestic programs such as drug interdiction. Under Title 10, Guard forces perform federal duties under the command of the president and are only then subject to the limitations of Posse Comitatus.

Responsibilities of Other Federal Agencies

Virtually every federal agency and department has some homeland security responsibilities. For example, FEMA has established a list of emergency support functions (ESFs). ESFs are functional areas of response activity established to facilitate the delivery of federal assistance required during the immediate response phase of a disaster to save lives, protect property and public health, and to maintain public safety. ESFs represent those types of federal assistance that states may need because of the specialized or unique nature of the assistance required or to supplement their available resources and response capabilities. ESFs are provided by a number of federal agencies. Additionally, many departments have unique response teams or participate in task forces that deal with terrorist threats or respond to disasters.

In addition to supporting emergency response activities, several departments have significant homeland security responsibilities. The Department of Health and Human Services is charged with overseeing bioterrorism preparedness programs including management of the National Strategic Stockpile, reserves of medicines and medical supplies that can be deployed for a range of emergencies. The Department of Energy manages the security of U.S. nuclear production facilities, laboratories, and information. The Department of Agriculture oversees initiatives for dealing with bioterrorism attacks on the U.S. food supply.

THE ROLE OF THE CONGRESS

In the wake of the September 11 attacks, Congress has only partially reorganized its homeland security responsibilities. Both the Senate and the House have established subcommittees within their appropriations committees who draft the DHS annual budget legislation. On the other hand, oversight of homeland security activities is still fragmented.

Congress's responsibilities related to homeland security and terrorism transcend all aspects of its traditional committee authority. The White House has identified 88 committees and subcommittees that currently exercise authority over homeland security policy. In the House, for example, at least 14 full committees and 25 separate subcommittees claim jurisdiction over some aspect of homeland security.[19]

The House has established a Homeland Security Committee to oversee operations of the DHS, but the committee does not have full jurisdiction. In the Senate, the Homeland Security Government Affairs Committee has some responsibility for overseeing matters related to the DHS.

There are persistent calls to reform the current committee system, but there is little agreement among Congressional leaders on how to best divide jurisdiction among various committees. Neither chamber gives committees full jurisdiction over all homeland security activities in the DHS.

STATE AND LOCAL GOVERNMENTS

The Tenth Amendment to the Constitution makes clear that each state retains substantial independent power with respect to the general welfare of its populace. States, territories, and U.S. tribal lands bear much of the responsibility for providing homeland security for their citizens.

Organization of State Operations

States direct some resources that are important for homeland security missions, including domestic counterterrorism operations, critical infrastructure protection, and disaster preparedness and response, such as statewide law enforcement agencies, public health officials, and state highway authorities. Since states have different geographic and demographic situations and varying resources, industries, and critical infrastructure, they face unique threats and vulnerabilities and capacities to respond.

The structure of each state's homeland security apparatus is also unique. According to the National Governors Association, after 9/11 all states created homeland security entities to prepare for a wide range of terrorist attacks. They accomplished this by facilitating the interaction and coordination needed among the governor's office, the homeland security director, the state emergency management office, other state agencies, local governments, the private sector, volunteer organizations, and the federal government. These were built on existing statewide response programs and resources.

There is no common model; however, in several states, the homeland security director serves as an advisor to the governor in addition to coordinating state emergency management, law enforcement, health, and related public safety functions. In some states, the homeland security advisor is also the state adjutant general, the commander of state National Guard troops. Rather than assigning the homeland security advisors oversight of state agencies, most governors have formed homeland security task forces, typically consisting of heads from law enforcement, fire and rescue, public health, National Guard, transportation, public works, and information technology agencies.[20]

Local Governments

Metropolitan cities, towns, villages, counties, and tribal council governments have significant homeland security responsibilities. In many cases, for example, mayors and county executives are owners or operators of public transportation systems and transport nodes (such as ports, subways, or airports) or participate in their management. The bulk of emergency response assets, including police, firefighter, public works, and emergency medical personnel are employees of state and local governments. In virtually every case, local government leaders will play a principal role in coordinating local security and directing on-scene emergency response.

Local governments represent a wide range of capacity to undertake homeland security measures and respond to disasters. Most communities employ an emergency manager and emergency operations center, which provide the instrument for a unified response of local assets. In addition, many communities maintain mutual support and cooperative agreements to share resources with nearby localities.

Emergency Responders

In the event of a terrorist incident, initial efforts to secure, protect, and assist at the scene are provided by emergency responders. The Homeland Security Act of 2002 defines emergency response providers as including "federal, state, and local public safety, law enforcement, emergency response, emergency medical (including hospital emergency facilities), and related personnel, agencies, and authorities."[21] These responders might include hazardous materials response teams, urban search and rescue assets, community emergency response teams, antiterrorism units, special weapons and tactics teams, bomb squads, emergency management officials, municipal agencies, and private organizations responsible for transportation, communications, medical services, public health, disaster assistance, public works, and construction.

CHAPTER SUMMARY

Homeland security is a national enterprise that requires the involvement of federal, state, and local governments as well as the private sector. Even within the federal government, each branch—the executive, legislative, and judicial—has an important role to play. Additionally, federal homeland security activities are not confined to the United States. Virtually every security activity has some international dimension that requires cooperation with other governments and international nongovernmental institutions.

The vital role of state and local governments cannot be overstated. State and local leaders play a critical role in all homeland security activities from finding and stopping terrorists to protecting critical infrastructure and responding to attacks. In particular, response activities will normally always be spearheaded by local officials, with state and federal assets providing support and reinforcement.

The complex nature of governance in the United States is a virtue, not a limitation. America is a large and diverse nation. Trying to run homeland security activities effectively out of an office in Washington, DC, would inevitably fail. The great strength of the decentralized nature of American governance is that it allows for innovation and flexibility and allows local leaders to lead, permitting them to adapt responses to local needs and conditions. This virtue, however, requires effective coordination between levels of government and the private sector to exploit the advantages of the American way of homeland security.

CHAPTER QUIZ

1. What is *federalism,* and how does it affect the conduct of homeland security?

2. How should the specific roles and responsibilities of federal, state, and local authorities be determined? Who should decide?

3. What is the difference between the National Security Council and Homeland Security Council? Should their functions be separate?

4. How does Congress influence the conduct of homeland security?

5. What is the appropriate role of the Department of Defense in homeland security?

NOTES

1. For a working definition, see the comments by Secretary of the Army Thomas White, *Secretary White Briefing on Homeland Security*, News Transcript (October 26, 2001), at defenselink.mil/news/Oct2001/t10262001_t1026sa.html.

2. The *National Strategy for Homeland Security*, p. 2. (See Note 1 in Introduction section.)

3. See PL 235-61 Stat. 496; USC 402. This law was amended by the National Security Act Amendments of 1949 (63 Stat. 579; 50 USC 401 et seq.). As part of the federal Reorganization Plan of 1949, the NSC was placed in the Executive Office of the President.

4. James Jay Carafano and Ha Nguyen, "Better Intelligence Sharing for Visa Issuance and Monitoring: An Imperative for Homeland Security," Heritage Backgrounder #1699 (October 27, 2003), www.heritage.org/Research/HomelandDefense/BG1699.cfm .

5. PL 42 USC 5121 et seq.

6. Presidential Homeland Security Directive 3 (March 2002), at www.whitehouse.gov/news/releases/2002/03/20020312-5.html. Responsibility for the HSAS was established by law in the Homeland Security Act of 2002. See Public Law 107-296, Sec. 201.

7. Membership in the U.S. Intelligence Community is defined in 50 USC 401a(4).

8. Loch K. Johnson, "The DCI and the Eight-Hundred Pound Gorilla." In *Intelligence and the National Security Strategist: Enduring Issues and Challenges*, edited by Roger Z. George and Robert D. Kline (Washington, DC: National Defense University Press, 2004), pp. 459–478.

9. John Brennan, Director, Terrorist Threat Integration Center, "Information Sharing and Coordination for Visa Issuance: Our First Line of Defense for Homeland Security," Testimony before the Committee on the Judiciary, U.S. Senate (September 23, 2003).

10. Established in 1987, TIPOFF is run through the Department of State's Bureau of Intelligence and Research as a clearinghouse for sensitive intelligence information provided by other agencies. It includes full biographic records on approximately 85,000 terrorist names, photos, fingerprints, and other source documentation. Testimony of Francis

X. Taylor before the Joint Congressional Intelligence Committee Inquiry (October 1, 2002), www.state.gov/s/ct/rls/rm/13891.htm.

11. For a list and discussion of the roles of the various federal law enforcement agencies see William Wechsler, "Law in Order: Reconstructing US National Security," *The National Interest* 67 (Spring 2002): 25–28.

12. Remarks prepared for delivery by Robert S. Mueller III, Director, Federal Bureau of Investigation, at a Press Availability on the FBI's Reorganization, Washington, DC (May 29, 2002), www.fbi.gov/pressrel/speeches/speech052902.htm; FBI Strategic Focus (May 29, 2002), www.fbi.gov/page2/52902.htm.

13. See Uniting and Strengthening America by Providing Appropriate Tools Required to Intercept and Obstruct Terrorism Act of 2001, Pub. L. 107-56, 115 Stat. 272 (October 26, 2001).

14. Charles Doyle, "The USA Patriot Act: A Sketch," Congressional Research Service, RS21203 (April 18, 2002).

15. The Inspector General for the Department of Justice has reported that there have been no instances in which the PATRIOT Act has been invoked to infringe on civil rights or civil liberties. See *Report to Congress on Implementation of Section 1001 of the USA Patriot Act* (January 27, 2004); see also "Report Finds No Abuses of Patriot Act," *Washington Post* (January 28, 2004): A2.

16. Title 10, USC, Secs. 331–334.

17. Title 18, USC, Sec. 381; Title 10, USC, Sec. 382.

18. Mathew Carlton Hammond, "The Posse Comitatus Act: A Principle in Need of Renewal," *Washington University Law Quarterly* (Summer 1997): 3, www.wulaw.wuslt.edu/75-2/752-10.html; Jeffrey D. Brake, "Terrorism and the Military's Role in Domestic Crisis Management: Background and Issues for Congress," Congressional Research Service (April 19, 2001), pp. 11–18; Craig T. Trebilcock, "Posse Comitatus—Has the Posse Outlived Its Purpose?" Center for Strategic and International Studies Working Group (2000), pp. 1–5.

19. Michael Scardaville, "The New Congress Must Reform Its Committee Structure to Meet Homeland Security Needs," Heritage Backgrounder #1612 (November 12, 2002), www.heritage.org/Research/HomelandDefense/bg1612.cfm.

20. National Governors Association, Overview of States Homeland Security Governance (January 2004), p. 1, www.nga.org/cda/files/homesecstructures.pdf. This overview provides a list of state homeland security directors and the organization of state homeland security activities as of January 2004.

21. PL 107-296, Sec. 2(6).

12

AMERICA'S NATIONAL STRATEGIES

The Plans Driving the War on Global Terrorism and What They Mean

War has been waged against us by stealth and deceit and murder. This nation is peaceful, but fierce when stirred to anger. The conflict was begun on the timing and terms of others. It will end in a way, and at an hour, of our choosing.

President George W. Bush, quoted in the National Security Strategy of the United States, *September 2002*

CHAPTER OVERVIEW

The United States has long relied on national strategies to focus federal efforts on dealing with national security issues from fighting World War II to the war on drugs. After 9/11, one of the first efforts of the Bush administration was to craft a family of strategies to guide the global war on terrorism. The *National Strategy for Homeland Security* was perhaps the most important of these documents, providing a framework for how the federal government would organize domestic security activities.

This chapter outlines the key points from each of the national strategies related to defeating terrorism and protecting the homeland. It builds on the information in the previous chapter, describing how the instruments of the federal government will be used to meet the threat of transnational terrorism, as well as the roles and responsibilities of state, local, and tribal governments and the private sector.

CHAPTER LEARNING OBJECTIVES

After reading this chapter, you should be able to

1. Define the critical mission areas in the *National Strategy for Homeland Security.*

2. Understand the role of the Department of Defense in homeland security.

3. Describe the roles the national strategies assign to state and local governments.

4. Describe the roles of the private sector in the national strategies.

5. Describe how the national strategies envision winning the war on terrorism.

WHAT IS A STRATEGY?

Strategy is the ends, ways, and means of achieving national objectives. The ends define the goals of the strategy. Ways comprise the methods that are employed to achieve the ends. Means describe the resources that are available to accomplish the goals. National strategies involve more than just the use of the armed forces. They consider all the economic, political, diplomatic, military, and informational instruments that might be used to promote a nation's interest or secure a state from its enemies.

The Purpose of Strategy

Strategies are intended to serve as guidance for the implementation of plans, programs, campaigns, and other activities. In practice, they may serve other purposes as well. Strategies released to the public may also serve political purposes designed to appeal to certain constituencies, influence public opinion, or intimidate an enemy.

The most influential strategies are those that make hard choices—allocating scarce resources, setting clear goals, or establishing priorities. U.S. strategy during World War II, which declared the allies would "defeat Germany first," offers a case in point. That simple declarative sentence drove a cascading series of decisions and actions that defined the conduct of the war. Likewise, the simple declaration of a U.S. policy of "containment" defined American policies toward the Soviet Union throughout the Cold War. Thus, there is no single definition of what makes a great strategy other than its ability to mobilize the country in pursuit of a national aim.

Crafting American Strategy

Some national strategies are required by law. Others are prepared at the direction of the president. Strategies can be drafted and coordinated by the National or Homeland Security Council or a lead federal agency, like the Defense or State Department, may be directed to prepare the document. Strategies remain in effect until they are revised or superseded by presidential direction.

National strategies are public documents, designed not only to guide government efforts but also to explain U.S. efforts to American citizens, friendly and allied nations, and potential enemies as well. Thus, while strategies might not detail everything being done (particularly classified actions such as spying and secret operations), they do outline current aspirations for future efforts.

Strategy and Homeland Security

National strategies are particularly important to the task of homeland security. While the task of defending the homeland is not new, merging the many activities that go into that task into a holistic mission is revolutionary. Likewise, determining how to set priorities, organize activities, and measure successes is an unprecedented challenge. Obtaining national unity requires the guiding vision of national strategies. Homeland security activities are guided by a number of overarching strategies. In the wake of the September 11 attacks eight new strategies were published, five of which were specifically developed to deal with the challenges of combating terrorism while the others were revisions of earlier strategies to account for the dangers of the post-9/11 world.

The national strategies comprise both offensive and defensive measures, though virtually all the national strategies provide guidance regarding both foreign and domestic affairs. Strategies for national security, combating terrorism, weapons of mass destruction, and the military are primarily focused on defeating terrorists overseas. The national homeland security strategy and strategies for critical infrastructure protection and cybersecurity principally focus on protecting the homeland. Strategies relating to drug control policy and money laundering focus on transnational criminal activities in which terrorists might also engage. These strategies contain components related to both domestic and overseas activities.

NATIONAL SECURITY STRATEGY

The *National Security Strategy* provides a broad framework for how all the instruments of national power will be employed including military power, intelligence, diplomacy, and law enforcement. It is required by law. President Reagan issued the first public national strategy in 1988. President Bush issued the first version of his strategy in September 2002, which included a specific section related to global terrorism.[1]

Prior to 9/11, combating transnational terrorism was primarily considered a law enforcement activity. The new strategy, which is Bush's *National Security Strategy*, shifts the priority from arrest and prosecution to preventing attacks and killing or capturing terrorists.

Importance of Offense

Bush's *National Security Strategy* was built on the assumption that the best defense is a good offense. The first priority of the strategy with regard to terrorism is disrupting and destroying terrorist organizations with global reach. Specific targets include leadership, their means of communicating, and controlling terrorist cells, financing, and material support.

The strategy assumes that a combination of ways will be required to achieve the goal of breaking up the capacity of transnational terrorist networks to reach across nations; preventing state sponsors of terrorism from gaining or using weapons of mass destruction; and destroying threats before they reach U.S. borders. Methods include invoking the nation's inherent right of self-defense to take direct action with conventional military forces as well as other means. In addition, the strategy calls for convincing or forcing states to deny sponsorship, support, and sanctuary for terrorists. In conducting these operations, the United States may act alone or in concert with other friendly nations and allies, though the strategy emphasizes that where possible America should work with other nations and existing alliances. This declaration is often referred to as the Bush Doctrine.

War of Ideas   Another component for Bush's national strategy calls for waging a "war of ideas." The goal of this campaign is to make clear that acts of terrorism are illegitimate and diminish the underlying conditions that support terrorism by promoting democratic values and economic freedom.

The Role of Defense   The final component of the president's national strategy with regard to terrorism emphasizes the specific role of homeland security, recognizing that a good offense is not sufficient for deterring, preventing, or mitigating every terrorist act. The *National Security Strategy* emphasizes improving the coordination and integration of domestic capabilities for combating terrorism.

NATIONAL STRATEGY FOR COMBATING TERRORISM

In February 2003 the United States promulgated its first public overall strategy for all national counterterrorism activities.[2] Though not required by law, the administration published the *National Strategy for Combating Terrorism*. This document built on the principles enunciated in Bush's *National Security Strategy*, providing additional details on the ways and means by which it would be employed—destroying terrorist networks, conducting a war of ideas, and strengthening security within the United States. The intent of the strategy for combating terrorism is not to end all terrorism everywhere, but specifically to defeat terrorist organizations "with global reach" and access to weapons of mass destruction.

The strategy for combating terrorism envisions a protracted campaign that will take many years and even if successful will require measures to maintain preparedness against new threats that might emerge in the future. The strategy calls for continuous action to disrupt terrorist activities, then degrade their supporting networks, and eventually destroy terrorist organizations. Rather than focusing specifically on al-Qaida the strategy is broad and open-ended, designed to be employed against any organization or state that employs transnational terrorism. The ways and means in the strategy for combating terrorism are defined by four tenets—defeat, deny, diminish, and defend.

Defeat   *Defeat* includes efforts to identify terrorists, locate their sanctuaries, and destroy their ability to plan and operate. It calls for the intelligence and law enforcement communities to work closely together to provide information on terrorist leaders, plans, intentions, modus operandi, finances, communications, and recruitment. Once terrorists have been identified and located, the United States intends to use every means available to disrupt, dismantle, and destroy their capacity to undertake terrorist acts.

Deny   The *deny* tenet of the strategy for combating terrorism refers to efforts to eliminate state sponsorship and sanctuaries. Emphasis on this component of the strategy was derived from the experience of al-Qaida's ability to use Afghanistan and the support of the ruling Taliban to create a base for training, planning, and directing terrorist actions. Activities under this tenet include encouraging all states to fulfill their responsibilities to combat terrorism, providing assistance to states that lack the means to conduct effective counterterrorism operations, and convincing states that are not meeting their obligations to change their policies. In addition to focusing on state activities, this tenet also includes efforts centered on breaking the nexus between terrorism and transnational crime.

Diminish   *Diminish* describes collective efforts to limit conditions that terrorists can exploit. This tenet includes all U.S. efforts to resolve regional disputes; foster economic, social, and political development; and promote market-based economies, good governance, and rule of law. In addition to these traditional elements of foreign policy, this tenet adds a discussion of the "war of ideas" called for in the national security strategy. In addition to general efforts to delegitimize terrorism and promote democratic, free-market alternatives, this tenet offers one area where the strategy focuses specifically on the threat of al-Qaida by calling for support to develop moderate and modern governments in the Muslim world. The goal is to ensure Muslims that American values and actions are not at odds with Islam. In particular, the strategy notes the importance of resolving the Israeli-Palestinian conflict as part of the war of ideas. The close U.S. relationship with Israel and the prevalence of extremist ideologies to use the conflict as a clarion call for attacks against America significantly affects the view of the

United States in the Muslim world. Promoting a lasting peace, the strategy argues, would result in greater U.S. influence and diminish criticisms of American policies.

Defend   *Defend*, the fourth tenet of the strategy for combating terrorism, encompasses the defense of U.S. territory and American interests abroad. The counterterrorism strategy relies heavily on the implementation of the national homeland security strategy (discussed subsequently) to provide the integration and coordination required to protect the United States from terrorist attacks. This tenet adds additional objectives to expand the global aspects of domestic security programs. In particular, the strategy calls for increasing "domain awareness," obtaining effective knowledge of activities, events, and persons in the dimensions of air, land, sea, and cyberspace. The emphasis on improving domain awareness is through sharing and fusing information and intelligence. This tenet also stresses improving the protection of citizens and infrastructure abroad by providing meaningful, up-to-date, and coordinated threat information.

NATIONAL STRATEGY TO COMBAT WEAPONS OF MASS DESTRUCTION

The *National Strategy to Combat Weapons of Mass Destruction*, which discussed ways to counter the potential use of weapons of mass destruction against the United States by states or nonstate groups, was released in December 2002. The unclassified version of the strategy was released as National Security Presidential Directive 17 and Homeland Security Presidential Directive 4.[3] There is also a classified version of the strategy that has not been released to the public.

The WMD strategy is based on three pillars—counterproliferation, nonproliferation, and consequence management. Counterproliferation includes measures to deter or defend against the use of WMD. Nonproliferation activities are those activities designed to prevent countries or groups from obtaining precursors that support WMD technologies, weapons, or delivery systems. Consequence management includes responding to reduce the extent of damage.

In addition to traditional nonproliferation instruments, such as arms control regimes like the Nuclear Nonproliferation Treaty, the strategy emphasizes three new major counterproliferation efforts. The first is the deployment of missile defense systems capable of interdicting ballistic missiles. The second is the establishment of a Counterproliferation Technology Coordination Committee consisting of senior members from federal agencies who will coordinate research and development. The third calls for targeting specific strategies to deal with different supplier and recipient states. One program resulting from this strategy is the Proliferation Security Initiative (PSI). This initiative seeks to engage any nation whose vessels, flags, ports, territorial waters, airspace, or land might be used for proliferation purposes. PSI agreements include, for example, the authority to inspect PSI-member ships on the high seas that are suspected of carrying WMD-related materials.

NATIONAL MILITARY STRATEGY

Though not required by law, since the late 1980s the United States has published a *National Military Strategy*. The latest version of the strategy published in 2004, established winning the global war on terrorism as its highest priority. Particularly, the strategy envisions that military assets, especially special operation forces, will be actively used in counterterrorism operations.[4]

In addition to the role of the armed forces in supporting offensive operations overseas and theater security activities to help the militaries of other countries build up their capacity to conduct counterterrorism activities, the strategy also calls for the Defense Department to work with other federal agencies, as well as Canada and Mexico, to form an integrated defense of the air, land, sea, and space approaches to U.S. sovereign territory. Additionally, the strategy calls for added emphasis on using military capabilities to secure and protect critical infrastructure that supports the deployment of U.S. forces from American soil and improving capabilities to provide military support to civilian authorities for mitigating the consequences of an attack on the United States. The emphasis placed on these tasks contrasts significantly with military strategy during the Cold War that envisioned U.S. forces being used almost exclusively to deter Soviet aggression.

NATIONAL STRATEGY FOR HOMELAND SECURITY

Issued by the president in July 2002, the *National Strategy for Homeland Security* provides overarching guidance for the protection of the United States against terrorist attacks.[5] The defense of the United States against more conventional military threats remains the responsibility of the Department of Defense, governed by the priorities established in the national security and national military strategies.

Perhaps the most important contribution of the homeland security strategy was the establishment of six critical mission areas. These areas serve to align federal efforts, responsibilities, and resources within the federal budgets to specific tasks for protecting the homeland. In fact, beginning in 2004 the president's annual budget proposal began to account for federal homeland security spending by department and overall by the mission areas listed in the strategy.

Intelligence and Early Warning

This mission area includes efforts to deny terrorists the element of surprise by detecting terrorist activities before they result in attacks on the homeland so that preemptive, preventive, and protective action can be taken. Intelligence and early warning activities relate to domestic information gathering and the analysis of intelligence gathered worldwide to identify threats against U.S. territory.

The 2004 strategy identified five major initiatives in this area: (1) enhancing the analytic capabilities of the FBI to evaluate the terrorist information collected; (2) building up the capabilities of the Information Analysis and Infrastructure Protection (IAIP) Directorate in the DHS; (3) implementing the Homeland Security Advisory System; (4) increasing analysis of dual-use technology that can be employed for both legitimate uses and terrorist acts; and (5) employing *red team* techniques, which uncover weaknesses in homeland security regimes by having analysts plan how terrorists might conduct attacks on the United States.

Border and Transportation Security

This critical mission area includes security of borders; activities at ports of entry into the United States; and conveyance on airlines, railroads, public transportation, highways, pipelines, and waterways. The objective is to establish layered security systems that will stop terrorists while safeguarding civil liberties and privacy and promoting the efficient and reliable flow of commerce and travel. Expectations are that no single initiative will be sufficient to impede every terrorist act, but that the cumulative effect of a number of measures employed in concert with one another will serve as a significant obstacle.

Major initiatives called for in the strategy include ensuring accountability of border and transportation security; creating "smart borders" through the better use of technology to identify threats; increasing the security of international shipping containers; implementing the Aviation and Transportation Security Act of 2001; recapitalizing the U.S. Coast Guard, whose shipping and aviation assets are wearing out from increased use; and reforming immigration services.

Domestic Counterterrorism

The activities of federal, state, and local law enforcement authorities comprise this critical mission area. The main objective of the strategy in this area is to reorient law enforcement on new counterterrorism objectives. While investigating and prosecuting criminal activities remains a responsibility, a priority is now assigned to preventing and interdicting terrorist activity within the United States. Equally important, however, is continued respect for the legal protections for civil liberties provided by U.S. laws. Domestic counterterrorism efforts are not supposed to trade off constitutional rights for added security, but to provide for both at the same time.

Major initiatives to be undertaken in this critical mission area include measures to improve intergovernmental law enforcement coordination; facilitate apprehension of potential terrorists; continue ongoing investigations and prosecutions against known terrorists; restructure the FBI to make the agencies capacity to undertake antiterrorism operations its top priority; target and attack terrorist financing; and track foreign terrorists and bring them to justice.

Defending against Catastrophic Threats

This critical mission area concerns harnessing science and technology for counterterrorism efforts. The goal of this mission area is to place particular emphasis on DHS research and development efforts to counter the threat of WMD, including detecting weapons and developing the means to limit casualties and economic damage.

The strategy calls for focusing research efforts on five key initiatives: (1) preventing the use of nuclear weapons through better sensors for detecting nuclear materials; (2) advancing means for detecting the presence of biological and chemical materials; (3) improving chemical detectors and decontamination techniques; (4) developing vaccines, antimicrobials, and antidotes that will be effective against a variety of biological threats; and (5) implementing the Select Agent Program, an effort to control the use of dangerous biological agents by academic and commercial research efforts.

Emergency Preparedness and Response

This critical mission area includes minimizing the damage and recovering from terrorist attacks. The objective of the strategy is to develop a national response system that brings together and coordinates all necessary response assets quickly and effectively.

The emergency preparedness and response critical mission area includes more than a dozen major initiatives. The two most important are integrating the half dozen separate federal response plans into a single all-discipline incident management plan and creating a national incident management system.

Protecting Critical Infrastructure and Key Assets

The strategy defines as critical those systems and assets whose incapacity or destruction would have a debilitating impact on security, national economic security, or national public health or safety. Sectors including critical infrastructure include agriculture, food, water, public health, emergency services, government, the defense industrial base, information and telecommunications, energy, transportation, banking and finance, the chemical industry, and postal and shipping. Key assets include monuments and places of national significance such as the Statue of Liberty.

Initiatives for protecting critical infrastructure include unifying national critical infrastructure efforts under the DHS; building and maintaining a complete and accurate assessment of critical assets; developing a national infrastructure protection plan; securing cyberspace; guarding against inside threats (attacks made by current or former employees); and partnering with the international community to protect transnational infrastructure, such as global commercial shipping.

Allocating Resources

In addition to delineating critical missions, the national homeland security strategy also establishes principles on how homeland security efforts will be funded. The strategy relies on the principles of federalism to establish the burden for funding programs by federal, state, and local governments. Thus, for example, intelligence, which is a national responsibility, will largely be carried out by federal agencies. On the other hand, the strategy expects that state and local governments will provide most of the resources and funding for emergency response and preparedness, while the private sector will bear the majority of the burden for critical infrastructure.

NATIONAL STRATEGY FOR THE PHYSICAL PROTECTION OF CRITICAL INFRASTRUCTURES AND KEY ASSETS

Published in February 2003, the *National Strategy for the Physical Protection of Critical Infrastructures and Key Assets,* amplifies the critical mission area of the homeland security strategy related to the protection of key capabilities for commerce, governance, and public services.[6] The physical infrastructure strategy delineates guiding principles including establishing responsibility and accountability; encouraging partnerships between different levels of government and between government and private industry; and encouraging market-oriented solutions to security and physical protection.

Objectives

The physical infrastructure strategy also establishes overall objectives—identifying and protecting the most critical assets with first priority to ensuring protection of assets facing specific, imminent threats and then pursuing collaborative measures to protect other assets that might be seen as lucrative targets in the future. The strategy defines the most critical assets as those systems and functions supporting public health and safety, governance, economic and national security, and public confidence.

Role of Private Sector

Since most critical national infrastructures are in private hands, the strategy envisions that the private sector will bear most of the responsibilities and cost of protecting infrastructure. The strategy also envisions that regulatory requirements should be kept to a minimum to allow the private sector the maximum flexibility to innovate and achieve the equally important goals of economic growth, dependability of service, and appropriate security.

NATIONAL STRATEGY TO SECURE CYBERSPACE

Closely related to the physical infrastructure strategy, the *National Strategy to Secure Cyberspace* was also issued by the president in February 2003.[7] The administration defines *cyberspace* as systems consisting of hundreds of thousands of interconnected computers, servers, routers, switches, and fiber-optic cables used to transmit data. Cyberspace, the strategy argues, is particularly critical since these information systems provide much of the backbone for the nation's critical infrastructure.

As with other components of critical infrastructure, the strategy calls for a combination of measures designed to prevent attacks, reduce vulnerabilities, and minimize the damage from cyberattacks that do occur.

Major Initiatives

The cyberspace strategy includes eight major initiatives: (1) establishing a public-private architecture for responding to national-level cyber incidents; (2) developing analysis of cyberattacks and vulnerability assessments; (3) encouraging the private sector to develop a synoptic view of cyberspace; (4) expanding the Cyber Warning and Information Network; (5) improving national incident management; (6) developing public-private contingency and continuity plans; (7) conducting national exercises; and (8) improving public-private information sharing.

Role of Private Sector

The cyberspace strategy finds that the private sector is best equipped and structured to meet cyberthreats since much of the infrastructure supporting national information systems is in private hands and the private sector is best able to leverage new technologies that can provide enhanced security and dependability.

Role of Government

In addition to promoting public-private solutions for cybersecurity, the cyberspace strategy also assigns roles and responsibilities to various federal agencies. Primary federal responsibilities are in the areas of forensics and attack attribution, protection of networks and systems critical to national security, provision of indications and warnings, and protection against organized attacks capable of inflicting debilitating damage on the national economy. The federal government is also tasked to support research and development in the private sector, with the DHS assigned the role of being the focal point for federal outreach to state and local governments and the private sector.

NATIONAL MONEY LAUNDERING STRATEGY

The *National Money Laundering Strategy*, a strategy for combating the illicit use of monetary instruments (including cash, gold, diamonds, stocks, bonds, wire transfers, and credit cards), is one of two national strategies which, while not exclusively related to the tasks of homeland security, include important counterterrorism activities. For over a decade, Congress has required the Department of Treasury to submit the *National Money Laundering Strategy*. The September 2002 strategy, prepared by the department in consultation with the Department of Justice reflects the increased focus on disrupting funding for terrorist operations.[8]

While the September 2002 money laundering strategy still focuses primarily on criminal activity, it outlines a major governmentwide strategy to combat terrorist financing, with emphasis on adapting the traditional methods of countering money laundering to the unconventional means often used by terrorist organizations. Among the initiatives being undertaken is the Financial Attack Center, being created jointly by the Justice, DHS, and Treasury departments to bring together their most experienced financial investigators and analysts to prioritize targets and develop plans to attack them.

NATIONAL DRUG CONTROL STRATEGY

By law, the president is required to produce an annual *National Drug Control Strategy* for countering the production, transport, sale, and use of illegal drugs. This strategy is developed by the Office of National Drug Control Policy in coordination with a number of federal agencies. It is extremely relevant to homeland security issues, though like the *National Money Laundering Strategy* it is not primarily designed to counter terrorist activities.[9] Trafficking in drugs has been used to fund terrorist organizations. Terrorists have also mimicked the activities of drug traffickers to smuggle illicit goods. Finally, many of the border and transportation security resources used to root out terrorists are also employed to track down drug smugglers. Sometimes security activities are dual-use, working to disrupt both drug smuggling and terrorist operations. In other cases, the two missions compete for resources and increasing effort in one area comes at the expense of operations conducted on the other. As a result, the goals and activities directed by the national drug control policy may have a significant impact on homeland security efforts.

Among the initiatives in the 2004 strategy most relevant to homeland security and counterterrorism are efforts to link drug and money laundering investigations, particularly through the creation of the Financial Attack Center.

Another significant initiative in the drug control strategy is efforts to accelerate antidrug efforts in Afghanistan. Afghanistan is not only the world's largest producer of opiates, but drug profits have been used in the past to support its terrorist operations. The main effort described in the strategy for combating the use of drug trafficking by global terrorists is a cooperative program with the United Kingdom to eradicate the farming of poppies, from which opium can be extracted and refined into heroin, and substitute the cultivation of alternative crops.

ASSESSING THE NATIONAL STRATEGIES

There is little question but that the framework of national strategies provide a comprehensive and nested set of guidelines for protecting the homeland. Since strategies have long-term implications for the direction of U.S. efforts, it may require years of implementation before a determination can be made over whether they are effective.

Evaluating the effectiveness and adequacies of the national strategies will be a significant challenge for policy makers in the years ahead and will no doubt remain a topic of discussion and debate. Evaluating the national strategies will likely fall into two areas. The first concerns the sufficiency of the strategies—whether they actually contain sufficient guidance to purposefully direct national policies and programs. The second area that will bear examination is the capacity of the strategies to reduce the threat of global terrorism and enhance homeland security. On the second point, much of the success of the strategies will turn on their underlying assumptions. While strategies can be modified and updated as lessons are learned, strategies based on faulty premises are unlikely to prove effective in achieving success in a protracted conflict.

The Fundamentals of Strategy

There is no universal agreement on the necessary components of strategy for describing ends, ways, and means. An initial analysis of the national strategies by the U.S. General Accounting Office (GAO) listed several useful criteria. The characteristics the GAO identified are (1) purpose, scope, and methodology; (2) problem definition and risk assessment; (3) goals, subordinate objectives, activities, and performance measures; (4) resources, investments, and risk management; (5) organizational roles, responsibilities, and coordination; and (6) integration and implementation. Overall, the strategies are generally good at establishing the purpose, scope, definition of the problem, and overall goals. The GAO, however, determined that none of the strategies addresses all the elements of resources, investments, and risk management; or integration and implementation. On the whole, the GAO found that the *National Strategy for Homeland Security* and the *National Strategy for the Physical Protection of Critical Infrastructure and Key Assets* address the greatest number of desirable characteristics, while the *National Security Strategy* and the *National Strategy to Combat Weapons of Mass Destruction* address the fewest.[10]

FROM THE SOURCE:

EVALUATING STRATEGY

In the wake of the many strategies published after 9/11, Congress tasked the General Accounting Office to identify and define the desirable characteristics of an effective national strategy and to evaluate whether the national strategies related to terrorism address those characteristics. Their report was published in February 2004 (see Figure 12.1).

National strategies and the extent they address GAO's desirable characteristics

National Strategy (short titles)	Purpose scope, and methodology	Problem definition and risk assessment	Goals, subordinate objectives, activities, and performance measures	Resources investments, and risk management	Organizational roles responsibilities and coordination	Integration and implementation
National Security	Does not address	Does not address	Partially addresses	Does not address	Does not address	Does not address
Homeland Security	Addresses	Addresses	Partially addresses	Partially addresses	Addresses	Partially addresses
Combating Terrorism	Partially addresses	Addresses	Partially addresses	Does not address	Partially addresses	Partially addresses
Weapons of Mass Destruction	Does not address	Does not address	Partially addresses	Does not address	Partially addresses	Partially addresses
Physical Infrastructure	Addresses	Addresses	Partially addresses	Partially addresses	Partially addresses	Partially addresses
Secure Cyberspace	Partially addresses	Addresses	Partially addresses	Partially addresses	Partially addresses	Partially addresses
Money Laundering	Partially addresses	Partially addresses	Partially addresses	Partially addresses	Partially addresses	Partially addresses

Source: (Combating Terrorism: Evaluation of Selected Characteristics of National Strategies Related to Terrorism by Randall A. Yim, managing director, homeland security and justice issues, before the Subcommittee on National Security, Emerging Threats, and International Relations, House Committee on Government Reform. GAO-04-408T, February 3, 2004.)

Questioning Assumptions

Another means for evaluating strategies is to examine the underlying premises on which they are based. By questioning underlying assumptions, one can evaluate whether a strategy has correctly diagnosed the nature of the problem and proposed adequate solutions. There are several issues that an assessment of the national strategies might explore.

Offense versus Defense

One key premise of the strategies is an emphasis on offense over defense. Rethinking the balance between offense and defense in the light of emerging threats should be a priority. Cold War strategy relied on deterrence. New strategies look to employ a mix of deterrence, preemption, retaliation, and homeland security. What constitutes the best balance, and what defenses best complement offensive measures, are open to debate. For example, some defenses might better enable the offense, allowing the United States to apply diplomatic, economic, or military means abroad without fear that an enemy could retaliate on the homeland. An optimum homeland security system would enhance freedom of action and be facile enough to deal with threats that are not easily countered by offensive measures that take the battle to the enemy.

War of Ideas

A particularly important assumption in the offensive strategies established by the Bush administration is the importance on waging a war of ideas. The administration argues that reducing global terrorism requires addressing underlying problems in the developing world including lack of good governance and poor economic growth. While there are many failed and failing states, however, not all have proved as harbingers for transnational terrorist threats. In addition, many of the world's most notorious terrorist leaders are well-educated and from families of some means. Some security analysts doubt that a strong nexus can be made between transnational threats and weak states. Others argue that even if such a nexus can be made the United States can only tangentially affect development in these countries and that significant reforms will require home-grown initiatives. In short, they argue the United States cannot conduct an effective war of ideas.

ISSUES:

THE WAR OF IDEAS

Announced by President Bush in November 2003, the goal of the Middle East Partnership Initiative is to support economic, political, and educational reform efforts in the Middle East by linking Arab, U.S., and global private-sector businesses, nongovernmental organizations, civil society elements, and governments together to develop innovative policies and programs that support reform in the region.

Supporters of the initiative claim it will undercut support for terrorism. Some detractors counter that the United States should not try to impose democracy from the outside. Others argue that these efforts are unlikely to address the root cause of terrorism.

Excerpt from the President's Speech

Some skeptics of democracy assert that the traditions of Islam are inhospitable to the representative government. This "cultural condescension," as Ronald Reagan termed it, has a long history. After the Japanese surrender in 1945, a so-called Japan expert asserted that democracy in that former empire would "never work." Another observer declared the prospects for democracy in post-Hitler Germany are, and I quote, "most uncertain at best"—he made that claim in 1957. Seventy-four years ago, the Sunday London Times declared nine-tenths of the population of India to be "illiterates not caring a fig for politics." Yet when Indian democracy was imperiled in the 1970s, the Indian people showed their commitment to liberty in a national referendum that saved their form of government.

Time after time, observers have questioned whether this country, or that people, or this group, are "ready" for democracy—as if freedom were a prize you win for meeting our own Western standards of progress. In fact, the daily work of democracy itself is the path of progress. It teaches cooperation, the free exchange of ideas, and the peaceful resolution of differences. As men and women are showing, from Bangladesh to Botswana, to Mongolia, it is the practice of democracy that makes a nation ready for democracy, and every nation can start on this path.

It should be clear to all that Islam—the faith of one-fifth of humanity—is consistent with democratic rule. Democratic progress is found in many predominantly Muslim countries—in Turkey and Indonesia, and Senegal and Albania, Niger and Sierra Leone. Muslim men and women are good citizens of India and South Africa, of the nations of Western Europe, and of the United States of America.

More than half of all the Muslims in the world live in freedom under democratically constituted governments. They succeed in democratic societies, not in spite of their faith, but because of it. A religion that demands individual moral accountability, and encourages the encounter of the individual with God, is fully compatible with the rights and responsibilities of self-government.

Yet there's a great challenge today in the Middle East. In the words of a recent report by Arab scholars, the global wave of democracy has—and I quote—"barely reached the Arab states." They continue: "This freedom deficit undermines human development and is one of the most painful manifestations of lagging political development." The freedom deficit they describe has terrible consequences, of the people of the Middle East and for the world. In many Middle Eastern countries, poverty is deep and it is spreading, women lack rights and are denied schooling. Whole societies remain stagnant while the world moves ahead. These are not the failures of a culture or a religion. These are the failures of political and economic doctrines.

1. Will the war of ideas work and will it address the issue of transnational terrorism?

2. What does the United States have to do to be successful in a war of ideas?

3. Are other U.S. actions around the world consistent with the goals of the war of ideas?

4. What are the alternatives to a war of ideas? Would they be more successful? If so, why?

Threat of WMD

The national strategies also assume that transnational terrorists may well obtain and employ WMD. To that end, emphasis in both offensive and defensive strategies is focused on responding to this challenge. Some national security analysts argue that this emphasis is unwarranted and the terrorists are likely to use more readily available means to threaten the homeland.[11] Others argue that the danger of WMD attacks is far graver than currently realized and that the Bush administration's efforts are inadequate.

Layered Defense

The defensive strategies also reflect a clear preference by the administration. The homeland security strategy and its supporting directives assume the United States will undertake a layered approach to its security system. This approach engenders both advantages and disadvantages. One advantage of multiple layers of security is that it complicates the obstacles facing terrorists. In addition, the redundancies provide multiple defenses that mitigate the requirement for any one system to function flawlessly. A disadvantage of multiple measures is that it could prove more expensive to maintain and coordinate numerous disparate security systems. Additionally, it may be unclear how much protection is achieved through layered security until all the systems supporting them are up and running.

Sufficient Strategies

One subject for debate is whether the current strategies sufficiently address all the critical mission areas related to homeland security. For example, maritime, border, and transportation security are interrelated, complex missions. While each element of these challenges is addressed in the various defensive strategies, it is not clear that they comprise a holistic solution to the terrorist threats shared in all these areas. Another area of concern is the nexus between terrorism and transnational crime. Although the national drug policy and money laundering strategies address these problems, terrorists have also used other manners of crimes including identity theft, insurance fraud, and human smuggling. Thus, a specific national strategy on transnational crime should be required to sufficiently address this problem.

Adequacy of Resources

Federal spending on homeland security more than doubled after the 9/11 attacks. The Bush administration's strategy for homeland security, however, did not envision substantial further increases in federal spending. The strategy's stated preference is to rely on the principles of federalism and cost sharing between the public and private sectors. This approach may not be sufficient to ensure adequate participation by cash-strapped state and local governments, as well as by a private sector that may prove reluctant to invest in improvements to protect critical infrastructure. On the other hand, the administration's proposed funding scheme may prove more sustainable over the long-term. In addition, this issue still begs the fundamental question of how much homeland security spending is sufficient to meet the threat of global terrorism.

CHAPTER SUMMARY

The national strategies provide comprehensive guidance on prosecuting the war on terror and protecting the homeland. Key concepts include the notion that the best means to defend the United States is to diminish the capacity of terrorist networks overseas to plan, prepare for, and conduct operations. In addition, the strategies acknowledge that securing the homeland is also important. They call for a "layered defense" that employs numerous organizations, programs, and activities. The strategies also envision shared responsibilities for federal, state, local, tribal, and private entities.

While the strategies offer a plethora of guidance, many questions remain over how effective they may prove. Key issues include adequacy of funding, the role of the war of ideas, and the potential threat of WMD.

CHAPTER QUIZ

1. What is meant by the *war of ideas*, and why is it important to U.S. strategy?
2. What does the concept of *layered defense* mean?
3. What are the critical missions in the *National Security Strategy*, and why are they important?
4. How does the United States plan to "win" the war against transnational terrorism?
5. Who will pay for providing homeland security?

NOTES

1. *National Security Strategy of the United States*, pp. 5–7, www.whitehouse.gov/nsc/nss.html.
2. *National Strategy for Combating Terrorism* (February 2004), www.whitehouse.gov/news/releases/2003/02/counter_terrorism/counter_terrorism_strategy.pdf.
3. *National Strategy to Combat Weapons of Mass Destruction* (December 2002), www.state.gov/documents/organization/16092.pdf.
4. U.S. Joint Chiefs of Staff, *National Military Strategy of the United States of America, 2004: A Strategy for Today, a Vision for Tomorrow* (Washington, DC: Joint Chiefs of Staff, 2004). In addition to the public *National Military Strategy* more specific direction on the use of the armed forces in the global war on terrorism is provided in the *National Military Strategic Plan for the War on Terrorism*. This document is classified.
5. *National Strategy for Homeland Security* (July 2002), www.whitehouse.gov/homeland/book.
6. *National Strategy for the Physical Protection of Critical Infrastructures and Key Assets* (February 2003), www.whitehouse.gov/pcipb/physical.html.
7. *National Strategy to Secure Cyberspace* (February 2003), www.us-cert.gov/reading_room/cyberspace_strategy.pdf.
8. *2002 National Money Laundering Strategy* (September 2002), www.ustreas.gov/press/releases/reports/js10102.pdf.

9. See, for example, *National Drug Control Policy 2002* (2002), www.whitehousedrugpolicy.gov/publications/policy/03ndcs/3priorities.html.

10. The U.S. General Accounting Office, "Combating Terrorism: Evaluation of Selected Characteristics in National Strategies Related to Terrorism," GAO-04-408T (February 3, 2004).

11. See, for example, Audrey Kurth Cronin, "Terrorist Motivations for Chemical and Biological Weapons Use: Placing the Threat in Context," Congressional Research Service (March 28, 2003).

13

DOMESTIC ANTITERRORISM AND COUNTERTERRORISM

The New Role for States and Localities and Supporting Law Enforcement Agencies

The attacks of September 11 . . . redefined the mission of federal, state, and local law enforcement authorities. While law enforcement agencies will continue to investigate and prosecute criminal activity, they should now assign priority to preventing and interdicting terrorist activity within the United States.

National Strategy for Homeland Security

CHAPTER OVERVIEW

The 9/11 attacks created a new focus on the roles of state and local officials in preventing terrorism in their communities and responding to it if it does occur. State and local officials are on the front lines of homeland security, and in many cases, local police will have the first opportunity to detect and prevent terrorism. Because of this, state and local governments are now undertaking programs of *antiterrorism*, generally used to describe passive or defensive measures against terrorism, and *counterterrorism*, which usually describes proactive measures, including targeting terrorist personnel and supporters. Should these programs fail, it will be local officers, firefighters, and emergency medical personnel who will be first on the scene of a terrorist attack.

State and local jurisdictions across the nation have been grappling with these responsibilities. Their success could mean preventing a major attack or lessening the human and financial toll when one occurs.

CHAPTER LEARNING OBJECTIVES

After reading this chapter, you should be able to

1. **Explain the role of state and local agencies in domestic counterterrorism.**
2. **Describe the role of intelligence in domestic counterterrorism.**
3. **List state and local strategies for preventing and interdicting terrorism.**
4. **Provide examples of state and local efforts to respond to terrorist events that do occur.**

THE FRONT LINES OF TERRORISM

As the 9/11 hijackers prepared for their mission, they managed to avoid the FBI, CIA, and other agencies viewed as America's front line of defense against terrorism. But some of them were stopped beforehand—for traffic violations. While these stops did not disrupt the terrorist plot, similar incidents have lead to the capture of terrorists. In 1988, a hardened Japanese Red Army terrorist, transporting bombs in his car as part of an apparent plot against New York City, was captured at a New Jersey Turnpike rest stop by a trooper who thought he was acting suspiciously. While Timothy McVeigh was not stopped before his attack, he was arrested soon after—by an Oklahoma Highway Patrol trooper who stopped him for missing a license plate, speeding, and failing to wear his seat belt. In other cases, investigations by local officials have uncovered organized crime and other support activities linked to terrorist groups. However, many of these cases were broken by luck rather than by a specific strategy. In the current environment, state and local officials are developing specific, proactive plans and programs to prevent and respond to terrorist acts in their jurisdictions.

JURISDICTIONS AND RESPONSIBILITIES

The Department of Homeland Security (DHS) is the lead agency for protecting the American homeland and has as a key mission to "prevent and deter terrorist attacks and protect against and respond to threats and hazards to the nation."[1] The DHS is assisted by numerous other federal agencies, most notably the FBI, which provides law enforcement, intelligence, and hostage rescue/special operations capabilities.

But it is state and local governments that have jurisdiction over most aspects of daily life. State criminal codes and state and local law enforcement agencies make up the bulk of the criminal justice system. It is up to governors, county supervisors, and mayors to protect the citizens in their jurisdictions. Many of the nation's critical infrastructures and key assets are either controlled by state and local governments (such as airports and ports) or regulated by them (like building codes governing skyscrapers and utilities).

STATE AND LOCAL PLANNING

After 9/11, many states created homeland security offices; most have developed specific homeland security plans. This model has been followed by local jurisdictions such as counties and cities. Because there are far more state and local first responders than federal ones, these state and local plans, and more specific operational and enforcement strategies, direct the majority of America's domestic counterterrorism activities. The federal government has attempted to coordinate state and local planning, including through the DHS which provides billions of dollars in funding—along with training, planning, exercise, and technical assistance programs—to state and local jurisdictions. In order to gain this support, states must develop and submit homeland security assessments and strategies. For example, the Commonwealth of Massachusetts developed a plan based on intelligence and warning;

transportation security; domestic counterterrorism; protecting critical infrastructures and key assets; defending against catastrophic threats (WMD); and emergency preparedness and response.[2]

While they vary from jurisdiction to jurisdiction, state and local strategies include many common elements. They are driven by requirements, plans, training, assessments and evaluations, and corrective actions. They often include prevention, protection, response, and recovery components and an emphasis on coordination, communication, and interoperability among jurisdictions.

Resources and Deployment

In the past, most state and local jurisdictions did not have substantial counterterrorism budgets. So in order to improve their security, they must reallocate existing resources and/or find new ones. This has proven extremely challenging, especially due to budget shortfalls that have hit many states over recent years.

This effort has often involved creating and equipping new security units and upgrading the capabilities of old ones. In some cases, they have been funded by federal grants; in others, existing functions have been reduced in order to support new security requirements. Some jurisdictions have also refocused the efforts of current programs. For example, intelligence units that once focused on a wide variety of organized crime now spend more time on terrorism. Or motor vehicle departments devote more resources to preventing applicants from falsely obtaining driver's licenses.

In some cases state and local resources are supplemented by federal grants. With the creation of the Department of Homeland Security an effort was made to consolidate most federal assistance involving domestic security in the new department under the Office of State and Local Government Coordination and Preparedness. Included in these grants are programs formerly administered by the Department of Justice to provide training and equipment assistance to state and local law enforcement for domestic counterterrorism operations.

Legal Preparation

States have also moved to increase the focus of their criminal justice and legal systems on terrorism. In the wake of 9/11, for example, New York, Pennsylvania, Virginia, and several other states enacted additional statutes to define terrorist crimes and provide enhanced law enforcement investigative authorities. Furthermore, legislation provided additional penalties for terrorist acts. The New York law, for example, allows for the death penalty in the case of murder committed during the commission of a terrorist act. In some cases, states have passed new laws to toughen regulations on gun and explosives possession.[3] Additional legal measures included establishing standards for action against suspected terrorists under existing laws such as conspiracy statutes.

Planning, Coordination, and Information Sharing

In the wake of 9/11, local officials have stepped up their coordination and information sharing with other government organizations. This includes sharing among different agencies in the same jurisdiction (i.e., police with fire department with private sector in the same city); different jurisdictions within the state (i.e., cities with counties with state); different states within a region (i.e., New York and New Jersey); and states with the federal government.

FBI's Joint Terrorism Task Forces

The lead federal agency for coordinating counterterrorism activities is the FBI. The FBI's Joint Terrorism Task Forces (JTTFs) represent one example of how activities at all levels of government can be integrated. The JTTFs bring together state and local law enforcement officers, FBI agents, and representatives from other federal agencies to work on common terrorist cases. They also provide a forum for intelligence sharing and coordination. As of 2004, more than 2,300 personnel were assigned to JTTFs at each of the FBI's 56 main field offices and 10 other locations.[4] A typical JTTF will include two divisions, one for intelligence collection and analysis and another for investigations.

Statewide Intelligence Offices

The JTTFs are not the only instruments for statewide coordination. Some states have established statewide intelligence offices. Others employ designated state homeland security offices to dispense information. Additionally a number of states have established regional state domestic counterterrorism task forces that mirror the federal JTTF. In other cases, such as Florida, local domestic counterterrorism task forces have been collocated or even integrated with the federal task forces.

Federal Data

State and local enforcement agencies can also obtain information from federal sources through database and federal coordination centers. The Department of Homeland Security, for example, distributes information to the major cities and state homeland security offices through its Homeland Security Operations Center. Most of this information deals with day-to-day activities. For information that might be directly relevant to a particular investigation, law enforcement services can query the National Criminal Investigation Center (NCIC). The NCIC is a computerized index of criminal justice information that is maintained by the FBI and available to federal, state, and local law enforcement and other criminal justice agencies. The database includes the agency's Interstate Identification Index (criminal history information); Wanted Persons File; Missing Persons File; Unidentified Persons File (to cross-reference unidentified bodies against records in the Missing Persons File); Foreign Fugitive File; and Violent Gang/Terrorist File (used to identify criminal gangs and their members to local, state, and federal law enforcement). The database also includes the U.S. Secret Service (now part of the Department of Homeland Security) Protective File, which maintains names and other information on individuals who are believed to pose a threat to the president. The law requires the agency to share information in the Interstate Identification Index and the Wanted Persons File as well as other files as agreed to by the attorney general and the FBI.

Federal Centers

In addition to the NCIC there are a number of other federal assets available to state and local governments. The El Paso Intelligence Center (EPIC), staffed by 14 federal agencies, has cooperative information-sharing agreements with every state on information regarding drug movement and immigration violations, data that might also be useful for related counterterrorism investigations. The Terrorist Screening Center is a one-stop point of contact for law enforcement agencies that can query all federal terrorist watch lists. The Department of Homeland Security's Law Enforcement Support Center provides immigration status and identity information to local, state, and federal law enforcement agencies on aliens suspected, arrested, or convicted of criminal activity.

Movement to Greater Dissemination

Today, many of these services are accessed by phone, fax, and e-mail. There are plans, however, to use information technology to create more Web-based, interactive, and collaborative services. Released in May 2004, the Department of Justice's *National Criminal Intelligence Sharing Plan* calls for developing a strategy to share information on a routine basis. Initiatives include creating an FBI Intelligence Web page as part of Law Enforcement Online to make information available at the unclassified level for FBI partners in state and local law enforcement. The FBI has also established a field intelligence group (FIG) in each FBI field office. The FIGs are the bridge that joins national intelligence with regional and local intelligence information through entities like the JTTFs. Meanwhile, the department is exploring how new technologies can be used to enhance information sharing.

Current Information-Sharing Systems

The Joint Regional Information Exchange System (JRIES) began in December 2002 as a pilot program to share counterterrorism information between state and local law enforcement and the Department of Defense. It came out of the Defense Intelligence Agency–led Joint Intelligence Task Force—Combating Terrorism (JITF-CT). The first participants included the New York Police Department Counter Terrorism Bureau and the California Department of Justice Anti-Terrorism Information Center; the number of states, localities, and federal agencies participating in the network increased once the program became operational.

In February 2004, the DHS started the Homeland Security Information Network, with the goal of connecting all U.S. states, five territories, the District of Columbia, and 50 urban areas with the Homeland Security Operations Center (HSOC). The DHS has continued using the JRIES infrastructure, but has expanded both its capabilities and users. Instead of having law enforcement as its sole user group, the program is broadening its real-time homeland security information sharing.

JRIES uses a secure virtual private network with encrypted communications to connect the participants' databases over the Internet. The system has commercial off-the-shelf components and Web-based software for user access to databases, analysis applications, secure e-mail, and collaborative environments in real time. Currently, participants may exchange sensitive but unclassified information. DHS plans to upgrade network security to allow for the exchange of certain classified-level information in the near future. There are also plans to connect JRIES to the Regional Information Sharing System and the FBI's Law Enforcement Online (LEO) Network.

The Regional Information Sharing System (RISS) Program comprises regional centers that share intelligence and coordinate efforts against criminals who may operate in multiple jurisdictions. The program supports prosecution of traditional crimes like drug trafficking, but also targets terrorism, violent crime, cybercrime, gang activity, and organized crime. There are member agencies in every state, Washington, DC, U.S. territories, and internationally. The program supplies information-sharing resources, analytical services, specialized equipment loans, training, and technical assistance.

The Department of Justice developed the RISS program in 1974 to assist police departments in the southern United States in exchanging information via computers. RISS has six regional centers: Mid Atlantic–Great Lakes Organized Crime Law Enforcement Network (MAGLOCLEN), Mid Atlantic Organized Crime Information Center (MOCIC), New England State Police Information Network (NESPIN), Rocky Mountain Information Network (RMIN), Regional Organized Crime Information Center (ROCIC), and the Western States Information Network (WSIN).

The primary information-sharing tool is RISSNET, a secure intranet, which allows members to share sensitive but unclassified information. Participants can have either a single computer attached to the intranet or act as a node to give access to more law enforcement personnel in that agency. RISSNET participants use a virtual private network (VPN) connection over the Internet to access the RISSNET gateway firewall, whereupon the user's identity is authenticated and access is granted to the secure intranet. The secure intranet is a dedicated network carried over frame relay circuits (a guaranteed amount of bandwidth carried over public telephone lines) connecting the RISS centers to the database resources. The data on the intranet are protected by encryption, smart cards, and other security protocols.

A recent addition is the RISS Anti-Terrorism Information Exchange (ATIX). This RISS subcomponent became operational in April 2003.

The ATIX communities differ from the typical RISS users; they include state, county, local, tribal, and federal government; law enforcement; emergency management; disaster relief; utilities; and, among others, the chemical, transportation, and telecommunication industries. The system includes secure ATIX Web pages, a bulletin board, a real-time communication tool, and e-mail. RISSNET is also connected to the FBI's LEO system.

Future Information-Sharing Systems

The Intelligence Reform and Terrorism Protection Act of 2004, commonly known as 9/11 Reform Bill, mandated that the president establish an information-sharing environment (ISE) to distribute intelligence regarding terrorism to appropriate federal, state, local, and private entities. Section 1016 of the law requires designating an organizational and management structure to establish and maintain the ISE and report back to Congress within one year on the plans for implementation. The law also called for creating an Information Sharing Council to advise the president and the ISE program manager on developing policies, procedures, guidelines, roles, and standards for establishing and maintaining the ISE.

Training and Equipment

Many jurisdictions have conducted special basic counterterrorism and response training; some have even added it to basic in-service training programs. While the federal government has been slow in promulgating training standards and best practices, it has provided significant financial support for local training efforts, along with courses and curricula provided by residential training facilities such as the National Emergency Training Center (NETC). Local institutions such as community colleges have also begun offering counterterrorism training to first responders.

Federal grants have also provided state and local organizations with the ability to purchase new equipment. In many cases this has consisted of gear designed for WMD attacks, such as personal protective equipment (PPE), detection devices, and decontamination devices and supplies. A major national push to help agencies at all levels of government procure equipment and adopt procedures to allow interoperable radio communications remains at an early stage.

**Intelligence
Gathering and
Exploitation**

One area in which many local jurisdictions, and even the FBI, lagged before 9/11 was in the advanced use of intelligence to prevent and solve crimes. While some intelligence is available through the federal resources described earlier, state and local jurisdictions are now creating clearinghouses for information and intelligence, sometimes called "all source intelligence fusion centers."[5] Such centers fuse intelligence from different sources, such as informers or radio intercepts; different organizations, such as police departments and federal agencies; and different types, such as written reports and imagery.

The aim of these centers, which must be established only with careful reference to state and federal law, is to discern the capabilities and intents of terrorists. Long used by federal intelligence agencies and military units, the intelligence process involves collecting, analyzing, evaluating, storing, and disseminating intelligence.

Collecting and Analyzing Intelligence

In order to get the raw data needed for analysis, jurisdictions create specific "intelligence requirements" for officers and others in the field. Departments may use community policing techniques to drive collection, reaching out to citizens and private-sector groups. There is often a focus on creating a clear line from the collector in the field to the intelligence center; more sophisticated organizations also find ways to reward collectors for providing information, which may require little more than giving them feedback on its value.

Officers should also be trained on specific clues of terrorist activities. For example, an officer who knows that castor beans are used to create the deadly poison ricin might be able to tell an improvised biological weapons project from a meth lab. An agent who knows the commercially available components used in chemical weapons might report them more quickly if he or she saw them at a crowded stadium.

Officers can also use traditional methods to generate intelligence, such as using seat-belt and sobriety checkpoints. Such efforts may be increasingly effective as the federal government updates the NCIC, adding subjects of terrorism investigations.[6]

Targeting scams used by terrorist fund-raisers is an excellent intelligence-gathering tactic for state and local authorities and is discussed subsequently. Some agencies also harness their own management systems for intelligence. For example, the theft of police uniforms or emergency vehicles could be key information.

Finally, state and local authorities, often working with federal officials, may use advanced sensing and surveillance equipment to gather intelligence.

Once the intelligence is collected, it may be graded for reliability and other factors. Then it must be analyzed through techniques such as spatial, association, and temporal charting; link analysis; and financial analysis.

Dissemination and Warnings

Once the data are received, analyzed, and turned into "intelligence products" such as reports and warnings, the information must be disseminated. This is a critical step in the process; ineffective information-sharing procedures and networks can waste even the best intelligence. For security reasons, the sharing of intelligence is typically done on a need-to-know basis, in which personnel receive only the intelligence they need to know to perform their assignments. Agencies may try to produce their reports with a *tear line*, the place at which more sensitive information—such as the sources and methods used to obtain the information—ends and the less sensitive information begins. In this way, it is easier to provide a wider audience with the report by simply providing them with the data "below the tear line."

Jurisdictions also develop an understanding of indications and warnings (I&W), red flags that signal the potential for an imminent attack. These red flags should trigger a planned response from the jurisdiction. For example, if police officers spot a suspicious person surveilling a chemical plant a week after explosives have been stolen from the local quarry, the plan should be set to respond with an automatic increase in security levels, which might include warnings to key members of the private sector.

Disrupting and Interdicting Terrorism

The most effective way for state and local authorities to prevent terrorism is to understand terrorist phases and operations and direct specific efforts at them. As discussed earlier, key terrorist support activities include recruitment and indoctrination; fund-raising; network building; training; logistics/supply/communication; and propaganda and psychological operations. Operational phases consist of target selection; intelligence, surveillance, and reconnaissance activities; operational planning of the attack; recruitment of specialized personnel; surveillance on the target; countersurveillance to ensure the plotters have not been detected; rehearsals/dry runs; training for specific elements of the attack; movement to the attack; the attack itself; escape/exfiltration from the site; exploitation of the attack through propaganda or intelligence techniques; and after-action reviews.

A strong counterterrorism strategy addresses countermeasures to all these phases and operations, plus creates target countermeasures based on likely terrorist tactics. For example, officer survival training should include scenarios based on the different threats posed by terrorists during varying phases of their operations. When some of 9/11 hijackers were stopped for traffic violations during their training and rehearsal stages, they did not resist. However, had they been pulled over on their way to the airport on September 11, their reaction might have been quite different.

Terrorists and their supporters in the United States may be especially vulnerable to detection during certain of these phases and operations, including surveillance and fund-raising.

Countersurveillance

Every jurisdiction has more critical facilities than could ever be protected all at once; the best way to prioritize is by letting the terrorists identify which potential target is most important. Al-Qaida and other terrorist groups have a record of meticulous surveillance of the targets; according to the FBI, terrorists may prepare "targeting packages" using photographs, CAD/CAM (computer-assisted design/computer-assisted mapping) software, and notes. They gather information from vehicles or by loitering near targets, perhaps in the guise of tourists or vendors. Jurisdictions with aggressive countersurveillance programs are in a position to detect such activities. Countersurveillance can include undercover observation and technical equipment such as cameras. Encouraging private security personnel and the public to watch for surveillance increases the chances of detecting it before an attack.

Fund-Raising and Organized Crime

As discussed earlier, the FBI has stated that operatives from such terrorist groups as Hizballah, HAMAS, and the PIJ are conducting fund-raising and support activities in the United States. Terrorist groups must have money to operate. Their funding sources can include fake charities, counterfeit apparel, robberies, blackmail, kidnapping for ransom, legitimate businesses, support from high-net-worth individuals, and money from foreign governments. Operatives linked to al-Qaida in the United States have also been linked to shoplifting, stealing luggage, picking pockets, and credit card fraud. However, organized crime and scams, often combined with money laundering, are key activities linked to terrorist supporters. In 2002, more than 500 Arab- and Muslim-owned small businesses across the United States, many of them convenience stores, were reportedly under investigation to determine if they were involved in such activities.[7] Terrorist supporters in the United States are accused of employing a range of criminal activities to raise funds.

Baby Formula Diversion. Texas authorities have estimated that criminal rings steal millions of dollars of formula per year in that state alone. Scammers exchange the formula for federal vouchers provided to poor mothers. The customer and baby may end up with improperly stored and outdated formula; the criminals get a hefty profit that, according to investigators, has sometimes been shipped to shadowy bank accounts in the Middle East. In 2003, Arizona's Joint Terrorism Task Force brought charges in connection with a baby formula case and related criminal activity estimated to have generated $22 million.[8]

Drugs. Arab-American criminal groups active in New York, Michigan, and Canada were implicated in a huge federal investigation called Operation Mountain Express. According to prosecutors, the group arranged for pseudoephedrine to be trucked from Canada into the United States, where it was sold to Mexican gangs who used it to create methamphetamine. The scheme made millions, some of it traced to Hizballah accounts.[9]

Coupon Fraud. Those tiny coupons can add up to millions of dollars in fraud. In the typical case, crooks clip coupons and deliver them to store employees with whom they are in cahoots. The employees redeem the coupons without selling the products. Coupon fraud has been connected to terrorism in several cases according to congressional testimony and news reports. Mahmud Abouhalima, an Islamic extremist also known as Mahmud the Red for his hair, allegedly ran a coupon scam before being arrested and convicted in the 1993 World Trade Center bombing.[10]

Cigarette Smuggling. A federal investigation called Operation Smokescreen, uncovered a group of Lebanese men who had entered the United States with illegal visas, engaged in marriage fraud to remain in the country, and engaged in organized crime, including credit card fraud and money laundering. They sold millions of dollars in smuggled cigarettes, bought in North Carolina where taxes were low and resold in Michigan at a hefty markup. Part of the proceeds was sent to Hizballah, and the plot also helped supply the terrorist group with laser range finders, night vision devices, stun guns, mine detection equipment, and other devices. The ringleader was sentenced in 2003, but several charged suspects, including the alleged chief of Hizballah procurement, escaped apprehension.[11]

ISSUE:

PREVENTING TERRORISM WHILE PROTECTING CIVIL LIBERTIES

The driving principle of domestic counterterrorism is to stop terrorism before it occurs. That requires good intelligence. But it's also critical that best practices be used to control how intelligence is collected, safeguarded, and employed. Civil libertarians and privacy advocates have raised serious concerns about domestic intelligence collection at the federal level, concerns that will certainly arise more and more frequently at the state and local levels. For example, by 2004 controversy over the federally supported MATRIX (Multistate Anti-Terrorism Information Exchange) database and information-sharing system had lead some states to drop out of the program. Other types of initiatives, including the installation of surveillance cameras and targeted law enforcement crackdowns on scams, have also drawn criticism.

Ethnic and religious profiling is another concern raised by aggressive intelligence collection. Not all terrorists are from Islamic extremist groups; as discussed earlier, many of the most dangerous extremists in the United States are members of domestic groups. While Islamic terrorists and their supporters are Muslims, the vast

---

majority of Americans who follow the Islamic faith has nothing to do with terrorism or its supporters. In addition, contrary to stereotypes about Arab terrorists, al-Qaida operatives and their supporters have included those with European, Asian, Hispanic, and African-American backgrounds. Muslim-Americans and Arab-Americans have expressed significant concerns about law enforcement and domestic intelligence-gathering activities many believe are disproportionately aimed at their communities. They point out that members of the Arab, Muslim, Sikh, and South-Asian community were not only victims of the 9/11 attacks themselves, but all too often endured vicious discrimination, public hostility, and bias crimes afterwards. By early 2004, the federal government had investigated 546 alleged hate crimes against these groups since 9/11, including not only personal attacks, but plots to bomb locations where Muslim-Americans gather.[12]

1. How should state and local jurisdictions meet the need to gather terrorism intelligence with the requirement to protect the civil rights of their citizens?

2. What types of data should state and local agencies be able to store in their data fusion centers? For how long? With what safeguards?

3. What policies should be in place to prevent racial, religious, and ethnic profiling?

4. How might state and local agencies use prevention policies to increase cooperation in local communities?

Document Fraud

Terrorists and other criminals often travel with fake or illegitimate documents. Detecting such documents, or uncovering their sources, can help uncover terrorist activity. The tools and skills required to reveal fake documents need not be complex. First, investigators must know what real ones look like; important types are birth certificates, Social Security cards, driver's licenses, INS documents (especially I-551s, or "green cards," and I-94s, or arrival/departure records), State

Department documents (U.S. passports and visas), and foreign passports. Then, by using magnifying glasses, officers can check pertinent documents for microlines, the tiny print found on Social Security cards, passports, and many driver's licenses. Because microlines require sophisticated printing, they are difficult for most criminals to counterfeit. The same is true for the images on many documents that can only be detected under ultraviolet lights.

Many of the 9/11 hijackers used legitimate documents, such as Virginia driver's licenses, they had obtained through the use of fraud. Government investigators believe they employed the licenses to board their flights in order to avoid suspicions raised by showing a foreign passport.[13] Terrorists may use bogus IDs such as fake birth certificates—known as breeder documents—to obtain real documents. In this case, careful examination and questioning can expose the subterfuge. In some cases, criminals have actually traveled with identification under multiple names, a dead give-away if detected. Investigators can ask suspicious people for multiple forms of identification, checking data from one against the other, asking questions and "peeling back the onion" to trip up even trained terrorists.

Target Hardening   A common and effective countermeasure is target hardening, which often focuses on high-risk and high-consequence structures such as bridges, tunnels, and stadiums. Facilities holding potential biological and radioactive weapons material, which exist at many universities, are also priorities.

Jurisdictions may employ the Crime Prevention through Environment Design (CPTED) principles at such locations. These include access control and surveillance, along with encouragement of "territoriality," or a sense of ownership and protectiveness, among citizens involved with the facility. Specific countermeasures often include obstacles to keep trucks from potential targets, security cameras, police and security presence, random inspections of vehicles, and searches of people.

The deterrent effect of target hardening is clear; for example, convicted al-Qaida operative Iyman Faris allegedly sent a message to the group's leadership that the "the weather is too hot," indicating security was too tight for a planned attack on the Brooklyn Bridge.[14]

FROM THE SOURCE:

WASHINGTON STATE'S TERRORISM PREVENTION PLAN

Excerpted from the Washington Statewide Homeland Security Plan

Objectives and Strategies

3.1   Develop and implement terrorism monitoring, threat assessment, and information sharing systems.

3.1.1 Partner regionally and nationally to develop and implement effective systems for terrorist threat monitoring and surveillance.

3.1.2 Define the essential elements of critical homeland security information.

3.1.3 Establish a system for dissemination of all relevant terrorism data and information to ensure reliable capability to alert officials and emergency response personnel of terrorist threats statewide.

3.1.4 Establish a statewide prevention information, analysis, and intelligence sharing and infrastructure protection capability.

3.1.5 Integrate daily use systems used in emergency response coordination into the information collection and dissemination system.

3.1.6 Create a central antiterrorism intelligence and analytical center [(Washington Joint Analytical Center—(WAJAC)].

3.1.7 Establish one additional regional intelligence group; strengthen capacities and capabilities of existing groups.

3.2   Coordinate statewide for prevention plans, assessments, procedures, infrastructure protection, and funding priorities.

3.2.1 Use the state homeland security structure to coordinate and facilitate the building prevention capacity.

3.3   Adopt or develop an apppropriate analytical "risk management" model to assess risk or vulnerability and identify methods to reduce risk.

3.3.1 Establish threat reduction "anti-terrorism" activities, assist and educate the private sector.

3.4   Improve threat recognition to halt the development of a terrorist threat before it is executed.

3.4.1 Create a system to regional system capability that consists of a full computerized file system that is integrated between regions; system capability should include analytical software and GIS imagery with law enforcement database sharing to collect, screen, and store relevant information with prevention investigative value.

3.4.2 Map threats and capabilities for preemptive action.

3.4.3 Explore the use of remotely sensed Geographic Information Systems (GIS) data in the effort to map statewide threats.

3.4.4 Establish a public and private community based pre-incident "threat indicator" training program.

3.5   Improve the northern border area security.

3.5.1 Define roles and responsibilities and work on actions to improve the northern border area security.

RESPONSE

If prevention fails, state and local law enforcement will be called to the scene. This can include tactical responses to suspected terrorists and terrorist attacks. Specialized units such as SWAT teams must be prepared to engage terrorists, but as discussed earlier, street officers also need a basic awareness of terrorist tactics. For example, domestic and international terrorists are known to use ambushes as a tactic. But many, perhaps most, police officers have not been trained to respond to a vehicular ambush, in which the natural reaction of many people may play right into the hands of the attacker.

More attention has been paid to training for WMD scenes. While similar in some ways to the HAZMAT (hazardous materials) disasters for which fire departments, emergency management agencies, and emergency medical technicians have traditionally prepared, WMD attacks present dramatic new challenges to state and local law enforcement. Not only do they need detection capabilities, protective equipment, decontamination equipment, and the plans and training to use them, but they must also be prepared to enter scenes in which criminal evidence, secondary explosive devices and booby traps, and even resisting terrorists may be found. The capabilities now recommended for law enforcement officers have stretched the resources of many jurisdictions.[15]

Recognizing an Attack

First, law enforcement must be able to identify a WMD attack. This can be challenging given the range of potential WMD attacks and the general confusion of most emergency situations. In some cases, terrorist violence may not be initially suspected. Responders—equipped with handheld detection devices and/or decision support software in more advanced jurisdictions—must recognize "signs and symptoms" or "indicators and effects" quickly or face the prospect of becoming victims themselves.

Following Self-Protection and Protection Measures

Once a WMD attack has been confirmed, officers must take action to protect themselves and those on the scene. This may require donning PPE, which if done improperly can lead to contamination and if done correctly causes an immediate decrease in mobility, visibility, and effectiveness.

An important step is to identify the *hot zone*, where the greatest danger exists; the *cold zone,* a safe area often downwind and downgrade where the weapon is not present; and the *warm zone,* where decontamination can occur.

Reporting Incident and Initiating Command Systems

Communicating the existence of a WMD attack as rapidly as possible is critical to successful response. Responders must know how to communicate, what to communicate, and to whom to communicate. They must also understand the procedures for establishing incident command (see Chapter 14).

Securing and Controlling the Scene

The nature of WMD attacks, including the potential of continued lethality and dispersion of agents to other locations, demands immediate and tight control of the scene. Law enforcement personnel need to establish perimeters, command posts, staging areas, medical monitoring stations, and isolation zones. They must also establish an immediate and effective media management operation.

Protecting Responders

While all this is going on, those on the scene may need to address other components of the attack, such as *secondary devices*, bombs timed to go off after responders gather at the scene.

Protecting the Crime Scene

In order to allow investigation and prosecution of the terrorists, plus preserve valuable intelligence information, responders must be able to recognize, protect, and collect evidence—from footprints to weapons containers—to the greatest extent possible while saving lives and preserving public safety and order.

Officials must be prepared with detailed plans to initiate "shelter in place" orders or evacuations. Aside from the normal emergency management component of such decisions, officials must be prepared to deal with crowds or disobedience of public safety directives.

Should a major nuclear, chemical, or biological attack occur, the challenge to public order may be significant and panic may pose the risk of additional loss of life.

After the Incident

While recovery is not typically considered part of counterterrorism, state and local officials will be required to address the health, economic, social, logistical, and other dimensions of an attack long after it occurs. This also includes critiques of their response to gain lessons learned that may help prevent or respond to future attacks.

CHAPTER SUMMARY

No longer can state and local officials leave the defense of their communities to the federal government. Their role in homeland security is now increasingly recognized by the federal government and the voting public. In many areas, officials are taking aggressive new measures to combat terrorism, especially by counterterrorism strategies. Their challenge is accomplishing this critical mission with limited resources, virtually unlimited vulnerabilities, and the need to protect the civil liberties of citizens while rooting out the terrorists who may be hiding among them.

CHAPTER QUIZ

1. Explain why state and local agencies have a key role in counterterrorism.
2. What is a data fusion center?
3. List two components of the risk management model.
4. Provide examples of organized crime activities linked to terrorism funding.
5. What are three skills law enforcement need at a WMD scene?

NOTES

1. Department of Homeland Security, "The DHS Strategic Plan—Securing Our Homeland" (February 24, 2004), www.dhs.gov/dhspublic/theme_home1.jsp.
2. Commonwealth of Massachusetts, "The Strategic Plan for Safeguarding the Commonwealth of Massachusetts against Terrorism and Related Threats" (December 2002), www.ifpa.org/pdf/mass-security.pdf.
3. National Conference of State Legislatures, "Protecting Democracy—The States Respond to Terrorism" (December 2001), www.ncsl.org/programs/press/2001/freedom/terrorism01.htm.
4. Federal Bureau of Investigation, "Federal Bureau of Investigation War on Terrorism: Partnerships," www.fbi.gov/terrorinfo/counterrorism/partnership.htm.
5. For best practices in law enforcement intelligence systems, see Department of Homeland Security, "The Office for Domestic Preparedness Guidelines for Homeland Security, Prevention and Deterrence" (June 2003), www.ojp.usdoj.gov/odp/docs/ODPPrev1.pdf.
6. *National Strategy for Homeland Security*," p. 26. While the *National Strategy for Homeland Security* (September 2002), p. xiii, reports the "United States spends roughly $100 billion per year on homeland security," the actual amount is open to debate. The cited estimate includes DHS agencies and federal, state, and local first responders and emergency services, but excludes most military spending. Private-sector estimates of total homeland security spending, which sometimes include international purchases of technology, range up to $138 billion a year. However, some far lower estimates focus on the increased spending due to the terrorist threat and exclude "normal" spending on law enforcement, fire fighting, and emergency services.

7. John Mintz and Douglas Farah, "Small Scams Probed for Terror Ties: Muslim, Arab Stores Monitored as Part of Post-Sept. 11 Inquiry," *The Washington Post* (August 12, 2002): A1.

8. Dennis Wagner. "Security, Rights Butting Heads," *The Arizona Republic* (September 14, 2003), www.azcentral.com/specials/special21/articles/0914terrorchase14.html.

9. Department of Justice, "President Bush Requests Substantial Funding Increases to Fight Illegal Drug Trafficking and Reduce Substance Abuse" (January 24, 2003), www.usdoj.gov/opa/pr/2003/January/03_ag_038.htm.

10. Rex A. Hudson, "The Sociology and Psychology of Terrorism: Who Becomes A Terrorist and Why?" A Report Prepared under an Interagency Agreement by The Federal Research Division, Library Of Congress, (September 1999), p. 77, www.fas.org/irp/threat/frd.html.

11. See, for example, Internal Revenue Service, "Other (IRS) Programs—Counterterrorism—FY 2003 Annual Business Report—Criminal Investigations (CI)," www.irs.gov/irs/article/0,,id=122539,00.html.

12. Department of Justice, Civil Rights Division, "Enforcement and Outreach Following the September 11 Terrorist Attacks" (February 18, 2004), www.stateline.org/stateline/?pa=issue&sa=showIssue&id=541.

13. Statement of Paul J. McNulty, United States Attorney, Eastern District of Virginia, before the Committee on the Judiciary, United States Senate (October 21, 2003), judiciary.senate.gov/testimony.cfm?id=965&wit_id=2742.

14. Department of Justice Press Release, "Lyman Faris Sentenced for Providing Material Support to Al Qaeda" (October 28, 2003), www.usdoj.gov/opa/pr/2003/October/03_crm_589.htm.

15. Office for Domestic Preparedness, "Emergency Responder Guidelines" (August 1, 2002), www.homelandone.com/docs/em-guidelines.pdf.

14

CRITICAL INFRASTRUCTURE PROTECTION AND KEY ASSETS

Protecting America's Most Important Targets

It is important to learn from the events of September 11. We now know that the symbols of our nation may be the targets of terrorist's plots.

Senator Arlen Spector

CHAPTER OVERVIEW

This chapter discusses the important roles of sector coordinating councils, information-sharing and analysis centers, and risk management in determining how to apply scarce resources to the challenges of protecting the nation's lifeblood—its vital economic and cultural centers. It also outlines the critical infrastructure sectors and key assets identified by the federal government. It addresses government and private-sector responsibilities, key concerns that have to be addressed, and ongoing initiatives to improve security.

CHAPTER LEARNING OBJECTIVES

After reading this chapter, you should be able to

1. Define critical infrastructure.

2. Describe the importance of information-sharing and analysis centers.

3. Understand the role of risk management in critical infrastructure protection.

4. Identify key concerns for protecting critical infrastructure.

5. Understand the roles and responsibilities for protecting critical infrastructure.

LIFEBLOOD OF THE U.S. ECONOMY

Concern over protecting the critical infrastructure of the United Stares from terrorists emerged long before the September 11 attacks. On May 22, 1998, President Bill Clinton issued Presidential Decision Directive (PDD) No. 63, which defined *critical infrastructure* as "those physical and cyber-based systems essential to the minimum operations of the economy and government." This set up a framework for organizing activities including establishing lead federal agencies to liaison with representatives of different private sectors; establishing interagency coordination on critical infrastructure matters; and assigning responsibility to federal agencies for protecting their own critical assets. Perhaps most importantly, the PDD reaffirmed the primacy of private-sector responsibilities for protecting commercial assets and established information-sharing and analysis centers (ISACs) for sharing information between the public and private sectors.

The September 11 attacks did much to expand the scope of national critical infrastructure protection initiatives. In some cases, specific acts were passed to immediately improve airline and maritime transportation security and strengthen the protection of the nation's food supply. In addition, national strategies specifically identified critical infrastructure and key asset protection as a critical mission area for homeland security. A directorate was also established within the Homeland Security Department with specific responsibilities for assessing the risks and vulnerabilities of national critical infrastructure.

FROM THE SOURCE:

PRESIDENTIAL DIRECTIVE

On December 17, 2004, President Bush issued HSPD 7, which established U.S. policy regarding critical infrastructure and key assets.

Excerpt from the Directive

Purpose

1. This directive establishes a national policy for Federal departments and agencies to identify and prioritize United States critical infrastructure and key resources and to protect them from terrorist attacks.

Background

2. Terrorists seek to destroy, incapacitate, or exploit critical infrastructure and key resources across the United States to threaten national security, cause mass casualties, weaken our economy, and damage public morale and confidence.

3. America's open and technologically complex society includes a wide array of critical infrastructure and key resources that are potential terrorist targets. The majority of these are owned and operated by the private sector and State or local governments. These critical infrastructures and key resources are both physical and cyber-based and span all sectors of the economy.

4. Critical infrastructure and key resources provide the essential services that underpin American society. The Nation possesses numerous key resources, whose exploitation or destruction by terrorists could cause catastrophic health effects or mass casualties comparable to those from the use of a weapon of mass destruction, or

could profoundly affect our national prestige and morale. In addition, there is critical infrastructure so vital that its incapacitation, exploitation, or destruction, through terrorist attack, could have a debilitating effect on security and economic well-being.

5. While it is not possible to protect or eliminate the vulnerability of all critical infrastructure and key resources throughout the country, strategic improvements in security can make it more difficult for attacks to succeed and can lessen the impact of attacks that may occur. In addition to strategic security enhancements, tactical security improvements can be rapidly implemented to deter, mitigate, or neutralize potential attacks.

MEANS FOR PROTECTING CRITICAL INFRASTRUCTURE

National efforts to ensure the protection of critical infrastructure and key assets against terrorist attacks center on coordinating public and private policies, sharing information, and risk-based planning. The cornerstone of these efforts is sector coordinating councils, information-sharing and analysis centers, and risk management.

Sector Coordinating Councils

These councils, which are to be established by representatives of the private sector, serve as the government's point of entry for coordinating infrastructure protection activities and issues. Sector coordinating council activities include efforts such as sectorwide planning, development of best practices, promulgation of programs and plans, development of requirements for effective information sharing, research and development, and cross-sector coordination.

Information-Sharing and Analysis Centers

Information-sharing and analysis centers (ISACs) are one of the primary means of promoting communications and threat warnings across public-private stakeholders. First called for in PDD 63 in May 1998, ISACs are voluntary organizations formed by various critical infrastructure sectors. Currently, 15 ISACs are in operation or in the process of being established. They include chemical, electricity, energy, emergency management and response, financial services, food, information technology, telecommunications, research and education, multistate government operations, public transit, surface transportation, highway, water, and real estate. (See Figure 14.1.)

The structure, operations, and level of activity among ISACs vary significantly. The basic ISAC model, however, usually finds the center managed and operated by a private organization. In many cases, an industry association has assumed responsibility for managing an ISAC or providing personnel and facilities to support its operations. The American Chemistry Council, for example operates the ISCA for its sector through CHEMTRAC, a 24-hour communications center run by the council to provide technical assistance for dealing with emergencies related to the distribution of chemicals. Some ISACs employ contractors to perform the day-to-day operations at their centers. The centers are funded through a variety of methods including association dues, fee-for-service, federal grants, and voluntary contributions. ISACs employ a variety of means for sharing information including Web sites, meetings and conferences, e-mails, faxes, and conference calls. Some ISACs maintain formal alert warning systems.

Risk Management

Many of the activities related to developing and implementing critical infrastructure protection measures are derived from employing risk management techniques. Risk management incorporates conducting threat and vulnerability assessments. These assessments identify potential security weaknesses and the likelihood that terrorists will exploit them. Based on this analysis, priorities are established for reducing risks by adopting measures to prevent, recover from, or mitigate the effects of a terrorist attack.

Effective strategies depend on careful cost-benefit analysis; there are not enough resources to waste money on programs that don't work or targets that do not merit protection.

Jurisdictions often attempt to prioritize through the use of risk management models. There is no commonly accepted risk-management methodology in either the government or the private sector. A common one, however, has five steps.

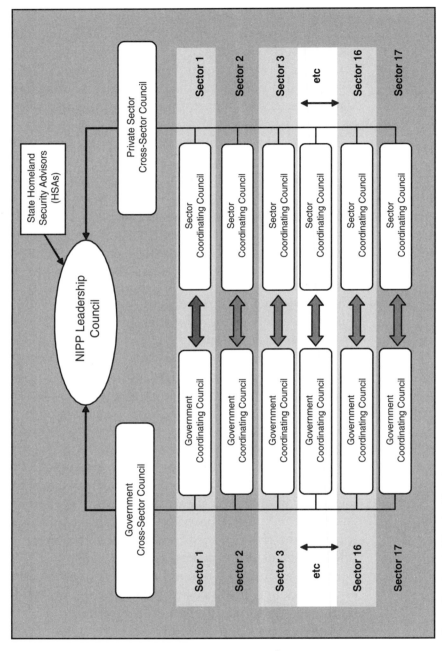

F I G U R E   1 4 . 1

National infrastructure protection plan, sector engagement framework

Source: Department of Homeland Security.

Asset Assessment

This step focuses on identifying the assets that are most valuable, those targets whose destruction would have the worst consequences. These potential targets might be people, facilities, or infrastructures—including computer networks. Consequences could include physical damage, such as the release of hazardous fumes from a destroyed chemical plant, or psychological, such as the assassination of a key leader or celebrity. Some jurisdictions use a "target value assessment" process to determine the damage that would be caused by the destruction of various assets.

Threat Assessment

This step entails determining who would want to attack certain targets and how these attacks might be undertaken. A good threat assessment includes analysis of the organization, its people, and its facility to assess whether any of these elements might be seen as social, cultural, or economic icons whose destruction would serve terrorist goals. The priority placed by the terrorists in attacking specific types of targets is also considered in this step. Analysis of terrorist strategies and intelligence on their planned activities is also a critical component of the threat assessment.

Vulnerability Assessment

During this process, planners determine security vulnerabilities in targets, trying to gauge how open they are to attack. Additionally, this assessment considers the likely consequences of a successful attack including potential casualties, physical destruction, and psychological consequences.

Risk Assessment

Combining and weighing the asset, threat, and vulnerability assessments produces a risk assessment. A target that has a high asset value, is threatened by terrorists, and is vulnerable merits protection.

Identification of Countermeasures

Once key potential targets are identified, planners can determine countermeasures to reduce the risks. Countermeasures should be evaluated for cost-effectiveness. These measures could be preemptive efforts to minimize threats, protection initiatives to lessen the danger of a successful strike, mitigation precautions to minimize disruptions or limit damage caused by an attack, and recovery efforts to ensure the rapid restoration of service after an attack.

TYPES OF CRITICAL INFRASTRUCTURE

U.S. critical infrastructure is defined by Homeland Security Presidential Directive 7.[1] The critical infrastructure of the United States is vast in scope and complexity including 2,800 power plants, 5,800 hospitals, 66,000 chemical plants, 120,000 miles of railroads, two million miles of pipeline, in addition to many other facilities. Critical infrastructure assets consist of people, physical assets, and information systems. Additionally, much of the national critical infrastructure is interdependent. In other words, the operation of one sector is dependent or related to the functioning of another. For example, the operations of many sectors depend on reliable energy supplies. In turn, power plants rely on transportation assets to deliver the fuel that drives the power plants.

Critical infrastructure assets are defined by three characteristics. The first is the production of essential goods and services. This includes sectors such as food and water production, public health, and emergency services. Also included in this category are sectors that sustain the U.S. economy including energy, transportation, and banking and financial services. A second category is assets that provide essential interconnectedness and operability among various sectors including information and telecommunications and postal services. Third, critical infrastructure also comprises sectors that are essential for public safety and security including public health, emergency services, the defense industrial base, and government.

Agriculture and Food

The agriculture and food sector includes the supply chains for feed, animals, and animal products; crop production and the supply chains for seed, fertilizer, and related materials; and the postharvesting components of the food supply from processing, production, and packaging through distribution to retail sales, food service, and home consumption.

Concerns

The greatest threat to the agricultural sector is disease and contamination of the food supply. Even without the threat of terrorism, food-borne disease causes on average 76 million illnesses each year, 325,000 hospitalizations, and 5,000 deaths, creating an economic cost that by some estimates ranges up to $32 billion.[2] Biological dangers can threaten plants and animals as well as people. Crop and livestock losses from contamination by mycotoxins (toxins produced by fungi) alone cost the United States on average $932 million. Humans can also be exposed to a range of deadly or debilitating toxins by ingesting contaminated plant and animal products, or less frequently by contact or inhalation.[3] Improper storage, poor sanitation, and cross-contamination during the production, transportation, processing, or storage of medicine, food supplies, or other consumables can further spread toxins or biological agents. For instance, in 1984, the Rajneeshee cult contaminated local salad bars in an Oregon town with salmonella, demonstrating the ease of conducting small-scale, indiscriminate terrorist attacks.[4]

Protecting the food supply from production to delivery in supermarkets and restaurants is an ongoing challenge. The responsibility for securing the food supply chain is divided among federal, state, and local authorities. The Public Health Security and Bioterrorism Preparedness and Response Act of 2002 called for a number of additional measures to strengthen protection of the food supply, including hiring additional inspectors, creating a registry of products manufactured abroad, increasing research and development, adding reporting requirements, and instituting new legal penalties and prohibitions.[5]

Initiatives

Planned enhancements include a complete review of risks in the agriculture and food sector by the DHS and the Department of Agriculture in conjunction with state and local governments and industry. Additionally, the Department of Agriculture is working on enhancing detection and testing capabilities and identifying incentives to encourage private-sector initiatives, as well as developing emergency response strategies specifically for the agricultural sector.

Water   The nation's critical water infrastructure includes systems for delivering fresh water and wastewater collection and management. Facilities that comprise these systems include reservoirs, wells, aquifers, treatment facilities, pumping stations, aqueducts, pipelines, storm water systems, and sewer lines.

Concerns

Concerns in this sector include the physical protection of assets including toxic chemicals used in water treatment, cyberattacks on the supervisory control and data acquisition (SCADA) systems that control water systems, disruption of services, and contamination of water supplies. Addressing all the possible means of threatening the U.S. water supply could be a serious fiscal challenge. Aging U.S. water systems could require over $500 billion in improvements, which if not provided, could leave them vulnerable to attack. Although contamination of water supplies attracts the most public concern, this threat is perhaps the least likely.

Initiatives

Currently, the Environmental Protection Agency and the DHS are jointly undertaking a national vulnerability and threat assessment of the water supply. This initiative includes identifying the highest-priority vulnerabilities and improving site security at high-threat locations and enhancing nationwide monitoring and sharing of information as well as integrating cross-sector response plans, particularly with the energy, chemical industry, and information and telecommunications sectors (see Figure 14.2).

Public Health   The public health sector consists of state and local health departments, hospitals, health clinics, mental health facilities, laboratories, mortuaries, pharmacies, and pharmaceutical stockpiles. The term *public health sector* is in part perhaps misleading. Significant portions of the public health sector are in private hands. For example, the overwhelming percentage of U.S. ambulance services is provided by commercial companies.

Concerns

Concerns in the public health sector are the protection of health facilities against physical attack, their great dependence on other critical infrastructure systems such as energy and information and

F I G U R E   1 4 . 2

FEDERAL GOVERNMENT ORGANIZATION
TO PROTECT CRITICAL INFRASTRUCTURE AND KEY ASSETS

President

Secretary of Homeland Security
Federal, state, local, and private sector coordination and integration
Comprehensive national infrastructure protection plan
Mapping threats to vulnerabilities and issuing warnings

Sector	Lead Agency
Agriculture	Department of Agriculture
Food: *Meat and poultry* *All other food products*	*Department of Agriculture* *Department of Health* * and Human Services*
Water	Environmental Protection Agency
Public Health	Department of Health and Human Services
Emergency Services	Department of Homeland Security
Government: *Continuity of government* *Continuity of operations*	*Department of Homeland Security* *All departments and agencies*
Defense Industrial Base	Department of Defense
Information and Telecommunications	Department of Homeland Security
Energy	Department of Energy
Transportation	Department of Homeland Security*
Banking and Finance	Department of the Treasury
Chemical Industry and Hazardous Materials	Environmental Protection Agency
Postal and Shipping	Department of Homeland Security
National Monuments and Icons	Department of the Interior

* Under the *Homeland Security Act of 2002*, the Transportation Security Administration, responsible for securing our Nation's transportation systems, will become part of the Department of Homeland Security. The new department will coordinate closely with the Department of Transportation, which will remain responsible for transportation safety.

telecommunications, and protection against spread of contamination from contaminated patients or health care workers. The control and protection of facilities may be the greatest challenge since medical centers are, by design, intended to be accessible.

Perhaps the greatest challenge in maintaining infrastructure over the long term will be the fiscal strains on the health care system. The advantages provided by any initiatives in public health preparedness could be overwhelmed by declines in the national health care structure driven by such factors as an increasingly aging population, the rising numbers of medically uninsured, and the cost of prescription drugs. The economic resources required to meet the nation's health needs are expected to rise from 14 to 16.8 percent of GDP by 2010.[6] Many states are already forecasting that future increases in Medicare and Medicaid costs could place an enormous strain on their budgets. Critical infrastructure will be of little use if the medical system lacks sufficient emergency medical technicians, doctors, nurses, and hospital facilities.[7]

Initiatives

Among the most vigorous ongoing initiatives being pursued are efforts to enhance the national capacity to respond to disasters—being able to quickly identify a crisis and surge response assets to meet critical medical challenges. Ongoing initiatives include efforts to enhance biomedical surveillance and communications capabilities, protecting emergency stockpiles of medical supplies, strengthening national disaster medical systems, and exploring options for providing incentives to the private sector to encourage improvement of the physical security of the medical infrastructure.

Emergency Services

Critical infrastructure supporting emergency services consists of fire, rescue, medical, and law enforcement organizations. These include both personnel and facilities. Emergency services are provided by federal, state, and local governments, as well as commercial firms and volunteer organizations.

Concerns

Among the greatest concerns for protecting emergency services is the potential for service providers or facilities to themselves become targets of terrorist attacks. One distinction between responding to deliberate attacks and responding to natural or technological disasters is that in order to exacerbate physical and psychological casualties, terrorists may deliberately target emergency response capabilities.

Terrorists could well use secondary devices specifically intended to harm first responders and civilian onlookers. Explosives are commonly used for this purpose, but other weapons might be employed as well.[8] Employing small amounts of various chemical, biological, toxin, or radiological agents in the ancillary strikes against first responders might further confuse a coordinated response.

Follow-on terrorist strikes may not be limited to the initial attack site. To complicate consequence management, attacks might be launched at hospitals, police stations, and emergency operations centers. Many state and city emergency operations centers are particularly vulnerable. Often, they lack physical security protection and redundant communications. Backup centers and mobile command posts usually do not exist.[9]

Another critical factor affecting the safety and capacity of emergency services to effectively respond at a disaster site is the state of interoperable communications. The lack of means to share information across the different systems used by responders has long been a barrier to effective interagency communications. In a typical metropolitan area, public safety agencies operate over frequencies ranging from VHF to UHF, 800 MHz, and low bands. It is not uncommon for responders from the same jurisdiction to have difficulty communicating at the scene of an incident or request neighboring jurisdictions to provide assistance.

Initiatives

Initiatives for strengthening the emergency service sector include developing programs to enhance interoperable and redundant communications networks and instituting a more robust national emergency preparedness exercise program to promote consistent protection planning and response protocols and encourage lesson learning and the sharing of best practices. Additionally, the DHS is strengthening mutual aid agreements among local communities so the communities can effectively share resources during a crisis.

Defense Industrial Base

Private-sector defense industries provide critical capabilities that are essential for the mobilization and deployment of military forces. These include manufacturing ammunition and equipment, as well as a range of support services.

Concerns

Market competition and consolidation have reduced or eliminated redundant sources for some critical products and services. In some cases, an individual vendor is the only supplier in the world capable of satisfying a unique requirement. In other cases, defense industries use so many subcontractors and suppliers that they are unable to map their supply chains and identify critical sources of supplies and services.

Protecting critical infrastructure that could be a bottleneck in the ability of the United States to project military power is a significant concern. As an example, the overwhelming bulk of American military power moves by ship. Most military supplies and hardware ship out from just 17 seaports. Only four of these ports are designated specifically for the shipment of arms, ammunition, and military units.[10] During the height of a foreign crisis, attacks could interfere with port operations and limit the access of combat forces to overseas theaters by preventing them from leaving the United States.

Initiatives

Coordination of defense industrial activities is largely the responsibility of the Department of Defense (with the exception that the Department of Energy is responsible for the security of infrastructure used in the production and maintenance of nuclear weapons). The Defense Department's main efforts center on including critical infrastructure protection requirements in contract processes; incorporating security concerns in defense-related commercial production and distribution processes; and improving information sharing between defense organizations and the private sector.

Telecommunications

This sector provides voice and data services through a complex public-private network comprising the Public Switch Telecommunications Network (PTSN), the Internet, and private enterprise networks. The PTSN includes a vast array of physical infrastructures including two billion miles of communications cables, 20,000 switches, access tandems, and other equipment, as well as cellular, microwave, and satellite technologies that provide access to mobile users. Internet service providers (ISPs) interconnect with the PTSN through points of presence (POPs), usually switches and routers. In addition, private enterprises have additional proprietary and leased telecommunication assets.[11]

Concerns

The challenge for telecommunications carriers is to balance the priorities of providing reliable service, cost, security, and privacy. One of the greatest difficulties is reaching a shared appreciation of acceptable risks among public and private stakeholders. Another concern is the cascading effects of attacks on communications systems, which might spread to other critical infrastructure sectors. For example, crippling telecommunications could greatly limit responders' capacities to effectively coordinate emergency services.

Terrorists, for example, might attempt to jam telecommunications systems to interfere with emergency service providers responding to a disaster. The technology for conducting electromagnetic jamming—the ability to interfere with radio, radar, television, and telecommunications signals—has been available for some time. Jamming is accomplished by broadcasting electromagnetic radiation on certain frequencies in order to create sufficient interference to prevent legitimate transmissions. It can also employ different tactics from intermittent jamming designed to make it appear that targeted systems are simply not operating properly or constant jamming to prevent the use of equipment altogether.[12]

Initiatives

Ongoing telecommunications sector initiatives include an effort by the DHS to map the overall national communications architecture, identify the most critical nodes, and then develop strategies to address security and reliability issues. Greater effort is also being made to coordinate with key allies and trading partners to address international communications issues.

Energy   The production and transmission of electricity, oil, and natural gas comprise the energy sector. The infrastructures in this sector includes production platforms, processing, and refining facilities; terminals and bulk storage stations; nuclear, coal, and oil-fired power plants;

and transmission, distribution, and control and communications systems. Pipelines, which might carry oil or natural gas are considered components of the transportation sector.

Concerns   Challenges in the energy sector center on its sprawling, complex, and interdependent infrastructure. The business configuration of the sector also presents obstacles to implementing security initiatives. Competition, structural changes, and regulatory regimes significantly affect the sectors capacity and requirements to upgrade security and complicate efforts to fix responsibilities and create incentives to improve security.

There are many assets in the energy sector that remain exposed to terrorist strikes. In some cases, disrupting a few critical nodes would have a significant effect on national energy production. For example, offshore oil platforms are especially vulnerable. Most of the oil extracted from the Gulf of Mexico is routed through a handful of offshore pumping stations. Bombing several key pumping stations could lead to serious economic disruption.[13]

Initiatives

Among the current national efforts to enhance the resilience of energy critical infrastructure is an effort by the DHS and the Department of Energy to inventory replacement and repair equipment and components and then identify means to speed restoration and recovery of services. There are also ongoing efforts to define consistent criteria for risk and vulnerability assessments and guidelines for physical security programs.

Transportation   This sector consists of all major national transportation nodes including aviation, maritime traffic, rail, pipelines, highways, trucking and busing, and public mass transit. Transportation assets are among the most diverse and robust of all the critical infrastructure sectors.

Concerns

Despite the vast capabilities of the transportation sector significant concerns remain. Many critical sectors are dependent upon the transportation sector, and disruptions can have a significant rippling effect throughout the economy. Moreover, al-Qaida has shown significant interest in attacking transportation assets. In addition to hijacking and attempting to blow up airplanes, its operatives have also explored attacking airports, bridges, tunnels, and railways.

Attacks against transportation assets could range from explosive devices, the most commonly used terrorist weapon, to new innovative threats. Of particular concern is the vulnerability of commercial aircraft to military shoulder-fired air defense weapons that might be obtained by terrorists.[14] No such attack in the United States has ever been confirmed.[15] However, shoulder-fired weapons have been used against commercial aircraft in other countries. In November 2002, for example, an airliner taking off from Monbasa, Kenya,was unsuccessfully fired on by terrorists with suspected links to al-Qaida.[16] Figures for how many attacks have been conducted vary, but there have likely been dozens of attempted attacks (mostly in areas of ongoing armed conflict), including successful strikes that claimed several hundred lives. For years, official studies of airline vulnerabilities have recognized that these weapons could pose a serious threat to U.S. aircraft.[17]

Initiatives

Major national programs in the transportation sector have been tailored to meet the unique needs of various nodes. New security initiatives in aviation center on implementation of the congressional legislation and researching options for protecting commercial airliners from shoulder-fired missiles. Similarly, the emphasis for improving maritime security has been on meeting the requirements established in post-9/11 legislation. Efforts in rail and mass transit security have centered on establishing national security practice standards. Likewise, developing standard protocols, practices, and guidelines has been the major focus in improving security for other forms of public transport. Research and development of new technologies for screening containers, baggage, and passengers has also been a priority.

Banking and Finance

The banking and financial services sector comprises retail and wholesale banking operations, financial markets, regulatory institutions, and repositories of documents and financial assets. Of particular concern is infrastructure that supports electronic financial services including computers and telecommunications networks. Also considered vital are financial services employees with highly specialized skills.

Concerns

Disruptions in this sector not only have the potential to disrupt financial activities, but also inflict significant rippling effects across the nation and the world including shaking public confidence. The September 11 attacks, for example, resulted in the longest closure of stock markets since the 1930s. The strikes demonstrated the vulnerability of financial institutions to wide-scale disruption.[18]

Initiatives

Currently, the Department of the Treasury is leading a sectorwide risk review. In addition, the department, in conjunction with the DHS, has established a national working group to address the challenges arising from the financial sector's dependency on information and telecommunications systems.

Chemical Industry and Hazardous Material

The nation's chemical sector provides products that are vital to virtually every sector of economic activity. Chemical manufacturing includes producing everything from fertilizer to medicines. In fact, the chemical sector is perhaps the most diverse with respect to size, geographic dispersion, and range of commercial activities conducted by different companies.

Concerns

Enhancing security across such a diverse and complex infrastructure could be extraordinarily expensive. Many companies lack even minimal security measures. Where precautions have been taken in the past they were primarily concerned with safety and environmental issues and gave scant attention to the prospects of deliberate sabotage. At the same time, many components of the sector operate on very slim profit margins. As a result, no single security blueprint would likely be practical to address the appropriate measures that should or could be taken by all chemical facilities.

Of greatest concern within this sector is the potential for chemical releases that could endanger a large number of lives. The most likely dangerous agents that could be released would be either toxic chemicals or flammable substances. Of the two, toxic chemicals could be potentially the more dangerous since they tend to represent a greater downwind hazard. Anhydrous ammonia and chlorine are the most widely used industrial chemicals that might be the target of a sabotage effort. Both can represent substantial vapor hazards. For instance, most chlorine in the United States is transported in 90-ton railcars. The downwind hazard for a release from a railcar in an urban setting is 22.5 kilometers.[19] The gas plume could kill outright any exposed individual up to six kilometers away and inflict permanent lung damage on those further downwind.

On the other hand, while flammable substances present less of a vapor hazard, they can still represent a substantial danger. For example, in 1989, a massive release of isobutene, ethylene, hexane, and hydrogen from a Phillips 66 chemical plant in Houston ignited in a fireball that exploded with a force of 2.3 kilotons. The disaster killed 23 and injured 130, leaving $750 million in damage at the plant and hurling debris 9.5 kilometers into neighboring communities.[20]

Initiatives

The current authorities provided to the Environmental Protection Agency to oversee the chemical industry are probably inadequate to meet homeland security needs. Thus, new legislation in this area is likely. In the meantime, current initiatives focus on improving information sharing, particularly with regard to threats.

ISSUES:

WHIFF OF DANGER

One of the most controversial areas for improving security relates to chemical and hazardous material facilities. In 2003 Senators James Inhofe (R-OK) and Zell Miller (D-GA) introduced the Chemical Facilities Security Act of 2003. The Inhofe bill called for

- Requiring companies to conduct vulnerability assessments and security plans.
- Authorizing the secretary of homeland security to require plant owners and operators to revise their plans and assessments to ensure adequate safety and protection.
- Allowing other agencies, including the Environmental Protection Agency (EPA), to provide the DHS with technical support.

- Requiring the DHS to perform routine oversight of facilities to ensure compliance with the law.
- Authorizing the secretary of the DHS to petition the courts for injunction relief in cases where companies fail to comply, which in practice could temporarily shut down a facility.
- Allowing the secretary of the DHS to impose civil penalties of $50,000 a day for each day a violation occurs and administrative penalties of up to $250,000.

A competing bill, The Chemical Security Act, was introduced by Senator Jon Corzine (D-NJ). The Corzine bill would require the EPA and DHS to identify high-priority chemical plants and *develop regulations* to require these high-priority chemical plants to conduct vulnerability assessments and to implement response plans that include security improvements and safer technologies. Neither bill was approved during the legislative year.

- Do the two bills represent different approaches to protecting critical infrastructure? If so, how?
- Which bill is more consistent with current national strategies?
- Which bill offers a better approach to improving security?

Postal Services   The U.S. postal system services more that 137 million addresses nationwide. The supporting infrastructure comprises almost 750,000 personnel and tens of thousands of facilities. Disruption of mail service could have a significant effect on economic activity. It might also have significant psychological effects increasing anxiety and apprehension.

Concerns

Challenges in the postal services not only include ensuring reliable maintenance of service and providing security for facilities, but also protecting employees. The 2001 anthrax attacks that inadvertently contaminated and killed two postal workers underscored this concern. Numerous points of entry into the mail system and the fact that the postal service does not always maintain custody of mail throughout the delivery process complicates the task of preventing attacks like the anthrax letters. The postal service must also be concerned about ensuring that constitutional rights of U.S. citizens (such as the rights to privacy and free speech) are not abridged by security procedures.

Initiatives

The U.S. Postal Service has several ongoing initiatives to improve security. These efforts include improving emergency response plans, adopting new health-risk reduction measures, and adopting new technologies to screen, identify, decontaminate, and investigate suspicious mail.

Key Assets   In addition to establishing critical sectors of the U.S. economy that must be protected from terrorist attack, national strategies identified several categories of key assets, specific facilities of critical importance. These include national monuments and icons, nuclear power plants, dams, government facilities, and key commercial assets (such as high-rise office buildings). Key assets represent facilities of high strategic value (like the Pentagon) or economic importance (such as the New York Exchange). A successful attack on any of these assets could result in catastrophic damage (e.g., dams and nuclear power plants) or significantly impact national prestige, morale, and confidence.

As with other aspects of critical infrastructure, key assets belong to a polyglot of federal, state, local community, and private entities. Federal agencies are responsible for securing their own key assets. For example, the Department of the Interior has oversight of national monuments. In addition, lead federal agencies have been assigned responsibility for coordinating security activities for various categories of key assets. The Nuclear Regulatory Commission, for example, is responsible for overseeing the security of commercial nuclear power plants.

CHAPTER SUMMARY

Protecting critical infrastructure and key assets is vital to the security of the United States. While initiatives are ongoing to better secure key infrastructures from terrorist attacks, significant concerns remain in all areas. Since most critical infrastructures are in private hands, public-private cooperation is essential. Effective coordination of policies and practices through the sector coordinating councils and better communications through the ISACs are important parts of that effort. Risk management is also a critical tool for determining how to apply scarce resources to the challenge of protecting critical infrastructure.

CHAPTER QUIZ

1. How does the government determine what are critical infrastructure and key assets?
2. What do you think is the most significant vulnerability?
3. How should the balance of government and private-sector responsibilities be determined?
4. What is an ISAC, and how does it work?
5. Describe the steps in risk management.

NOTES

1. The Office of the President, HSPD-7, "Critical Infrastructure Identification, Prioritization, and Protection" (December 17, 2003), www.whitehouse.gov/news/releases/2003/12/20031217-5.html.

2. For an overview of the threat of biological agroterrorism see Anne Kohnen, "Responding to the Threat of Agroterrorism: Specific Recommendations for the United States Department of Agriculture," BCSIA Discussion Paper 2000-29, ESDP Discussion Paper ESDP-2000-04, John F. Kennedy School of Government, Harvard University (October 2000). Estimates for the cost of food-borne illness vary considerably based on what criteria are used. See Jean C. Buzby, et al., "Bacterial Foodborne Disease: Medical Costs and Productivity Losses," *Agricultural Economics* 741(August 1996), www.ers.usda.gov/publications/Aer741/index.htm.

3. John L. Richard, et al., *Mycotoxins: Risks in Plant, Animal, and Human Systems* (Ames, IA: Council for Agricultural Science and Technology, January 2003), pp. 10, 48–57.

4. Judith Miller, et al., *Germs: Biological Weapons and America's Secret War* (New York: Simon & Schuster, 2001), pp. 13–32. See also W. Seth Carus, "The Rajneeshees (1984)." *In Toxic Terror*, edited by Jonathan B. Tucker (Cambridge, MA: MIT Press, 2000), pp. 115–137.

5. For additional information see www.fda.gov/oc/bioterrorism/bioact.html.

6. Stephen Heffler, et al., "Trends: Health Spending Projections for 2001-2011: The Latest Outlook," *Health Affairs* 21/2 (March/April 2002), 130.94.25.113/1130_abstract_c.php?ID=http://130.94.25.113/Library/v21n2/s25.pdf.

7. A recent study by the Institute of Medicine found major deficiencies in the national health care system. These included outdated and vulnerable technologies; health work force lacking training and reinforcements; antiquated laboratory capacity; lack of real-time surveillance and epidemiological systems; ineffective and fragmented communications networks; incomplete domestic preparedness and emergency response capabilities; and communities without access to essential public health services. Institute of Medicine, *The Future of the Public's Health in the 21st Century* (Washington, DC: The National Academies Press, 2002), p. 3.

8. Paul M. Maniscalco and Hank T. Christen, *Understanding Terrorism and Managing the Consequences* (Upper Saddle River, NJ: Prentice Hall, 2002), p. 228.

9. Committee on Science and Technology for Countering Terrorism, *Making the Nation Safer: The Role of Science and Technology in Countering Terrorism* (Washington, DC: National Academy Press, 2002), pp. 8-2, 8-3.

10. For an overview of the military's reliance on ports and associated security risks, see U.S. General Accounting Office, "Combating Terrorism: Preliminary Observations on Weaknesses in Force Protection for DOD Deployments through Domestic Seaports," GAO-02-955TNI, July 23, 2002; Statement of William G. Schubert before the Subcommittee on National Security, Veterans Affairs, and International Relations, Senate Government Reform Committee, July 23, 2002, www.marad.dot.gov/Headlines/testimony/homesecurity.html. See also U.S. General Accounting Office, "Combating Terrorism: Actions Needed to Improve Force Protection for DOD Deployments through Domestic Seaports," GAO-03-15 (October 2002), pp. 5–10.

11. *National Strategy for the Physical Protection of Critical Infrastructure and Key Assets*, p. 47. http://www.whitehouse.gov/pcipb/physical.html

12. Naval Air Warfare Center, *Electronic Warfare and Radar Handbook*, ewhdbks.mugu.navy.mil/contents.htm.

13. Gary Hart, et al., *America Still Unprepared——Still in Danger* (New York: Council on Foreign Relations, 2002), p. 26.

14. Also prominently mentioned as a source of concern is the U.S. shoulder-launched "stinger" surface-to-air missile which has an effective range of about 5,500 meters. In the 1980s, the United States supplied up to 500 or more missiles to the Mujahedin to combat Soviet-occupation troops in Afghanistan. After the conflict, all the missiles were not accounted for and may have fallen into the hands of the Taliban, al-Qaida, or other terrorist groups or arms traders. Allegedly, a dozen of the missiles were obtained by Iran. The United States has had an active program to buy back these missiles where they are found. Nevertheless, it is likely that dozens are still unaccounted for. How much of a threat these missiles represent is questionable since any remaining weapons would be a decade old and are unlikely to have been well maintained. Given their wide availability, other missiles, such as the SA-7, represent much more likely threats.

15. There have been claims that the July 17, 1996, TWA crash was caused by a shoulder-fired missile, but the FBI found no forensic evidence to support this conclusion. Statement of Lewis D. Schiliro before the Subcommittee on Administrative Oversight and the Courts, Senate Judiciary Committee (May 10, 1999), www.fbi.gov/congress/congress99/twa800c.htm.

16. Richard Evans, "Authorities Make Arrest in Hunt for Kenyan Terrorists," *Jane's Intelligence Digest* (November 29, 2002), www.janes.com/regional_news/africa_middle_east/news/twr/twr021129_1_n.shtml.

17. See, for example, *White House Commission on Aviation Safety and Security: Final Report to the President* (February 12, 1997), api.hq.faa.gov/strategicgoals/docs/WHCrpt.html.

18. U.S. General Accounting Office, "Potential Terrorist Attacks: Additional Actions Needed to Better Prepare Critical Financial Market Participants,"GAO-03-414 (February 12, 2003), www.gao.gov/atext/d03414.txt.

19. James C. Belke, "Chemical Accident Risks in U.S. Industry—A Preliminary Analysis of Accident Risk Data from U.S. Hazardous Chemical Facilities," Environmental Protection Agency (September 25, 2000).

20. Jack Yates, *Phillips Petroleum Chemical Plant and Fire: Pasadena, TX* (October 23, 1989), U.S. Fire Administration, Report 035, p. 1.

15

INCIDENT MANAGEMENT AND EMERGENCY MANAGEMENT

Preparing for When Prevention Fails

We're in uncharted territory.

New York Mayor Rudolph Giuliani to
Police Commissioner Bernard Kerik
at the World Trade Center Site, September 11

CHAPTER OVERVIEW

This chapter outlines the roles and responsibilities of federal, state, local, and tribal agencies in responding to a terrorist attack. It addresses the all-hazards approach to planning for and responding to all kinds of disasters, including acts of terrorism. In particular, the chapter outlines the guidance provided in the National Response Plan and the National Incident Management System.

CHAPTER LEARNING OBJECTIVES

After reading this chapter, you should be able to

1. Understand the key concepts in the National Response Plan.
2. Define what is meant by an *all-hazards* approach.
3. Describe the incident management system.

4. Describe the principles and components of emergency management.

5. Understand future requirements for improving the national response system.

THINKING . . . AND EXPERIENCING THE UNTHINKABLE

On the morning of September 11, 2001, New York City was the most prepared city in the nation. City leaders had spent four years rewriting plans and revamping emergency response procedures. A swath of local, state, and federal representatives was invited to coordination meetings. The city's emergency planning office held drills and training exercises with high-ranking officials, including the mayor.[1] But it was not enough. On the day of the incident, lack of communications and coordination made it impossible to establish unified command at the scene. The city's Office of Emergency Management headquarters on the 23rd floor of 7 World Trade Center had to be evacuated. After the collapse of the South Tower, officials ordered responders to abandon the North Tower. Not everyone got the word. At least one police officer, five Port Authority police officers, and 121 firefighters died when the second tower collapsed.[2]

THE EMERGENCY RESPONSE CHALLENGE

The heroic, but flawed, response to the September 11 attacks; efforts in the wake of natural disasters; and recent major counterterrorist training exercises suggest there is already enough known about the homeland security challenge to conclude that the national response system in place before 9/11 was inadequate to deal with a large-scale terrorist threat. In each case, three major shortfalls consistently emerge in preventing, protecting against, and responding to large-scale disasters, which can, in part, be addressed through improved planning and management.[3]

Interagency Coordination

Operations are frequently plagued by a lack of information sharing and confusion over responsibilities among policy makers, law enforcement, emergency managers, first responders, public health workers, physicians, nonprofit organizations, and federal agencies. The necessity for speed can exacerbate the coordination challenge. Effectively negating threats in many cases requires a rapid response capability, and operating on compressed time lines leaves little room for miscues in coordination.[4] One significant requirement, for example, is quickly emplacing an incident response structure that can detect and assess threats and mobilize appropriate resources. In particular, for a chemical or biological attack, actions taken in the first hours to identify, contain, and treat victims may significantly reduce the scope of casualties. Major exercises, however, are frequently marred by potentially crippling flaws. For example, during TOPOFF I (which stands for top officials), the first of congressionally mandated "no-notice" exercises conducted to evaluate the federal response to a major strike, the Coast Guard asked for the assistance of the U.S. Marine Chemical and Biological Incident Response Forces (CBIRF). The Defense Department rejected the request, arguing that Federal Emergency Management Agency (FEMA), as lead response agency, was the only agency authorized to request department resources. This dispute delayed the CBIRF deployment by almost 24 hours.[5] Even determining which agency is in charge can be a major problem. A National Capital Region exercise conducted in Washington, DC, in conjunction with TOPOFF simulated the explosion of a radiological dispersion device. Initially, hours were lost in confusion over whether the Energy Department or the EPA should lead the response.[6]

Organization and Communication

Virtually every large-scale exercise or response experiences problems in agency notification; mobilization; information management; communication systems; and administrative and logistical support. Organizations have particular difficulty in optimizing flexibility and the capacity to decentralize operations and conduct rapid problem solving, often a key requirement for responding effectively to major disasters.[7] Significant organizational deficiencies, such as failing to provide redundant capabilities or alternative means for responding to a crisis, are frequently not discovered until the onset of a major operation. For example, when the New York City Emergency Operations Center was destroyed, the city had no adequate backup command and control capability available. It took three days to reconstitute all the functions and capabilities lost by the destruction of the emergency operations center.[8]

Convergence

Convergence is a phenomenon that occurs when people, goods, and services are spontaneously mobilized and sent into a disaster-stricken area.[9] Although convergence may have beneficial effects, like rushing resources to the scene of a crisis, it can also lead to congestion, put additional people at risk, create confusion, hinder the delivery of aid, compromise security, and waste scarce resources. This proved to be a major concern during the response to the September 11 attack on the World Trade Center. When the first tower was struck, firefighters, police officers, and emergency medical technicians from all over the metropolitan area streamed to the site, leaving other parts of the city vulnerable and, after the towers collapsed, creating tremendous problems in accounting for emergency personnel.

All these problems would be greatly exacerbated by the scale of a truly catastrophic attack requiring the mobilization of resources nationwide. Advanced planning, more funding, training, better communications systems, and operational experience can help address some of these challenges, but they alone are not sufficient preparation for catastrophic disasters. Welding resources and capabilities together requires an overall emergency management system.

MANAGEMENT OF DOMESTIC INCIDENTS

The U.S. system for dealing with the threat and aftermath of catastrophic disasters continues to evolve in the wake of the September 11 tragedies, but the basic framework of responsibilities remains unchanged from its pre-9/11 structure. Consistent with the dictates of federalism and the authorities in the U.S. Constitution the response for managing emergencies, including responding to terrorist threats, falls to local and state governments.[10] Federal authorities provide assistance at the direction of the president when dangers exceed the capacity of local officials to deal with the problems and state or territory officials request federal assistance. Only in extreme cases of national emergency, such as insurrection, loss of the continuity of government, or to enforce federal laws does the president have the authority to assume command of response activities.

Modifications to the national management of terrorist incidents and other disasters also builds on approaches and principles that have been in place for decades. The United States maintains a single system for dealing with all forms of hazards comprising standardized elements.

FROM THE SOURCE:

THE CHALLENGE OF COMMAND

HSPD 5, issued in February 2003, defines federal responsibilities for responding to a terrorist attack.

Excerpt from Homeland Security Presidential Directive 5

(4) The Secretary of Homeland Security is the principal Federal official for domestic incident management. Pursuant to the Homeland Security Act of 2002, the Secretary is responsible for coordinating Federal operations within the United States to prepare for, respond to, and recover from terrorist attacks, major disasters, and other emergencies. The Secretary shall coordinate the Federal Government's resources utilized in response to or recovery from terrorist attacks, major disasters, or other emergencies if and when any one of the following four conditions applies: (1) a Federal department or agency acting under its own authority has requested the assistance of the Secretary; (2) the resources of State and local authorities are overwhelmed and Federal assistance has been requested by the appropriate State and local authorities; (3) more than one Federal department or agency has become substantially involved in responding to the incident; or (4) the Secretary has been directed to

assume responsibility for managing the domestic incident by the President.

(5) Nothing in this directive alters, or impedes the ability to carry out, the authorities of Federal departments and agencies to perform their responsibilities under law. All Federal departments and agencies shall cooperate with the Secretary in the Secretary's domestic incident management role.

(6) The Federal Government recognizes the roles and responsibilities of State and local authorities in domestic incident management. Initial responsibility for managing domestic incidents generally falls on State and local authorities. The Federal Government will assist State and local authorities when their resources are overwhelmed, or when Federal interests are involved. The Secretary will coordinate with State and local governments to ensure adequate planning, equipment, training, and exercise activities. The Secretary will also provide assistance to State and local governments to develop all-hazards plans and capabilities, including those of greatest importance to the security of the United States, and will ensure that State, local, and Federal plans are compatible.

(7) The Federal Government recognizes the role that the private and nongovernmental sectors play in preventing, preparing for, responding to, and recovering from terrorist attacks, major disasters, and other emergencies. The Secretary will coordinate with the private and nongovernmental sectors to ensure adequate planning, equipment, training, and exercise activities and to promote partnerships to address incident management capabilities.

(8) The Attorney General has lead responsibility for criminal investigations of terrorist acts or terrorist threats by individuals or groups inside the United States, or directed at United States citizens or institutions abroad, where such acts are within the Federal criminal jurisdiction of the

United States, as well as for related intelligence collection activities within the United States, subject to the National Security Act of 1947 and other applicable law, Executive Order 12333, and Attorney General-approved procedures pursuant to that Executive Order. Generally acting through the Federal Bureau of Investigation, the Attorney General, in cooperation with other Federal departments and agencies engaged in activities to protect our national security, shall also coordinate the activities of the other members of the law enforcement community to detect, prevent, preempt, and disrupt terrorist attacks against the United States. Following a terrorist threat or an actual incident that falls within the criminal jurisdiction of the United States, the full capabilities of the United States shall be dedicated, consistent with United States law and with activities of other Federal departments and agencies to protect our national security, to assisting the Attorney General to identify the perpetrators and bring them to justice. The Attorney General and the Secretary shall establish appropriate relationships and mechanisms for cooperation and coordination between their two departments.

(9) Nothing in this directive impairs or otherwise affects the authority of the Secretary of Defense over the Department of Defense, including the chain of command for military forces from the President as Commander in Chief, to the Secretary of Defense, to the commander of military forces, or military command and control procedures. The Secretary of Defense shall provide military support to civil authorities for domestic incidents as directed by the President or when consistent with military readiness and appropriate under the circumstances and the law. The Secretary of Defense shall retain command of military forces providing civil support. The Secretary of Defense and the Secretary shall establish appropriate relationships and mechanisms for cooperation and coordination between their two departments.

(10) The Secretary of State has the responsibility, consistent with other United States Government activities to protect our national security, to coordinate international activities related to the prevention, preparation, response, and recovery from a domestic incident, and for the protection of United States citizens and United States interests overseas. The Secretary of State and the Secretary shall establish appropriate relationships and mechanisms for cooperation and coordination between their two departments.

THE ALL-HAZARDS APPROACH

The term *all hazards* includes concern for both natural disasters and technological or human-made incidents. Natural disasters include floods, hurricanes, tornadoes, and earthquakes, while human-made incidents include inadvertent accidents, such as an industrial accident, that result in an emergency situation, or deliberate acts, including terrorism.

There is some debate among emergency response experts on the best means for planning to respond to the breadth of emergencies that could threaten the lives and property of Americans. Some argue for a "specific hazards approach," developing unique plans, training, and equipment for responding to different kinds of disasters. They contend that a one-size-fits-all method may miss the crucial difference necessary for meeting different threats. For example, an earthquake and a nuclear bomb may both topple buildings and put streets to flame, but an earthquake will not present radiological hazards. Likewise, infectious disease and biological threats that are not contagious may require different responses since diseases may quickly spread beyond the initial victims of an attack.

Additionally, there are concerns an all-hazards approach may divert too many resources to one kind of threat. Some fear that all-hazards preparedness will be used as an excuse for state and local governments to supplement normal public safety resources with federal grants intended to strengthen antiterrorism measures. Others worry that obsessive concerns about terrorist threats could lead officials to neglect preparedness for more common dangers like fire and floods.

In contrast, an all-hazards approach argues that the initial response to all threats be based on a common framework because many events create similar dangers, though the cause of the incidents may vary. In short, they contend that the initial response in most cases will be the same. For example, regardless of the nature of the incident, officials will have to determine how to secure the area, actions that will be as important to protecting a potential crime scene (in the case of a terrorist attack) as they will be to ensuring the safety of victims, responders, and bystanders. Advocates of an all-hazards approach contend that it is the most efficient means for preparing to respond to multiple dangers and simplifies the challenge of coordinating an integrated response among multiple agencies at the local, state, and federal level.

FEMA has long supported an all-hazards approach to disaster management.[11] After the agency was integrated into the Department of Homeland Security, the department adopted the FEMA approach as a guide to structuring national response efforts. In the wake of the September 11 disasters, however, there was wide recognition that after the initial response to an incident, a capability was required to adjust the response and the resources available to the specific needs of each disaster. Thus, national planning now emphasizes an all-hazards approach, but continues to develop supporting plans and capabilities to respond to unique threats, particularly those that might result from a terrorist threat.

PRINCIPLES AND COMPONENTS OF EMERGENCY MANAGEMENT

There are four components to all-hazards disaster management. They include mitigation, preparedness, response, and recovery.

Mitigation   Mitigation involves adopting measures to reduce exposure and potential loss from hazardous events. Building guidelines and restrictions (such as zoning and building codes) are frequently used as mitigation techniques. Mitigation may also involve educating businesses and the public on measures they can take. In the case of preventing terrorism, mitigation measures might include educating the public on safety precautions and first-aid techniques.

Preparedness Preparedness includes activities undertaken before an event to ensure an effective response. These may involve hiring staff; conducting training, tests, and drills; stockpiling equipment; and establishing facilities, such as emergency operations centers. A key element of preparedness is the development of plans that link together all the aspects and resources committed to emergency management.

Response Response measures are the time-sensitive actions to save lives and property at the onset of an incident. They include issuing warnings, notifying emergency management personnel of the crisis, aiding victims, providing security and traffic control, assessing the extent of damage and estimating support needs, evacuating and sheltering affected populations, keeping people informed, and requesting help from outside the jurisdiction.

Recovery Recovery is the effort to restore infrastructure and the social and economic life of a community. In the short term, it may comprise establishing essential critical infrastructure such as power, communication, water and sewage, and public transportation. It may also include providing humanitarian assistance such as food and clothing. Long-term recovery involves restoring economic activity and rebuilding community facilities and family housing. This might involve emergency economic aid, consulting services, business loans, environmental monitoring, and mental health services such as treatment and counseling.

EMERGENCY MANAGEMENT SYSTEMS AND OPERATIONS

The current U.S. national response system is guided by Homeland Security Presidential Directive 5 (HSPD-5).[12] HSPD-5 required the establishment of a National Response Plan and a National Incident

Management System (NIMS). Under HSPD-5, the secretary of homeland security is the principal federal officer for domestic incident management, responsible for drafting, coordinating, and implementing the National Response Plan and the NIMS and coordinating federal operations within the United States to prepare, respond, and recover from terrorist attacks, major disasters, and other emergencies.

The National Response Plan

The National Response Plan replaces the Federal Response Plan. Originally developed in 1992, the Federal Response Plan was a cooperative agreement signed by 27 federal departments and agencies to detail a mechanism for the delivery of assistance to state and local governments overwhelmed by major disasters and other emergencies. The Federal Response Plan was later revised to include an annex for responding to terrorist attacks. The revised plan established two categories of emergency management—crisis management and consequence management. Crisis management included measures to anticipate, prevent, or resolve a threat or act of terrorism. It was considered predominantly a federal law enforcement responsibility with state and local law enforcement playing supporting roles. The Federal Bureau of Investigation was assigned primary responsibility for crisis management. Consequence management included measures to protect public health and safety, restore essential government services, and provide emergency relief for the consequences of terrorist acts. States had primary responsibility for consequence management with the federal government providing assistance. FEMA had responsibility for directing federal consequence management.

The Federal Response Plan was the subject of some controversy. It was not clear under the plan when federal responsibility for managing responses to terrorist incidents would shift from the FBI to FEMA. Another concern was whether the plan accounted for all the emergency response functions (ERFs) that might be required in support of a national emergency. Finally, the relationship between the Federal Response Plan and other national plans for dealing with emergencies such as the release of radiological material or hazardous material spills was unclear.

HSPD-5 directed that crisis and consequence management be treated as a single, integrated function rather than two separate activities. The plan's main purpose is to define the roles and responsibilities for supporting a domestic incident. In addition, the directive required the National Response Plan to establish protocols for different threats and threat levels, as well as incorporate existing federal emergency and incident management plans. It also called for the upgrading of ERFs to include public affairs, intergovernmental communications, and other necessary functions.

Drafting of a National Response Plan to replace the Federal Response Plan engendered more controversy. The initial draft of the plan was considered by many to be too cumbersome and complex. A second draft proved overly simplistic. The Department of Homeland Security then settled on a simple basic plan with supporting annexes, in effect making the National Response Plan an umbrella for a family of plans covering natural disasters, technological emergencies, and terrorist attacks including the U.S. Government Interagency Domestic Terrorism Concept of Operations Plan, the Federal Radiological Emergency Response Plan, Mass Migration Response Plan, and the National Oil and Hazardous Substances Pollution Contingency Plan.

While the National Response Plan was being finalized, the Department of Homeland Security released an Initial National Response Plan that superseded the Federal Response Plan. The Initial National Response Plan accounts for the role of the Department of Homeland Security in managing domestic incidents including the function of the Homeland Security Operations Center (HSOC), which now serves as the primary national center for operational communications and information. The HSOC includes provisions for an Interagency Incident Management Group (IIMG). The IIMG is made up of senior representatives from federal departments and agencies, nongovernmental organizations, and the DHS. It is their task to coordinate support for their organizations for national operations.

The National Response Plan also calls for the secretary of homeland security to establish a principal federal official (PFO). The PFO acts as the local DHS representative during an incident and will oversee and coordinate federal activities and work with local authorities to determine requirements and provide timely assistance. The PFO also directs the joint field office (JFO). Federal activities at a local incident site will be integrated with state and local authorities through a JFO. The JFO incorporates existing entities such as the joint operations center, the disaster field office, and other federal offices and teams that provide on-scene support.

While the Initial National Response Plan integrated all federal activities under the authority of the Department of Homeland Security, the attorney general retains lead responsibility for the criminal investigation of terrorist acts inside the United States.[13] Generally acting through the Federal Bureau of Investigation, the attorney general also retains responsibility for coordinating with other members of the law enforcement community. HSPD-5 requires the attorney general and the secretary of homeland security to establish appropriate mechanisms for coordination between their two departments.

The National Incident Management System

HSPD-5 also called for the development of the NIMS. Approved by the secretary for homeland security in March 2004, NIMS provides a framework for ensuring interoperability among federal, state, and local assets. It establishes procedures for managing operations, conducting training, and setting requirements, standard terminology, and common procedures. State and local governments must adopt the NIMS to receive federal preparedness assistance through grants, contracts, and other fund allocations.

The NIMS has six components: command and management, preparedness, resource management, communications and information management, supporting technologies, and ongoing management and maintenance.

Command and Management

The NIMS standardizes incident management for all hazards and across all levels of government. It provides detailed instructions on the organization and responsibilities and procedures for incident command systems (ICS), multiagency coordination systems, and public information systems.

First developed by U.S. fire departments, the ICS has become the principal means used by responders to direct field operations. ICS is a standardized on-scene emergency management concept that allows for multiple agencies, including responders from different jurisdictions to operate under an integrated command structure. Once established the ICS organization has five functions: command, operations, planning, logistics, and finance and administration. If required, an information and intelligence section may also be established.

When the response to an incident involves support from different governmental and geographic jurisdictions with different functional and legal responsibilities, a unified command structure is established. Supporting agencies integrate their efforts through a collaborative process, usually at an incident command post located at or near the scene of the disaster.

The purpose of multiagency coordination systems is to provide support for field operations being directed by the incident commander. Primary activities include providing logistical support, tracking resources, directing incident-related information, and coordinating interagency and intergovernmental issues. These activities are usually directed at an emergency operations center (EOC).

Public information systems include means for communicating timely and accurate information to the public during periods of crisis or emergencies. Operations may call for the establishment of a joint information center, a location where public affairs professionals representing various agencies can coordinate their activities and share information.

Preparedness

The NIMS establishes specific measures and capabilities that jurisdictions and agencies should develop and incorporate into an overall system to enhance preparedness for managing all hazards. The measures include programs for planning, training, exercises, personnel and equipment qualifications and certification, publications management, and mutual aid. Mutual aid agreements provide the means for one jurisdiction to supply resources, facilities, services, and other required support to another jurisdiction during an incident.

Resource Management

According to the NIMS, *standardized* means to classify, inventory, track, and dispatch resources before, during, and after an incident. It establishes how operations are funded and reimbursed. Generally, resource management activities are prescribed in appropriate emergency operations plans.

Communications and Information Management

The NIMS communications and information systems enable the essential functions needed to provide a common operating picture and interoperability for incident management. Information that must be shared over these systems include disseminating indicators and early warnings, communicating operational decisions, and developing and maintaining overall awareness of response activities.

Supporting Technologies

In addition to providing a framework for preparing and responding to domestic incidents, the NIMS serves to help develop new technologies that will better support implemention of the national response system. It provides an architecture for how the Department of Homeland Security's S&T Directorate will help develop supporting technologies.

Ongoing Management and Maintenance

As part of the NIMS, the DHS will establish a multijurisdictional, multidisciplinary NIMS Integration Center. This center will provide oversight of the NIMS. All users and stakeholders, including various levels of government and the private sector, will be asked to participate in NIMS Integration Center activities.

THE FUTURE OF NATIONAL DOMESTIC INCIDENT MANAGEMENT

While the establishment of the National Response Plan and the NIMS provides the framework for establishing an integrated national system for responding to terrorist attacks and other national disasters, there are many issues involving the implementation that have yet to be resolved. Changes and modifications will likely be a hallmark of the national response for years to come.

Establishing the ICS

The implementation of the ICS concept offers a case in point. State and local governments have considerable flexibility in how they choose to implement the system. In most incidents usually the local police or fire service representative is in charge. For some emergencies, such as a fire or hostage-taking, there would be little dispute over which agency should take the lead. For others, for example, a combination of incidents, establishing the lead responsibility would be more difficult. In some cases, different command traditions, local political disputes, or disagreements between agencies or leaders might complicate the process of establishing an effective ICS.

The Role of the PFO

Another issue to be resolved in the NIMS is the role of the principal federal officer (PFO), who is supposed to take charge of national assets at the scene of an incident. There are, for example, questions about the extent of the PFO's authority at the site, particularly in relation to the role of the FEMA regional director, who has traditionally served as the senior federal official at the scene of a major disaster.

Developing Supporting Technologies

The state of supporting technologies is also a major issue of concern. The lack of interoperable communications both between emergency responders and across different government jurisdictions remains a cause of great concern.[14] While NIMS requires interoperable communications standards, neither the standards nor the supporting equipment are available. The DHS has established a SAFECOM program to coordinate the development of an interoperable wireless communications network.[15]

Also complicating an emergency response is that many first responders such as uniformed police are ill-organized and ill-equipped to rapidly address terrorist attacks that might require assets or equipment not normally employed during a tour of duty. Police officers, for example, lack the capacity to carry a lot of additional emergency response equipment in the trunk of their patrol cars. Officers on foot, bicycle, or equine patrol have even less capacity. Undercover agents and antiterrorism squads trying to blend into their surroundings and trying to appear inconspicuous have problems carrying additional equipment as well.[16]

Even when equipment is available, first responders find they have significant limitations. Clothing, gloves, and masks are bulky, heavy, and demanding on physical labor. Most protective gear is too uncomfortable for extended wear. Routine activities such as communicating, pushing buttons, and observing surroundings cannot be easily accomplished in protective gear.[17]

Finally, it is often extremely difficult to extend the situational awareness that must be extant in the emergency response system to the frontline responders. For example, fire personnel need to know hydrant and standpipe locations, as well as utility and building designs and hazardous material inventories. Often, critical information is stored in locations or formats (e.g., paper records) that prevent them from being readily on hand.

Taken together, these challenges will present enormous obstacles to responders that may well have to deal with multiple catastrophic attacks requiring the integration of multiple assets across multiple regions and multiple layers of government. To effectively address such threats, the United States will require better technology to support the national response system.

ISSUES:

ORGANIZED CHAOS

The National Commission on Terrorist Attacks upon the United States, popularly known as the 9/11 Commission, found significant problems with the response to the disaster at the World Trade Center on September 11. The staff prepared a detailed report of the events on that fateful day.

Excerpt from the Commission's Staff Statement

As we turn to the events of September 11, we will try to describe what happened in the following one hundred minutes. . . . [North Tower] The plane cut through floors 93/94 to 98/99 of the building. All three of the building's stairwells became impassable from the 92nd floor up. Hundreds of civilians were killed instantly by the impact. Hundreds more remained alive but trapped. A jet fuel fireball erupted upon impact, and shot down at least one bank of elevators. The fireball exploded onto numerous lower floors, including the 77th , 50th , 22nd , West Street lobby level, and the B4 level, four stories below ground. . . . Within minutes,

New York City's 9-1-1 system was flooded with eyewitness accounts of the event. Most callers correctly identified the target of the attack. . . .

Because of damage to the building's systems, civilians did not receive instructions on how to proceed over the public address system. Many were unable to use the emergency intercom phones as instructed in fire drills. Many called 9-1-1. 9-1-1 operators and FDNY dispatchers had no information about either the location or magnitude of the impact zone and were therefore unable to provide information. . . . Although the default guidance to stay in place may seem understandable in cases of conventional high rise fires, all the emergency officials that morning quickly judged that the North Tower should be evacuated.

Shortly before 9:00 a.m. . . . Impressed by the magnitude of the catastrophe, fire chiefs had decided to clear the whole WTC complex, including the South Tower. Just after the South Tower impact, chiefs in the North Tower lobby huddled to discuss strategy for the operations and communication in the two towers. . . . At 9:05 a.m., two FDNY chiefs tested the WTC complex's repeater system. This was the system installed after the 1993 bombing in order to enable firefighters operating on upper floors to maintain consistent radio communication with the lobby command. The system had been activated for use on portable radios at 8:54 a.m., but a second button which would have enabled the master hand-set was not activated at that time. The chief testing the master handset at 9:05 a.m. did not realize that the master handset had not been activated. When he could not communicate, he concluded that the system was down. . . .

The emergency response effort escalated with the crash of United 175 into the South Tower. With that escalation, communications and command-and-control became increasingly critical and increasingly difficult. First responders assisted thousands of civilians in evacuating the towers, even as incident commanders from responding agencies lacked knowledge of what other agencies and, in some cases, their own responders were doing.

The North Tower collapsed at 10:26 a.m. The FDNY Chief of Department and the Port Authority Police Department Superintendent and many of their senior staff were killed. The Fire Department of New York suffered the largest loss of life of any emergency response agency in U.S. history. The Port Authority Police Department suffered the largest loss of life of any American police force in history. The New York Police Department suffered the second largest loss of life of any police force in U.S. history, exceeded only by the loss of Port Authority police the same day. The nation suffered the largest loss of civilian life on its soil as a result of a domestic attack in its history.

1. Does this excerpt of the staff report of the 9/11 attack reflect any of the problems commonly associated with responding to a major incident? Which ones?

2. What contributed to problems?

3. How might the response have been organized?

CHALLENGES FOR STATE AND LOCAL GOVERNMENT EMERGENCY OPERATIONS PLANNING

Even with increasing federal guidance and involvement, state and local jurisdictions face many challenges in adopting common command and control standards, ensuring equipment interoperability, and implementing mutual aid agreements. In many cases, emergency plans also must be revised to address continuity of operations and continuity of state and local government/services, ensuring that operations and governmental authority are not disrupted as a result of a terrorist attack or other major disaster.[18]

Many state and local jurisdictions had emergency operations plans in place before the September 11 attacks, but many of these plans required updating to account for the guidance in the newly established NIMS and mutual aid agreements, the threat of terrorist acts, and the potential for catastrophic threats including weapons of mass destruction.

Dealing with Terrorist Threats

Updating of plans may require adding roles and responsibilities for assessing terrorist threats; information on nuclear, biological, chemical, radiological, and agroterrorism agents and cyberthreats; actions in regard to changes in the Homeland Security Advisory System; mass casualty care; and responses to potential terrorist attacks.[19]

Critical Infrastructure

State and local governments may also find they must give greater consideration to the identification and protection of critical infrastructures. Local officials are primarily responsible for ensuring the continuation of critical services in communities affected by disasters. Protecting critical infrastructures will also be essential for enabling rescue operations and ensuring the continuity of government operations. Emergency operations plans must inventory and assess the vulnerability of critical infrastructures and develop suitable mitigation and preparedness measures.[20]

Interstate and Intrastate Mutual Aid Agreements

In the wake of September 11 many state and local governments have added new capabilities or are seeking to expand their capacity to respond to disasters through cooperative agreements. This is often accomplished through intrastate (communities within a state) and interstate (among two or more states) mutual aid pacts, such as emergency management assistance compacts (EMACs).

Establishing and updating mutual aid agreements should be a priority for revising emergency operations plans. An effective mutual aid agreement should address liability and reimbursement, as well as rapidly identify the availability and location of needed resources, and provide a means to accurately track the resources. Emergency operations plans should also account for the reception and employment of national resources that might support state and local efforts. These resources might include the Strategic National Stockpile, National Medical Disaster System, civil support teams, and urban search and rescue task forces.

Strategic National Stockpile

The Strategic National Stockpile is a supply of medications and medical/surgical equipment maintained by the Department of Health and Human Services to supplement and resupply state and local public health agencies in the event of a national emergency. The stockpile includes push packages located around the country that can be deployed to a designated place within 12 hours. Follow-on supplies can be delivered within 24 to 36 hours. Currently, many state and local governments lack robust plans or capabilities to distribute supplies from the Strategic National Stockpile.

The National Medical Disaster System

The National Medical Disaster System (NMDS) coordinates hospital support to supplement state and local needs and assists in the evacuation of patients from a disaster area. The NMDS also includes a number of emergency response teams. Disaster medical assistance teams (DMATs) are professional medical personnel and support staffs that can be deployed to provide emergency medical care during a disaster. Veterinary medical assistance teams (VMATs) can provide emergency medical treatment of animals and conduct disease surveillance. National pharmacist response teams (NPRTs) will be employed to assist in mass chemoprophylaxis or vaccination in response to an infectious disease threat. National medical response teams–weapons of mass destruction (NMRTs–WMD) are specialized response forces designed to provide medical care following nuclear, biological, and/or chemical incidents. The national nurse response team (NNRT) can be used to deploy hundreds of nurses to the site of an emergency. Disaster mortuary operational response teams (DMORTs) that work under the guidance of local authorities, provide technical assistance and personnel to recover, identify, and process deceased victims.

Civil Support Teams

Civil support teams (CSTs) are teams of 22 National Guard personnel that are available to support civil authorities in the event of a chemical, biological, radiological, nuclear, or high-yield explosive (CBRNE) incident by identifying hazardous agents, assessing the spread of contamination, advising on response measures, and coordinating further military support.

Urban Search and Rescue Task Force

Urban search and rescue (US&R) task forces conduct search and rescue operations in damaged or collapsed structures, perform hazardous materials evaluations, and provide stabilization of damaged structures. They can also provide emergency medical care. A US&R task force is a partnership between local fire departments, law enforcement agencies, federal and local governmental agencies, and private companies.

Continuity of Government and Operations

Emergency operations plans must account for the continued performance of state and local government and essential services during a crisis. According to FEMA, planning goals should include the ability to operate within 12 hours of activation, as well as sustain operations for up to 30 days. Elements of a viable capability include a line of succession, delegation of authorities, establishment of alternate facilities, safeguarding of vital records, providing for communications, and ensuring adequate logistical support for essential activities.

CHAPTER SUMMARY

The concept of national response management has evolved significantly since the 9/11 attacks. Governments at all levels have responsibility for responding to terrorist attacks. The national response is guided by the framework provided by the National Response Plan and the National Incident Management System. The principle of all-hazards response, including establishing an on-scene incident commander for each event, guides the U.S. approach to emergency response.

Though significant progress has been made since 9/11 in building a more structured national emergency response system, much work remains to be done. There are technical, organizational, and doctrinal issues that must be resolved at all levels of government.

CHAPTER QUIZ

1. What is an all-hazards approach?
2. What are the principles of emergency response? Why are they important?

3. What are the most significant challenges in emergency response?
4. Who will be in charge at the scene of a terrorist attack?
5. Describe the components of NIMS.

NOTES

1. Testimony of Jerome M. Hauer before the National Commission on Terrorist Attacks upon the United States (May 19, 2004), p. 1, www.9-11commission.gov/hearings/hearing11/hauer_statement.pdf.

2. The National Commission on Terrorist Attacks upon the United States, "Crisis Management," Staff Statement No. 14, p. 6, www.9-11commission.gov/hearings/hearing11/staff_statement_14.pdf; Testimony of Dennis Smith before the National Commission on Terrorist Attacks upon the United States (May 19, 2004), p. 4, www.9-11commission.gov/hearings/hearing11/smith_statement.pdf.

3. See, for example, FEMA, *Responding to Incidents of National Consequence* (2004), http://www.usfa.fema.gov/downloads/pdf/publications/fa-282.pdf.

4. For example, an analysis that modeled the economic consequences of a biological attack found that the speed of the response was the single most important variable in reducing casualties. Arnold F. Kaufmann, et al., "The Economic Impact of Bioterrorist Attack: Are Prevention and Postattack Intervention Programs Justifiable?" *Emerging Infectious Diseases* (April–June 1997), www.cdc.gov/ncidod/eid/vol3no2/kaufman.htm.

5. Environmental Protection Agency, *Exercise TOPOFF 2000 and National Capital Region (NCR) After-Action Report,* The National Response Team, Final Report (Washington, DC: August 2000), p. 10. For other shortfalls see Thomas V. Inglesby, "The Lessons from TOPOFF," Comments at the Second National Symposium on Medical and Public Health Response to Terrorism (Washington, DC, November 28–29, 2000); Thomas V. Inglesby, et al., "A Plague on Your City: Observations from TOPOFF," *Clinical Infectious Diseases* (February 2001): 436–445; Richard E. Hoffman and Jane E. Norton, "Lessons Learned from a Full-Scale Bioterrorism Exercise," *Emerging Infectious Diseases* (November/December 2000), www.cdc.gov/ncidod/eid/vol6no6/hoffman.htm.

6. Environmental Protection Agency, *Exercise TOPOFF 2000 and National Capital Region (NCR) After-Action Report,* p. 17.

7. For a discussion on the importance of decentralized execution and flexibility see Kathleen J. Tierney, "Disaster Preparedness and Response: Research Findings and Guidance from the Social Science Literature," Disaster Research Center, University of Delaware, pp. 13–14, www.udel.edu/DRC.

8. James Kendra and Tricia Wachtendorf, "Elements of Resilience in the World Trade Center Attack," Disaster Research Center, University of Delaware, pp. 6–9, www.udel.edu/DRC.

9. For a discussion of convergence, see Julie L. Demuth, *Countering Terrorism: Lessons Learned from Natural and Technological Disasters* (Washington, DC: National Academy of Sciences, 2002), p. 7.

10. FEMA, *Guide for All Hazard Emergency Operations Planning: State and Local Guide*, Annex G (April 2001), p. G-1, www.fema.gov/doc/rrr/allhzpln.doc.

11. FEMA, *Guide for All Hazard Emergency Operations Planning: State and Local Guide* (September 1996), pp. 1–3.

12. Homeland Security Presidential Directive/HSPD-5 (February 28, 2003), www.whitehouse.gov/news/releases/2003/02/20030228-9.html.

13. The attorney general is also responsible for terrorist acts directed at U.S. citizens or institutions abroad, where such acts are within the federal criminal jurisdiction of the United States, as well as for related intelligence collection activities within the United States, subject to the National Security Act of 1947 and other applicable law, Executive Order 12333, and Attorney General-approved procedures pursuant to that Executive Order. See Homeland Security Presidential Directive/HSPD-5 (February 28, 2003), www.whitehouse.gov/news/releases/2003/02/20030228-9.html.

14. National Task Force on Interoperability, "Why Can't We Talk: Working Together to Bridge the Communications Gap to Save Lives, A Guide to Public Officials" (February 2003), www.agileprogram.org/ntfi/ntfi_guide.pdf.

15. Department of Homeland Security, "Statement of Requirements for Public Safety Wireless Communications and Interoperability" (March 10, 2004), www.safecomprogram.gov/files/PSCI_Statement_of_Requirements_v1_0.pdf.

16. Tom LaTourrette, et. al., *Protecting Emergency Responders*, Vol. 2: *Community Views of Safety and Health Risks and Personal Protection Needs* (Santa Monica, CA: RAND, 2003), p. 53.

17. Brian A. Jackson, et al., *Protecting Emergency Responders: Lessons Learned from Terrorist Attacks* (Arlington, VA: RAND Science and Technology Institute, nd), Proceedings of a conference held on December 9–11, 2001, pp. xii, 8.

18. FEMA, *Introduction to State and Local EOP Planning Guidance* (August 2002), www.fema.gov/preparedness/introstate.shtm.

19. See FEMA, *Toolkit for Managing the Emergency Consequences of Terrorist Incidents* (July 2002), www.fema.gov/pdf/onp/toolkit_toc.pdf.

20. FEMA, *How-to Guide #7: Integrating Manmade Hazards into Mitigation Planning* (September 2003), www.fema.gov/txt/fima/howto7.txt.

16

BUSINESS PREPAREDNESS, CONTINUITY, AND RECOVERY

Private Sector Responses to Terrorism

Immediately after Sept. 11, there was urgency to rethink disaster planning, risk assumptions, and preparation contingencies.

Robert C. Chandler and J. D. Wallace, "Business Continuity Planning after September 11"

CHAPTER OVERVIEW

When the role of the private sector in homeland security is discussed, most think of its impact on big office towers and major industries. This perception is simply wrong. Disasters, including terrorism, can strike at any business no matter how small. This chapter surveys the measures that companies can take to protect their operations, facilities, and employees.

CHAPTER LEARNING OBJECTIVES

After reading this chapter, you should be able to

1. Understand how September 11 has changed private-sector perceptions toward preparedness.
2. Describe what is meant by disaster recovery and continuity of operations.

3. Understand the legal implications of preparedness planning.

4. Describe the steps in preparedness planning.

NEW WORLD OF DISORDER

Terrorists strike at more than nations and people; companies, large and small, can fall victim as well. An estimated 1,200 to 2,000 small businesses, including about 600 in the Twin Towers, were wiped out by the 9/11 attack on New York City. The attack also affected over 15,000 businesses in the area and 13.4 million square feet of real estate. Lower Manhattan lost more than 100,000 employees to death, relocation, or unemployment. Companies disrupted by the collapse of the World Trade Center buildings ranged from rich, multinational corporations to small mom-and-pop stores. Robert Garber's Bits, Bites and Baguettes that stood in the shadow of the Twin Towers was a typical casualty. On September 10, 2001, Bits and Bites had its busiest day ever, revenues were up 35 percent, and staff had quadrupled since the small restaurant and catering service had been established in 1997. After September 11, the business was barricaded for two months, pushing Garber's company to the edge of insolvency.[1]

Acts of terrorism are not the only threat to private enterprise; businesses can also suffer from the effects of all sorts of natural and technological (human-made) disasters including fires, floods, earthquakes, tornadoes, and industrial accidents. Many of the practices and precautions recommended for preventing, responding to, and mitigating these kinds of events are equally applicable to preparing for terrorist strikes. In other cases, additional precautions and measures are required to safeguard business practices against deliberate acts that may interfere with the normal course of everyday commerce.

Failure to undertake disaster preparedness could have a dramatic impact on business practices. For example, according to a 1998 survey by Strategic Research Corporation, the financial impact of a major outage would have a significant impact on America's largest companies including costing brokerage operations $6.5 million per hour. A breakdown in the credit-card sales authorization system would cost $2.6 million per hour. The effects of disaster are perhaps most significant on small businesses. Data collected by FEMA suggest that half the small companies that experience a disaster go out of business within two years. As the National Red Cross emphasizes: No business should risk operating without a disaster plan.

Indeed, business continuity and disaster response and recovery planning have become an integral component of modern business practices. In the 1980s as companies became increasingly dependent on computers, disaster recovery emerged as a formal disciple. The main focus of effort was on protecting data. Over time the emphasis has shifted and expanded to include supply chain management, the physical security of property and personnel, and securing information networks.

DEFINITIONS AND STANDARDS

Business continuity involves developing measures and safeguards that will allow an organization to continue to produce or deliver goods or services under adverse conditions. Disaster response and recovery includes responding to, mitigating, and recovering or reconstituting personnel, infrastructure, and business capabilities in the wake of an event. The main difference between the two efforts is that continuity planning is meant to prevent business interruptions, while disaster planning involves dealing with major interruptions that occur as a result of a sudden, calamitous event that causes significant damage or loss. Collectively, these activities are often referred to as contingency planning.

There are no universal standards for preparedness in the private sector. Many groups, however, have endorsed standards promulgated by the National Fire Protection Association in NFPA 1600 as an appropriate model for standards on disaster/emergency management and business continuity programs. The NFPA offers descriptions of the basic criteria for a comprehensive program that addresses disaster recovery, emergency management, and business continuity.

CHANGING BUSINESS ENVIRONMENT: THE USAMA EFFECT

There are still significant gaps and great disparities in how companies prepare for future contingencies. A 2002 survey of 1,057 medium and large businesses (more than 100 employees) by Digital Research Inc. found that about one in four companies do not have business continuity/disaster recovery plans. Twenty percent of the businesses that do have plans, have not tested them in five years. The larger the company in terms of revenues and employees, the more likely they were to have plans in place and to have tested them, at least annually.

According to the survey, the al-Qaida attacks on New York City and Washington DC convinced more businesses to undertake planning and caused nearly three-quarters of businesses with plans in place to update and improve plans. On the other hand, according to the survey the majority of companies with business continuity/disaster plans implemented their planning prior to 9/11. The impact of 9/11 on small-business planning is less clear. Despite the dramatic example of the impact of attacks in New York on small enterprises, it is not clear that preparedness among the small-business community has improved significantly.

Thus, it appears that the "Usama effect," as it is referred to by some disaster recovery experts, may have made only a temporary and transitory impact on the likelihood that companies will prepare for a terrorist attack or indeed any kind of disaster. Nevertheless, the general trend, especially for medium and large companies, is that commercial enterprises are increasingly recognizing the need to pay greater attention to ensuring the continuity of their business practices in the face of adversity.

LEGAL ISSUES

Sound business practices and concern over the safety of employees, the surrounding community, and the environment are not the only motivation for undertaking contingency planning. Federal, state, and local laws may also require companies to undertake some preparedness measures. Occupational Safety and Health Administration (OSHA) regulations offer a case in point. OSHA Standard 29 CFR 1910.38 requires plans that designate actions that employers and employees must take to ensure safety in the event of "fire and other emergencies."[2]

In addition, other legal requirements may impact on the need for contingency planning as well. There are a number of federal laws that regulate hazardous materials, including the Superfund Amendments and Reauthorization Act of 1986 (SARA), the Resource Conservation and Recovery Act of 1976, the Hazardous Materials Transportation Act, the Occupational Safety and Health Act, the Toxic Substances Control Act, and the Clean Air Act. SARA, for example, regulates the packaging, labeling, handling, storage, and transportation of hazardous materials. The law requires a facility to furnish information about the quantities and health effects of materials used at the facility and to promptly notify local and state officials whenever a significant release of hazardous materials occurs.

OSHA has also established equipment and training requirements for fire brigades and other response teams that might be employed in dealing with hazardous materials. Some employee training such as fire drills is also mandatory.[3] Detailed definitions as well as lists of hazardous materials and training and equipment requirements can be obtained from the Environmental Protection Agency and OSHA.

ISSUES:

LEADERSHIP AND LIABILITY

In the wake of a series of devastating corporate scandals Congress adopted new legislation that required chief executive officers (CEO) to certify that they had reviewed the financial practices of their companies. In addition to requiring corporate officers to take responsibility for the accuracy of financial statements, the Public Accounting Reform and Investor Protection Act of 2002 (Sarbanes-Oxley) requires that companies certify they understand the risks that may impact the financial reporting process.

Some security experts argue that Sarbanes-Oxley may implicitly require sound contingency plans. A proper assessment of risk might be construed to include operational risks resulting from inadequate business continuity or disaster recovery plans.

Companies should recognize that they may incur legal or criminal liability if response plans are absent or inadequate. For example, courts determine liability by weighing the probability of the loss compared to the magnitude of harm, balanced against the cost of protection. Courts will use this standard to determine if companies and individuals took reasonable precautions, in legal terms showed "due diligence" in mitigating the effects of a disaster on business operations. Thus, a sound business contingency plan would account for potential liabilities that might be incurred by the company or its representatives.

1. Should companies be held culpable for injuries and losses that occur from a terrorist attack?
2. What kinds of measures should they be expected to take?
3. Should Sarbanes-Oxley require companies to certify they have taken precautions against disasters? Should the federal and state governments provide more regulation?

PLANNING FOR THE WORST

Most specialists in the field agree that the centerpiece of preparations for any size company is the development of a business continuity/disaster recovery program, built around a sound contingency plan. A contingency plan is a comprehensive statement of actions to be taken before, during, and after a disaster. A successful planning process must achieve three goals: (1) create awareness of potential disasters, (2) define actions and activities that will minimize disruptions of critical functions, and (3) develop the capability to reestablish business operations. Experts also agree that for the plan to be effective it must be documented, tested, and updated periodically as part of a comprehensive contingency program.

The cost and resources invested in contingency planning will vary with the size of the business and the scope of its resources, risks, and vulnerabilities. Small and medium-size businesses may face a number of challenges in developing and implementing plans, such as limited employee time that can be dedicated to the tasks of maintaining a preparedness program.[4]

Business continuity and disaster recovery planning professionals generally recommend a sequential planning process that could be applied to most companies regardless of their size and number of employees. Many aspects of the contingency planning process are equally applicable to nongovernmental and governmental organizations. There are many different recommended versions of the planning process. Most contain the following basic elements: obtain management commitment, establish a planning committee, perform a risk assessment, establish operational priorities, determine continuity and recovery options, develop a contingency plan, and implement the plan.[5]

Obtain Management Commitment

Senior management should be responsible for coordinating planning activities. Among the most critical activities that they perform are ensuring that sufficient time and resources (such as a budget for research, printing, seminars, consulting services, and other expenses that may be necessary during the planning process) are committed to developing an effective plan and that developing the plan is a priority.

Establish a Planning Committee

Since a disaster could well affect every aspect of a company's business practices from the acquisition of raw materials to public relations and advertising, representatives from every facet of the company need to be involved in the planning process. A planning committee should be appointed to develop and implement the business continuity/disaster recovery plan. The CEO or plant manager should head the group. Committee members might also include operations managers; union representatives; information technology or data processing managers; legal, purchasing, and financial management representatives; engineering and maintenance personnel; public information and human resources personnel; safety, health, and environmental affairs representatives; sales and marketing and community relations representatives; suppliers; and service providers.

The committee's purpose is to develop and document the contingency plan. Duties for the committee would include drafting a mission statement, budget, work plan, and time line for various planning activities. The committee would also be responsible for research, engaging consultants, meeting with outside groups, and supervising planning activities.

**Perform a Risk
Assessment**

Most specialists consider this step to be the most vital task for establishing an effective business continuity/disaster recovery plan. Typically, the risk assessment will comprise an evaluation of threats, vulnerabilities, and costs.

Threats are the things that can go wrong or that can "attack" a company's personnel, property, products, or systems. Threats include natural disasters like earthquakes and floods and human-made disasters such as industrial accidents, fraud, and sabotage, or the loss of a key supplier or customer. An assessment would not only include what threats a company might face, but how likely it would be that different threats will actually happen.

Vulnerabilities are those things that make the company more prone to a disaster or more likely to suffer damage in the event of an incident. For example, in the advent of a fire, the presence of a vast amount of flammable material, like fuel oil, would be a significant vulnerability.

Costs include assessment of the financial impact of various disaster scenarios. An assessment should consider both direct costs, such as the loss of revenues due to an interruption in sales, and indirect costs, like a devaluation of a company's stock as the result of a loss of confidence by stockholders in how the management team responded to a particular disaster. This part of the risk assessment is often called the *business impact analysis*.

Evaluations of threat, vulnerability, and cost are not only used to determine what dangers to prepare for and how to meet them, but also to prioritize preparedness efforts. As part of the planning process, organization leadership will have to decide which threats are the most likely and the most dangerous, and consequently with regards to safety and sound business practices, where they should invest their time and effort in preparing to deal with the consequences of various dangers.

The assessment should define the possible disasters that a business might encounter and their potential impact on the company's business practices. Traditionally, fire is the most common form of disaster experienced by businesses, but depending on geographical location, enterprises might be particularly vulnerable to other kinds of danger as well including floods, tornadoes, or wildfires. Usually accurate and fairly complete information on likely hazards can be obtained through local and state organizations such as emergency management offices, floodplain management, public or commercial geospatial information services, geological surveys, and universities and colleges.

Determining if a company is susceptible to a terrorist attack is more problematic. Location and activity might suggest if a business is more likely to become a victim of a terrorist incident. For example, given the number of terrorist incidents involving commercial aviation, businesses involved in this sector, including tourism, travel services, and airport vendors, might have greater concern over how their practices might be affected by a terrorist attack. Organizations involved in politically controversial activities might also consider the potential for becoming victims of a terrorist act. Sources of information for conducting a terrorist risk assessment might include local law enforcement, industry associations, or a business sector information-sharing and analysis center.

As part of risk assessment, each area of an organization (such as billing, shipping, advertising, utilities, and information technology services) should be assessed to determine the potential consequences of different kinds of disasters. Impacts that should be considered are the cost of repairing or replacing equipment; loss of worker productivity and the expense of replacing and training new personnel; impact on customers; violations of contractual agreements; the imposition of fines and penalties or legal costs; and interruption of supplies or distribution of products.

Establish Operational Priorities

Before the planning team begins to decide how to best prepare for different threats and mitigate vulnerabilities, it must first identify the critical needs of each element within the company. Critical elements are those resources, leadership, or capabilities whose loss would stop or significantly degrade essential business activities, such as the delivery of goods or services. The analysis of operational priorities should determine the maximum amount of time that the organization can operate without each critical element. This step is essential for ensuring that the most important parts of the business are addressed first. An assessment of operational priorities might include determining essential activities and systems, key personnel, and vital records and documents. Examples of critical operational priorities might include sole-source vendors; lifeline services like water, oil, or gas; and irreplaceable equipment. The assessment usually ranks personnel, facilities, and services as essential, important, or nonessential.

Determine Continuity and Recovery Options

Another critical task for the planning committee is to determine the practical alternatives for preparing the organization to deal with a disaster. The main focus in developing continuity and recovery options should be protecting the operational priorities identified by the planning committee.

As part of this process, the committee will collect critical data that would be needed to respond to a disaster including critical and backup personnel listings; essential telephone numbers; inventories of equipment, office supplies, and documents; lists of vendors and customers; storage locations; software and data files backup/retention schedules; and important contracts.

The committee should also gather information about current capabilities that are already available by reviewing existing plans, policies, and programs including evacuation and fire plans, safety and health programs, environmental policies, security procedures, finance and purchasing procedures, employee manuals, hazardous materials plans, capital improvement programs, and mutual aid agreements.

In particular, any assessment should include a rigorous evaluation to determine if insurance policies are adequate to meet the liabilities that might be incurred as a result of a disaster. Most small-business insurance policies include basic property and liability insurance. Basic property insurance generally covers losses from fire or a lightning strike. Additionally, small-business policies usually cover damage from windstorm, hail, explosion, riot and civil commotion, and destruction caused by vehicles or vandalism. Coverage against earthquakes, floods, and building collapse is usually optional. Liability insurance protects business assets in the event the company is sued.

In addition to examining pertinent documents, the planning committee should review the status of internal assets available to respond to an emergency. These might include resources and capabilities that could be needed in an emergency such as materials response teams, emergency medical services, security, and the company's public information officer. The committee should also be aware of any specialized emergency equipment or facilities like fire protection and suppression equipment, communications equipment, first aid supplies, emergency supplies, warning systems, emergency power equipment, decontamination equipment, shelter areas, and first aid stations. Finally, the committee should know what backup services are available such as payroll, customer service, shipping and receiving, and information technology systems.

As part of this process, the committee will also have to review applicable federal, state, and local regulations to ensure that the plans in place and options being developed are consistent with the law and the industry and a company's stated policies. Documents that might be reviewed include occupational safety and health regulations, environmental regulations, fire codes, seismic safety codes, transportation regulations, zoning regulations, and corporate policies.[6]

Meetings should also be held with outside groups to determine what kind of support and resources may be available and what coordination would be required in the event of a disaster. Sources of information might include the community emergency management office, the office of the mayor or a community administrator, a local emergency planning committee, fire and police departments, emergency medical services organizations (such as an ambulance service), the public works department or local planning commission, telephone, electric and other local utilities, hospitals, contractors, neighboring businesses, the American Red Cross, and the National Weather Service.

Finally, options for processing data and conducting business activities in case of a disaster should be researched and evaluated. There are four types of preparedness measures that might be undertaken to reduce the risk of a disaster. Deterrent measures reduce the likelihood of a disaster or deliberate attack. Preventive measures protect vulnerabilities and make an attack unsuccessful or reduce its impact. Corrective measures reduce the effect of an attack. Detective measures discover attacks and trigger preventive or corrective controls. These measures may require new practices, personnel, or equipment. As part of the planning process, the committee will determine the costs and benefits of implementing these measures and their value for ensuring business continuity or responding to an attack.

Develop a Contingency Plan

Once the committee has decided what measures will be incorporated into the plan, the measures need to be documented in a comprehensive written product. The plan should include detailed procedures to be used before, during, and after a disaster, with specific responsibilities assigned to a management team covering all the important areas of the organization. Once completed, the plans should be approved by management.

The plan should establish an emergency management group. Detailing the responsibilities of the management team is especially critical since it will be in charge of the response and recovery process. This group will be the company leaders responsible for managing the "big picture," controlling all incident-related activities. The mission of the emergency management group is to support the incident commander whose task it will be to oversee the technical aspects of the response. The incident commander is responsible for frontline management, making decisions on the scene regarding how to respond to the disaster and relaying requests for additional resources if they are needed. The group supports the incident commander by allocating resources and by interfacing with the community, the media, outside response organizations, and regulatory agencies. The emergency director, who should be the facility manager, heads the emergency management group.

Plans may also require establishing an emergency operations center (EOC). The EOC serves as the center used by the emergency management group to coordinate the response to a disaster. It should be located in a facility that is not likely to be involved in an incident.

Business contingency plans normally include an executive summary that provides a brief overview of the purpose of the plan; the facility's emergency management policy; authorities and responsibilities of key personnel; the types of emergencies that could occur; and where response operations will be managed. A second portion of the plan should briefly describe how the core elements of emergency management will be organized within the organization. These include communications; safety; property protection; community outreach; recovery and restoration of systems, operations, and facilities, administration and logistics. The third portion of the plan spells out how the organization will respond to emergencies.

In addition to the basic plan, support documents that might be needed in an emergency should also be developed. They might include building and site maps that indicate utilities and shutoff locations, floor plans, escape routes, emergency equipment inventories and location, alarm system plans, and the location of hazardous materials and critical items. Other documents might include emergency procedures, personnel lists, and emergency-call rosters.

Implement the Plan

After the plans are drafted, they should be tested. Procedures should also be established for maintaining and updating the plan. Implementation procedures should also allow for a regular review of the plan by key personnel.

Finally, means for exercising and training must be established. Exercises could include everything from "table-top" exercises where the disaster management team reviews their responsibilities to full-scale drills.

Training plans should include worker orientations and periodic classes that contain information on individual roles and responsibilities; threats, hazards, and protective actions; notification, warning, and communications procedures; means for locating family members in an emergency; emergency response procedures; evacuation, shelter, and accountability procedures; location and use of common emergency equipment; and emergency shutdown procedures.

The importance of training in implementing contingency planning cannot be overstated. Research finds that employees who have participated in drills and classroom training respond faster and make better decisions when responding to an emergency.[7]

FROM THE SOURCE:

GETTING ORGANIZED

FEMA provides a number of resources to assist businesses in contingency planning, including an online emergency management business guide (www.fema.gov/library/bizindex.shtm).

Excerpt from the FEMA Guide Describing the Requirements for a Company Emergency Operations Center

Emergency Operations Center (EOC)

The EOC serves as a centralized management center for emergency operations. Here, decisions are made by the company's emergency management group. Regardless of size or process, every facility should designate an area where decision makers can gather during an emergency.

The EOC should be located in an area of the facility not likely to be involved in an incident, perhaps the security department, the manager's office, a conference room or the training center. An alternate EOC should be designated in the event that the primary location is not usable.

Each facility must determine its requirements for an EOC based upon the functions to be performed and the number of people involved. Ideally, the EOC is a dedicated area equipped with communications equipment, reference materials, activity logs and all the tools necessary to respond quickly and appropriately to an emergency.

In a hazardous materials accident, an off-site medic was exposed to the spilled material and required hospitalization. It was determined that the person was able to enter the hazardous area unprotected because no one among a host of managers and facility responders was "in charge" at the scene.

EOC Resources:
- Communications equipment
- A copy of the emergency management plan and EOC procedures
- Blueprints, maps, status boards
- A list of EOC personnel and descriptions of their duties
- Technical information and data for advising responders
- Building security system information
- Information and data management capabilities
- Telephone directories
- Backup power, communications and lighting
- Emergency supplies

SUPPLY CHAIN SECURITY

One aspect of contingency planning gaining greater attention is the challenge of supply chain continuity. In order to reduce the high costs of maintaining large inventories of products, many companies have adopted the concept of just-in-time delivery of goods and services. Quick and responsive delivery lessens the need to have large stockpiles on hand, thus reducing operating costs.[8] As a consequence, supply chains have become increasingly fragile. Unexpected delays in the delivery of products can negate the advantages of inventories that are managed by the speed in which orders are filled rather than by the size of a company's warehouse. For instance, in the wake of the 9/11 attacks security at the borders and Canada was significantly upgraded. As a result, many truckers were delayed at border crossings for several hours. Since many truckers are only permitted to drive 10 hours per day, significant delays at the border can add an extra day to delivery time. After the attacks on the World Trade Center, Ford Motor Company idled five U.S. manufacturing plants because of slow delivery from parts suppliers in Canada.[9]

Visibility and Control

Two issues regarding supply chain management are particularly problematic. Companies often have reduced visibility and control over the delivery of goods. Visibility represents the organization's capacity to know where goods are and when they will be delivered. Control reflects the means companies have at their disposal to change how and when goods are delivered. A study conducted by Michigan State University identified four key components for an effective contingency plan for supply chain continuity.[10]

Risk Assessment

The first is a thorough risk assessment that identifies the supply chain's susceptibility to potentially crippling disruption. This assessment should include steps in the supply chain internal to the company, as well as the role of customers and suppliers. One common technique employed in developing continuity plans is supply chain mapping. Mapping helps identify bottlenecks, important transportation nodes, and critical suppliers within the supply chain.

Reducing and Monitoring Risks

The second key effort is developing preventative measures for reducing and monitoring risks. These are tasks undertaken to reduce the likelihood or impact of supply chain disruptions. Monitoring includes watching changes in the supply that may increase or decrease risks, such as sudden shifts in the availability of raw materials or the cost of transportation.

Contingency Plans

Third, contingency plans should include remediation plans for recovery from disruptions that do occur. Measures might include shortening the period of disruption or minimizing the impact on business practices.

Knowledge Management

The fourth component of effective supply contingency planning is establishing "knowledge management" or learning from disruptions in the supply chain that do occur. Knowledge management employs postevent audits and analysis of supply chain disruptions to determine lessons that can be applied to future activities.

PHYSICAL SECURITY

Increasing concern over terrorism has made physical security an increasingly relevant concern and an important factor in mitigating risks and vulnerabilities.[11] Most experts cite three basic means for mitigating physical security risks. The first includes adding mechanical systems. Additional security hardware might include access control systems such as electronic card readers and door locks, closed-circuit television and other surveillance and monitoring systems, biometrics, emergency call boxes and intrusion alarms, as well as command and control systems including working stations capable of monitoring various security systems. A second category of mitigating measures includes improvements in organization including reviewing the adequacy of security staff and procedures as well as security policies governing management, tenants, and employees. The third element of security mitigation is sometimes referred to as "natural" security, including the architectural elements of facilities and the surrounding area. Such elements might include, for example, removing trash cans during heightened periods of alert to limit the risk that they might be used as drops for improvised explosive devices.

Experts also agree that regular security surveys and assessments, implementing practical cost-effective measures, developing easily understood policies and procedures, and periodic training for employees and security staff are central to establishing security mitigation measures. For example, only about 1 percent of the triggering of automatic alarms represents actual emergencies or intrusions. The remainder results from mechanical faults, human error, or the disregard of established security procedures. Thus, establishing effective maintenance and education programs are essential for reducing the number of false alarms and ensuring that security personnel appropriately respond to automatic warnings.

INFORMATION TECHNOLOGY CONTINUITY AND RECOVERY

Protecting data and the information technology systems that support business practices continues to be an increasingly important component of private-sector contingency programs. The current trend in information technology continuity and recovery is to focus on the "survivability" of systems. *Survivability* is usually defined as the capability of a system to fulfill its mission in the presence of cyberattacks, physical disruptions, failures, or accidents.[12] Rather than protecting the computer system per se, contingency planning focuses on security of the information and the capability to conduct specific mission critical business practices, such as billing or inventory control.

Businesses of all sizes will find a plethora of vendors, consultants, and support services offering assistance in planning and implementing information technology contingency programs. For example, some vendors provide *hot sites*, an operationally ready data center that could serve as an alternative computer center for key business activities. The use of hot sites, particularly for financial firms, continues to grow. According to one survey from 1982 to 2004 over 582 successful business recoveries have been conducted at 25 different hot sites throughout the United States.

Another tool becoming increasing relied on by industry is *quick shipping*, the emergency shipment of computers from third-party leasing vendors to immediately replace lost equipment. Some companies also contract for small portable computer sites or mobile emergency office suites that can be delivered to the work location. Finally, many vendors offer various PC-based continuity and disaster recovery planning tools or consulting services to assist in the development and implementation of contingency plans.

CHAPTER SUMMARY

This chapter emphasizes the importance of business contingency planning. Good planning is based on a disciplined planning process directed by key leaders and managers. As with critical infrastructure protection activities, risk management is an important tool for planning preparedness activities.

CHAPTER QUIZ

1. Why should companies undertake contingency planning?
2. What effect did the September 11 attacks have on how businesses viewed the importance of contingency planning?
3. What is the most important step in contingency planning? Why?
4. Why is risk management important?

NOTES

1. National Community Capital Association, "2 Years after 9/11: A Report on the Unique Role Community Development Financial Institutions Are Playing in the Rebuilding of Lower Manhattan" (October 15, 2003), p. 4.
2. For more details see, Guy Colonna, ed., *Introduction to Employee Fire and Life Safety* (Quincy, MA: National Fire Protection Association, 2001), pp. 2–8.
3. Guy Colonna, ed., *Introduction to Employee Fire and Life Safety,* p. 10.
4. For estimates of the time and resources required for medium and small-business contin-

gency planning see Norm Koehler, "The Small and Medium Size Businesses Guide to a Successful Continuity Program," www.drj.com/special/smallbusiness/article1-01.html.

5. See, for example, FEMA, *Emergency Management Guide for Business and Industry* (2002), www.fema.gov/pdf/library/bizindst.pdf.

6. See, for example, Claire Lee Reiss, *Risk Management for Small Business* (Fairfax, VA: Public Entity Risk Institute, 2004), pp. 43–46.

7. Guy Colonna, ed., *Introduction to Employee Fire and Life Safety*, p. 13.

8. For an introduction to just-in-time supply management see B. Modarress and Abdolhossein Ansari, *Just-in-Time Purchasing* (New York: The Free Press, 1990).

9. Joseph Martha, "Just-in-Case Operations," *Warehouse Forum* 17/2 (January 2002), www.warehousing-forum.com/news/2002_01.pdf.

10. George A. Zsidisin, et al., "Effective Practices in Business Continuity Planning for Purchasing and Supply Chain Management," Michigan State University (July 2003), http://www.bus.msu.edu/msc/documents/AT&T%20full%20paper.pdf.

11. Building Owners and Managers Institute "BOMI Institute Corner: Building an Effective Security Program," *Today's Facility Manager* (October 2001), www.facilitycity.com/tfm/tfm_01_10_news3.asp.

12. Howard F. Lipson and David A. Fisher, "Survivability—A New Technical and Business Perspective on Security," *Proceedings of the 1999 New Security Paradigms Workshop, Ontario, Canada* (September 22–24, 1999), p. 1.

17

PUBLIC AWARENESS AND PERSONAL AND FAMILY PREPAREDNESS

Simple Solutions, Serious Challenges

All Americans should begin a process of learning about potential threats so we are better prepared to react during an attack. While there is no way to predict what will happen, or what your personal circumstances will be, there are simple things you can do now to prepare yourself and your loved ones.

U.S. Department of Homeland Security, www.ready.gov

CHAPTER OVERVIEW

There are many simple and inexpensive precautions that Americans can take to help fight terrorism, prevent themselves from becoming the victim of a terrorist strike, or mitigate the effects of an attack. The far greater challenge is getting individuals to undertake these measures. Individuals, families, and households have little propensity to care about disasters before they occur. Everyday concerns will always far outweigh preparing for a terrorist attack.

This chapter outlines the difficulties faced in getting individuals to adopt personal preparedness and security measures. It also describes the means to alert citizens to take preparedness measures. Finally, it describes practical measures that should be taken.

CHAPTER LEARNING OBJECTIVES

After reading this chapter, you should be able to

1. Understand why it is difficult to get individuals to adopt personal preparedness measures.
2. Understand the limitations of current risk communications systems.
3. Describe critical preparedness activities that individuals should adopt.
4. Know what should be in a disaster preparedness kit.
5. Describe individual measures that can be taken to combat terrorism.

THE PREPAREDNESS CHALLENGE

Disasters happen in America every day. Yet, few of us prepare for them. That's a problem. Convincing Americans to prepare for disasters, any kind of disasters, is no easy task. The disasters of 9/11 largely happened at the workplace, and physical damage did not extend far beyond the confines of the attack site. America might not be so lucky next time.

Why We Don't Prepare

There is a considerable body of research suggesting that many individuals change patterns of behavior or take precautionary measures in preparation for disasters only after they have had some personal experience with that threat. Additionally, the perceived need for preparedness recedes as the event becomes more remote.[1] Given that few Americans have experienced, or are likely to experience, a terrorist attack, such findings do not bode well for convincing a significant number of Americans to take commonsense precautions in anticipation of a terrorist attack over threat periods that may span several years between major attacks.

The diverse character of the American public significantly exacerbates the challenge of promoting individual preparedness. Differences in socioeconomic status, gender, race, ethnicity, age, culture, and language all affect an individual's predisposition to undertake preparedness.

Value of Preparedness

Nevertheless, personal preparedness is vitally important. If a disaster occurs, local responders may not be able to reach all the affected population immediately, or they may lack the resources to address every problem or concern. Basic services such as electricity, gas, telephones, or sewage may not be available or people may be forced to evacuate their homes. When individuals can care for themselves, they may greatly reduce the prospects for life-threatening illness or injury and limit the losses that occur in the wake of a tragedy. In addition, being prepared and understanding how to respond will also reduce fear and anxiety, important for both short- and long-term recovery.

While the prospects for encouraging families to undertake preparedness measures are daunting, the payoff could be substantial. There are many popular assumptions, largely influenced by television or disaster movies,[2] suggesting how people will react in the face of disasters. These are largely myths. According to a survey of behavioral science research, panic during community disasters is extremely rare. Panic flight only occurs in extreme situations, such as fleeing fires in confined spaces like narrow hallways. Nor do people tend to act dazed or helpless in the aftermath of tragedy or turn on another for their self-preservation. Rather in the aftermath of tragedy people will tend to look after themselves and actively assist neighbors and kin.[3]

Given that local communities are generally likely to act positively toward a disaster situation, taking even simple measures recommended by emergency preparedness professionals is likely to have a dramatic impact on limiting the extent of damage and casualties and, equally important, allowing emergency responders to focus their assets on the most life-threatening problems.

RISK COMMUNICATIONS

Research does suggest that individuals are far more likely to take action when they are forewarned and they perceive the threat is fairly certain and imminent. One of the most significant challenges for authorities in attempting to mobilize public preparedness is crafting and communicating appropriate warnings that will motivate individuals to prepare for a terrorist attack.

Homeland Security Advisory System

There is no single, integrated national system of communicating terrorist risks to the general public. A national Homeland Security Advisory System (HSAS) was established by President Bush in March 2002. The U.S. attorney general assumed overall responsibility for implementing the system. Subsequently, the Homeland Security Act of 2002 placed responsibility for early warning activities squarely on the shoulders of the secretary of the Department of Homeland Security (DHS). Section 201 of the law also assigns the Directorate of Information Analysis and Infrastructure Protection (IAIP) the responsibility for administering the HSAS.

The HSAS employs a series of color codes to designate various levels of national preparedness in anticipation of a terrorist attack. Associated with each threat condition are a range of suggested protective measures (such as implementing various contingency plans), with federal, state, and local agencies responsible for developing and implementing their own specific response activities.[4]

The primary purpose of the HSAS is to direct federal preparedness activities, though it is widely perceived by many as primarily a warning system for the general public. That's a problem. The HSAS does not meet all the expectations of an effective public alert system.

Public alerts must be credible, specific, understandable, and actionable by individuals.[5] Arguably, the change in color code, which dominates the public perception of what the HSAS represents, is none of these. For example, when the national alert level is changed, local officials may take no publicly discernable action because they have no specific information of threats in their area. In February 2003, when the federal government changed the national threat condition to code orange, the governor of Hawaii chose to maintain a blue level of alert. The governor of Arizona suggested that Arizona might do the same, depending on threats to the state.[6] For average citizens, these responses are incongruous, raising questions about the overall credibility of the HSAS.

The lack of specificity over the nature of the alert and the absence of clear guidance on what actions need to be taken by individual citizens is problematical as well. The American Red Cross, recognizing the public confusion over the color-coded system, has issued its own guide-lines for preparedness by the general public.[7] While the measures it recommends are relatively simple and straightforward, absent more specific information, it is unlikely they will motivate significantly greater numbers of people to undertake preparedness measures.

The Emergency Alert System

There are national systems to provide more targeted emergency alerts. The Emergency Alert System (EAS) is one of two national systems for providing specific alerts and early warnings to the general public. The other is the National Oceanic and Atmospheric Administration's Severe Weather Radio System operated by the National Weather Service. The EAS replaced the Cold War–era Emergency Broadcast System and its monthly announcements "This is a test of the Emergency Alert System—this is only a test. . . ." EAS provides the means with the capability to address the country during emergencies. If used at the national level, only the president, or his representative, can activate EAS; however, state and local governments can also use the system. All AM, FM, and TV broadcast stations participate in EAS as well as cable systems and wireless cable networks. EAS codes can also travel on nonbroadcast frequencies and telephone lines and provides the option to allow new specially equipped cellular phones, pagers, and eventually Internet broadband messages.

EAS messages could include identification of precautionary protective actions for special populations (school children and transportation-dependent individuals) or by location (public parks, beaches, etc.); identification of protective actions (if any) for the general public using familiar landmarks (political jurisdictions, major highways, rivers, railroads, zip codes, etc.); identification of evacuation routes; identification of reception centers for radiological monitoring of evacuees and congregate care centers for lodging of evacuees; instructions on how to maximize protection when sheltering (remain inside, close all windows and doors, shut off any forced air heating or cooling systems); provision of information addressing and responding to false or misleading rumors, as well as the provision of rumor control numbers to the public; ingestion-related instructions and information (how to avoid ingesting contaminated particles); reminders on what to take along when evacuating; and pet information. EAS messages are required to be under two minutes in duration.

A sample message might be

This is an Emergency Alert System announcement concerning a General Emergency at the Duckworth Nuclear Power Plant located near Duckworth, Virginia. The Commonwealth of Virginia Division of Emergency Services, with the authority of Governor Gerald Robinson, issues this message:

At 10:30 this morning, Governor Gerald Robinson issued an Emergency declaration in response to this situation. Because of the potential for release of radioactivity from the Duckworth Nuclear Power Plant, Governor Robinson has ordered the evacuation of public and private schools near the plant. The Governor also requests that all persons within about 5 miles of the plant remain inside, close all windows and doors, and shut off any forced air heating or cooling systems. Please stay tuned to this station for additional information. Also refer to your red and blue "Public Awareness" brochure or to Page X of the Duckworth Telephone directory for further information. This concludes this broadcast.[8]

An EAS message such as this would be followed by more detailed special news broadcasts.

Today, the EAS is primarily used to disseminate weather warnings and Amber (abducted child) alerts. While the system is well-established, there are concerns over the security, funding, and management of the EAS, which is shared by the Federal Communications Commission (FCC), National Weather Service, the DHS, states, and volunteer state and local EAS committees.[9] Nor is participation in the EAS mandatory for state and local governments.

In addition to the EAS there are a plethora of state and local emergency systems ranging from bells and sirens to automatic calling services. There are also a wide variety of commercially available alert systems. Still more likely, many individuals will receive risk communications through the filter of the public media via radio, cable news, or the Internet.

The Media   Many residents are more than likely to receive disaster information from the public media via broadcast or cable television, radio, or the Internet. In the United States, for example, the dramatic drop in death tolls as the result of tornadoes over the last two decades has been attributed in part to the more effective use of warnings issued over the public media.

Public media outlets can be used to disseminate disaster preparedness and response information, stimulate volunteerism (such as giving blood and food), and counteract rumors and inaccurate information.[10]

The Challenges of Risk Communication

Every form of alert system has both advantages and disadvantages in terms of reaching its intended audience and ensuring the message is understood. Of all the means available, telephonic alerts are considered the most accurate, dependable, and capable of reaching most sectors of the population.

Lack of Specific Information

Even with appropriate means to transmit risk communications, providing early warning of terrorist attacks is especially problematic. Unlike weather alerts, for example, authorities may lack sufficient specific information or the time to craft a warning that elicits an appropriate public response.

Lack of Practice

Another challenge is that many authorities are simply not well practiced in risk communications. It is often not clear to them what information is required by different segments of the population, and it is often difficult to get timely feedback that citizens are actually receiving and acting on the information.[11]

Lack of Capacity

There are not adequate systems for individuals to query officials during times of emergency to ask questions or clarify instructions. People will generally call the organizations they are most familiar with (such as the local police station) rather than the entity with the right information and will most certainly, in the event of a major disaster, overload officials with their inquiries. For example, within the United States, the three-digit telephone number "911" has been designated as the universal emergency number. About 96 percent of the United States is covered by some form of 911 system. The FCC has also instituted a program to require wireless carriers to provide 911 services. Efforts are also under way to provide 911 access using voice over the Internet protocols. But 911 services could be overwhelmed during a large-scale emergency.

Limitations of the Media

The use of the media as an alert system may also be a challenge. Most media members want to be professional and accurate. On the other hand, in today's real-time news environment, they are also under a great deal of pressure to get stories out fast and make them as dramatic and timely as possible. Rather than serving as a responsible conduit for risk communications, the media may exacerbate the problem with inaccurate or misleading information. Reporters, for example, may lack the knowledge or expertise to properly cover an event. The media can also control how much time is devoted to a subject matter and to some extent can dictate what types of subject matter public officials can discuss on the air. Studies also show that the amount of media coverage of a disaster can directly affect audience response, prompting the public to take preparedness measures or exacerbating anxiety and stress.[12]

Principles of Effective Communication

Regardless of the means of delivery, the key to successfully motivating the public to undertake preparedness or response measures is to adhere to the principles of effective communication. These are essential for communicating messages both directly to the public and through the media to a general audience.

Clear Goals

Communication efforts must have clear goals and key messages to support them. For example, a goal of "educating the public on bioterrorism and preparing them for any eventuality" is not realistic; informing people of specific dangers is a more achievable goal.

Consistent Message

Another fundamental of effective risk communications is to "stay on message." In other words the message should be focused, consistent, and received by the intended audience.

Appropriate Information

Information must be timely, accurate, and simple to understand; this is particularly important for communicating complex or scientific data. It is equally important to acknowledge uncertainty. Loss of credibility will significantly degrade effectiveness. If the audience does not perceive communications as credible, they will be unlikely to act on them. Key factors that the public assesses in judging credibility are empathy and caring, competence and expertise, honesty and openness, and dedication and commitment.[13]

ISSUES:

MYTHS

Popular myths often interfere with establishing effective risk communications. One is that warnings are more likely to alarm than calm people. In fact, research suggests the opposite is true. When individuals receive information, can express concern, ask questions, and receive accurate answers, they are far more likely to act in a positive manner and experience less stress and apprehension.

Another myth is that the form of risk communications is less important than the content. In contrast, research suggests that the process of structuring and transmitting the message is as vital as the content of the information.

Finally, many believe that issues that arise during a crisis or disaster may be too difficult for the public to understand. However, while individuals may lack the knowledge to grasp technical issues, many of the key issues they must understand and the precautions needed to prepare or respond to a terrorist attack can be explained in plain, understandable language.[14]

1. Are there other myths concerning personal security and preparedness?
2. What is the best way to combat myths?
3. What can be done to get individuals to better prepare for terrorist threats?

INDIVIDUAL, FAMILY, AND COMMUNITY ANTITERRORISM MEASURES

Personal antiterrorism measures for the most part parallel the recommendations by public safety experts for preventing crime. The basic principles are taking steps to properly secure the home, workplace, and personal property; being alert and aware of surroundings and alert to conspicuous or unusual behavior; reporting suspicious activities through appropriate channels; supporting Neighborhood Watch programs; creating liaisons between neighborhood groups and local law enforcement authorities; and developing a system to disseminate information rapidly throughout the neighborhood.[15]

Encouraging individuals to adopt good security practices requires that they understand the threat and perceive it as relevant to their community. Thus, learning about the nature of terrorism will increase the likelihood that good security practices are adopted. Individuals must understand how terrorists look for visible targets where they can avoid detection before or after an attack such as international airports, large cities, major international events, resorts, and high-profile landmarks. Communities must understand the different types of terrorist weapons including explosives, kidnappings, hijackings, arson, and shootings and that the best practice is to deal with a terrorist incident by adapting many of the same techniques used to counter criminal activity. In addition, there are specific skills and practices that can serve as useful antiterrorism measures.

Specific Antiterrorism Measures

The most useful individual antiterrorist precautions are knowing the techniques to respond to bomb threats and suspicious packages, vehicles, and individuals; the most likely terrorist threats that may be encountered; and ones where the public can play a significant role in helping to deter, prevent, or mitigate terrorist acts.

Bomb Threats

If a bomb threat is received, individuals should know how to properly respond. Try to get as much information from the caller as possible. Keep the caller on the line and record everything that is said. Notify the police and the building management.

Individuals should know how to respond to terrorist bombings of high-rise buildings or public conveyances such as subways. These are often favorite bombing targets for terrorists. Individuals should learn where emergency exits and staircases are located. Individuals should think ahead about how to evacuate a building, subway, or congested public area in a hurry. They should also know where fire extinguishers are located and how to use them.

In the event of an incident, to avoid being hurt by debris that might be loosed by an explosion, individuals should take cover against a desk or table. Move away from file cabinets, bookshelves, or other things that might fall. Face away from windows and glass. Move away from exterior walls.

If evacuation of a high-rise building or subway is required, do not use elevators. Elevator shafts could act as a chimney spreading fire or contamination throughout a structure. Rather, building residents should go down the stairwells staying to the right to allow emergency workers to come up.

Suspicious Packages

Law enforcement agencies have identified a number of characteristics that might indicate a suspicious package containing a bomb or other hazardous material. Items to watch for include inappropriate or unusual labeling; excessive postage; handwritten or poorly typed addresses; misspellings of common words; strange return address or no return address; incorrect titles or title without a name; not addressed to a specific person; marked with restrictions, such as "Personal," "Confidential," or "Do not x-ray"; marked with any threatening language; or postmarked from a city or state that does not match the return address.

Suspicious packages can also be identified by appearance. Packages should be inspected for powdery substances felt through or appearing on the package or envelope; oily stains, discolorations, or odors; lopsidedness or unevenness; excessive packaging material such as masking tape, string, etc; excessive weight; and protruding wires or aluminum foil. Packages should also be checked for suspicious sounds like ticking.

If an individual encounters a suspicious package, the following steps are recommended. Put the package or envelope down on a stable surface; do not sniff, touch, taste, or look closely at it or at any contents that may have spilled. Alert others in the area. Leave the area and close any doors. If possible, shut off the ventilation system. Anyone who handled the package should immediately wash their hands with soap and water to prevent spreading potentially hazardous material. Notify a supervisor, security officer, or a law enforcement official. Make a list of persons who were in the room and persons who also may have handled this package or letter.

Responding to Suspicious Activity

Individuals must use their best judgment to identify activities that are extraordinary or suspicious. Suspect activities might include looking lost and/or wandering around; appearing to be conducting surveillance (using cameras/video); abandoning an item and leaving the area quickly; or openly possessing a weapon or any prohibited or dangerous item.

In all cases, the appropriate action is to notify a responsible person such as a superior, security official, or local enforcement. Suspected terrorist activities can also be reported to the FBI's hotline at tips.fbi.gov.

PRINCIPLES OF EMERGENCY PREPAREDNESS PLANNING

Many of the measures applicable to preparing the general public to respond to any kind of a terrorist attack are the same as those necessary to respond to other human-made or technological disasters. Thus, preparing for a terrorist strike is little different from getting ready to deal with virtually any kind of public emergency. Almost none of these efforts require specialized equipment or training. For the most part, emergency planning professionals eschew stockpiling specialized equipment such as gas masks or antibiotics, since most individuals lack the training and experience to maintain and use these items appropriately and safely. Rather, extensive research suggests that simple and commonsense precautions are usually effective at protecting individuals in most cases until emergency response services can be brought to bear.

There are many commercial and public service products to assist in emergency planning and education. The most readily available source of information is the American Red Cross. Individuals can obtain copies of the disaster education material from a local Red Cross chapter. They can also be consulted on the national Red Cross Web site or a special Web site established by the Department of Homeland Security at www.ready.gov.

Virtually all disaster preparedness guides include the following basic components: a disaster supply kit, a family emergency and communication plan, and a shelter-in-place or evacuation scheme.

Disaster Supply Kits Fundamental to any personal response is the establishment of an emergency cache of supplies. These are items that will allow individuals to limit the potential for injury or illness. Federal Emergency Management Agency (FEMA) recommends maintaining sufficient supplies to survive for three days. Items should be kept together in an easy-to-carry container, such as a trash bag, backpack, or duffle bag, not just so they are easy to find in the event of an emergency, but also to ensure that they are easily transportable in case evacuation is required. Disaster preparedness kits should be prepared for the workplace as well as the home. In addition, individuals should include a smaller disaster supply kit in the trunk of their cars. The six basics recommended for home disaster kits include water, food, first aid supplies, clothing and bedding, tools and emergency supplies, and special items.

Water

Stockpiling water must be an absolute rule priority. Water is not only essential for sustaining life and helping the body heal itself in case of injury or illness, but necessary for sanitation. Proper hydration will help individuals think and act and maintain stamina, all essential attributes for responding to what may be stressful, demanding, and chaotic conditions in the aftermath of an attack. A rule of thumb is one gallon of water per person per day for drinking, food preparation, and sanitary purposes. Physical condition, high altitude, and hot weather may significantly increase fluid requirements. For example, children, nursing mothers, and injured or ill individuals may need more. Water should be stored in clean, nontoxic, plastic containers rather than in something that might decompose or break like cardboard milk containers or glass. Stored water should be changed every six months. Containers should be sealed to limit contamination.

Food

Food stored for emergency situations should not require refrigeration, cooking, or extensive food preparation. These supplies should be stored in a cool, dry place in tightly sealed containers and can include the staples normally found on a typical kitchen shelf, such as canned food or packaged goods. In the wake of an attack, individuals should take care to clean containers and food utensils before consuming food to ensure that they do not inadvertently consume contaminated particles that might be in the air. Unlike water, food, except for children and pregnant women can be rationed, with individuals surviving on half their normal intake.

FROM THE SOURCE:

RED CROSS RECOMMENDED DISASTER AID KIT

Flashlight with extra batteries
> Use the flashlight to find your way if the power is out. Do not use candles or any other open flame for emergency lighting.

Battery-powered radio
> News about the emergency may change rapidly as events unfold. You also will be concerned about family and friends in the area. Radio reports will give information about the areas most affected.

Food
> Enough nonperishable food to sustain you for at least one day (three meals), is suggested. Select foods that require no refrigeration, preparation, or cooking, and little or no water. The following items are suggested:
>
> Ready-to-eat canned meals, meats, fruits, and vegetables.
> Canned juices.
> High-energy foods (granola bars, energy bars, etc.).

Water

Keep at least one gallon of water available, or more if you are on medications that require water or that increase thirst. Store water in plastic containers such as soft-drink bottles. Avoid using containers that will decompose or break, such as milk cartons or glass bottles.

Medications

Include usual nonprescription medications that you take, including pain relievers, stomach remedies, etc.

If you use prescription medications, keep at least three-day's supply of these medications at your workplace. Consult with your physician or pharmacist on how these medications should be stored, and your employer about storage concerns.

First aid supplies

If your employer does not provide first aid supplies, have the following essentials:

(20) adhesive bandages, various sizes

(1) 5" x 9" sterile dressing

(1) conforming roller gauze bandage

(2) triangular bandages

(2) 3 x 3 sterile gauze pads

(2) 4 x 4 sterile gauze pads

(1) roll 3" cohesive bandage

(2) germicidal hand wipes or waterless alcohol-based hand sanitizer

(6) antiseptic wipes

(2) pair of large medical-grade nonlatex gloves

Adhesive tape, 2" width

Antibacterial ointment

Cold pack

Scissors (small, personal)

Tweezers

CPR breathing barrier, such as a face shield

Tools and Supplies
    Emergency "space" blanket (Mylar).
    Paper plates and cups, plastic utensils.
    Nonelectric can opener.
    Personal hygiene items, including a toothbrush, toothpaste,
        comb, brush, soap, contact lens supplies, and feminine
        supplies.
    Plastic garbage bags, ties (for personal sanitation uses).
    Include at least one complete change of clothing and
        footwear, including a long-sleeved shirt and long pants,
        as well as closed-toed shoes or boots.
    If you wear glasses, keep an extra pair with your workplace
        disaster supplies.

First Aid Supplies

Recommendations on what first aid supplies should be stockpiled vary. The Red Cross has issued a list of suggested medical supplies. These include items normally found in most commercially available first aid kits or ones that can be purchased in any grocery store or pharmacy. In the wake of a disaster, the greatest concern of emergency responders is addressing potentially life threatening illness or injury, until professional medical service can be provided. These actions include preventing shock, stopping bleeding and maintaining an appropriate level of body fluids, and limiting the risk of infection or contamination. As such, the first aid supplies are principally those that can be used to stop bleeding, clean skin and wounds, and provide comfort. Medications recommended are nonprescription, ones that can be safely administered without expert medical advice, such as pain-relief, antidiarrhea, or stomachache tablets.

Clothing and Bedding

These items can be important for preserving heath and safety after an attack. For example, clothing may be contaminated by particles or debris. Wet clothing will make individuals more vulnerable to illness. Bedding may be required to help treat shock. Safety clothing may be required to recover injured people or remove damage. Individuals should have one complete change of clothing and footwear for each member of the household, including sturdy work shoes, gloves, hats, socks, underwear, sunglasses, and rain gear. Bedding could include blankets or sleeping bags.

Tools and Emergency Supplies

Individuals should assume that public services may be disrupted by a terrorist attack and that they will have to go without television, Internet services, telephony, electricity, and sewage. Thus, tools and emergency supplies are necessary to get emergency information and provide basic services. As a result, recommended lists include items such as portable battery-powered radios and batteries, signal flares, matches, battery-operated clocks, manual can opener, paper and pens, and sanitation and hygiene items like bleach, insect repellent, soap, toothpaste, and toothbrushes. Also recommended are tools and supplies that might be useful for emergency repairs to limit damage or risk of contamination, including wrenches, pliers, and shovels; eye protection; dust masks; duct tape, plastic sheeting, and scissors; and fire extinguishers.

Special Items

The most critical items are those needed to meet the special needs of individuals who would be at higher risk including older persons, children, and pregnant women. Equally vital are preserving important family documents. These might include wills, insurance policies, contract deeds, stocks and bonds, passports, social security cards, immunization records, bank account numbers, credit card account numbers and companies, inventory of valuable household goods, password information, household inventories, important telephone numbers, family records (birth, marriage, death certificates). These materials should be kept in a sealed, waterproof container that can be easily transported.

Family Disaster and Communications Plan

Preparedness experts agree stockpiling supplies alone is not sufficient. Families may not be together when disaster strikes, so they will require a plan on how to contact one another as well as relatives and associates. Families also need to review what needs to be done in different situations and what local plans and services are in place to assist them in times of emergencies.

The first step in crafting individual plans is to gather relevant information. Individuals should find out what kinds of disasters, both natural and human-made, are most likely to occur in the local area and how residents will be notified of impending emergency. The local chapter of the Red Cross is usually the best source of this information. Individuals should also inquire about site-specific emergency plans at schools, day-care providers, workplaces, neighborhoods, public transportation, apartment buildings, and other places where individuals spend most of their day.

Communications planning includes ensuring all family members have means of contacting one another. Often during an emergency it is easier to contact someone outside the disaster area. Many plans call for contacting an out-of-state friend, relative, or associate. Plans also call for picking a safe meeting place located outside the neighborhood or workplace where family members can assemble if they cannot return home.

A most critical element of the plan is to meet with family members and coworkers to discuss what kinds of emergencies might occur and how response will be implemented. Finally, the plan should be practiced.

Evacuation and Shelter in Place

One of the most critical components of emergency response is the decision of whether to shelter in place or evacuate. In most cases, security professionals recommend that unless individuals are in immediate physical danger (fires, explosions, or contamination released inside a building may require evacuation), then it is safer to remain indoors. Fires, conventional explosions, as well as biological, radiological, and chemical incidents may all release dangerous contaminants into the atmosphere. Sheltering in place is perhaps the best method to avoid any hazards that may be present at the scene of a disaster, including dangerous materials that might be in the air or a debris cloud. The best safety practice is to limit exposure to contamination by remaining indoors.

Sheltering in place means taking refuge in a small, interior room or basement with no or few windows in the house, school, or workplace. In the case of a chemical threat, an aboveground shelter is preferable since some chemicals are heavier than air and will sink to lower levels. In addition, other precautions might include closing windows, vents, and flues, and sealing cracks around doors and vents with plastic sheeting and duct tape. Sheltering-in-place under these conditions is usually required for only a few hours, so there is little threat of suffocating.

Unless individuals are under immediate physical danger, they should only evacuate under an order from local government officials. It is, therefore, essential to listen to local radio and television reports when disaster threatens. If evacuation is required, residents should know how to shut off electricity, gas, and water supplies at main switches or values. Residents should secure their homes, let their out-of-state points of contact know where they are going, and evacuate with their disaster preparedness kits using evacuation routes recommended by the authorities. In an evacuation, individuals will have to be mindful that local authorities could make mistakes or misjudge the situation. In the absence of instructions or if individuals are threatened or endangered, they will have to use their best judgment.

Special Needs Preparedness plans must give special consideration to persons with disabilities or special needs. For example, the hearing impaired or non–English speaking may require special arrangements to receive emergency warning information. Mobility impaired individuals or households with single working parents may require assistance in responding to disasters or getting family members to shelters. People with special dietary or medical needs should have specially tailored emergency supplies. Children, older individuals, and persons with depressed immune systems as a result of illness, such as HIV/AIDS, or medical treatment, like chemotherapy, may require additional attention when at risk of injury or contagious disease.

Measures taken to address special needs could include finding out about special assistance programs that might be available in local communities or registering with the local office of emergency services or fire department, so that needed help can be provided quickly in an emergency. Networks of relatives, friends, caregivers, or coworkers can be organized to provide aid in the case of an emergency. People in support networks should know how to operate specialized medical equipment or administer medicines. Supplies to support specialized equipment like batteries for wheelchairs, diapers for children, catheters, or food for hearing and guide dogs should be stockpiled. Individuals may also wear medical alert tags or bracelets to help identify their disability. Those requiring prescription medications might consider maintaining a three-day supply at their workplace in case they cannot get home during an emergency. A physician or pharmacist should be consulted about stockpiling medication to ensure issues such as storage requirements or expiration dates are addressed.

INDICATIONS OF A TERRORIST ATTACK

Obvious signs of physical destruction will not mark all disasters. Symptoms of an event involving hazardous chemical materials might include observing a large number of people in physical distress, such as vomiting, convulsions, or unconsciousness. The presence of strange or out-of-place odors, such as the smell of new-mown hay in a subway or dead birds or small animals might also indicate the release of dangerous chemicals. Incidences of biological or radiological agents might be far less obvious to observe. The initial onset of effects may resemble something similar to that of a cold or flu.

Immediate Actions in the Case of an Emergency

If a terrorist attack does occur, the Red Cross recommends a standard response that would be applicable to any kind of emergency situation. Remain calm and be patient. Follow the advice of local emergency officials. Listen to radio or television for news and instructions. If the disaster occurs in proximity, check for injuries. Give first aid and get help for seriously injured people. Care should be taken to avoid eating or drinking anything that might be contaminated with hazardous material. Check for damage using a flashlight. Do not light matches or candles or turn on electrical switches. Check for fires, fire hazards, and other household hazards. Sniff for gas leaks, starting at the water heater. If a gas leak is suspected, turn off the main gas valve, open windows, and get everyone outside quickly. Shut off any other damaged utilities. Confine or secure your pets. Implement the family emergency communications plan, and check on neighbors or coworkers, especially those who are elderly or disabled.

CHAPTER SUMMARY

For a variety of social, cultural, economic, and psychological reasons it is difficult to get individuals to undertake personal preparedness and security measures. In addition, the national systems for risk communication are inadequate. These limitations aside, there are simple, inexpensive, and effective precautions that individuals can undertake to improve their personal security. Many of these measures are all-hazards; in other words, they are effective for all kinds of disasters from fires to WMD attacks.

CHAPTER QUIZ

1. Why is it difficult to get people to prepare?
2. Why is it important to have individuals undertake personal security and preparedness measures?
3. List the categories of items in an emergency preparedness kit.
4. How does a family communication plan work?
5. How can individuals help combat terrorism?

NOTES

1. Kathleen J. Turner, et al., *Facing the Unexpected: Disaster Preparedness and Response in the United States* (Washington, DC: Joseph Henry Press, 2001), pp. 34–43.
2. E. L. Quarantelli, "The Study of Disaster Movies: Research Problems, Findings, and Implications" (University of Delaware, Disaster Research Center, 1980), passim.
3. E. L. Quarantelli, "How Individuals and Groups Act During Disasters: Planning and Managing Implications for EMS Delivery," Preliminary Paper #138 (University of Delaware, Disaster Research Center, 1989), pp. 4–10.
4. Homeland Security Presidential Directive 3 (March 2002), www.whitehouse.gov/news/releases/2002/03/20020312-5.html.
5. Kathleen J. Turner, et al., *Facing the Unexpected*, p. 30.
6. Advisory Panel to Assess Domestic Response Capabilities for Terrorism Involving Weapons of Mass Destruction, *Forging America's New Normalcy: Securing Our Homeland, Preserving Our Liberty*, Santa Monica, CA: RAND, December 15, 2003), p. 27.
7. "American Red Cross Homeland Security Advisory System Recommendations for Individuals, Families, Neighborhoods, Schools, and Businesses," www.redcross.org/services/disaster/beprepared/hsas.html.

8. FEMA, "Background on Emergency Alert System," www.fema.gov/rrr/rep/easrep.shtm.

9. Partnership for Public Warning, "The Emergency Alert System: An Assessment" (February 2004), p. 26, www.partnershipforpublicwarning.org/ppw/docs/eas_assessment.pdf.

10. Ruth Seydlitz, J. William Spencer, and George Lundskow, "Media Presentations of a Hazard Event and the Public's Response: An Empirical Examination." *International Journal of Mass Emergencies and Disasters* 12/3 (November 1994): 279–301.

11. E. L. Quarantelli, "How Individuals and Groups Act During Disasters," pp. 25, 27, 31.

12. Defense Treat Reduction Agency, "Human Behavior and WMD Crisis/Risk Communications Workshop" (March 2001), p. 21.

13. U.S. Department of Health and Human Services, "Communicating in a Crisis: Risk Communication Guidelines for Public Officials" (2002), pp. 9–18, 25.

14. U.S. Department of Health and Human Services, "Communicating in a Crisis," pp. 24–25.

15. Jean F. O'Neil, "Crime Prevention Can Spur and Support Homeland Security in Neighborhoods and Communities," *Topics in Crime Prevention* (Winter 2003), pp. 2–3.

18

THE FUTURE OF HOMELAND SECURITY

Adapting and Responding to the Evolving Terrorist Threat While Balancing Safety and Civil Liberties

America is prepared but can become better prepared.

Governor James Gilmore III, Chairman of the Advisory Panel to Assess Domestic Response Capabilities for Terrorism Involving Weapons of Mass Destruction

CHAPTER OVERVIEW

This chapter offers a glimpse of what Americans may face in the future both in terms of new threats and new capabilities to counter them. It discusses how both transnational and domestic terrorism may evolve in the future. The chapter also looks at possible changes in tactics terrorists might adopt to make their attacks more deadly, even without obtaining WMD materials. It also looks at significant technological innovations that might be adopted to provide better homeland security or create even more insidious threats. Finally, it examines organizational reforms that might be undertaken to improve security.

CHAPTER LEARNING OBJECTIVES

After reading this chapter, you should be able to

1. Understand how transnational and domestic terrorism may change in the future.
2. Understand the role of technology in shaping the future of homeland security.
3. Understand why the structure of national homeland security organizations may change in the future.

THE FUTURE OF TERRORISM

There is little question but that the terrorist threats the United States will face in the years ahead will be different from the al-Qaida network that launched the September 11 attacks. Global terrorism is in transition. Terrorist sanctuaries have been destroyed. Leaders captured. Money seized. New homeland security regimes and counterterrorism measures have been put in place. Now the terrorists are trying to adapt—sponsoring attacks by others, recruiting, fund-raising, inspiring religious and ethnic hatred, and debating new strategies for attacking the West as well as regimes in the Middle East.[1]

How terrorism will evolve in the future is far from certain. The war on terrorism, like all wars, is a contest of action and counteraction that can't be predicted with certainty. There are no rule books or guidelines that can provide a guaranteed blueprint for success. While the future will always remain a foreign country, there are emerging trends and wild cards that could significantly turn the course of future events. Two of the most significant could be a resurgence of domestic terrorism and a new terrorist tactic—weapons of mass disruption.

Domestic Terrorism   While it is far from clear how terrorist organizations will evolve in the future, there is one aspect of the threat that may not be receiving sufficient attention as an emerging danger, the threat of domestic terrorism. While the events of September 11 focused America's attention on foreign foes, concern over domestic groups that perpetrate violence should not be ignored. Before the 9/11 attacks, the most deadly strike on U.S. soil by a nonstate actor was the bombing of the Alfred P. Murrah Federal Office Building, an act carried out by domestic extremists. There are many groups that could provide the foundation for the next wave of terrorism. By some counts, over 600 groups have demonstrated the potential to conduct violent acts with memberships ranging from a handful to hundreds.[2] In addition, individuals and small ad hoc groups have shown the capability to launch attacks that take lives and destroy or damage property. Today, these groups represent lesser dangers than organizations like al-Qaida, but that may not always be so. As homeland security measures overwhelmingly focus on threats from overseas, enemies may be anxious to seek alliances within the United States. Domestic groups that act in sympathy or as offshoots of transnational networks, extending their reach inside the United States, could represent particularly serious future security risks.

In the 1980s the activity level of domestic groups declined significantly and the nature of these factions shifted from predominantly left-wing movements that had been involved with the anti-Vietnam War movement and civil rights protests to right-wing organizations espousing racial supremacy and antigovernment ideology. The activities of right-wing groups reached a plateau by the mid-1990s. In the last several years, groups associated with animal rights, antiglobalization, and environmental extremism have been on the rise. For example, the FBI has estimated that since 1996 the Earth Liberation Front, an ecological terrorist group, has committed 600 criminal acts costing over $42 million.[3] Though such groups are primarily responsible for the increase in terrorist acts since 1999, right-wing extremist organizations, which often target people as well as property, are considered potentially more formidable and dangerous.

This pattern of domestic terrorism suggests that it is broadly linked to mainstream contemporary political, religious, and social movements, where small factions have attempted to radicalize broad-based, activist social agendas. For complex political and cultural movements, like the "antiglobalization" campaign, future threats could come from a strange admixture of factions from the right and the left.

While these groups currently present a notable, but secondary class of risk, they can be a significant domestic security problem. The greatest danger for the United States is concerted operations by multiple groups—domestic organizations, individuals, and transnational actors acting together—to maximize the strain on intelligence, law enforcement, defense, and consequence management resources. Such a "coalition" attack might also increase the range of weapons and tactics available to both foreign and domestic groups. This cooperation might occur not out of shared motivations or planning, but rather out of a desire to achieve the common ends of public violence and destruction. Alternatively, it is possible that transnational organizations and domestic groups might intentionally work closely together, driven by ideological motivations or for financial gain.

Cooperation between domestic and foreign groups would not be unprecedented. Nor would it be impossible for such alliances to be forged without notice. For example, only during the first half of the 1950s were communist activities in the United States an issue of widespread popular concern. Claims of vast domestic spy networks, however, were soon dismissed. Recently, however, searches of formerly classified communication intercepts, USA Communist Party records, and former Soviet Bloc archives have revealed that the American Communist Party's covert activities from the 1930s to the 1950s were far larger and well-organized than most assumed and that agents worked in close cooperation with or under the direct supervision of Soviet military and intelligence organizations.[4] Thus, while the recent attention given transnational terrorist organizations and potential aggressor states is not misplaced, over the long term the threat of domestic groups can also not be ignored.

Weapons of Mass Disruption

In addition to the many known tactics and methods for conducting terrorist attacks, a new danger may appear in the future by enemies seeking new ways to inflict mass casualties, even if they cannot obtain weapons of mass destruction. Terrorists have never before grouped multiple means of attack against multiple locations, but they have good reason to consider such tactics as a means for achieving greater levels of damage and disruption. Such a strike might be called a "weapon of mass disruption."

A weapon of mass disruption would incorporate existing weapons and delivery systems. Terrorists could maximize their effects by conducting orchestrated strikes. These might be several attacks with the same kind of weapon striking at several geographically dispersed areas to place maximum strain on resources and create a heightened sense of vulnerability. Alternatively, an attack might combine different targets and weapons into a single coordinated operation at one or several locations. By placing the same amount of effort dedicated to several attacks into one synchronized operation, an enemy might achieve far greater effects than what could be achieved by several disparate attacks. Even without inflicting mass casualties, a well-orchestrated series of attacks could be a significant threat, in effect creating "mass disruption."

A mass attack might include strikes on multiple urban centers in relatively close proximity to maximize the difficulty of coordinating responses and overtax local resources. For example, an enemy might choose to strike Tampa, Florida, a major urban area, as well as the home of two critical major military commands. At the same time, strikes might hit Orlando, Florida, a relatively dense population area that also contains several national entertainment venues including Walt Disney World, and Jacksonville, a major urban, port, and industrial area. These targets might be chosen because the North Florida area is untested in dealing with major terrorist strikes.

Preparatory activities may well pave the way for an attack to increase its effectiveness. In the case of the hypothetical Florida attack, for example, strikes might be preceded by an arson campaign, setting a series of forest fires in the southern part of the state. Forest fires are often a serious problem in Florida, and the natural response would be to shift assets to deal with the threat. Thus, the bulk of the state's first-responder capabilities might be out of position when the rest of the strikes occur. At the same time, small diversionary terrorist strikes might also be conducted in other parts of the country to distract national responders and slow rapidly dispatching support to the actual attack site. Indeed, creating the impression of a national terror campaign might make federal and state authorities reluctant to dispatch some resources to the scene. They could be tempted to husband assets for subsequent attacks.

These attacks might target critical infrastructure as a means of magnifying a strike's disruptive effects. In the example of the hypothetical

North Florida strike, all three cities include seaports, airports, and major road systems. Attacks could begin with immobilizing the transportation networks. Hazardous material at the ports or being transported by highway could be hijacked or sabotaged to start the attack. Shoulder-fired precision-guided weapons or suicide attacks might have the best prospects for penetrating existing security barriers and fences. Immediate mass casualties might be inflicted by an arson strike on a major fertilizer factory or sabotage at the Crystal River nuclear power plant.

To complicate consequence management, small attacks might be launched at hospitals, police stations, and emergency operations centers. Many state and city emergency operations centers are particularly vulnerable. Often they lack physical security protection and redundant communications. Backup centers and mobile command posts usually do not exist.[5] For example, the New York City Emergency Operations Center was on the 23rd floor of 7 World Trade Center. When the building was destroyed during the 9/11 attacks, the city had no adequate secondary command and control capability available. It took three days to reconstitute all the functions and capabilities lost by the destruction of the emergency operations center.[6]

Another vulnerability that might be exploited is the tendency of local first responders to rush to the scene of a disaster. Often people, supplies, and services are spontaneously mobilized and sent into a disaster-stricken area. This phenomenon is called *convergence.*[7] It can lead to congestion, create confusion, hinder the delivery of aid, compromise security, and waste scarce resources. This proved to be a major concern during the response to the September 11 attack on the World Trade Center. When the first tower was struck, firefighters, police officers, and emergency medical technicians from all over the metropolitan area streamed to the site, leaving other parts of the city vulnerable and, after the towers collapsed, creating tremendous problems in accounting for emergency personnel.[8]

By sequencing strikes in an attack, responders can also be targeted, creating additional casualties and chaos. For example, the timing of the strikes on the World Trade Center resulted in the loss of 343 fire personnel and destroyed 91 pieces of equipment. Included in the casualties were virtually the entire complement of the New York City

Fire Department's trained cadre of hazardous material (Hazmat) response specialists.[9]

In addition, attacks could well use "secondary devices" specifically intended to harm first responders and civilian onlookers. Explosives are commonly used for this purpose,[10] but other weapons might be employed as well. Employing small amounts of various chemical, biological, toxin, or radiological agents in the ancillary strikes against first responders might further confuse a coordinated response. In this manner, an enemy lacking robust delivery systems, such as cruise missiles and UAVs, or large amounts of deadly agents could still achieve the disruptive effects and psychological casualties that might be caused by the use of unconventional weapons.

Information warfare could be a particularly useful instrument to supplement a mass disruption attack. For example, in 1992, the London Ambulance Service installed a faulty computer dispatch service. Delays resulting from dispatching snafus resulted allegedly in the deaths of 20 to 30 patients. An intentional disruption of computer dispatching services during a crisis might result in even far greater chaos and disruption. Alternatively, electronic jamming might be used to interrupt emergency frequencies. Meanwhile the Internet, as was the case after the 9/11 attacks, could be employed to spread rumors and disinformation or be the target of denial-of-service attacks.[11] In fact, this should be expected as a matter of course. The increasing likelihood of cyberstrikes following physical attacks appears to be becoming an established trend.[12] Additionally, as after the September 11 strikes, a mass disruption attack would likely generate unprecedented local levels of user demand, severely stressing servers and some Web sites such as popular news portals.[13]

In practice, mass disruption attacks could take many forms. Vulnerabilities that might make choice targets for a coordinated attack can vary significantly from region to region. Sections of the country with high populations, heavy industry, and concentrated transportation networks will present different kinds of targets than areas with dispersed populations and scattered infrastructure. For example, urban centers, with large populations, commuters, and tourists that could spread an infectious disease quickly, would be better targets for an orchestrated series of contagious biological agent attacks.

Given the many potential variables involved, predicting the balance of advantage between attacker and defender in this form of competition is difficult. A major attack would probably be difficult and costly to execute, but might reap substantial damage. Elements of this tactic, however, could be employed on a smaller scale and used very effectively for limited cost and at much less risk. Indeed, it may be only a matter of time before the United States faces such threats. Most of the means to launch such attacks are within the grasp of many potential state and nonstate enemies. A skilled and determined leader may be the only element missing from the mix of capabilities required to launch such an attack. Leadership, in fact, could be the key variable in determining whether these attacks against the United States ever become a reality. If such enemies do arise, they may well find that the element of surprise is on their side.

THE FUTURE OF TECHNOLOGY

Much effort has been made to harness technology in the war on terrorism. Most of the technology being applied is "off-the-shelf." In other words, existing equipment and technical capabilities are being applied to address new problems. As research in science and technology looks to develop new, cutting-edge long-term solutions there may be some technologies that provide dramatic new advantages. Technology may, however, also unleash unprecedented threats. Among the new innovations to consider closely are those resulting from new biotechnologies and directed energy weapons.

Nanotechnologies and the Revolution in Biosecurity

One of the promising areas for enhancing homeland security is in the area of biotechnology. In particular, advances in biotechnology may offer up dramatic new opportunities to improve defenses against chemical, biological, and toxin agents. Nanotechnologies, or more likely microelectrical mechanical systems (MEMS) that might employ nanotechnologies, in particular, hold tremendous promise for creating incredibly small machines that could become an arsenal for fighting bioweapons. Devices could be manufactured on an industrial scale and used virtually anywhere. Once the technology has matured, it might be applied to a variety of purposes, produced and employed relatively cheaply, and widely proliferated.

Advances in chemistry and biology could result in cheap and widely proliferated systems that can provide screening and early detection.[14] For example, "lab-on-a-chip" technologies that duplicate operations performed in a conventional laboratory with specially designed chip architectures consisting of interconnected fluid reservoirs and pathways that can be used to assay cells or individual molecules are currently being commercially developed as diagnostic tools. Potentially, such technologies could provide treatments as well.[15]

The list of other innovations that could potentially aid biodefenses is rather substantial, including high-throughput laboratories for testing and experimentation that could vastly expand the national capacity to screen and analyze materials as well as support vaccine and other antigen development programs.[16] New detectors capable of better screening against infectious diseases or smuggling bioweapons may become available.[17] Remote detection of bioattacks employing spectral imagery and new forms of radar could also mature over the next decade.[18]

The uncertainty surrounding these new defenses relates to how soon they will mature from experimental systems to full-scale commercial and military use. Some of these technologies, particularly those relying on advances in the rapidly growing field of bioinformatics, may be available in the near term. Others may not appear before the end of the decade.[19]

Adversarial Uses of Advanced Technologies

As with most advances in biotechnology, innovations that enhance U.S. defenses might also be used to fashion better weapons. The proliferation of biological and toxin threats will likely only grow with time. Biotechnology is one of the fastest growing commercial sectors in the world. The number of biotechnology companies in the United States alone has tripled since 1992. These firms are research-intensive, bringing new methods and products to the marketplace every day, and many of the benefits of this effort are largely dual-use, increasing the possibility that knowledge, skills, and equipment could be adopted to a biological agent program. As the global biotechnology industry expands, nonproliferation efforts will have a difficult time keeping pace with the opportunities available to field a bioweapon.[20]

In addition, biological science and the commercial applications of biotechnology innovations are evolving rapidly. An analysis done less than a decade ago may already be out of date in capturing the growing capability of even moderately skilled and equipped actors to produce new and more effective weapons. The pharmaceutical industry, for example, has invested enormous effort in making drugs more stable for oral or aerosol delivery and thus, unintentionally, is developing the tools for producing the next generation of easily deliverable biological weapons.[21]

Although there are already many obtainable pathogens that could serve as effective biological weapons, in the future there could be other dangers as well. A sophisticated and reasonably well financed enemy could introduce previously unknown and potentially very deadly threats. Advances in molecular and biological engineering open up the possibility of fashioning new organisms or modifying existing diseases by means such as transferring pathogenic properties between different agents. Enemies might, for example, breed strains of bacteria resistant to commonly used antibiotics.[22]

In particular, genomics and genetic engineering could serve as tools for developing new weapons.[23] Upwards of 200 bacterial genomes have already been sequenced, and gene survey techniques are being used to identify unique characteristics that determine virulence and pathology.[24] This information can be used to craft new weapons as well as new cures. One way that this can be done is through recombinant DNA technology. Recombinant DNA is created by incorporating material from two or more sources into a single recombinant molecule. Currently, recombinant DNA processes are difficult and have a low success rate. When new DNA is created, there is no guaranteed way to pass the genetically altered organism's newly obtained trait on to subsequent generations. However, recombinant DNA technology, in turn, enables new forms of genetic engineering. Through cloning, for example, sections of DNA can be inserted into a cell, in effect, creating new organisms.[25]

The science behind recombinant DNA technology is widely known, and legitimate scientific experiments have demonstrated how this knowledge can be misused. In 2001, a team of Australian scientists inadvertently altered a strain of mousepox creating a highly virulent microorganism that proved deadly, even to laboratory mice already vaccinated against the disease.[26] This accident demonstrated the potential for malevolent research to create new and unexpected threats. Further highlighting the potential for creating recombinant biological weapons was the successful effort of a team of researchers in New York who reconstituted a polio virus from DNA samples, suggesting that new designer diseases or extinct diseases could be assembled from basic genetic material.[27] It cannot be assumed that enemies will not have access to the technical skills required to conduct similar research. Of particular concern is the proliferation of the research and skills of thousands of Russian scientists trained under the former Soviet Union's extensive bioweapons program.[28]

Recent advances in biotechnology could also eventually lead to pathogens designed to cause disease in only certain types of people or even unique individuals, depending on their genetic makeup, sometimes called an "ethnic bullet."[29] The difficulties in perfecting such a weapon, however, might be significant. An enemy would have to identify a genetic marker that was unique to the targeted population. Such an approach might work well against an isolated group. The United States, with its diverse and genetically mixed population, on the other hand, would represent a problematic target, though an enemy might perhaps attempt to target a particular subgroup in the country. Given the many variables and difficulties of developing such a bioagent, it could well take decades to develop a practical weapon.[30]

Biotechnology might also be used to produce genetically engineered antimaterial weapons. Through the application of recombinant DNA technologies and cloning techniques, it could eventually be possible to develop fast-acting microbes with particular behaviors that can be targeted against certain materials. For example, biodegradative microorganisms might be created that can damage hydrocarbons, concrete, plastics, rubber, composite materials, or even metals.[31] Such weapons might be used to attack critical infrastructure, such as rupturing power cables or pipelines. Unlike a conventional bomb that might breech one point in a pipeline, an antimaterial bioweapon might infect and incapacitate an entire system.[32]

Directed Energy   Directed energy technologies are used in the production of concentrated beams of electromagnetic energy, such as lasers. Future directed energy weapons may have their greatest impact on improving protection of critical infrastructure. American military developments in mobile high-energy lasers, for example, could produce, within a decade, prototype weapons capable of providing point defenses of areas against artillery, rockets, mortars, missiles, and low-flying unmanned aerial vehicles (UAVs). Ground-based lasers are being designed not only for battlefield uses, but also to protect Israeli population centers from terrorist attacks using *Katyusha* rockets and other improvised rocket, artillery, and mortar systems.[33] There is no reason these systems could not be employed in the United States as well.

Directed energy technologies may have a number of homeland security applications. They might, for example, be used at airports to defend planes taking off and landing from attack by shoulder-fired missiles or provide defenses for critical infrastructure, government buildings, or public events against strikes by makeshift rockets or missiles. Eventually, tactical lasers may also be useful against low-flying cruise missiles or UAVs. It is, however, not likely that these capabilities would be widely available before the end of the decade.

THE FUTURE OF HOMELAND SECURITY STRUCTURES

While there will likely be changes in the war on terrorism resulting from the changing nature of the terrorist threat and the emergence of new technologies, there will also no doubt be innovations resulting from efforts to enhance and upgrade homeland security regimes. Indeed, history suggests changes are inevitable. The National Security Act of 1947 created the National Security Council, the Department of Defense, and the Central Intelligence Agency, the primary weapons used in the Cold War. In practice, however, most of the instruments used to fight the Cold War from NATO to nuclear deterrence and containment evolved over a decade through a process of experimentation, improvisation, and trial and error. Much as during the Cold War, it is unrealistic to believe that the United States could establish all the right instruments to fight a complex global war on terrorism in short order.

Organizational Innovation

One area that will likely gain increased attention in the years ahead is the organization of the Department of Homeland Security. Among the issues that will likely be addressed are the appropriate roles and missions of the department. Policy makers will have to decide, for example, if all the appropriate critical homeland security missions have been consolidated in the department or, in some cases, if consolidation has gone too far.

Consolidation of biomedical homeland security response assets offers an example of the challenge of getting the right balance of responsibilities. The Homeland Security Act transferred the operational resources of several agencies to the DHS, including oversight of the Strategic National Stockpile. Managed by the Centers for Disease Control and Prevention (CDC) in the Department of Health and Human Services (HHS), the Strategic National Stockpile provides for the storage and deployment of pharmaceuticals, supplies, and equipment for responding to a national health emergency or disaster. The DHS also oversees the Metropolitan Medical Response System and the National Disaster Medical System, including national disaster medical assistance teams, veterinary medical assistance teams, and disaster mortuary support teams—formerly administered by the HHS. In addition, the DHS has assumed the functions of the HHS's Office of Emergency Preparedness, which manages and coordinates federal health, medical, and health-related social services for major emergencies and disasters. While the DHS has overall supervision for these programs, the HHS retains responsibility for the day-to-day running of many of the key biomedical response programs.[34]

Bifurcating responsibility for medical response programs such as the National Strategic Stockpile between the HHS and DHS was probably a mistake. Managing complex programs through interagency memoranda of understanding is bureaucratic, inefficient, and unnecessary. Clearly, efficiencies could be gained by transferring responsibility and budgetary oversight of these efforts into one department or the other.

The DHS lacks the expertise and experience to oversee large medical emergency response programs. It could well make more sense to shift responsibility for overseeing the National Strategic Stockpile, the Metropolitan Medical Response System, and the National Disaster Medical System to HHS.

Recognizing that the DHS had little to contribute to managing the National Strategic Stockpile, in 2004, the department turned management of the program back over to the HHS. The need for further changes and consolidation is still being debated.

CHAPTER SUMMARY

The future is a foreign country. Nothing is predetermined. Nothing is inevitable. Yet, there are two predictions that might be made with confidence. The threat of terrorism will remain with us for some years to come, and homeland security organizations, programs, and activities will have to evolve to keep up, or better yet, stay ahead of the terrorists.

In the future, terrorists will likely change their tactics, organizations, and, perhaps, goals—searching for new ways to undermine U.S. security. Technology will almost certainly be a critical dynamic in this competition. Likewise, U.S. security systems will grow as lessons learned and new initiatives are adopted to meet the threat of global terrorism.

NOTES

1. Bruce Hoffman, "Al Qaeda, Trends in Terrorism and Future Potentialities: An Assessment," (Santa Monica: Rand, 2003), www.rand.org/publications/P/P8078/P8078.pdf.

2. See the findings of the Southern Poverty Law Center, www.splcenter.org/intelligence-project/ip-index.html.

3. Statement of Dale L. Watson before the Senate Select Intelligence Committee (February 6, 2002).

4. Allen Weinstein and Alexander Vassiliev, *The Haunted Wood: Soviet Espionage in America—The Stalin Era* (New York: Random House, 1999), passim; Harvey Klehr and John Earl Haynes, *Venona: Decoding Soviet Espionage in America* (New Haven, CT: Yale University Press, 2000), passim.

5. Committee on Science and Technology for Countering Terrorism, *Making the Nation Safer: The Role of Science and Technology in Countering Terrorism* (Washington, DC: National Academies Press, 2002), pp. 8-2, 8-3.

6. James Kendra and Tricia Wachtendorf, "Elements of Resilience in the World Trade Center Attack," Disaster Research Center, University of Delaware, pp. 6–9, www.udel.edu/DRC. See also Brian A. Jackson, et al., *Protecting Emergency Responders: Lessons Learned from Terrorist Attacks* (Santa Monica, CA: Rand, 2002).

7. For a discussion of convergence, see Julie L. Demuth, *Countering Terrorism: Lessons Learned from Natural and Technological Disasters* (Washington, DC: National Academy of Sciences, 2002), p. 7.

8. The problem of organizations, units, and individuals "self-dispatching" themselves without the knowledge or permission of the on-scene incident commander was also a problem at the site of the attack on the Pentagon. Arlington County, *After Action Report on the Response to the September 11 Terrorist Attack on the Pentagon* (Arlington, VA: Arlington County, 2002), p. 12.

9. *Learning from Disasters: Weapons of Mass Destruction Preparedness Through Worker Training* (Washington, DC: The National Clearinghouse for Worker Safety and Health Training, 2002), p. 18.

10. Paul M. Maniscalco and Hank T. Christen, *Understanding Terrorism and Managing the Consequences* (Upper Saddle River, NJ: Prentice Hall, 2002), p. 228.

11. National Infrastructure Protection Center, "Cyber Protests Related to the War on Terrorism: The Current Threat," (November 2001), www.nipc.gov/publications/nipcpub/cyberprotests1101.pdf. This report concluded that post-9/11 illicit computer activity was not particularly damaging.

12. "Cyber Attacks During the War on Terrorism: A Predictive Analysis" (Institute for Security and Technology Studies, September 22, 2001), p. 1.

13. *The Internet under Crisis Conditions: Learning from September 11* (Washington, DC: National Academies Press, 2002), p. 2.

14. *Lab-on-a-Chip: The Revolution in Portable Instrumentation*, 4th ed. (Englewood, NJ: Technical Insights, January 10, 2002), passim.

15. For discussions on nanotechnologies see Executive Office of the White House, Office of Science and Technology, *Leading to the Next Industrial Revolution: A Report by the Interagency Working Group on Nanoscience, Engineering and Technology* (February 2000); Philip S. Antón, et al., *The Global Technology Revolution: Bio/Nano/Material Trends and Their Synergies with Information Technology by 2015* (Santa Monica: Rand, 2001). The Defense Advanced Projects Research Agency has pursued some of these technologies for biodefense, including the use of biofluidic chips that would be capable of regulating complex cellular and molecular processing. Such chips, for example, might be capable of imitating the human immune system. Acting as remote sensors they could be used to alert to the presence of deadly pathogens.

16. J. Craig Venter, "High-Throughput Sequencing, Information Generation, and the Future of Biology," in *Firepower in the Lab: Automation in the Fight against Infectious Diseases and Bioterrorism*, edited by Scott P. Layne, Tony J. Beugelsdijk, and C. Kumar N. Patel (Washington, DC: Joseph Henry Press, 2001), pp. 261–66.

17. For example, one proposal under consideration is a pass-through portal that reads the thermal plume surrounding each individual, which carry hundreds of bioafflunets and skin particles. These could be sampled and provide evidence of biological weapons or illnesses, as well as chemicals and explosives. Gary S. Settles, et al., "Potential for Portal Detection of Human Chemical and Biological Contamination," *SPIE Aerosense* 4378 (April 2001): 1–9.

18. Hyperspectral imaging examines the light reflection of different kinds of atoms to determine material composition. LIDAR (light detection and ranging) is a form of radar that

operates at very high frequencies, sending out two nearly simultaneous beams of light at slightly different wavelengths. The beams are absorbed by chemicals and biological material at slightly different levels, and measuring the comparative strength of the reflected beams is used to identify the composition of the material. LIDAR is already used to monitor air pollution. The U.S Army has developed a prototype system, the Long Range-Biological Standoff Detection System (LR-BSDS) mounted on a UH-60 helicopter designed to detect and track biological aerosol clouds at distances up to 30 kilometers. Future systems could be employed using satellites, aircraft, unmanned aerial vehicles, or aerostats. There are also many other candidate technologies for biological agent detection. See North American Technology and Industrial Base Organization, *Biological and Detection System Technologies, Technology and Industrial Base Study: A Primer on Biological Detection Systems* (February 2001), pp. 4-1 to 4-20, www.dtic.mil/natibo. Still, no single system or technology promises a ready solution that could detect all types of agents and methods of attack or provide comprehensive national coverage. In addition, most of these technologies are expensive and require significant support requirements.

19. Jonathan R. Davis and Joshua Lederberg, *Public Health Systems and Emerging Infections: Assessing the Capabilities of the Public and Private Sector* (Washington, DC: National Academies Press, 2000), pp. 1–23; *Biological Threats and Terrorism: Assessing the Science and Response Capabilities: Workshop Summary* (Washington, DC: National Academies Press, 2002), pp. 1–19.

20. Jonathan B. Tucker, "Putting Teeth in the Biological Weapons Convention," *Issues in Science and Technology* (Spring 2002): 71–77.

21. Fifth Review Conference of the States Parties to the Convention on the Prohibition of Development, Production and Stockpiling of Bacteriological (Biological) and Toxin Weapons and on Their Destruction, Background Paper on New Scientific and Technological Developments Relevant to the Convention on the Prohibition of the Development, Production and Stockpiling of Bacteriological (Biological) and Toxin Weapons and on Their Destruction, (September 14, 2001), p. 11, www.brad.ac.uk/acad/sbtwc/revconf/5conv4.pdf.

22. Peter H. Gilligan, "Therapeutic Challenges Posed by Bacterial Bioterrorism Threats," *Current Opinion in Microbiology* 5/5(2002): 489–495.

23. Claire M. Fraser and Malcolm R. Dando, "Genomics and Future Biological Weapons: The Need for Preventive Action by the Biomedical Community," *Nature Genetics* 29 (November 2001): 254.

24. Thomas S. Whittam and Alyssa C. Bumbaugh, "Inferences from Whole-genome Sequences of Bacterial Pathogens," *Current Opinion in Genetics and Development* 12/6 (November 2002): 719–725.

25. Michael T. Madigan, et al., "Amplifying DNA: The Polymerase Chain Reaction." In *Brock Biology of Microoganisms*, edited by Paul F. Corey (Upper Saddle River, NJ: Prentice Hall, 1997), pp. 374–375.

26. "The Need for Oversight of Hazardous Research," *Issues in Science and Technology* (Spring 2002): 74.

27. Jeronimo Cello, et al., "Chemical Synthesis of Poliovirus DNA: Generation of Infectious Virus in the Absence of Natural Template," *Science Express Reports* (July 11, 2002).

28. Jonathan Tucker, "Biological Weapons Proliferation from Russia: How Great a Threat?" Paper presented to the 7th Carnegie International Non-Proliferation Conference (Washington, DC, January 11–12, 1999).

29. British Medical Association, *Biotechnology, Weapons, and Humanity* (Canada: Harwood Academic Publishers, 1999), pp. 53–67.

30. Testimony of Raymond Zilinskas before the Subcommittee on National Security, House Veterans Affairs, and International Relations Committee (October 20, 1999), passim.

31. Many such microorganisms already exist, but natural processes of degradation and deterioration by them are normally slow-acting. See, for example, Patricia A. Wagner, et al., "Biodegradation of Composite Materials," *International Biodeterioration & Biodegradation* 38/2 (September 1996): 125–132.

32. Some commercial research has been made in this area in the form of bioremediation, such as developing fast-acting microbes that can consume oil spills. See, for example, G. Saylor, "Field Applications of Genetically Engineered Microorganisms for Bioremediation Processes," *Current Opinion in Biotechnology* 11 (2000): 288–289. The U.S. military has studied the possibility of biodegradation as a military weapon. See, for example, James R. Campbell, "Defense against Biodegradation of Military Materiel," Paper presented to the Non-Lethal Defense Conference (February 1, 1998).

33. Josef Schwartz, et al., "Tactical High Energy Laser," Paper presented to the SPIE Proceedings on Laser and Beam Control Technologies (January 21, 2002), pp. 1–6. A fixed-site Tactical High Energy Laser (THEL) was developed by TRW Inc. under a $89 million contract. In tests, the system has successfully shot down 25 rockets. It is, however, not capable of being deployed for operational use. The U.S. Army is developing a mobile version and has requested additional funding for the program. In February 2004, the Army's tactical laser project was formally transitioned into an acquisition program. The first prototype of the mobile laser is due to appear in 2008. See also, *Directed Energy Weapons: Technologies, Applications, and Implications* (Washington, DC: The Lexington Institute, 2003), pp. 11–12, 24–25.

34. James Jay Carafano, "Improving Federal Response to Catastrophic Bioterrorist Attacks: The Next Steps," Heritage Backgrounder #1705 (November 13, 2003), www.heritage.org/Research/HomelandDefense/BG1705.cfm.

1

PROFILES OF SIGNIFICANT ISLAMIC EXTREMIST AND INTERNATIONAL TERRORIST GROUPS AND STATE SPONSORS

The following profiles are adopted from the U.S. State Department's report *Patterns of Global Terrorism—2003* published in 2004. While these profiles are generally recognized as reliable, it is important to recall they reflect the analysis and opinions of the U.S. government.[1]

PROFILES OF SIGNIFICANT ISLAMIC EXTREMIST TERRORIST GROUPS

Sunni Extremist Terrorist Organizations

Al-Qaida a.k.a. Qa'idat al-Jihad

DESCRIPTION

Established by Usama Bin Ladin in the late 1980s to bring together Arabs who fought in Afghanistan against the Soviet Union. Helped finance, recruit, transport, and train Sunni Islamic extremists for the Afghan resistance. Current goal is to establish a pan-Islamic Caliphate throughout the world by working with allied Islamic extremist groups to overthrow regimes it deems "non-Islamic" and expelling Westerners and non-Muslims from Muslim countries—particularly Saudi Arabia. Issued statement under banner of "the World Islamic Front for Jihad Against the Jews and Crusaders" in February 1998, saying it was the duty of all Muslims to kill US citizens—civilian or military—and their allies everywhere. Merged with Egyptian Islamic Jihad (Al-Jihad) in June 2001. . . .

ACTIVITIES

In 2003, carried out the assault and bombing on 12 May of three expatriate housing complexes in Riyadh, Saudi Arabia, that killed 20 and injured 139. Assisted in carrying out the bombings on 16 May in Casablanca, Morocco, of a Jewish center, restaurant, nightclub, and hotel that killed 41 and injured 101. Probably supported the bombing of the J.W. Marriott Hotel in Jakarta, Indonesia, on 5 August that killed 17 and injured 137. Responsible for the assault and bombing on 9 November of a housing complex in Riyadh, Saudi Arabia, that killed 17 and injured 100. Conducted the bombings of two synagogues in Istanbul, Turkey, on 15 November that killed 23 and injured 200 and the bombings in Istanbul of the British Consulate and HSBC Bank on 20 November that resulted in 27 dead and 455 injured. Has been involved in some attacks in Afghanistan and Iraq.

In 2002, carried out bombing on 28 November of hotel in Mombasa, Kenya, killing 15 and injuring 40. Probably supported a nightclub bombing in Bali, Indonesia, on 12 October that killed about 180. Responsible for an attack on US military personnel in Kuwait, on 8 October, that killed one US soldier and injured another. Directed a suicide attack on the MV Limburg off the coast of Yemen, on 6 October that killed one and injured four. Carried out a firebombing of a synagogue in Tunisia on 11 April that killed 19 and injured 22. On 11 September 2001, 19 al-Qaida suicide attackers hijacked and crashed four US commercial jets—two into the World Trade Center in New York City, one into the Pentagon near Washington, DC, and a fourth into a field in Shanksville, Pennsylvania, leaving about 3,000 individuals dead or missing. Directed the attack on the USS Cole in the port of Aden, Yemen, on 12 October 2000 killing 17 US Navy members and injuring another 39.

Conducted the bombings in August 1998 of the US Embassies in Nairobi, Kenya, and Dar es Salaam, Tanzania, that killed at least 301 individuals and injured more than 5,000 others. Claims to have shot down US helicopters and killed US servicemen in Somalia in 1993 and to have conducted three bombings that targeted US troops in Aden, Yemen, in December 1992.

Al-Qaida is linked to the following plans that were disrupted or not carried out: to assassinate Pope John Paul II during his visit to Manila in late 1994, to kill President Clinton during a visit to the Philippines in early 1995, to bomb in midair a dozen US transpacific flights in 1995, and to set off a bomb at Los Angeles International Airport in 1999. Also plotted to carry out terrorist operations against US and Israeli tourists visiting Jordan for millennial celebrations in late 1999. (Jordanian authorities thwarted the planned attacks and put 28 suspects on trial.) In December 2001, suspected al-Qaida associate Richard Colvin Reid attempted to ignite a shoe bomb on a transatlantic flight from Paris to Miami. Attempted to shoot down an Israeli chartered plane with a surface-to-air missile as it departed the Mombasa airport in November 2002.

STRENGTH

Al-Qaida probably has several thousand members and associates. The arrests of senior-level al-Qaida operatives have interrupted some terrorist plots. Also serves as a focal point or umbrella organization for a worldwide network that includes many Sunni Islamic extremist groups, some members of al-Gama'a al-Islamiyya, the Islamic Movement of Uzbekistan, and the Harakat ul-Mujahidin.

LOCATION/AREA OF OPERATION

Al-Qaida has cells worldwide and is reinforced by its ties to Sunni extremist networks. Was based in Afghanistan until Coalition forces removed the Taliban from power in late 2001. Al-Qaida has dispersed in small groups across South Asia, Southeast Asia, and the Middle East and probably will attempt to carry out future attacks against US interests.

EXTERNAL AID

Al-Qaida maintains moneymaking front businesses, solicits donations from likeminded supporters, and illicitly siphons funds from donations to Muslim charitable organizations. US and international efforts to block al-Qaida funding has hampered the group's ability to obtain money.

Abu Sayyaf Group (ASG)

DESCRIPTION

The ASG is a small, brutally violent Muslim separatist group operating in the southern Philippines. Some ASG leaders allegedly fought in Afghanistan during the Soviet war and are students and proponents of radical Islamic teachings. The group split from the much larger Moro National Liberation Front in the early 1990s under the leadership of Abdurajak Abubakar Janjalani, who was killed in a clash with Philippine police on 18 December 1998. His younger brother, Khadaffy Janjalani, has replaced him as the nominal leader of the group, which is composed of several semiautonomous factions. . . .

ACTIVITIES

Engages in kidnappings for ransom, bombings, beheadings, assassinations, and extortion. Although from time to time it claims that its motivation is to promote an independent Islamic state in western Mindanao and the Sulu Archipelago—areas in the southern Philippines heavily populated by Muslims—the ASG has primarily used terror for financial profit. Recent bombings may herald a return to a more radical, politicized agenda, at least among the factions. The group's first large-scale action was a raid on the town of Ipil in Mindanao in April 1995. In April of 2000, an ASG faction kidnapped 21 persons—including 10 Western tourists—from a resort in Malaysia. Separately in 2000, the group briefly abducted several foreign journalists, three Malaysians, and a US citizen. On 27 May 2001, the ASG kidnapped three US citizens and 17 Filipinos from a tourist resort in Palawan, Philippines. Several of the hostages, including one US citizen, were murdered. During a Philippine military hostage rescue operation on 7 June 2002, US hostage Gracia Burnham was wounded but rescued, and her husband Martin Burnham and Filipina Deborah Yap were killed during the operation. Philippine authorities say that the ASG had a role in the bombing near a Philippine military base in Zamboanga on 2 October that killed three Filipinos and one US serviceman and wounded 20 others. It is unclear what role ASG has played in subsequent bombing attacks in Mindanao.

STRENGTH

Estimated to have 200 to 500 members.

LOCATION/AREA OF OPERATION

The ASG was founded in Basilan Province and operates there and in the neighboring provinces of Sulu and Tawi-Tawi in the Sulu Archipelago. It also operates in the Zamboanga peninsula, and members occasionally travel to Manila. In mid-2003, the group started operating in the major city of Cotobato and on the coast of Sultan Kudarat on Mindanao. The group expanded its operational reach to Malaysia in 2000 when it abducted foreigners from a tourist resort.

EXTERNAL AID

Largely self-financing through ransom and extortion; may receive support from Islamic extremists in the Middle East and South Asia. Libya publicly paid millions of dollars for the release of the foreign hostages seized from Malaysia in 2000.

Ansar al-Islam (AI) a.k.a Partisans of Islam, Helpers of Islam, Supporters of Islam, Jund al-Islam, Jaish Ansar al-Sunna

DESCRIPTION

Ansar al-Islam is a radical Islamist group of Iraqi Kurds and Arabs who have vowed to establish an independent Islamic state in Iraq. It was formed in December 2001 and is closely allied with al-Qaida. Some of its members trained in al-Qaida camps in Afghanistan, and the group provided safehaven to al-Qaida fighters before Operation Iraqi Freedom (OIF). Since OIF, it has been one of the leading groups engaged in anti-Coalition attacks. (Ansar al-Islam was designated on 20 February 2003, under E.O. 13224. The UNSCR 1267 Committee designated Ansar al-Islam pursuant to UNSCRs 1267, 1390, and 1455 on 27 February 2003.) . . .

ACTIVITIES

The group has primarily fought against one of the two main Kurdish political factions—the Patriotic Union of Kurdistan (PUK)—and has mounted ambushes and attacks in PUK areas. AI members have been implicated in assassinations and assassination attempts against PUK officials and work closely with both al-Qaida operatives and associates in Abu Mus'ab al-Zarqawi's network. Before OIF, some AI members claimed to have produced cyanide-based toxins, ricin, and alfatoxin.

STRENGTH

Approximately 700 to 1000 members.

LOCATION/AREA OF OPERATION

Central and northern Iraq.

EXTERNAL AID

The group receives funding, training, equipment, and combat support from al-Qaida and other international jihadist backers.

'Asbat al-Ansar

DESCRIPTION

'Asbat al-Ansar—the League of the Followers or Partisans' League—is a Lebanon-based, Sunni extremist group, composed primarily of Palestinians and associated with Usama Bin Ladin's al-Qaida organization. The group follows an extremist interpretation of Islam that justifies violence against civilian targets to achieve political ends. Some of those goals include overthrowing the Lebanese Government and thwarting perceived anti-Islamic and pro-Western influences in the country. . . .

ACTIVITIES

'Asbat al-Ansar has carried out multiple terrorist attacks in Lebanon since it first emerged in the early 1990s. The group assassinated Lebanese religious leaders and bombed nightclubs, theaters, and liquor stores in the mid-1990s. The group raised its operational profile in 2000 with two attacks against Lebanese and international targets. It was involved in clashes in northern Lebanon in December 1999 and carried out a rocket-propelled grenade attack on the Russian Embassy in Beirut in January 2000. 'Asbat al-Ansar's leader, Abu Muhjin, remains at large despite being sentenced to death in absentia for the murder in 1994 of a Muslim cleric.

In 2003, suspected 'Asbat al-Ansar elements were responsible for the attempt in April to use a car bomb against a McDonald's in a Beirut suburb. By October, Lebanese security forces arrested Ibn al-Shahid, who is believed to be associated with 'Asbat al-Ansar, and charged him with masterminding the bombing of three fast food restaurants in 2002 and the attempted attack in April 2003 on the McDonald's. 'Asbat forces were involved in other violence in Lebanon in 2003, including clashes with members of Yassir Arafat's Fatah movement in the 'Ayn al-Hilwah refugee camp and a rocket attack in June on the Future TV building in Beirut.

STRENGTH

The group commands about 300 fighters in Lebanon.

LOCATION/AREA OF OPERATION

The group's primary base of operations is the Ayn al-Hilwah Palestinian refugee camp near Sidon in southern Lebanon.

EXTERNAL AID

Probably receives money through international Sunni extremist networks and Usama Bin Ladin's al-Qaida network.

Al-Gama'a al-Islamiyya (Islamic Group, IG)

DESCRIPTION

Egypt's largest militant group, active since the late 1970s, appears to be loosely organized. Has an external wing with supporters in several countries worldwide. The group issued a cease-fire in March 1999, but its spiritual leader, Shaykh Umar Abd al-Rahman—sentenced to life in prison in January 1996 for his involvement in the World Trade Center bombing of 1993 and incarcerated in the United States—rescinded his support for the cease-fire in June 2000. The IG has not conducted an attack inside Egypt since August 1998. Senior member signed Usama Bin Ladin's *fatwa* in February 1998 calling for attacks against the United States.

Unofficially split in two factions: one that supports the cease-fire led by Mustafa Hamza, and one led by Rifa'i Taha Musa, calling for a return to armed operations. Taha Musa in early 2001 published a book in which he attempted to justify terrorist attacks that would cause mass casualties. Musa disappeared several months thereafter, and there are conflicting reports as to his current whereabouts. In March 2002, members of the group's historic leadership in Egypt declared use of violence misguided and renounced its future use, prompting denunciations by much of the leadership abroad. In 2003, the Egyptian Government released more than 900 former IG members from prison.

For members still dedicated to violent jihad, the primary goal is to overthrow the Egyptian Government and replace it with an Islamic state. Disaffected IG members, such as those potentially inspired by Taha Musa or Abd al-Rahman, may be interested in carrying out attacks against US interests. . . .

ACTIVITIES

Group conducted armed attacks against Egyptian security and other government officials, Coptic Christians, and Egyptian opponents of Islamic extremism before the cease-fire. From 1993 until the cease-fire, IG launched attacks on tourists in Egypt—most notably the attack in November 1997 at Luxor that killed 58 foreign tourists. Also claimed responsibility for the attempt in June 1995 to assassinate Egyptian President Hosni Mubarak in Addis Ababa, Ethiopia. The IG never has specifically attacked a US citizen or facility but has threatened US interests.

STRENGTH

Unknown. At its peak the IG probably commanded several thousand hard-core members and a like number of sympathizers. The cease-fire of 1999 and security crackdowns following the attack in Luxor in 1997 and, more recently, security efforts following September 11, probably have resulted in a substantial decrease in the group's numbers.

LOCATION/AREA OF OPERATION

Operates mainly in the Al-Minya, Asyut, Qina, and Sohaj Governorates of southern Egypt. Also appears to have support in Cairo, Alexandria, and other urban locations, particularly among unemployed graduates and students. Has a worldwide presence, including in the United Kingdom, Afghanistan, Yemen, and various locations in Europe.

EXTERNAL AID

Unknown. The Egyptian Government believes that Iran, Usama Bin Ladin, and Afghan militant groups support the organization. Also may obtain some funding through various Islamic nongovernmental organizations.

Islamic Movement of Uzbekistan (IMU)

Description

Coalition of Islamic militants from Uzbekistan and other Central Asian states. The IMU is closely affiliated with al-Qaida and, under the leadership of Tohir Yoldashev, has embraced Usama Bin Ladin's anti-US, anti-Western agenda. The IMU also remains committed to its original goals of overthrowing Uzbekistani President Islom Karimov and establishing an Islamic state in Uzbekistan. . . .

Activities

The IMU in recent years has participated in attacks on US and Coalition soldiers in Afghanistan and plotted attacks on US diplomatic facilities in Central Asia. In May 2003, Kyrgyzstani security forces disrupted an IMU cell that was seeking to bomb the US Embassy and a nearby hotel in Bishkek, Kyrgyzstan. The IMU primarily targeted Uzbekistani interests before October 2001 and is believed to have been responsible for five car bombs in Tashkent in February 1999. Militants also took foreigners hostage in 1999 and 2000, including four US citizens who were mountain climbing in August 2000 and four Japanese geologists and eight Kyrgyzstani soldiers in August 1999.

Strength

Probably fewer than 700 militants.

Location/Area of Operation

Militants are scattered throughout South Asia, Tajikistan, and Iran. Area of operations includes Afghanistan, Iran, Kyrgyzstan, Pakistan, Tajikistan, Kazakhstan, and Uzbekistan.

External Aid

Support from other Islamic extremist groups and patrons in the Middle East and Central and South Asia.

Jemaah Islamiya (JI)

Description

Jemaah Islamiya is a Southeast Asian–based terrorist network with links to al-Qaida. The network recruited and trained extremists in the late 1990s, ~~following the stated goal of creating an Islamic state comprising Brunei, Indonesia, Malaysia, Singapore, the southern Philippines, and southern Thailand.~~ . . .

ACTIVITIES

JI was responsible for the bombing of the J. W. Marriott Hotel in Jakarta on 5 August 2003, the Bali bombings on 12 October 2002, and an attack against the Philippine Ambassador to Indonesia in August 2000. The Bali plot, which left more than 200 dead, was reportedly the final outcome of meetings in early 2002 in Thailand, where attacks against Singapore and soft targets such as tourist spots in the region were also considered. In December 2001, Singapore authorities uncovered a JI plot to attack the US and Israeli Embassies and British and Australian diplomatic buildings in Singapore, and in June 2003, Thai authorities disrupted a JI plan to attack several Western embassies and tourist sites there. Investigations also linked the JI to bombings in December 2000 where dozens of bombs were detonated in Indonesia and the Philippines, killing 22 in the Philippines and 15 in Indonesia.

The capture in August of Indonesian Riduan bin Isomoddin (a.k.a. Hambali), JI leader and al-Qaida Southeast Asia operations chief, damaged the JI, ~~but the group maintains its ability to target Western interests in the region and to recruit new members through a network of radical Islamic schools based primarily in Indonesia~~.

STRENGTH

Exact numbers are currently unknown, and Southeast Asian authorities continue to uncover and arrest additional JI elements. ~~Elements of total JI members vary widely from the hundreds to the thousands~~.

LOCATION/AREA OF OPERATION

JI is believed to have cells spanning Indonesia, Malaysia, the Philippines, southern Thailand, and Pakistan and may have some presence in neighboring countries.

EXTERNAL AID

Investigations indicate that, in addition to raising its own funds, JI receives money and logistic assistance from Middle Eastern and South Asian contacts, nongovernmental organizations, and other groups—including al-Qaida.

Al-Jihad a.k.a. Jihad Group, Egyptian Islamic Jihad (EIJ)

DESCRIPTION

This Egyptian Islamic extremist group merged with Usama Bin Ladin's al-Qaida organization in June 2001. Active since the 1970s, the EIJ's primary goals traditionally have been to overthrow the Egyptian Government and replace it with an Islamic state and to attack US and Israeli interests in Egypt and abroad. EIJ members who didn't join al-Qaida retain the capability to conduct independent operations. . . .

ACTIVITIES

Historically specialized in armed attacks against high-level Egyptian Government personnel, including cabinet ministers, and car bombings against official US and Egyptian facilities. The original Jihad was responsible for the assassination in 1981 of Egyptian President Anwar Sadat. Claimed responsibility for the attempted assassinations of Interior Minister Hassan al-Alfi in August 1993 and Prime Minister Atef Sedky in November 1993. Has not conducted an attack inside Egypt since 1993 and has never successfully targeted foreign tourists there. Responsible for Egyptian Embassy bombing in Islamabad in 1995, and in 1998 an attack against US Embassy in Albania was thwarted.

STRENGTH

Unknown, but probably has several hundred hard-core members.

LOCATION/AREA OF OPERATIO

Historically operated in the Cairo area, but most of its network is outside Egypt, including Yemen, Afghanistan, Pakistan, Lebanon, and the United Kingdom, and its activities have been centered outside Egypt for several years.

EXTERNAL AID

Unknown. The Egyptian Government claims that Iran supports the Jihad. Received most of its funding from al-Qaida after early 1998—close ties that culminated in the eventual merger of the two groups. Some funding may come from various Islamic nongovernmental organizations, cover businesses, and criminal acts.

Lashkar-i-Jhangvi (LJ) (Army of Jhangvi)

DESCRIPTION

Lashkar I Jhangvi (LJ) is the militant offshoot of the Sunni sectarian group Sipah-i- Sahaba Pakistan (SSP). The group focuses primarily on anti-Shia attacks and was banned by Pakistani President Musharraf in August 2001 as part of an effort to rein in sectarian violence. Many of its members then sought refuge with the Taliban in Afghanistan, with whom they had existing ties. After the collapse of the Taliban, LJ members became active in aiding other terrorists with safehouses, false identities, and protection in Pakistani cities, including Karachi, Peshawar, and Rawalpindi. In January 2003, the United States added LJ to the list of Foreign Terrorist Organizations. . . .

ACTIVITIES

LJ specializes in armed attacks and bombings. The group attempted to assassinate former Prime Minister Nawaz Sharif and his brother Shabaz Sharif, Chief Minister of Punjab Province, in January 1999. Pakistani authorities have publicly linked LJ members to the kidnap and murder of US journalist Daniel Pearl in early 2002. Police officials initially suspected LJ members were involved in the two suicide car-bombings in Karachi in 2002—against a French shuttle bus in May and the US Consulate in June—but their subsequent investigations have not led to any LJ members being charged in the attacks. Similarly, press reports have linked LJ to attacks on Christian targets in Pakistan, including a grenade assault on the Protestant International Church in Islamabad in March 2002 that killed two US citizens, but no formal charges have been filed against the group. Pakistani authorities believe LJ was responsible for the bombing in July 2003 of a Shiite mosque in Quetta, Pakistan.

STRENGTH

Probably fewer than 100.

LOCATION/AREA OF OPERATION

LJ is active primarily in Punjab and Karachi. Some members travel between Pakistan and Afghanistan.

EXTERNAL AID

Unknown.

Shiite Terrorism: Hizballah and State Sponsor Iran

Hizballah (Party of God) a.k.a. Islamic Jihad, Revolutionary Justice Organization, Organization of the Oppressed on Earth, and Islamic Jihad for the Liberation of Palestine

DESCRIPTION

Also known as Lebanese Hizballah, this group was formed in 1982 in response to the Israeli invasion of Lebanon; this Lebanon-based radical Shi'a group takes its ideological inspiration from the Iranian revolution and the teachings of the late Ayatollah Khomeini. The *Majlis al-Shura,* or Consultative Council, is the group's highest governing body and is led by Secretary General Hassan Nasrallah. Hizballah is dedicated to liberating Jerusalem and eliminating Israel and has formally advocated ultimate establishment of Islamic rule in Lebanon. Nonetheless, Hizballah has actively participated in Lebanon's political system since 1992. Hizballah is closely allied with, and often directed by, Iran but has the capability and willingness to act alone. Although Hizballah does not share the Syrian regime's secular orientation, the group has been a strong ally in helping Syria advance its political objectives in the region. . . .

ACTIVITIES

Known or suspected to have been involved in numerous anti-US and anti-Israeli terrorist attacks, including the suicide truck bombings of the US Embassy and US Marine barracks in Beirut in 1983 and the US Embassy annex in Beirut in September 1984. Three members of Hizballah—'Imad Mughniyah, Hasan Izz-al-Din, and Ali Atwa—are on the FBI's list of 22 Most-Wanted Terrorists for the hijacking in 1985 of TWA Flight 847 during which a US Navy diver was murdered. Elements of the group were responsible for the kidnapping and detention of US and other Westerners in Lebanon in the 1980s. Hizballah also attacked the Israeli Embassy in Argentina in 1992 and the Israeli cultural center in Buenos Aires in 1994. In fall 2000, Hizballah operatives captured three Israeli soldiers in the Shab'a Farms and kidnapped an Israeli noncombatant whom may have been lured to Lebanon under false pretenses.

In 2003, Hizballah appeared to have established a presence in Iraq, but for the moment its activities there are limited. Hizballah Secretary General Hassan Nasrallah stated in speeches that "we are heading . . .

toward the end and elimination of Israel from the region" and that the group's "slogan is and will continue to be death to America." Hizballah's television station, al-Manar, continued to use inflammatory images and reporting in an effort to encourage the *intifadah* and promote Palestinian suicide operations.

rebellion

STRENGTH

Several thousand supporters and a few hundred terrorist operatives.

LOCATION/AREA OF OPERATION

Operates in the southern suburbs of Beirut, the Bekaa Valley, and southern Lebanon. Has established cells in Europe, Africa, South America, North America, and Asia.

EXTERNAL AID

Receives financial, training, weapons, explosives, political, diplomatic, and organizational aid from Iran and diplomatic, political, and logistic support from Syria. Receives financial support from sympathetic business interests and individuals worldwide, largely through the Lebanese diaspora. movement away from homeland

[Authors' note: In 2004 the FBI reported that Hizballah has an "ongoing capability to launch terrorist attacks inside the U.S," although it was using the United States for fund-raising, recruitment, and procurement. According to one report, Hizballah members were believed to have left the United States for terrorist training in Lebanon and then returned to the United States.[2]]

Iran

Iran remained the most active state sponsor of terrorism in 2003.[3] Its Islamic Revolutionary Guard Corps and Ministry of Intelligence and Security were involved in the planning of and support for terrorist acts and continued to exhort a variety of groups that use terrorism to pursue their goals.   urge strongly

Iran's record against al-Qaida remains mixed. After the fall of the Taliban regime in Afghanistan, some al-Qaida members fled to Iran where they have found virtual safehaven. Iranian officials have acknowledged that Tehran detained al-Qaida operatives during 2003, including senior members. Iran's publicized presentation of a list to the United Nations of deportees, however, was accompanied by a refusal to publicly identify senior members in Iranian custody on the grounds of "security." Iran has resisted calls to transfer custody of its al-Qaida detainees to their countries of origin or third countries for further interrogation and trial.

During 2003, Iran maintained a high-profile role in encouraging anti-Israeli activity, both rhetorically and operationally. Supreme Leader Khamenei praised Palestinian resistance operations, and President Khatami reiterated Iran's support for the "wronged people of Palestine" and their struggles. Matching this rhetoric with action, Iran provided Lebanese Hizballah and Palestinian rejectionist groups—notably HAMAS, the Palestine Islamic Jihad, and the Popular Front for the Liberation of Palestine–General Command—with funding, safehaven, training, and weapons. Iran hosted a conference in August 2003 on the Palestinian *intifadah*, at which an Iranian official suggested that the continued success of the Palestinian resistance depended on suicide operations.

Iran pursued a variety of policies in Iraq aimed at securing Tehran's perceived interests there, some of which ran counter to those of the Coalition. Iran has indicated support for the Iraqi Governing Council and promised to help Iraqi reconstruction.

Shortly after the fall of Saddam Hussein, individuals with ties to the Revolutionary Guard may have attempted to infiltrate southern Iraq, and elements of the Iranian Government have helped members of Ansar al-Islam transit and find safehaven in Iran. In a Friday Prayers sermon in Tehran in May (2003), Guardian Council member Ayatollah Ahmad Jannati publicly encouraged Iraqis to follow the Palestinian model and participate in suicide operations against Coalition forces.

Iran is a party to five of the 12 international conventions and protocols relating to terrorism.

[Authors' note: While revelations of Tehran's nuclear and missile programs have focused attention on the nation's strategic threat, concerns about the potential for Iranian-supported terrorism remain. For example, the United States expelled Iranian security guards from the nation's UN mission in 2004 after claiming they were videotaping New York landmarks and transportation infrastructure.[4]]

**Groups Active in
the Kashmir
Conflict (Muslim
area disputed by
Pakistan and
India)**

Harakat ul-Mujahidin (HUM) (Movement of Holy Warriors)

DESCRIPTION

The HUM is an Islamic militant group based in Pakistan that operates primarily in Kashmir. It is politically aligned with the radical political party, Jamiat Ulema-i-Islam Fazlur Rehman faction (JUI-F). Longtime leader of the group, Fazlur Rehman Khalil, in mid-February 2000 stepped down as HUM emir, turning the reins over to the popular Kashmiri commander and his second in command, Farooq Kashmiri. Khalil, who has been linked to Usama Bin Ladin and signed his *fatwa* in February 1998 calling for attacks on US and Western interests, assumed the position of HUM Secretary General. HUM operated terrorist training camps in eastern Afghanistan until Coalition airstrikes destroyed them during fall 2001. In 2003, HUM began using the name Jamiat ul-Ansar (JUA), and Pakistan banned the successor JUA in November 2003. . . .

ACTIVITIES

Has conducted a number of operations against Indian troops and civilian targets in Kashmir. Linked to the Kashmiri militant group al-Faran that kidnapped five Western tourists in Kashmir in July 1995; one was killed in August 1995, and the other four reportedly were killed in December of the same year. The HUM is responsible for the hijacking of an Indian airliner on 24 December 1999, which resulted in the release of Masood Azhar—an important leader in the former Harakat ul-Ansar imprisoned by the Indians in 1994—and Ahmed Omar Sheik, who was convicted of the abduction/murder in January-February 2002 of US journalist Daniel Pearl.

STRENGTH

Has several hundred armed supporters located in Azad Kashmir, Pakistan, and India's southern Kashmir and Doda regions and in the Kashmir valley. Supporters are mostly Pakistanis and Kashmiris and also include Afghans and Arab veterans of the Afghan war. Uses light and heavy machine guns, assault rifles, mortars, explosives, and rockets. HUM lost a significant share of its membership in defections to the Jaish-i-Mohammed (JIM) in 2000.

LOCATION/AREA OF OPERATION

Based in Muzaffarabad, Rawalpindi, and several other towns in Pakistan, but members conduct insurgent and terrorist activities primarily in Kashmir. The HUM trained its militants in Afghanistan and Pakistan.

EXTERNAL AID

Collects donations from Saudi Arabia and other Gulf and Islamic states and from Pakistanis and Kashmiris. The HUM's financial collection methods also include soliciting donations from magazine ads and pamphlets. The sources and amount of HUM's military funding are unknown. In anticipation of asset seizures in 2001 by the Pakistani Government, the HUM withdrew funds from bank accounts and invested in legal businesses, such as commodity trading, real estate, and production of consumer goods. Its fundraising in Pakistan has been constrained since the government clampdown on extremist groups and freezing of terrorist assets.

Jaish-e-Mohammed (JEM) (Army of Mohammed) a.k.a. Tehrik ul-Furqaah, Khuddam-ul-Islam

DESCRIPTION

The Jaish-e-Mohammed is an Islamic extremist group based in Pakistan that was formed by Masood Azhar upon his release from prison in India in early 2000. The group's aim is to unite Kashmir with Pakistan. It is politically aligned with the radical political party, Jamiat Ulema-i-Islam Fazlur Rehman faction (JUI-F). The United States announced the addition of JEM to the US Treasury Department's Office of Foreign Asset Control (OFAC) list—which includes organizations that are believed to support terrorist groups and have assets in US jurisdiction that can be frozen or controlled—in October 2001 and the Foreign Terrorist Organization list in December 2001. By 2003, JEM had splintered into Khuddam ul-Islam (KUI) and Jamaat ul-Furqan (JUF). Pakistan banned KUA and JUF in November 2003. . . .

ACTIVITIES

The JEM's leader, Masood Azhar, was released from Indian imprisonment in December 1999 in exchange for 155 hijacked Indian Airlines hostages. The HUA kidnappings in 1994 by Omar Sheik of US and

British nationals in New Delhi and the HUA/al-Faran kidnappings in July 1995 of Westerners in Kashmir were two of several previous HUA efforts to free Azhar. The JEM on 1 October 2001 claimed responsibility for a suicide attack on the Jammu and Kashmir legislative assembly building in Srinagar that killed at least 31 persons but later denied the claim. The Indian Government has publicly implicated the JEM—along with Lashkar-i-Tayyiba—for the attack on 13 December 2001 on the Indian Parliament that killed nine and injured 18. Pakistani authorities suspect that perpetrators of fatal anti-Christian attacks in Islamabad, Murree, and Taxila during 2002 were affiliated with the JEM.

STRENGTH

Has several hundred armed supporters located in Pakistan and in India's southern Kashmir and Doda regions and in the Kashmir valley, including a large cadre of former HUM members. Supporters are mostly Pakistanis and Kashmiris and also include Afghans and Arab veterans of the Afghan war. Uses light and heavy machine guns, assault rifles, mortars, improvised explosive devices, and rocket grenades.

LOCATION/AREA OF OPERATION

Pakistan. The JEM maintained training camps in Afghanistan until the fall of 2001.

EXTERNAL AID

Most of the JEM's cadre and material resources have been drawn from the militant groups Harakat ul-Jihad-i-Islami (HUJI) and the Harakat ul-Mujahidin (HUM). The JEM had close ties to Afghan Arabs and the Taliban. Usama Bin Ladin is suspected of giving funding to the JEM. The JEM also collects funds through donation requests in magazines and pamphlets. In anticipation of asset seizures by the Pakistani Government, the JEM withdrew funds from bank accounts and invested in legal businesses, such as commodity trading, real estate, and production of consumer goods.

Lashkar-Tayyiba (LT) (Army of the Righteous)

DESCRIPTION

The LT is the armed wing of the Pakistan-based religious organization, Markaz-ud-Dawa-wal-Irshad (MDI)—a Sunni anti-US missionary organization formed in 1989. The LT is led by Hafiz Muhammad Saeed and is one of the three-largest and best-trained groups fighting in Kashmir against India; it is not connected to a political party. The United States in October 2001 announced the addition of the LT to the US Treasury Department's Office of Foreign Asset Control (OFAC) list—which includes organizations that are believed to support terrorist groups and have assets in US jurisdiction that can be frozen or controlled. The group was banned, and the Pakistani Government froze its assets in January 2002. The LT is also known by the name of its associated organization, Jamaat ud-Dawa (JUD). Musharraf placed JUD on a watchlist in November 2003. . . .

ACTIVITIES

The LT has conducted a number of operations against Indian troops and civilian targets in Jammu and Kashmir since 1993. The LT claimed responsibility for numerous attacks in 2001, including an attack in January on Srinagar airport that killed five Indians along with six militants; an attack on a police station in Srinagar that killed at least eight officers and wounded several others; and an attack in April against Indian border-security forces that left at least four dead. The Indian Government publicly implicated the LT—along with JEM—for the attack on 13 December 2001 on the Indian Parliament building, although concrete evidence is lacking. The LT is also suspected of involvement in the attack on 14 May 2002 on an Indian Army base in Kaluchak that left 36 dead. Senior al-Qaida lieutenant Abu Zubaydah was captured at an LT safehouse in Faisalabad in March 2002, suggesting some members are facilitating the movement of al-Qaida members in Pakistan.

STRENGTH

Has several thousand members in Azad Kashmir, Pakistan, and in southern Jammu and Kashmir and Doda regions and in the Kashmir valley. Almost all LT cadres are Pakistanis from madrassas across Pakistan and Afghan veterans of the Afghan wars. Uses assault rifles, light and heavy machine guns, mortars, explosives, and rocket-propelled grenades.

LOCATION/AREA OF OPERATION

Based in Muridke (near Lahore) and Muzaffarabad.

EXTERNAL AID

Collects donations from the Pakistani community in the Persian Gulf and United Kingdom, Islamic NGOs, and Pakistani and other Kashmiri business people. The LT also maintains a Web site (under the name of its associated organization Jamaat ud-Daawa), through which it solicits funds and provides information on the group's activities. The amount of LT funding is unknown. The LT maintains ties to religious/military groups around the world, ranging from the Philippines to the Middle East and Chechnya through the fraternal network of its parent organization Jamaat ud-Dawa (formerly Markaz Dawa ul-Irshad). In anticipation of asset seizures by the Pakistani Government, the LT withdrew funds from bank accounts and invested in legal businesses, such as commodity trading, real estate, and production of consumer goods.

[Authors' note: A handful of American citizens, nicknamed the "Virginia jihad network" for their U.S. location, trained with this group, and some were convicted in connection with their plans to fight American troops in Afghanistan.[5]]

Groups Involved in the Algerian Conflict

Armed Islamic Group (GIA)

DESCRIPTION

An Islamic extremist group, the GIA aims to overthrow the secular Algerian regime and replace it with an Islamic state. The GIA began its violent activity in 1992 after the military government suspended legislative elections in anticipation of an overwhelming victory by the Islamic Salvation Front, the largest Islamic opposition party. . . .

ACTIVITIES

Frequent attacks against civilians and government workers. Since 1992, the GIA has conducted a terrorist campaign of civilian massacres, sometimes wiping out entire villages in its area of operation, although the group's dwindling numbers have caused a decrease in the number of attacks. Since announcing its campaign against foreigners living in Algeria in 1993, the GIA has killed more than 100 expatriate men and women—mostly Europeans—in the country. The group uses assassinations and bombings, including car bombs, and it is known to favor kidnapping victims. The GIA highjacked an Air France flight to Algiers in December 1994. In 2002, a French court sentenced two GIA members to life in prison for conducting a series of bombings in France in 1995.

STRENGTH

Precise numbers unknown; probably fewer than 100.

LOCATION/AREA OF OPERATION

Algeria and Europe.

EXTERNAL AID

None known.

Salafist Group for Call and Combat (GSPC)

DESCRIPTION

The Salafist Group for Call and Combat (GSPC), an outgrowth of the GIA, appears to have eclipsed the GIA since approximately 1998 and is currently the most effective armed group inside Algeria. In contrast to the GIA, the GSPC has gained some popular support through its pledge to avoid civilian attacks inside Algeria. Its adherents abroad appear to have largely co-opted the external networks of the GIA and are particularly active throughout Europe, Africa, and the Middle East. . . .

ACTIVITIES

The GSPC continues to conduct operations aimed at government and military targets, primarily in rural areas, although civilians are sometimes killed. A faction within the GSPC held 31 European tourists hostage in 2003 to collect ransom for their release. According to press reporting, some GSPC members in Europe maintain contacts with other North African extremists sympathetic to al-Qaida. In late 2003, the new GSPC leader issued a communique declaring the group's allegiance to a number of jihadist causes and movements, including al-Qaida.

STRENGTH

Unknown; probably several hundred fighters with an unknown number of support networks inside Algeria.

LOCATION/AREA OF OPERATION

Algeria, Northern Mali, Northern Mauritania, and Northern Niger.

EXTERNAL AID

Algerian expatriates and GSPC members abroad, many residing in Western Europe, provide financial and logistic support. In addition, the Algerian Government has accused Iran and Sudan.

PROFILES OF SIGNIFICANT INTERNATIONAL TERRORIST GROUPS

Nationalist-Palestinian–Israeli Conflict

HAMAS a.k.a. Islamic Resistance Movement

DESCRIPTION

Formed in late 1987 as an outgrowth of the Palestinian branch of the Muslim Brotherhood. Various HAMAS elements have used both violent and political means—including terrorism—to pursue the goal of establishing an Islamic Palestinian state in Israel. Loosely structured, with some elements working clandestinely and others openly through mosques and social service institutions to recruit members, raise money, organize activities, and distribute propaganda. HAMAS's strength is concentrated in the Gaza Strip and the West Bank. . . .

ACTIVITIES

HAMAS terrorists, especially those in the Izz al-Din al-Qassam Brigades, have conducted many attacks—including large-scale suicide bombings—against Israeli civilian and military targets. HAMAS maintained the pace of its operational activity during 2002-03, claiming numerous attacks against Israeli interests. HAMAS has not yet directly targeted US interests, although the group makes little or no effort to avoid targets frequented by foreigners. HAMAS continues to confine its attacks to Israel and the territories.

STRENGTH

Unknown number of official members; tens of thousands of supporters and sympathizers.

LOCATION/AREA OF OPERATION

HAMAS currently limits its terrorist operations to Israeli military and civilian targets in the West Bank, Gaza Strip, and Israel. The group's leadership is dispersed throughout the Gaza Strip and West Bank, with a few senior leaders residing in Syria, Lebanon, Iran, and the Gulf States.

EXTERNAL AID

Receives some funding from Iran but primarily relies on donations from Palestinian expatriates around the world and private benefactors, particularly in Western Europe, North America, and the Persian Gulf region.

The Palestine Islamic Jihad (PIJ)

DESCRIPTION

Originated among militant Palestinians in the Gaza Strip during the 1970s. Committed to the creation of an Islamic Palestinian state and the destruction of Israel through holy war. Also opposes moderate Arab governments that it believes have been tainted by Western secularism. . . .

ACTIVITIES

PIJ activists have conducted many attacks including large-scale suicide bombings against Israeli civilian and military targets. The group decreased its operational activity in 2003 but still claimed numerous attacks against Israeli interests. The group has not yet targeted US interests and continues to confine its attacks to Israelis inside Israel and the territories. US citizens have died in attacks mounted by the PIJ.

STRENGTH

Unknown.

LOCATION/AREA OF OPERATION

Primarily Israel, the West Bank, and Gaza Strip. The group's leadership resides in Syria and Lebanon, as well as other parts of the Middle East.

EXTERNAL AID

Receives financial assistance from Iran and limited logistic support assistance from Syria.

Al-Aqsa Martyrs Brigade (al-Aqsa)

DESCRIPTION

The al-Aqsa Martyrs Brigades consists of an unknown number of small cells of Fatah-affiliated terrorists that emerged at the outset of the current *intifadah* to attack Israeli targets. It aims to drive the Israeli military and settlers from the West Bank, Gaza Strip, and Jerusalem and to establish a Palestinian state. . . .

ACTIVITIES

Al-Aqsa has carried out shootings and suicide operations against Israeli civilians and military personnel and has killed Palestinians suspected of collaborating with Israel. At least five US citizens—four of them dual US-Israeli citizens—were killed in al-Aqsa's attacks. In January 2002, al-Aqsa claimed responsibility for the first suicide bombing carried out by a female.

STRENGTH

Unknown.

LOCATION/AREA OF OPERATION

Al Aqsa operates in Israel, the West Bank, and Gaza Strip and has claimed attacks inside all three areas. It may have followers in Palestinian refugee camps in southern Lebanon.

EXTERNAL AID

Unknown.

Palestine Liberation Front (PLF)

DESCRIPTION

Broke away from the PFLP-GC in the late 1970's. Later, split again into pro-PLO, pro-Syrian, and pro-Libyan factions. Pro-PLO faction led by Muhammad Abbas (a.k.a. Abu Abbas) had been based in Baghdad. Abbas himself was detained by Coalition Forces in April 2003 and subsequently died in custody of natural causes in March 2004. . . .

ACTIVITIES

The Abu Abbas–led faction is known for aerial attacks against Israel. Abbas's group also was responsible for the attack in 1985 on the Italian cruise ship Achille Lauro and the murder of US citizen Leon Klinghoffer. Has become more active since the start of the al-Aqsa *intifadah,* and several PLF members have been arrested by Israeli authorities for planning attacks in Israel and the West Bank.

STRENGTH

Unknown.

LOCATION/AREA OF OPERATION

Based in Iraq since 1990 and has a presence in Lebanon and the West Bank.

EXTERNAL AID

Had received support mainly from Iraq. Has received support from Libya in the past.

Popular Front for the Liberation of Palestine (PFLP)

DESCRIPTION

Marxist-Leninist group founded in 1967 by George Habash—as a member of the PLO—when it broke away from the Arab Nationalist Movement. The PFLP does not view the Palestinian struggle as a religious one, seeing it instead as a broader revolution against Western imperialism. The group earned a reputation for spectacular international attacks, including airline hijackings that have killed at least 20 US citizens. The PFLP is opposed to the Oslo process. . . .

ACTIVITIES

Committed numerous international terrorist attacks during the 1970s. Since 1978 has conducted attacks against Israeli or moderate Arab targets, including killing a settler and her son in December 1996. The PFLP has stepped up its operational activity since the start of the current *intifadah* highlighted by its assassination of the Israeli Tourism Minister in October 2001 to avenge Israel's killing of the PFLP Secretary General earlier that year.

STRENGTH

Unknown.

LOCATION/AREA OF OPERATION

Syria, Lebanon, Israel, West Bank, and Gaza Strip.

EXTERNAL AID

Receives safe haven and some logistic assistance from Syria.

Popular Front for the Liberation of Palestine–General Command (PFLP-GC)

DESCRIPTION

Split from the PFLP in 1968, claiming it wanted to focus more on fighting and less on politics. Violently opposed to Arafat's PLO. Led by Ahmad Jabril, a former captain in the Syrian Army. Jabril's son, Jihad, was killed by a car bomb in May 2002. Closely tied to both Syria and Iran. . . .

ACTIVITIES

Carried out dozens of attacks in Europe and the Middle East during the 1970s and 1980s. Known for cross-border terrorist attacks into Israel using unusual means, such as hot air balloons and motorized hang gliders. Primary focus now on guerrilla operations in southern Lebanon and small-scale attacks in Israel, West Bank, and Gaza Strip.

STRENGTH

Several hundred.

LOCATION/AREA OF OPERATION

Headquartered in Damascus with bases in Lebanon.

EXTERNAL AID

Receives logistic and military support from Syria and financial support from Iran.

Kahane Chai a.k.a. Kach

DESCRIPTION

Stated goal is to restore the biblical state of Israel. Kach (founded by radical Israeli-American rabbi Meir Kahane) and its offshoot Kahane Chai, which means "Kahane Lives," (founded by Meir Kahane's son Binyamin following his father's assassination in the United States) were declared terrorist organizations in March 1994 by the Israeli Cabinet under the 1948 Terrorism Law. This followed the groups' statements in support of Dr. Baruch Goldstein's attack in February 1994 on the al-Ibrahimi Mosque—Goldstein was affiliated with Kach—and their verbal attacks on the Israeli Government. Palestinian gunmen killed Binyamin Kahane and his wife in a drive-by shooting in December 2000 in the West Bank. . . .

ACTIVITIES

The group has organized protests against the Israeli Government. Kach has harassed and threatened Arabs, Palestinians, and Israeli Government officials. Has vowed revenge for the deaths of Binyamin Kahane and his wife. Suspected of involvement in a number of low-level attacks since the start of the al-Aqsa *intifadah*.

STRENGTH

Unknown.

LOCATION/AREA OF OPERATION

Israel and West Bank settlements, particularly Qiryat Arba' in Hebron.

EXTERNAL AID

Receives support from sympathizers in the United States and Europe.

Nationalist—Other

Liberation Tigers of Tamil Eelam (LTTE); Other known front organizations: World Tamil Association (WTA), World Tamil Movement (WTM), the Federation of Associations of Canadian Tamils (FACT), the Ellalan Force, and the Sangilian Force

DESCRIPTION

Founded in 1976, the LTTE is the most powerful Tamil group in Sri Lanka and uses overt and illegal methods to raise funds, acquire weapons, and publicize its cause of establishing an independent Tamil state. The LTTE began its armed conflict with the Sri Lankan Government in 1983 and has relied on a guerrilla strategy that includes the use of terrorist tactics. The LTTE is currently observing a cease-fire agreement with the Sri Lankan Government. . . .

ACTIVITIES

The Tigers have integrated a battlefield insurgent strategy with a terrorist program that targets not only key personnel in the countryside but also senior Sri Lankan political and military leaders in Colombo and other urban centers. The Tigers are most notorious for their cadre of suicide bombers, the Black Tigers. Political assassinations and bombings are commonplace.

STRENGTH

Exact strength is unknown, but the LTTE is estimated to have 8,000 to 10,000 armed combatants in Sri Lanka, with a core of trained fighters of approximately 3,000 to 6,000. The LTTE also has a significant overseas support structure for fundraising, weapons procurement, and propaganda activities.

LOCATION/AREA OF OPERATIONS

The Tigers control most of the northern and eastern coastal areas of Sri Lanka but have conducted operations throughout the island. Headquartered in northern Sri Lanka, LTTE leader Velupillai Prabhakaran has established an extensive network of checkpoints and informants to keep track of any outsiders who enter the group's area of control.

EXTERNAL AID

The LTTE's overt organizations support Tamil separatism by lobbying foreign governments and the United Nations. The LTTE also uses its international contacts to procure weapons, communications, and any other equipment and supplies it needs. The LTTE exploits large Tamil communities in North America, Europe, and Asia to obtain funds and supplies for its fighters in Sri Lanka.

Real IRA (RIRA) a.k.a. 32 County Sovereignty Committee

DESCRIPTION

Formed in early 1998 as the clandestine armed wing of the 32-County Sovereignty Movement, a "political pressure group" dedicated to removing British forces from Northern Ireland and unifying Ireland. RIRA also seeks to disrupt the Northern Ireland peace process. The 32-County Sovereignty Movement opposed Sinn Fein's adoption in September 1997 of the Mitchell principles of democracy and nonviolence and opposed the amendment in December 1999 of Articles 2 and 3 of the Irish Constitution, which laid claim to Northern Ireland. Despite internal rifts and calls by some jailed members—including the group's founder Michael "Mickey" McKevitt—for a cease-fire and the group's disbandment, the group pledged additional violence in October 2002 and continued to conduct attacks. . . .

ACTIVITIES

Bombings, assassinations, and robberies. Many Real IRA members are former Provisional IRA members who left that organization following the Provisional IRA cease-fire and bring to RIRA a wealth of experience in terrorist tactics and bombmaking. Targets have included civilians (most notoriously in the Omagh bombing in August 1998), the British military, the police in Northern Ireland, and Northern Ireland Protestant communities. Since October 1999, RIRA has carried out more than 80 terrorist attacks. RIRA's most recent fatal attack was in August 2002 at a London Army Base that killed a construction worker. In June 2003 raids, Irish national police interdicted two large-scale vehicle-born improvised explosive devices, each weighing more than 1,000 lbs. Five RIRA members and a senior Continuity Irish Republican Army member (CIRA) also were arrested during the raids.

STRENGTH

100 to 200 activists plus possible limited support from IRA hardliners dissatisfied with the IRA cease-fire and other republican sympathizers. Approximately 40 RIRA members are in Irish jails.

LOCATION/AREA OF OPERATION

Northern Ireland, United Kingdom, and Irish Republic.

EXTERNAL AID

Suspected of receiving funds from sympathizers in the United States and of attempting to buy weapons from US gun dealers. RIRA also is reported to have purchased sophisticated weapons from the Balkans. In May 2002, three Irish nationals associated with RIRA pleaded guilty to charges of conspiracy to cause an explosion and trying to obtain weapons following their extradition from Slovenia to the United Kingdom.

Religious   *Aum Supreme Truth (Aum) a.k.a. Aum Shinrikyo, Aleph*

DESCRIPTION

A cult established in 1987 by Shoko Asahara, the Aum aimed to take over Japan and then the world. Approved as a religious entity in 1989 under Japanese law, the group ran candidates in a Japanese parliamentary election in 1990. Over time, the cult began to emphasize the imminence of the end of the world and stated that the United States would initiate Armageddon by starting World War III with Japan. The Japanese Government revoked its recognition of the Aum as a religious organization in October 1995, but in 1997, a government panel decided not to invoke the Anti-Subversive Law against the group, which would have outlawed the cult. A 1999 law gave the Japanese Government authorization to continue police surveillance of the group due to concerns that the Aum might launch future terrorist attacks. Under the leadership of Fumihiro Joyu, the Aum changed its name to Aleph in January 2000 and claimed to have rejected the violent and apocalyptic teachings of its founder. . . .

ACTIVITIES

On 20 March 1995, Aum members simultaneously released the chemical nerve agent sarin on several Tokyo subway trains, killing 12 persons and injuring up to 6,000. The group was responsible for other mysterious chemical accidents in Japan in 1994. Its efforts to conduct attacks using biological agents have been unsuccessful. Japanese police arrested Asahara in May 1995. Asahara was sentenced in February 2004 and received the death sentence for his role in the attacks of 1995. Since 1997, the cult continued to recruit new members, engage in commercial enterprise, and acquire property, although it scaled back these activities significantly in 2001 in response to public outcry. The cult maintains an Internet home page. In July 2001, Russian authorities arrested a group of Russian Aum followers who had planned to set off bombs near the Imperial Palace in Tokyo as part of an operation to free Asahara from jail and then smuggle him to Russia.

STRENGTH

The Aum's current membership is estimated to be less than 1,000 persons. At the time of the Tokyo subway attack, the group claimed to have 9,000 members in Japan and as many as 40,000 worldwide.

LOCATION/AREA OF OPERATION

The Aum's principal membership is located only in Japan, but a residual branch comprising perhaps a few hundred followers has surfaced in Russia.

External Aid

None.

Basque Fatherland and Liberty (ETA) a.k.a. Euzkadi Ta Askatasuna, Batasuna

Description

Founded in 1959 with the aim of establishing an independent homeland based on Marxist principles encompassing the Spanish Basque provinces of Vizcaya, Guipuzcoa, Alava, as well as the autonomous region of Navarra, and the southwestern French Departments of Labourd, Basse-Navarra, and Soule. Recent Spanish counterterrorism initiatives are hampering the group's operational capabilities. Spanish police arrested 125 ETA members and accomplices in 2003; French authorities arrested 46, including the group's top leadership; several other members were arrested in Latin America, Germany, and the Netherlands. In March 2003, a Spanish Supreme Court ruling banned ETA's political wing, Batasuna. Spain currently holds 572 ETA members in prison, while France holds 124. . . .

Activities

Primarily involved in bombings and assassinations of Spanish Government officials, security and military forces, politicians, and judicial figures. During the summer of 2003, ETA targeted Spanish tourist areas. In 2003, ETA killed three persons, a similar figure to 2002's death toll of five, and wounded dozens more. The group has killed more than 850 persons and injured hundreds of others since it began lethal attacks in the early 1960s. ETA finances its activities primarily through extortion and robbery.

Strength

Unknown; hundreds of members plus supporters.

Location/Area of Operation

Operates primarily in the Basque autonomous regions of northern Spain and southwestern France but also has attacked Spanish and French interests elsewhere.

External Aid

Has received training at various times in the past in Libya, Lebanon, and Nicaragua. Some ETA members allegedly have received sanctuary in Cuba while others reside in South America.

Kongra-Gel (KGK) (Kurdistan Workers' Party, PKK, KADEK) a.k.a. Kurdistan People's Congress, Kurdistan Freedom and Democracy Congress (KADEK), Freedom and Democracy Congress of Kurdistan

DESCRIPTION

Founded in 1978 as a Marxist-Leninist insurgent group primarily composed of Turkish Kurds. The group's goal has been to establish an independent, democratic Kurdish state in the Middle East. In the early 1990s, the PKK moved beyond rural-based insurgent activities to include urban terrorism. Turkish authorities captured Chairman Abdullah Ocalan in Kenya in early 1999; the Turkish State Security Court subsequently sentenced him to death. In August 1999, Ocalan announced a "peace initiative," ordering members to refrain from violence and requesting dialogue with Ankara on Kurdish issues. At a PKK Congress in January 2000, members supported Ocalan's initiative and claimed the group now would use only political means to achieve its public goal of improved rights for Kurds in Turkey. In April 2002 at its 8th Party Congress, the PKK changed its name to the Kurdistan Freedom and Democracy Congress (KADEK) and proclaimed a commitment to nonviolent activities in support of Kurdish rights. Despite this pledge, a PKK/KADEK spokesman stated that its armed wing, The People's Defense Force, would not disband or surrender its weapons for reasons of self-defense. In late 2003, the group sought to engineer another political face-lift, renaming the group Kongra-Gel (KGK) and brandishing its "peaceful" intentions, while continuing to commit attacks and refuse disarmament. . . .

ACTIVITIES

Primary targets have been Turkish Government security forces in Turkey, local Turkish officials, and villagers who oppose the organization in Turkey. Conducted attacks on Turkish diplomatic and commercial facilities in dozens of West European cities in 1993 and again in spring 1995. In an attempt to damage Turkey's tourist industry, the then PKK bombed tourist sites and hotels and kidnapped foreign tourists in the early-tomid 1990s. KGK continued to engage in violent acts—including at least one terrorist attack—against the Turkish state in 2003. Several members were arrested in Istanbul in late 2003 in possession of explosive materials.

STRENGTH

Approximately 4,000 to 5,000, most of whom currently are located in northern Iraq. Has thousands of sympathizers in Turkey and Europe.

LOCATION/AREA OF OPERATION

Operates primarily in Turkey, Europe, and the Middle East.

EXTERNAL AID

Has received safehaven and modest aid from Syria, Iraq, and Iran. Syria and Iran appear to cooperate with Turkey against KGK in a limited fashion when it serves their immediate interests. KGK uses Europe for fundraising and conducting political propaganda.

Ideological   *Communist Party of Philippines/New People's Army (CPP/NPA)*

DESCRIPTION

The military wing of the Communist Party of the Philippines (CPP), the NPA is a Maoist group formed in March 1969 with the aim of overthrowing the government through protracted guerrilla warfare. The chairman of the CPP's Central Committee and the NPA's founder, Jose Maria Sison, reportedly directs CPP and NPA activity from the Netherlands, where he lives in self-imposed exile. Fellow Central Committee member and director of the CPP's overt political wing, the National Democratic Front (NDF), Luis Jalandoni also lives in the Netherlands and has become a Dutch citizen. Although primarily a rural-based guerrilla group, the NPA has an active urban infrastructure to conduct terrorism and uses city-based assassination squads. Derives most of its funding from contributions of supporters in the Philippines, Europe, and elsewhere and from so-called revolutionary taxes extorted from local businesses and politicians.

ACTIVITIES

The NPA primarily targets Philippine security forces, politicians, judges, government informers, former rebels who wish to leave the NPA, rival splinter groups, and alleged criminals. Opposes any US military presence in the Philippines and attacked US military interests, killing several US service personnel, before the US base closures in 1992. Press reports in 1999 and in late 2001 indicated that the NPA is again targeting US troops participating in joint military exercises as well as US Embassy personnel. The NPA claimed responsibility for the assassination of two congressmen from Quezon in May 2001 and Cagayan in June 2001 and many other killings. In January 2002, the NPA publicly expressed its intent to target US personnel if discovered in NPA operating areas.

STRENGTH

Slowly growing; estimated at more than 10,000. This number is significantly lower than its peak strength of around 25,000 in the 1980s.

LOCATION/AREA OF OPERATIONS

Operates in rural Luzon, Visayas, and parts of Mindanao. Has cells in Manila and other metropolitan centers.

EXTERNAL AID

Unknown.

Sendero Luminoso (Shining Path or SL)

DESCRIPTION

Former university professor Abimael Guzman formed SL in Peru in the late 1960s, and his teachings created the foundation of SL's militant Maoist doctrine. In the 1980s, SL became one of the most ruthless terrorist groups in the Western Hemisphere approximately 30,000 persons have died since Shining Path took up arms in 1980. The Peruvian Government made dramatic gains against SL during the 1990s, but reports of recent SL involvement in narcotrafficking and kidnapping for ransom indicate it may have a new source of funding with which to sustain a resurgence. Its stated goal is to destroy existing Peruvian institutions and replace them with a communist peasant revolutionary regime. It also opposes any influence by foreign governments. In January 2003, Peruvian courts granted approximately 1,900 members the right to request retrials in a civilian court, including the imprisoned top leadership. Counterterrorist operations targeted pockets of terrorist activity in the Upper Huallaga River Valley and the Apurimac/Ene River Valley, where SL columns continued to conduct periodic attacks. Peruvian authorities captured several SL members in 2003. . . .

ACTIVITIES

Conducted indiscriminate bombing campaigns and selective assassinations. In June 2003, an SL column kidnapped 71 Peruvian and foreign employees working on the Camisea gas line in Ayacucho Department.

STRENGTH

Membership is unknown but currently estimated to be 400 to 500 armed militants.

LOCATION/AREA OF OPERATION

Peru, with most activity in rural areas.

EXTERNAL AID

None.

Revolutionary People's Liberation Party/Front (DHKP/C) a.k.a. Devrimci Sol, Revolutionary Left, Dev Sol

DESCRIPTION

Originally formed in 1978 as Devrimci Sol, or Dev Sol, a splinter faction of Dev Genc (Revolutionary Youth). Renamed in 1994 after factional infighting; "Party" refers to the group's political activities, while "Front" is a reference to the group's militant operations. The group espouses a Marxist-Leninist ideology and is virulently anti-US, anti-NATO, and anti-Turkish establishment. It finances its activities chiefly through donations and extortion. . . .

ACTIVITIES

Since the late 1980s, the group has targeted primarily current and retired Turkish security and military officials. It began a new campaign against foreign interests in 1990, which included attacks against US military and diplomatic personnel and facilities. To protest perceived US imperialism during the Gulf war, the DHKP/C assassinated two US military contractors; wounded an Air Force officer; and bombed more than 20 US and NATO military, commercial, and cultural facilities. In its first significant terrorist act as DHKP/C in 1996, it assassinated a prominent Turkish businessman and two others. DHKP/C added suicide bombings to its repertoire in 2001, with successful attacks against Turkish police in January and September. Security operations in Turkey and elsewhere have weakened the group, however. DHKP/C did not conduct any major terrorist attacks in 2003, although a DHKP/C operative prematurely detonated her explosive belt in May.

STRENGTH

Probably several dozen terrorist operatives inside Turkey, with a large support network throughout Europe.

LOCATION/AREA OF OPERATION

Turkey, primarily Istanbul. Raises funds in Europe.

EXTERNAL AID

Unknown.

Mujahedin-e Khalq Organization (MEK or MKO) a.k.a. The National Liberation Army of Iran (NLA, the militant wing of the MEK), the People's Mujahedin of Iran (PMOI), National Council of Resistance (NCR), the National Council of Resistance of Iran (NCRI), Muslim Iranian Student's Society (front organization used to garner financial support)

DESCRIPTION

The MEK philosophy mixes Marxism and Islam. Formed in the 1960s, the organization was expelled from Iran after the Islamic Revolution in 1979, and its primary support came from the former Iraqi regime of Saddam Hussein since the late 1980s. The MEK's history is filled with anti-Western attacks as well as terrorist attacks on the interests of the clerical regime in Iran and abroad. The MEK now advocates the overthrow of the Iranian regime and its replacement with the group's own leadership. . . .

ACTIVITIES

The group's worldwide campaign against the Iranian Government stresses propaganda and occasionally uses terrorism. During the 1970s, the MEK killed US military personnel and US civilians working on defense projects in Tehran and supported the takeover in 1979 of the US Embassy in Tehran. In 1981, the MEK detonated bombs in the head office of the Islamic Republic Party and the Premier's office, killing some 70 high-ranking Iranian officials, including chief Justice Ayatollah Mohammad Beheshti, President Mohammad-Ali Rajaei, and Premier Mohammad-Javad Bahonar. Near the end of the war with Iran during 1980-88, Baghdad armed the MEK with military equipment and sent it into action against Iranian forces. In 1991, it assisted the Government of Iraq in suppressing the Shia and Kurdish uprisings in southern Iraq and the Kurdish uprisings in the north. In April 1992, the MEK conducted near-simultaneous attacks on Iranian Embassies and installations in 13 countries, demonstrating the group's ability to mount large-scale operations overseas. In April 1999, the MEK targeted key military officers and assassinated the deputy chief of the Armed Forces General Staff. In April 2000, the MEK attempted to assassinate the commander of the Nasr Headquarters—Tehran's interagency board responsible for coordinating policies on Iraq. The normal pace of anti-Iranian operations increased during the "Operation Great Bahman" in February 2000, when the group launched a dozen attacks against Iran. In 2000 and 2001, the MEK was involved regularly in mortar attacks and hit-and run raids on Iranian military and law-enforcement units and government buildings near the Iran-Iraq border, although MEK terrorism in Iran declined throughout the remainder of 2001. In February 2000, for example, the MEK launched a mortar attack against the leadership complex in Tehran that houses the offices of the Supreme Leader and the President. Coalition aircraft bombed MEK bases during Operation Iraqi Freedom, and the Coalition forced the MEK forces to surrender in May 2003. The future of the MEK forces remains undetermined with Coalition forces.

STRENGTH

Some 3,800 members are confined to Camp Ashraf, the MEK's main compound near Baghdad, where they remain under Coalition control. As a condition of the cease-fire agreement, the group relinquished its weapons, including tanks, armored vehicles, and heavy artillery.

LOCATION/AREA OF OPERATION

In the 1980s, the MEK's leaders were forced by Iranian security forces to flee to France. On resettling in Iraq in 1987, almost all of its armed units were stationed in fortified bases near the border with Iran. Since Operation Iraqi Freedom, the bulk of the group is limited to Camp Ashraf though an overseas support structure remains with associates and supporters scattered throughout Europe and North America.

EXTERNAL AID

Before Operation Iraqi Freedom, the group received all of its military assistance, and most of its financial support, from the former Iraqi regime. The MEK also has used front organizations to solicit contributions from expatriate Iranian communities.

Revolutionary Nuclei (RN) a.k.a. Revolutionary Cells

DESCRIPTION

Revolutionary Nuclei (RN) emerged from a broad range of antiestablishment and anti-US/NATO/EU leftist groups active in Greece between 1995 and 1998. The group is believed to be the successor to or offshoot of Greece's most prolific terrorist group, Revolutionary People's Struggle (ELA), which has not claimed an attack since January 1995. Indeed, RN appeared to fill the void left by ELA, particularly as lesser groups faded from the scene. RN's few communiques show strong similarities in rhetoric, tone, and theme to ELA proclamations. RN has not claimed an attack since November 2000 nor has it announced its disbandment. . . .

ACTIVITIES

Since it began operations in January 1995, the group has claimed responsibility for some two-dozen arson attacks and low-level bombings targeting a range of US, Greek, and other European targets in Greece. In its most infamous and lethal attack to date, the group claimed responsibility for a bomb it detonated at the Intercontinental Hotel in April 1999 that resulted in the death of a Greek woman and injured a Greek man. Its modus operandi includes warning calls of impending attacks, attacks targeting property vice individuals, use of rudimentary timing devices, and strikes during the late evening–to–early morning hours. RN may have been responsible for two attacks in July against a US insurance company and a local bank in Athens. RN's last confirmed attack against US interests in Greece was in November 2000 with two separate bombings against the

Athens offices of Citigroup and the studio of a Greek/American sculptor. Greek targets have included judicial and other government office buildings, private vehicles, and the offices of Greek firms involved in NATO-related defense contracts in Greece. Similarly, the group has attacked European interests in Athens, including Barclays Bank in December 1998 and November 2000.

STRENGTH

Group membership is believed to be small, probably drawing from the Greek militant leftist or anarchist milieu.

LOCATION/AREA OF OPERATION

Primary area of operation is in the Athens metropolitan area.

EXTERNAL AID

Unknown but believed to be self-sustaining.

Revolutionary Organization 17 November a.k.a. 17 November

DESCRIPTION

Radical leftist group established in 1975 and named for the student uprising in Greece in November 1973 that protested the ruling military junta. Anti-Greek establishment, anti-United States, anti-Turkey, and anti-NATO group that seeks the ouster of US bases from Greece, the removal of Turkish military forces from Cyprus, and the severing of Greece's ties to NATO and the European Union (EU). . . .

ACTIVITIES

Initially conducted assassinations of senior US officials and Greek public figures. Added bombings in the 1980s. Since 1990 has expanded its targets to include EU facilities and foreign firms investing in Greece and has added improvised rocket attacks to its methods. Supports itself largely through bank robberies. A failed 17 November bombing attempt in June 2002 at the Port of Piraeus in Athens coupled with robust detective work led to the first-ever arrests of this group. In December 2003, a Greek court convicted 15 members—five of whom were given multiple life terms—of hundreds of crimes. Four other alleged members were acquitted because of a lack of evidence.

STRENGTH

Unknown but presumed to be small. Police arrested 19 suspected members of the group in 2002.

LOCATION/AREA OF OPERATION

Athens, Greece.

EXTERNAL AID

Unknown.

**Conflict in
Colombia and
Narco-Terrorism**

Revolutionary Armed Forces of Colombia (FARC)

DESCRIPTION

Growing out of the turmoil and fighting in the 1950s between liberal and conservative militias, the FARC was established in 1964 by the Colombian Communist Party to defend what were then autonomous Communist-controlled rural areas. The FARC is Latin America's oldest, largest, most capable, and best-equipped insurgency of Marxist origin. Although only nominally fighting in support of Marxist goals today, the FARC is governed by a general secretariat led by longtime leader Manuel Marulanda (a.k.a. "Tirofi jo") and six others, including senior military commander Jorge Briceno (a.k.a. "Mono Jojoy"). It is organized along military lines and includes several units that operate mostly in key urban areas such as Bogota. In 2003, the FARC conducted several high profile terrorist attacks, including a February car-bombing of a Bogota nightclub that killed more than 30 persons and wounded more than 160, as well as a November grenade attack in Bogota's restaurant district that wounded three Americans. . . .

ACTIVITIES

Bombings, murder, mortar attacks, narcotrafficking, kidnapping, extortion, hijacking, as well as guerrilla and conventional military action against Colombian political, military, and economic targets. In March 1999, the FARC executed three US Indian rights activists on Venezuelan territory after it kidnapped them in Colombia. In February 2003, the FARC captured and continues to hold three US contractors and killed one other American and a Colombian when their plane crashed in Florencia. Foreign citizens often are targets of

FARC kidnapping for ransom. The FARC has well-documented ties to the full range of narcotics trafficking activities, including taxation, cultivation, and distribution.

STRENGTH

Approximately 9,000 to 12,000 armed combatants and several thousand more supporters, mostly in rural areas.

LOCATION/AREA OF OPERATION

Primarily in Colombia, with some activities—extortion, kidnapping, weapons sourcing, logistics, and R&R—in neighboring Brazil, Venezuela, Panama, and Ecuador.

EXTERNAL AID

Cuba provides some medical care and political consultation. A trial is currently underway in Bogota to determine whether three members of the Irish Republican Army—arrested in Colombia in 2001 upon exiting the FARC-controlled demilitarized zone (*despeje*)—provided advanced explosives training to the FARC. The FARC and the Colombian National Liberation Army (ELN) often use the border area for cross border incursions and use Venezuelan territory near the border as a safe haven.

National Liberation Army (ELN)–Colombia

DESCRIPTION

Marxist insurgent group formed in 1965 by urban intellectuals inspired by Fidel Castro and Che Guevara. In October 2003, the Colombian Government released top ELN leader Felipe Torres from prison, hoping to spur the ELN to accept government demands to declare a cease-fire and come back to the negotiating table, but by year's end peace talks had not commenced. . . .

ACTIVITIES

Kidnapping, hijacking, bombing, and extortion. Minimal conventional military capability. Annually conducts hundreds of kidnappings for ransom, often targeting foreign employees of large corporations, especially in the petroleum industry. Derives some revenue from taxation of the illegal narcotics industry. Frequently assaults energy infrastructure and has inflicted major damage on pipelines and the electric distribution network. In September (2003), the ELN kidnapped eight foreign tourists, but they have all since either escaped or been released.

STRENGTH

Approximately 3,000 armed combatants and an unknown number of active supporters.

LOCATION/AREA OF OPERATION

Mostly in rural and mountainous areas of north, northeast, and southwest Colombia and Venezuela border regions.

EXTERNAL AID

Cuba provides some degree of safe haven, medical care, and political consultation. Reports persist that ELN members are often able to obtain safe haven inside Venezuelan territory near the Colombian border.

United Self-Defense Forces/Group of Colombia a.k.a. AUC–Autodefensas Unidasde Colombia

DESCRIPTION

The AUC—commonly referred to as the paramilitaries—is a loose umbrella organization formed in April 1997 to consolidate most local and regional self-defense groups each with the mission to protect economic interests and combat FARC and ELN insurgents locally. The AUC is supported by economic elites, drug traffickers, and local communities lacking effective government security and claims its primary objective is to protect its sponsors from insurgents. Some elements under the AUC umbrella, under its political leader Carlos Castano's influence, have voluntarily agreed to a unilateral cease-fire though violations of the cease-fire do occur. Parts of the AUC loyal to Castano currently are in negotiations with the Government of Colombia to demobilize. To date, approximately 1,000 AUC fighters have demobilized. . . .

ACTIVITIES

AUC operations vary from assassinating suspected insurgent supporters to engaging FARC and ELN combat units. Castano has publicly claimed that 70 percent of the AUC's operational costs are financed with drug-related earnings, the rest from "donations" from its sponsors. The AUC generally avoids actions against US personnel or interests.

STRENGTH

Estimated 8,000 to 11,000 and an unknown number of active supporters.

LOCATION/AREAS OF OPERATION

AUC forces are strongest in the northwest in Antioquia, Cordoba, Sucre, and Bolivar Departments. Since 1999, the group demonstrated a growing presence in other northern and southwestern departments. Clashes between the AUC and the FARC insurgents in Putumayo in 2000 demonstrated the range of the AUC to contest insurgents throughout Colombia.

EXTERNAL AID

None.

Cuba   Cuba remained opposed to the US-led Coalition prosecuting the global war on terrorism and actively condemned many associated US policies and actions throughout 2003. Government-controlled press reporting about US-led military operations in Iraq and Afghanistan were consistently critical of the United States and frequently and baselessly alleged US involvement in violations of human rights. Government propaganda claimed that those fighting for self-determination or against foreign occupation are exercising internationally recognized rights and cannot be accused of terrorism. Cuba's delegate to the UN said terrorism cannot be defined as including acts by legitimate national liberation movements—even though many such groups clearly employ tactics that intentionally target innocent civilians to advance their political, religious, or social agendas. In referring to US policy toward Cuba, the delegate asserted, "acts by states to destabilize other states is a form of terrorism."

The Cuban Government did not extradite nor request the extradition of suspected terrorists in 2003. Cuba continued to provide support to designated Foreign Terrorist Organizations, as well as to host several terrorists and dozens of fugitives from US justice. The Government refuses to return suspected terrorists to countries when it alleges that a receiving government could not provide a fair trial because the charges against the accused are "political." Cuba has publicly used this argument with respect to a number of fugitives from US justice, including Joanne Chesimard, wanted for the murder of a New Jersey State Trooper in 1973. Havana permitted up to 20 ETA members to reside in Cuba and provided some degree of safe-haven and support to members of FARC and the ELN. Bogota was aware of the arrangement and apparently acquiesced; it has publicly indicated that it seeks Cuba's continued mediation with ELN agents in Cuba. A declaration issued by the Cuban Ministry of Foreign Affairs in May 2003 maintained that the presence of ETA members in Cuba arose from a request for assistance by Spain and Panama and that the issue is a bilateral matter between Cuba and Spain. The declaration similarly defended its assistance to the FARC and the ELN as contributing to a negotiated solution in Colombia.

Dozens of fugitives from US justice have taken refuge on the island. In a few cases, the Cuban Government has rendered fugitives from US justice to US authorities. The salient feature of Cuba's behavior in this arena, however, is its refusal to render to US justice any fugitive whose crime is judged by Cuba to be "political."

With respect to domestic terrorism, the Government in April 2003 executed three Cubans who attempted to hijack a ferry to the United States. The three were executed under Cuba's 2001 "Law Against Acts of Terrorism."

Cuba became a party to all 12 international conventions and protocols relating to terrorism in 2001.

[Authors' note: According to government and media reports, Cuba continues to harbor a number of accused and convicted U.S. terrorists in addition to Joanne Chesimard. Michael Robert Finney and Charles Hill, formerly radical black nationalists, are alleged hijackers wanted in connection with the murder of a New Mexico state police officer.

Cuba also provides refuge to accused Puerto Rican terrorist Victor Manuel Gerena, one of the FBI's Ten Most Wanted Fugitives for his alleged role in a 1983 $7 million robbery in Connecticut by the Puerto Rican nationalist terrorist group Los Macheteros; and convicted bomb maker William Guillermo Morales of the allied FALN Puerto Rican terrorist group. Evidence suggests Cuba provided training, operational, and occasional financial support to Puerto Rican terrorists and at least once even moved their loot via diplomatic pouch.[6] Cuba was also connected with leftist and black separatist groups in the United States, although the historical record remains unclear on the communist government's level of support. A variety of anti-American international terrorist organizations also received training and other forms of assistance from the Cubans.]

Syria The Syrian Government in 2003 continued to provide political and material support to Palestinian rejectionist groups. HAMAS, the PIJ, the Popular Front for the Liberation of Palestine-General Command, and the Popular Front for the Liberation of Palestine operate from Syria, although they have lowered their public profiles since May, when Damascus announced that the groups had voluntarily closed their offices. Many of these groups claimed responsibility for anti-Israeli terrorist acts in 2003; the Syrian Government insists that their Damascus offices undertake only political and informational activities. Syria also continued to permit Iran to use Damascus as a transshipment point for resupplying Hizballah in Lebanon.

Syrian officials have publicly condemned international terrorism but continue to make a distinction between terrorism and what they consider to be the legitimate armed resistance of Palestinians in the Occupied Territories and of Lebanese Hizballah. The Syrian Government has not been implicated directly in an act of terrorism since 1986.

During the past five years, there have been no acts of terrorism against US citizens in Syria. Despite tensions between the United States and Syria about the war in Iraq and Syrian support for terrorism, Damascus has repeatedly assured the United States that it will take every possible measure to protect US citizens and facilities. Damascus has cooperated with the United States and other foreign governments against al-Qaida, the Taliban, and other terrorist organizations and individuals; it also has discouraged signs of public support for al-Qaida, including in the media and at mosques.

In 2003, Syria was instrumental in returning a sought-after terrorist planner to US custody. Since the end of the war in Iraq, Syria has made efforts to tighten its borders with Iraq to limit the movement of anti-Coalition foreign fighters into Iraq, a move that has not been completely successful.

Syria is a party to seven of the 12 international conventions and protocols relating to terrorism.

North Korea
The Democratic People's Republic of Korea (DPRK) is not known to have sponsored any terrorist acts since the bombing of a Korean Airlines flight in 1987.

Following the attacks of September 11, Pyongyang began laying the groundwork for a new position on terrorism by framing the issue as one of "protecting the people" and replaying language from the Joint US-DPRK Statement on International Terrorism of October 2000. It also announced to a visiting EU delegation that it planned to sign the international conventions against terrorist financing and the taking of hostages and would consider acceding to other antiterrorism agreements.

At a summit with Japanese Prime Minister Koizumi in Pyongyang in September 2002, National Defense Commission Chairman Kim Jong II acknowledged the involvement of DPRK "special institutions" in the kidnapping of Japanese citizens and said that those responsible had already been punished. Pyongyang has allowed the return to Tokyo of five surviving abductees and is negotiating with Tokyo over the repatriation of their family members remaining in North Korea. The DPRK also has been trying to resolve the issue of harboring Japanese Red Army members involved in a jet hijacking in 1970—allowing the repatriation of several family members of the hijackers to Japan.

Although it is a party to six international conventions and protocols relating to terrorism, Pyongyang has not taken substantial steps to cooperate in efforts to combat international terrorism.

Sudan
Sudan in 2003 deepened its cooperation with the US Government to investigate and apprehend extremists suspected of involvement in terrorist activities. Overall, Sudan's cooperation and information sharing has improved markedly, producing significant progress in combating terrorist activity, but areas of concern remain.

Domestically, Khartoum stepped up efforts to disrupt extremist activities and deter terrorists from operating in Sudan. In May (2003), Sudanese authorities raided a probable terrorist training camp in Kurdufan State, arresting more than a dozen extremists and seizing illegal weapons. The majority of the trainees captured were Saudi citizens and were extradited to Saudi Arabia to face charges in accordance with a bilateral agreement. In June, the Sudanese Government detained several individuals linked to the publication of an alleged "hit list" attributed to the terrorist group al-Takfir wa al-Hijra. The list called for the killing of 11 prominent Sudanese Christian and leftist politicians, jurists, journalists, and others. In September, a Sudanese court convicted a Syrian engineer and two Sudanese nationals of training a group of Saudis, Palestinians, and others to carry out attacks in Iraq, Eritrea, Sudan, and Israel. A court statement said the Syrian was training others to carry out attacks against US forces in Iraq.

There were no international terrorist attacks in Sudan during 2003. Khartoum throughout the year placed a high priority on the protection of US citizens and facilities in Sudan. In November, the authorities stepped up their efforts to protect the US Embassy, which temporarily suspended operations in response to a terrorist threat that was deemed credible. Earlier in the year, Sudanese authorities closed a major Khartoum thoroughfare to enhance the Embassy's security and further upgraded security measures during Operation Iraqi Freedom.

The Sudanese Government also took steps in 2003 to strengthen its legislative and bureaucratic instruments for fighting terrorism by ratifying the International Convention for the Suppression of the Financing of Terrorism. Sudan also ratified the African Union's Convention on the Prevention and Combating of Terrorism and the Convention of the Organization of the Islamic Conference on Combating Terrorism. In June, Sudanese Minister of Justice Ali Mohamed Osman Yassin issued a decree establishing an office for combating terrorism. In 2003, Sudan signed a counterterrorism cooperation agreement with the Algerian Government, which during the 1990s accused Sudan of harboring wanted Algerian terrorists. Sudan also signed a counterterrorism agreement with Yemen and Ethiopia.

In response to ongoing US concern over the presence in Sudan of the Islamic Resistance Movement (HAMAS) and the Palestine Islamic Jihad (PIJ), Foreign Minister Mustafa Osman Ismail in June said the Sudanese Government would limit HAMAS to conducting political activities. Visiting Sudanese peace talks in Kenya in October, Secretary Powell said Sudan had yet to shut down the Khartoum offices of HAMAS and the PIJ.

President Umar al-Bashir in an interview with Al-Arabiyah television maintained that the Sudanese Government could not expel HAMAS because it has a political relationship with the group and stated there was no PIJ office in Sudan. Responding to press reports that its Sudan office had closed, HAMAS officials in Khartoum and Gaza in November said that the office remained open but that the main representative had been replaced.

Sudan also has participated in regional efforts to end its long-running civil war—a US policy priority that complements the US goal of denying terrorists safe haven in Sudan.

Sudan is a party to all 12 of the international conventions and protocols relating to terrorism.

Libya   In 2003, Libya held to its practice in recent years of curtailing support for international terrorism, although Tripoli continues to maintain contact with some past terrorist clients. Libyan leader Muammar Qadhafi and other Libyan officials continued their efforts to identify Tripoli with the international community in the war on terrorism. During an interview in January, Qadhafi stated that Libyan intelligence had been sharing information on al-Qaida and other Islamic extremists with Western intelligence services and characterized such cooperation as "irrevocable." In a speech marking the 34th anniversary of his revolution, he declared that Libya and the United States had a common interest in fighting al-Qaida and Islamic extremism.

unalterable

Regarding its own terrorist past, Libya took long-awaited steps in 2003 to address the UN requirements arising out of the bombing of Pan Am Flight 103 but remained embroiled in efforts to settle international political and legal disputes stemming from other terrorist attacks Tripoli conducted during the 1980s.

In August, as required by the UN Security Council, the Libyan Government officially notified the UN Security Council that it accepted responsibility for the actions of its officials in connection with Pan Am Flight 103 (Abdel Basset Ali al-Meghrahi, a Libyan intelligence agent, was convicted by a Scottish court in 2001 for his role in the bombing). Libya further confirmed that it had made arrangements for the payment of appropriate compensation to the families of the victims: a total of up to $2.7 billion or $10 million for each victim. Further, Libya renounced terrorism and affirmed its adherence to a

refused

number of UN declarations and international conventions and protocols that the Libyan Government had signed in the past. Libya also pledged to cooperate in good faith with any further requests for information in connection with the Pan Am Flight 103 investigation. In response, the Security Council voted on 12 September to permanently lift sanctions that it had imposed against Libya in 1992 and suspended in 1999.

In August, the Qadhafi Foundation pledged to compensate victims wounded in the bombing in 1986 of La Belle Discotheque, a Berlin nightclub, after a German court issued its written opinion finding that the Libyan intelligence service had orchestrated the attack. The original trial had concluded in 2001 with the conviction of four individuals for carrying out the attack, in which two US servicemen and a Turkish woman were killed and 229 persons wounded. Leaders of the Qadhafi Foundation indicated, however, that their compensation was a humanitarian gesture that did not constitute Libyan acceptance of responsibility. In September, the German Government indicated that it was engaged in talks with Libyan representatives, but at the end of the year, no announcement had yet been made regarding a final compensation deal.

On 19 December, Colonel Qadhafi announced that Libya would eliminate its weapons of mass destruction programs and MTCR-class missiles and took immediate steps to implement this public commitment with the assistance of the United States, United Kingdom, and relevant international organizations. The Libyan decision to reveal its programs to the international community shed important light on the international network of proliferators intent on subverting nonproliferation regimes.

Libya is a party to all 12 international conventions and protocols relating to terrorism.

NOTES

1. *Patterns of Global Terrorism*, Appendix B: "Background Information on Designated Foreign Terrorist Organizations," released by the Office of the Coordinator for Counterterrorism, U.S. Department of State (April 29, 2004).

2. Cam Simpson and Howard Witt, "U.S. Warns Terrorist Groups Against Retaliatory Attacks: Effort Aims to Stem Strikes During War," *Chicago Tribune* (March 20, 2003): 5

3. *Patterns of Global Terrorism*, Appendix B.

4. Warren Hoge, "Two Iranian Guards at U.N. Expelled for Filming New York Sites," *New York Times* (June 30, 2004): A1.

5. U.S. Department of Justice Press Release, "Randall Todd Royer and Ibrahim Ahmed Al-Hamdi Sentenced for Participation in Virginia Jihad Network," (Washington, DC, April 9, 2004), www.usdoj.gov/opa/pr/2004/April/04_crm_225.htm.

6. On Cuban support for the FALN, see, for example, Edmund Mahoney, "A Man and a Movement in Cuba's Grip," *The Harford Courant* (November 7, 1999): A1.

2

VOLUNTEER SERVICES

VOLUNTEERS ARE "FIRST RESPONDERS" TOO

It didn't take long. While in the movies people frequently frantically run from a disaster scene, in real life it's very different. Within minutes after clouds of debris washed over the site of the collapsed towers, volunteers began arriving at the World Trade Center. They were there to help, heedless of the risks. College students handed out bottles of water to rescue workers. Businessmen in suits helped people from the scene. So many unsolicited volunteers showed up they had to be turned away. Elsewhere, an estimated 300,000 or more people escaped the smoke and fire of lower Manhattan on a flotilla of disparate boats—all with no report of fatalities or major mishaps. The operation was a logistical marvel. Yet the evacuation was unplanned and often unsupervised, spurred by the spontaneous actions and cooperation of fleeing citizens and individual boat captains. No single individual or agency was "in charge."[1] Meanwhile, professional volunteer disaster teams began to quickly arrive from all over the United States and other countries as well. The Javits Convention Center was turned into their makeshift headquarters. By September 14, there was simply no more room for volunteers.

The selfless acts of the 9/11 volunteers are more typical than exceptional. Americans have strong volunteer traditions. This legacy could serve the nation well in the war on terror. Many volunteer organizations, like the Red Cross, are expected to play critical roles in responding to natural and human-made disasters. Volunteer groups should be consulted and integrated into emergency management planning and training. Individuals wishing to serve in a volunteer capacity have a number of options. Some are listed here.

THE CITIZENRY ORGANIZED—VOLUNTEERS

Hundreds of thousands of U.S. citizens have agreed to accept additional responsibilities in securing the homeland. These volunteers have joined a wide range of public and private organizations.

Government Volunteer Programs

In early 2002 the Bush Administration announced the creation of the USA Freedom Corps to marshal volunteers to "focus on three areas of need: responding in case of crisis at home; rebuilding our communities; and extending American compassion throughout the world."[2] A cornerstone of the plan was the Citizen Corps, established to support homeland security missions. Organized via a national network of Citizen Corps Councils, the organization reported serving almost half of the U.S. population by early 2004.

Community Emergency Response Team

One of the most aggressive Citizen Corps projects is the Community Emergency Response Team (CERT) program, which trains citizens in basic disaster response skills such as medical operations, fire safety, and search and rescue. Trained volunteers are expected to help prepare their communities and workplaces and provide assistance during an event. Information on forming CERTs can be obtained from FEMA.

Medical Reserve Corps

The Medical Reserve Corps (MRC) program enlists medical and public health professionals in homeland security. These volunteers, often retired or practicing doctors and nurses, can work with emergency response and public health programs, both in supporting ongoing efforts such as blood and immunization drives and during emergencies. The program is administered by the Department of Health and Human Services.

Volunteers in Police Service

The Voluteers in Police Service (VIPS) program extends the capabilities of law enforcement agencies by providing citizen volunteers to perform tasks that can assist or free up sworn officers. These duties could include helping with clerical work, assisting with agency outreach efforts, or conducting citizen patrols. VIPS is funded by the Department of Justice and managed by the International Association of Chiefs of Police.

Neighborhood Watch

Already a crime-fighting staple in many neighborhoods before 9/11, the Neighborhood Watch Program (NWP) now includes terrorism awareness education in its existing crime prevention mission. The program also attempts to encourage community emergency education and preparedness. Neighborhood Watch is administered by the National Sheriffs' Association and funded by the Department of Justice.

Private-Sector Volunteer Groups

From Boy Scouts handing out brochures at minor-league baseball games to multimillion-dollar Red Cross campaigns, the contributions of private, volunteer-centered organizations play a key role in supporting homeland security missions.

The Fire Corps

This program promotes volunteer efforts to help fire and rescue departments with safety education, administrative tasks, and needs.

Red Cross

With some 1,300 local chapters across the United States, the American Red Cross is one of the nation's most significant humanitarian organizations. Staffed in large part by volunteers, it follows the principles of the International Red Cross Movement and among its missions is helping people prevent, prepare for, and respond to emergencies. After a disaster, the Red Cross provides food, shelter, and health services. It also renders financial assistance to victims and programmatic support for projects involving disaster prevention, response, and recovery. For example, the Red Cross said it provided more than $800 million in assistance related to 9/11 in the two years after the attacks, including mental health assistance to more than 55,400 people in 48 states and 57 countries.[3] In addition, recognizing the public confusion over the federal government's color-coded HSAS system, the Red Cross issued its own guidelines for public preparedness.[4]

American Safety and Health Institute

An official partner of the Citizen Corps, the American Safety and Health Institute (ASHI) is a nonprofit organization that reports having 30,000 safety educators and supports Citizen Corps Councils across the United States.

Salvation Army

An international religious organization, the Salvation Army responds to calamities of all types and sizes, from home fires to natural disasters. The group estimates that almost 40,000 of its volunteers assisted in the aftermath of 9/11, providing supplies, counseling, and several million meals.

State Defense Forces

Some states maintain State Guard forces. These are state-managed volunteer organizations, authorized by the U.S. Constitution. The units are of volunteers and do not maintain stocks of equipment and supplies. State Guards may replace or supplement the National Guard when unavailable or inadequate for state service. The New York Naval Militia, for example, assisted in the response to the 9/11 attacks. More information on State Guards can be obtained from the State Guard Association of the United States.

Other Organizations

Many other groups, from the United States Junior Chamber of Commerce to the Civil Air Patrol have active programs in support of homeland security. Citizen Corps affiliates have included the American Radio Relay League; E9-1-1 Institute; Mercy Medical Airlift; National Association for Search and Rescue; National Crime Prevention Council; National Fire Protection Association; National Safety Council; National Volunteer Fire Council; National Voluntary Organizations Active in Disaster; Points of Light Foundation and the Volunteer Center National Network; Save A Life Foundation; and Veterans of Foreign Wars

NOTES

1. E. L. Quarantelli, "The Study of Disaster Movies: Research Problems, Findings, and Implications" (University of Delaware, Disaster Research Center, 1980), passim.

2. The President's State of the Union Address, The United States Capitol, Washington, DC (January 29, 2002), www.whitehouse.gov/news/releases/2002/01/20020129-11.html.

3. See Press Release, "Organizations Announce New Online Enrollment for 9/11 Mental Health and Substance Abuse Program" (New York, NY, September 10, 2003), www.red-cross.org/pressrelease/0,1077,0_314_1580,00.html. See also Red Cross Document, "Response to September 11, 2001 Terrorist Attacks; Statistics as of December 31, 2003," www.redcross.org/news/ds/0109wtc/donationwork/SRPStats.pdf.

4. American Red Cross Homeland Security Advisory System Recommendations for Individuals, Families, Neighborhoods, Schools, and Businesses, redcross.org/services/disaster/beprepared/hsas.html.

3

THE MEDIA AND ISSUES
FOR HOMELAND SECURITY

THE MEDIA

The news media are such an important component of homeland security that some suggest they should be considered a national critical infrastructure for information. "The interconnectedness of these modern infrastructure systems allows greater efficiency, but it also creates new vulnerabilities. And the news media may be the weakest link in this system," concluded one observer.[1] Whether the media are the weakest link, or one of the strongest, they have the undisputed capability to do both great harm and good to America's homeland security.

Influencing Policy and Defining Reality

On a policy level, the news media influence the national agenda. Some have suggested the United States would have been far better prepared for 9/11 had the media concentrated as much on the threat from al-Qaida as they did on political sex scandals, shark attacks, and the British Royal Family in the months and years before the attack.

Once events occur, especially specific attacks that are not personally experienced by most citizens and government officials, the media have the power to define the experience. What actually happened? How terrible was the event? Why did it happen? Most Americans can only answer these questions based on information they have gathered through the filter of the media. Media coverage has a direct impact on the perceived risk of becoming a victim of terrorism (often creating unrealistically high fears) and thereby has economic impacts on sectors such as the travel industry.[2]

A Tool of Terrorism

Because terrorists attack one group of people in order to influence another, they require the active participation of the news media to make their strategy a success. Media coverage, it has been said, is the oxygen of terrorism. That is a key reason U.S. officials issued a highly unusual call for American media executives to refrain from presenting Usama bin Ladin's full statements after the 9/11 attack.

"My message to them (the media) was that it's not (up) to me to judge news value of something like this," said Bush administration National Security Advisor Condoleeza Rice, "but it is to say that there's a national security concern about an unedited, 15 or 20 minute spew of anti-American hatred that ends in a call to go out and kill Americans, and I think that that was fully understood."[3] Despite opposition by some free-speech advocates, the request was heeded by media leaders such as the president of CBS News, who said: "This is absolutely unprecedented in my experience. The story is unique; the attack on the U.S. is unique. Nobody took umbrage at this. We are all giving the government the benefit of the doubt; the propaganda issue is a legitimate issue."[4]

Bin Ladin gloated, "They forgot all about fair and objective reporting and reporting the other side of the issue. I tell you freedom and human rights in America are doomed."[5] Objective observers praised the responsibility of the media, but wondered if their restraint did much good, especially since bin Ladin's message was carried to the rest of the world by non-U.S. outlets.

In their defense, media leaders often note that while they commit huge amounts of space to terrorism, their coverage almost always casts it in a negative light. While true, this misses the point. The essential message of intimidation always gets through to the viewer. Indeed, studies have indicated citizens dramatically overestimated their risk of being the victim of terrorism after saturation coverage by the media. Finally, the supporters of terrorist groups may simply disregard condemnatory editorial messages carried with the video of successful attacks.

The Message as a Weapon

Not only does media coverage offer terrorists the opportunity to spread their message to a huge number of people, but the immediacy and blanket coverage of modern electronic media can transform news into an actual weapon that creates tangible harm among consumers.

As seen earlier in this book, research indicates millions of Americans who were nowhere near the scenes of the 9/11 attacks suffered negative psychological symptoms based on their reaction to media coverage of the events.

More sophisticated future terrorists might attempt to exploit the media for psychological or intelligence warfare. Well-planned hoaxes could prompt spontaneous evacuations, runs on emergency supplies, or the consumption of unneeded drugs, such as anthrax treatments, that often pose serious side effects. In a certain way, the news has the potential to kill. But in a very real way, it can also save lives.

A Tool of Homeland Security

Just as the media could engender panic, it could also prevent it. Because of advances in television and digital technology, journalists can interact with the participants in terrorist events as never before and can certainly provide more extensive and rapid information than the government. On 9/11, information obtained from the media informed the actions of the passengers on United Airlines Flight 93. In many cases, according to media reports and government investigations, people trapped in the World Trade Center were more likely to get helpful information from a news radio station than New York's 911 emergency center. While there have been celebrated cases of media misinformation during emergencies, in many disasters, both natural and human-made, media warnings and the rapid information provided to citizens and officials have saved lives. Media reports have also helped authorities gather important information on terrorists and other criminals. Finally, news media coverage has certainly encouraged many citizens to increase their level of preparedness.[6]

Media Errors: The Cost of Doing Business

As discussed, in the case of terrorism news, deliberate disinformation or faulty information could cause news consumers to take incorrect action and even prompt panic. This presents a challenge for the media, because as in many other industries, journalistic organizations are designed to operate with an acceptable level of flawed outputs. Most daily newspapers and television shows choose not to invest the money or time to conduct exhaustive fact checking on every report. In the case of extemporaneous television and radio news shows, such standards are impossible. One only has to recall hoax phone calls from the fans of radio disk jockeys to realize how false information can reach the airwaves during breaking stories. A more troubling, if older, example was the appearance of bogus pictures of the Chernobyl nuclear disaster on American national television.

Media quality-control systems are often focused on preventing errors with financial implications, such as libelous reports, and are usually thorough enough to avoid repeated and significant factual mistakes as well. The less serious but numerous inaccuracies that do slip through can be corrected or not, depending on the organization's standards and consumer reaction. While this system works for general news, the margin of error in terrorism coverage is narrower and the impact greater.

Need to Be First and Fill the News Hole

The opportunity for errors and missteps is exacerbated by the competitive industry imperatives in most newsrooms. Journalists are under pressure both to get the story first and get it right; all too often the former prevails. It is not just mistakes that occur because of this competition; it also leads to the distribution of accurate reports that under other circumstances might have been withheld. For example, in the late 1990s, according to government officials, bin Ladin stopped using his satellite phone after a media leak that U.S. intelligence was able to track him by it.[7] Certainly media executives have shown restraint in declining to publish stories because of their potential harm to national security. And history has shown the publication of some stories the government wished to keep secret was a public service. But the tendency to publish more than less, and faster rather than more carefully, is driven by another important media imperative—the requirement for constant updates by a multiplying number of media outlets. These shows and publications require more and more information simply to fill what is called the "news hole." Often this involves a series of hastily arranged live interviews; the lower standards of accuracy and heightened levels of conjecture accepted during such broadcasts create an environment ripe for hyperbole, error, and faulty advice.

Ratings and the Emotional Appeal

It is not enough for media executives just to fill their news hole; they must fill it in a way that attracts as many viewers as possible. The drive for viewers, especially by electronic media, has created an emphasis on production methods that grip the audience emotionally and/or appeal to morbid curiosity. Violent events usually fit the bill nicely; for years journalists have joked about the saying, If it bleeds, it leads (the newscast). While many news managers reject that dictum, most would agree that fear, sorrow, and anger are emotions that produce compelling television. A rapid trip through the television news lineup usually reveals a litany of stories focused on tragedy and often based on the premise that "it could have been you (the viewer)" who suffered this fate. This type of coverage can amplify the fear produced by terrorist attacks and their threat.

Lack of Expertise

Exacerbating all these factors is a lack of technical expertise among journalists, who usually move from assignment to assignment and rarely have advanced technical or scientific training. Journalists pride themselves on their ability to simplify complicated issues, but the more reflective among them admit that many of these simplifications come at the price of accuracy. The current solution among many media outlets is to hire "experts," often selected as much for their television personas as professional qualifications. The problem of expertise is especially pronounced during news events when journalists are required to evaluate complex technical issues in real time. Such an event was Pennsylvania's Three Mile Island nuclear accident in 1979, where the lack of knowledge among some journalists—aggravated by the poor communication skills and impaired credibility of official spokespersons—contributed to confusion and sensationalism, which in turn increased public anxiety.[8] Such factors would be much more common, and serious, in the event of a bioterrorist attack or similar event.

Improvements Are Being Made

Across the United States, media outlets and government emergency managers have increased their cooperation since 9/11. The integration of media representatives into homeland security exercises is considered a best practice and improves the preparedness of first responders and reporters alike. The federal government and media organizations have also cooperated in conducting training seminars designed to increase technical skills and enhance understanding on both sides. While much work remains to be done, there has been progress.

In addition, many media organizations have taken steps to enhance their own preparations for a terrorist attack. The 1993 World Trade Center bombing disabled the antennae of several New York television stations, temporarily putting them off the air. The 2001 attack tested the operational capabilities of numerous media organizations. Learning from these events, media outlets have taken measures such as creating alternative editorial and publishing or broadcasting locations. Many have also outfitted their video crews and reporters with personal protective equipment to help them escape from WMD attack zones.

Bypassing the Traditional Media

Many in the media pride themselves as gatekeepers who determine what is news. This sometimes frustrates government officials, whose statements during disasters are often edited or simply disregarded by editors and producers. However, the role of the news media as a gatekeeper of information is in decline as news consumers, especially young ones, move to interactive and alternative information sources. In May 2004, American Nick Berg was beheaded in Iraq, and his killing put on the Internet. When major news outlets declined to run video or still pictures of the actual murder, many consumers turned to the Internet. After the killing was revealed, "Nick Berg video" became the number one search term on the Lycos search engine and "Nick Berg" became the second most searched phrase (after "American Idol") on Google for the month.[9] Uncounted individuals across the globe downloaded video of the beheading, bypassing the editorial judgment of the major media and in many cases no doubt inflicting at least minor psychological trauma on themselves.

In order to enlist the citizenry in homeland security, government planners must not only work to improve the preparedness of the mainstream news media. They must also understand that official messages carried on major media outlets will be competing with a vast array of data for the attention of the American people.

NOTES

1. Randy Atkins, "The News Media Could Be Our Weakest Link," *Washington Post* (January 26, 2003): B3.

2. See various studies cited in Bruce Hoffman, *Inside Terrorism* (New York: Columbia University Press, 1998).

3. NewsHour, "Censoring the Enemy" (October 15, 2001), www.pbs.org/newshour/bb/media/july-dec01/cens_10-15.html.

4. Mike Allen and Lisa de Moraes, "TV Networks to Limit Use of Tapes from Bin Laden: White House to Reinstate Some Congressional Briefings," *Washington Post* (October 11, 2001): A8.

5. CNN.Com, "Transcript of Bin Laden's October Interview" (February 5, 2002), www.cnn.com/2002/WORLD/asiapcf/south/02/05/binladen.transcript/index.html

6. LaVerie Berry, et al., "Media Interaction with the Public in Emergency Situations: Four Case Studies" (Washington, DC: Congressional Research Service, August 1999), p. 31.

7. CNN.Com, "Anti-leak Bill Awaits President's Action" (October 31, 2000), www.cnn.com/2000/US/10/31/leak.penalties.

8. Berry, "Media Interaction," p. 7.

9. Lycos Daily 50, "Report with Dean," 50.lycos.com/051304.asp; Google, "Zeitgeist," www.google.com/press/zeitgeist.html.

4

MEDICAL AND PUBLIC HEALTH SERVICES EMERGENCY AND DISASTER PLANNING AND RESPONSE

PUBLIC HEALTH AND MEDICAL ORGANIZATIONS HAVE UNIQUE AND DEMANDING RESPONSIBILITIES FOR PREPARING AND RESPONDING TO TERRORIST ATTACKS

The mission of public health services includes monitoring the public health status to identify community health problems; diagnosing and investigating health hazards; conducting public information and education activities; developing plans and policies and organizing community partnerships to respond to health issues; enforcing health and safety laws and regulations; advising officials on health policies; coordinating emergency public health activities; and conducting research on health problems.

Medical services and facilities include emergency medical services, hospitals, clinics, ambulance services, medical laboratories, pharmacies, managed health-care facilities, nursing homes, poison control centers, medical academic institutions, and veterinary services.

FEDERAL SUPPORT FOR MEDICAL RESPONSES

Before the creation of the Department of Homeland Security (DHS) in January 2002, numerous federal departments and agencies bore responsibility for medical preparedness and response. Today, at least four federal departments still retain significant responsibilities for providing coordinating support and providing resources to assist in state and local medical responses for terrorist attacks, disasters, and other emergencies.

The Department of Homeland Security

The DHS provides oversight of the Metropolitan Medical Response System and the National Disaster Medical System. In addition, the DHS has assumed the functions of the Department of Health and Human Services' Office of Emergency Preparedness, which manages and coordinates federal health, medical, and health-related social services for major emergencies and disasters. Responsibility for coordinating the federal response to any terrorist attack or major disaster (including medical support) falls to the Federal Emergency Management Agency (FEMA) under the oversight of the DHS under the secretary for Emergency Preparedness and Response. Formerly an independent agency but now part of the DHS, FEMA manages national mitigation and disaster assistance programs, including coordinating the types and levels of support provided by all federal departments and agencies in the response to and recovery from a terrorist strike.

Department of Health and Human Services

The Department of Health and Human Services' Centers for Disease Control (CDC) oversees national biosurveillance efforts, and its Laboratory Response Network provides specialized, rapid-detection capabilities to state and local health agencies. Along with the Health and Human Resources administration, the CDC provides funding directly to state and local health organizations to upgrade their overall capabilities and conduct training exercises. Finally, the CDC continues to manage the National Strategic Stockpile in coordination with the DHS through a memorandum of understanding agreed to by the two departments. In addition, the Public Health Security and Bioterrorism Preparedness and Response Act of 2002 established an assistant secretary for public health emergency preparedness to serve as the DHS secretary's principal advisor on matters related to bioterrorism and to coordinate interagency activities with other federal agencies and the state and local officials responsible for emergency preparedness.

Department of Defense

The Department of Defense is also a cosponsor of the National Disaster Medical System, and under certain circumstances its hospitals can be used to treat civilian disaster victims. In addition to hospital facilities, a number of defense assets might be deployed in response to a catastrophic bioterrorist attack. In particular, the department is able to provide technical and personnel support to the DHS and state authorities during a declared biological or other terrorist disaster. These include the U.S. Army's Medical Research Institute for Infectious Diseases' (USAMRIID) Aeromedical Isolation Team and the U.S. Marine Corps' Chemical and Biological Incident Response Force (CBIRF).

Additionally, Congress established an assistant secretary of defense for homeland defense to oversee programs and policies providing military assistance to civilian authorities (MACA). The Pentagon also established the U.S. Northern Command (NORTHCOM), which has responsibilities for both MACA and defense of the United States.

Department of Veterans Affairs

The Department of Veterans Affairs' Emergency Preparedness Act of 2002 assigned preparedness and response functions to the nationwide system of hospitals and clinics operated by the Department of Veterans Affairs (VA). The act created an assistant secretary of operations, preparedness, and security to act as the VA's liaison with the DHS, and it directs that all VA facilities be made available for use during a declared national emergency. The VA is also creating four regional emergency preparedness research centers to aid in developing federal medical response strategies.

ORGANIZING STATE AND LOCAL ACTIVITIES

State and local medical and health-care providers can be divided into the preparedness activities (actions taken before an emergency occurs) and response operations.

Activities to Be Conducted Prior to an Emergency

In preparation for a terrorist attack, medical providers and public health officials should conduct assessments, develop systems and plans, and conduct training and exercises.

Conduct an Assessment of Medical Capacity

An important first step in any preparedness program is to conduct an inventory of the resources that might be available in the event of a crisis. This should include assets that might be available locally, provided through mutual aid agreements, and those available from state and federal governments. This assessment might include medical supplies and equipment, personnel and facilities, laboratory assets, pharmacological support, and medical transport.

Coordinate with Other Agencies

Public health officials and medical service providers cannot respond to terrorist attacks, disasters, or other emergencies in a vacuum. They should establish contacts, coordinate planning, establish mutual aid agreements, and conduct training exercises with emergency medical services and agencies; medical, public health, and veterinary providers; fire and law enforcement agencies; state, local, and tribal governments; local emergency planning committees, neighboring health jurisdictions; volunteer and nongovernmental organizations; private businesses, 911 centers, poison control centers, and medical academic institutions.

Participate in Risk Assessments

Medical and public health providers should actively seek to join in risk assessment conduct by government, nongovernmental agencies, and the private sector, ensuring that there is an understanding of how available medical resources may affect the threats and vulnerabilities identified while conducting assessments of risks and appropriate risk-reduction measures. Medical and public health providers should conduct their own risk assessments, including determining their reliance on critical infrastructure (such as information systems, telecommunications, and utilities) and physical security needs.

Develop a Medical Surveillance System

Establishing systems for conducting mortality, morbidity, syndromic, and mental and behavioral surveillance and registries of affected populations are the foundation of a proactive medical response system.

Medical surveillance is the analysis of health information to look for problems that may signal the onset of a biological or chemical attack or identify unique health problems related to a crisis or disaster. Surveillance may identify trends or unusual health events in a community that may indicate the need for an emergency medical response. Medical surveillance is already conducted in many workplaces to identify health risks. For example, Department of Defense Manual 6055.5-M details minimum standards for programs that are used to help occupational health professionals and others recognize and evaluate health risks associated with specific workplace exposures. In the wake of 9/11, a number of efforts are under way to expand medical surveillance to provide local, regional, and national surveillance to help identify possible terrorist threats and infectious disease hazards.

Develop Plans, Procedures, Guidelines, and Training

A basic all-hazards operations plan should be developed as well as incident-specific annexes to account for the unique requirements for responding to different types of hazards. Incident-specific annexes should cover potential natural disasters (such as avalanche and drought); infectious disease outbreaks; technological or human-made disasters like airplane crashes and chemical accidents; critical infrastructure failures (such as loss of sanitation, water supplies, or electricity); and terrorist chemical, biological, radiological, nuclear, high-yield explosive events. Plans should also include procedures to ensure a command and communications scheme, contingencies for continuity of operations of medical and health-care services; public affairs and risk communications guidelines; and means to respond to mass casualties including surge capacity to accomplish basic health-care missions, means for the delivery of assets such as distributing National Strategic Stockpile supplies and dispensing prophylaxes (for example, vaccines).

A medical response program should also provide orientation, training, and exercises to ensure that personnel are properly trained and certified; equipment and systems function properly; emergency plans are validated; and levels of readiness are measured. Exercises should conclude with after-action reviews to identify planning, training, or equipment shortfalls that must be addressed.

Response   The first 24 hours of a response to a terrorist attack or other major emergency are considered the *acute phase* of responding to a crisis. The tasks performed during this period are thought to be the most critical for ensuring an effective response to a disaster. The Centers for Disease Control recommends that the response to the acute phase of a disaster be divided into immediate, intermediate, and extended responses.

Immediate Response (0 to 2 Hours)

The immediate response to a medical disaster begins with assessment of the situation. This usually occurs during the first two hours of a response. The assessment includes estimating how many people have been injured, killed, or exposed and the geographic boundaries of the impacted area. Assessments should consider the effects of current and forecasted weather conditions. They should also evaluate factors that impact on response capabilities, including the state of critical infrastructure, whether incident command systems and emergency operations centers have been activated, what agencies and organizations are responding to the threat, what response measures have already been taken, and what information has been communicated to responders and the public.

An initial response also includes contacting and mobilizing key health-care personnel that have emergency management responsibilities. In addition to medical staff, these might include administrators, environmental health specialists, epidemiologists, laboratory personnel, safety and health experts, medical examiners, animal control officers, and public information officers. A key element of an immediate response is to ensure that medical personnel are available to evaluate and treat casualties. Health-care representatives should also be assigned to provide appropriate support to emergency operations centers. This may require dedicated liaison personnel or establishing lines of communications to ensure continuous and close coordination with other response activities.

The emergency management team should formulate a health response action plan. This plan should include specific, measurable, and achievable goals based on the initial assessment of the situation. The plan should assign responsibilities for accomplishing these goals.

Public health officials should establish contact with health and safety officers to ensure hazards or unsafe conditions are identified at the scene and appropriate supervisors are notified of what precautions or safety measures to take. These measures will include as a minimum site safety briefings for response personnel.

Communications should be established with key health and medical organizations that have emergency response responsibilities. These agencies might include hospitals and clinics, laboratories, nursing homes, mental health and social service providers, and state and county medical societies.

A means should be established to address requests for assistance and information on health- and medical-related issues. As part of this effort, a joint information center (JIC) may be established at emergency operations centers. The JIC will manage a joint information system (JIS). Public health officials should participate in the JIS. They may also operate public health hotlines to answer questions or issue public health messages.

Intermediate Response (2 to 6 Hours)

During the intermediate response phase, public health officials must ensure that critical medical infrastructure is being properly mobilized to support emergency medical response efforts. Public health officials should verify that medical surveillance systems are operational, collecting, processing, analyzing, and storing information as intended.

Laboratory facilities needed to support a response should be made operational. Public health officials should also begin to ensure that needs of special populations, such as children, disabled persons, and individuals with unique medical needs (like dialysis patients) are being addressed. Procedures and operations should be established to ensure volunteer health services and donations are properly managed. Finally, public health officials should determine requirements to sustain medical responses and coordinate for the reception of additional state and federal assets as needed.

Extended Response (12 to 24 Hours)

Emphasis during this phase shifts to establishing plans for long-term support for emergency response. Efforts include beginning preparations to provide for mental and behavioral health services and establishing personnel and equipment needs for 24-hour operations. Health and medical needs assessments should set requirements for epidemiological and health surveillance, contamination and infectious disease control, sanitation, veterinary services, mortuary support, food and water safety, evacuation, and sheltering.

Bioterrorism Preparedness

The medical preparedness and response can be particularly crucial when responding to a terrorist bioterrorism attack or infectious disease outbreak. Public health and medical organizations can enhance their response to bioterrorism by establishing plans, facilities, and resources to provide medical surveillance monitoring that detects unusual health events; provide laboratory services that can diagnose biological agents; develop treatment protocols; develop a capacity to identify secondary victims or exposed individuals; maintain current pharmaceutical inventories and stockpiles; establish effective risk communication; and ensure responsive links to adjacent jurisdictions, state governments, and federal agencies.

5

PREPARING AND RESPONDING TO THREATS AGAINST THE AGRICULTURE SECTOR

Protecting infrastructure from terrorist threats and preparedness and response in the agricultural sector includes activities affecting farms, production and processing facilities, restaurants and food services, retail, warehousing, transportation, and supporting logistics.

FEDERAL AGRICULTURAL SECURITY AND RESPONSE RESOURCES

Homeland Security Presidential Directive 9, promulgated by the president on January 30, 2004, established roles and responsibilities for federal agencies to enhance national defenses against threats to agriculture and the food supply. The measures directed include improving surveillance and warning systems, conducting vulnerability assessments, developing mitigation strategies, and enhancing laboratory capacity. Among the new capabilities required to be developed were a National Veterinary Stockpile (NVS) containing sufficient amounts of animal vaccine, antiviral, or therapeutic products to appropriately respond to the most damaging animal diseases affecting human health and the economy and a National Plant

Disease Recovery System (NPDRS) capable of responding to a high-consequence plant disease with pest control measures and the use of resistant seed varieties.

Several federal agencies provide significant resources and coordination in support of the agricultural sector. These include the Department of Homeland Security, Department of Health and Human Services, Department of Agriculture, Environmental Protection Agency, and public-private partnerships.

The Department of Homeland Security

The secretary of homeland security is responsible for coordinating the overall national effort to enhance the protection of the critical infrastructure and key resources of the United States, including agriculture. The Federal Emergency Management Agency (FEMA) coordinates national response operations, while the DHS's Information Analysis and Infrastructure Protection Directorate provides national threat and vulnerability assessments, and the Office of State and Local Government Coordination and Preparedness is responsible for coordinating DHS activities with state and local governments, managing homeland security grants, and coordinating a range of education and training activities. The DHS also took over the Department of Agriculture's Plum Island Animal Disease Center, which conducts research and experiments on a wide range of animal pathogens, and the Animal and Plant Health Inspection Service, which conducts border inspections. The department is also establishing a National Biodefense Analysis and Countermeasures Center (NBACC). The center will provide new capabilities to conduct bioforensics, the means to determine the source of a biological agent used in an attack.

Food security is monitored as part of the information analysis and infrastructure protection focus of the Homeland Security Operations Center (HSOC). The HSOC collects information from a variety of sources, issues advisories and threat bulletins, and manages response activities. The HSOC includes real-time representation of over 35 agencies, including the Department of Agriculture.

The Department of Health and Human Services

The Department of Health and Human Services' Food and Drug Administration (FDA) with its Office of Crisis Management and the Centers for Disease Control (CDC) all play important roles in the federal response to agricultural threats. The FDA's Office of Crisis Management works with state and local food safety agencies to identify possible food supply contamination. The FDA also issues guidelines and regulations on security measures. The CDC may also play a role in responding to agricultural threats. The centers may be involved because some animal diseases are zoonotic, in other words they can be transferred to humans from other species.

Department of Agriculture

Several offices and agencies with the Department of Agriculture (USDA) assist in preparedness and response for the agricultural sector. The Offices of Food Security and Emergency Preparedness were established by the USDA to coordinate activities to prevent and respond to an intentional attack on the food supply. The USDA's Food Safety and Inspection Service (FSIS) is responsible for ensuring the safety of commercial meat, poultry, and egg supplies. The FSIS issues guidelines, conducts inspections and monitoring, and coordinates response activities.

The USDA is also working with states to expedite the development and implementation of a National Animal Identification System to help stop the spread of animal diseases, either as an accidental act or through malicious activity. Meanwhile, the USDA has developed a National Animal Health Reserve Corps to mobilize close to 300 private veterinarians from around the United States to assist during an emergency.

Environmental Protection Agency

The Environmental Protection Agency (EPA) provides information, guidelines, and regulations concerning the handling and response to incidents involving hazardous materials, including pesticides and other chemicals and by-products related to agriculture operations. The EPA's National Agriculture Compliance Assistance Center provides information about environmental requirements that affect the agricultural community. The agency's Office of Pesticide Programs coordinates with the pesticide industry, and agriculture facilities review existing security measures. The office also issues voluntary guidelines for improving safety and security and coordinating response activities.

Public-Private Partnerships

The president has designated the agriculture sector as a critical infrastructure. As part of this effort a Food and Agriculture Information Sharing Analysis Center (ISAC) has been established. In addition to industry participation, the National Association of State Departments of Agriculture (NASDA) and the Association of State and Territorial Health Officers (ASTHO) serve as part of a joint federal-state food and agriculture sector team, providing a government sector counterpart to the private-sector participation through the ISAC. Additionally, a sector coordinating council is being established supported by food and agriculture subcouncils, that represent the key components of the agriculture industry and food chain (such as prefarm input, farm operations and producers, food processors, food transporters, dairy operations, warehouse and wholesale operators, and retail sectors).

PROTECTION OF CRITICAL AGRICULTURE INFRASTRUCTURE

Enhancing the protection of critical infrastructure is an essential component of limiting terrorist threats against agriculture. Measures include physical security, limiting access to agricultural facilities, and effective monitoring and surveillance, including reporting of suspicious activity and suspected cases of contamination or disease outbreaks.

Farmland Security

Like other aspects of critical infrastructure, farmland security relies on conducting risk assessments and developing and implementing appropriate plans and measures to mitigate risks. Assessments and plans include identifying areas or activities where threats might occur and increasing security in those areas. Consulting with local experts such as veterinarians, crop consultants, extension agents, and state agricultural officers should be part of the assessment process. Most farmland security plans will focus on preventing tampering with animals, crops, supplies, chemicals, and water and energy sources.

Security programs should also establish requirements for screening, orienting, and training employees. The primary purpose of orientation and training is to make employees aware of the signs of possible tampering of crops, livestock, equipment, or facilities and how to report suspicious incidents. Employees should also be trained to report sudden, unexplained deaths or unusual behavior of animals in herds or flocks. Programs should include requirements for periodic refresher training.

Physical security is also an important part of a complete program. This might include inventorying and securing hazardous materials, safeguarding feed supplies, securing water wells, securing facility boundaries to prevent unauthorized access, and providing outdoor lighting. In some cases it may be appropriate to establish means to credential and identify employees, maintenance personnel, and visitors and maintain access control, including registering arrivals and departures from facilities.

Biosecurity

Biological security measures are becoming standard in many agricultural sectors. These controls are meant to minimize the risk of introducing and spreading disease. The object of biosecurity measures is to stop transmission of disease-causing agents by preventing, minimizing, or controlling cross-contamination (through feces, urine, saliva, and other organic materials) between animals, through contact with feed or equipment, or through contact with humans.

Biosecurity management practices are designed to prevent the spread of disease by minimizing the movement of biologic organisms and vectors (such as viruses, bacteria, rodents, and flies). They are the cheapest and most effective means of disease control available.

Biosecurity has three major components: (1) isolation, (2) traffic control, and (3) sanitation. Isolation limits contact between animals within a controlled environment. Traffic control includes managing traffic to manage access to animals by ensuring that vehicles, people, and animals are directed in a way that avoids spreading infectious organisms. Traffic control should be designed to minimize contamination of animal, feed, and feed-handling equipment. Sanitation addresses the disinfection of materials, people, and equipment entering the operation and the cleanliness of the people and equipment on the operation.

Security of Production Facilities

Many federal and state agencies have issued regulations or guidelines governing safety and security requirements for agriculture processing facilities. For example, the Food Safety and Inspection Service (FSIS) has prepared voluntary guidelines to assist federal- and state-inspected plants that produce meat, poultry, and egg products in identifying ways to strengthen biosecurity protection.

Transportation Security

The USDA has established voluntary guidelines for the security of transporting agricultural products. Available on the department's Web site, the guidelines recommend a risk-based approach to developing plans and procedures for commercial agriculture and food transportation companies. The guidelines also encourage sharing information on security practices. The department's guide also provides security checklists and tips for drivers.

PREPAREDNESS AND RESPONSE

Each state has its own structure to manage preparedness and response activities for agricultural emergencies. In some states, for example, state and local emergency operations may be coordinated through a state department of agriculture, board of animal health, or animal health commission. The federal government, however, is working with states to ensure that organizations, policies, and procedures are consistent with the National Incident Management System.

Planning

Emergency management coordinators should develop annexes or additional plans to respond to emergencies related to the agricultural sector. These plans will have to coordinate with key support agencies including state and local veterinary groups, humane organizations, animal rescue societies, and the private sector. Planning must include developing mutual aid agreements with neighboring jurisdictions, government agencies, and private organizations.

Preparedness Operational Activities

Key operational activities that should occur prior to a terrorist attack or other disaster include conducting surveillance of potential animal or plant diseases, invasive species, chemicals, poisons, or toxins that could represent a substantial threat to agricultural industries, commerce, or public health. Training and exercises incorporating public and private entities that might be involved in a response are also critical to an effective preparedness program.

Response and Recovery

These activities include efforts to limit the impact of a terrorist attack by minimizing the spread of damage or speeding the recovery of supplies or services. As part of the response effort, agencies directing emergency operations must have the authority to order the evacuations of, restrict movement of, or detain animals, agricultural products, equipment, and personnel in order to prevent the spread of disease. Emergency managers must also have special authorities to direct technical assistance and establish shelters for animals.

INDEX

Page numbers followed by an italic *n* refer to a specific note that appears within the text.

Abbas, Muhammad, 414
Abd al-Rahman, Shaykh Umar, 397
Abortion and pro-life extremists, 120, 123, 126–128
Abouhalima, Mahmud, 273
Abu Sayyaf Group (ASG), 26, 78, 143–144, 394–395
Achille Louro, 107, 414
Afghanistan, 27, 28, 30, 37, 44, 47, 75, 93, 96, 99, 110, 251
African embassy bombings (1998), 28, 97, 149, 393
Agriculture, Department of (USDA), 230, 291, 293, 463, 466
Agriculture critical infrastructure, xvi, 290–292, 293, 461–467
AI (Ansar al-Islam), 99, 395–396
Air India Boeing 747 bombing (1985), 148
Air-based attacks, xiii, 16, 56, 80, 106–108, 144–150, 393, 438
  (*See also* 9/11/2001 attacks)
Airport attacks, 14, 105, 106, 147
al-Alfi, Hassan, 401
Al-Aqsa Martyrs Brigade, 112, 413–414
al-Bashir, Umar, 438
Al-Dawa, 93
ALF (Animal Liberation Front), 128–129
Alfred P. Murrah Federal Building bombing, Oklahoma
  City (1995), 16, 56, 77, 122–123, 135, 149, 176–177, 375
Al-Gama'a al-Islamiyya Group (IG), 397–398
Algeria, 26, 150, 410–412
Al-Jihad, 26, 401
All hazards disaster approach, 314–316
Allah, 86
  (*See also* Islam and Islamic extremists)
al-Mihdhar, Khalid, 31
al-Qaida
  historical view, 15–19, 25–36, 37, 44, 47, 96
  and homeland security, 241, 242, 272–273, 275, 276,
    298–299, 334, 374, 375
  tactics, 135, 138–149, 152, 178, 192
  terrorist manual, 31, 35, 90, 99, 133, 138, 141–143, 178
  as terrorist organization, 77, 80, 81, 85, 87, 88, 90, 91,
    96–99, 104, 108, 110, 113, 120, 124, 130, 391–405
  (*See also* bin Ladin, Usama; 9/11/2001 attacks)
al Saud family, 88
al-Shahid, Ibn, 396
al-Zarqawi, Abu Mus'ab, 99, 396
Ambush, as technique, 143
America (*see specific topics*)
American Communist Party, 376

American Red Cross, 333, 341, 354, 363–366, 368, 370, 441,
  443
American Safety and Health Institute (ASHI), 443
Amtrak derailment, Arizona (1995), 143
Anarchists, 123, 125–126
Anarchist's Cookbook, The, 135, 193
Animal Liberation Front (ALF), 128–129
Ansar al-Islam (AI), 99, 395–396
Anthrax letters (2001), 32, 36, 48–49, 147–148, 150–151, 303
Antiaircraft weapons, as technique, 144–147
Anti-semitism, 85, 96, 97, 119, 124–125, 130, 149, 392
Antiterrorism, 261
  (*See also specific topics*)
Anti-Terrorism Information Exchange (ATIX), 268–269
Apostate Muslim rulers, 87, 88, 90, 96
Arafat, Yasir, 70, 397
Argentina, Jewish attacks, 96, 403
Armed Islamic Group (GIA), 26, 410–411
Army of God, 126, 127–128
Arson, eco-terrorism, 128
Aryan Brotherhood, 126
Aryan Nations, 121, 122, 126
Asahara, Shoko, 24, 419
Asbat al-Ansar, 396–397
ASG (Abu Sayyaf Group), 26, 78, 143–144, 394–395
ASHI (American Safety and Health Institute), 443
Assessment
  contingency planning, 338–340
  critical infrastructure protection, 289
  emergency management, 456
  of national strategies, 251–258
  risk, 287, 289–290, 338–339, 345–346, 353–359
ATIX (Anti-Terrorism Information Exchange), 268–269
Atlanta Olympics bombing (1996), 123
Atta, Muhammad, 31
Attack planning and execution, 133–152
  ideology, doctrine and tactics, 134–136
  leadership organization, 136–139
  operational phase and tactics, 142–151
  recognition and response, xv, 279, 370
  support organization, 139
  tactics, 134–136
  target selection and timing, 140–141
  (*See also* 9/11/2001 attacks; *specific attacks*)

Atwa, Ali, 403
AUC (United Self-Defense Forces of Columbia), 432–433
Aum Shinrikyo, 16–17, 23–25, 68, 80, 81, 113, 155, 156, 166, 173, 419–421
Australia Group, 156, 163
Azhar, Masood, 406, 407

Baader-Meinhof gang, 25, 27, 106
Baby formula scam, fund raising, 273
Bahonar, Mohammad-Javad, 427
Bali nightclub bombing (2002), 147, 400
Banking and finance critical infrastructure, xvi, 293, 299–300
Basque Fatherland and Liberty (ETA), 106, 109, 192, 421
Beamer, Todd, xiii
Bedding, emergency supplies, 366–367
Beheadings, 144, 450
Beheshti, Mohammad, 427
Beirut bombings, Lebanon (1983), 70, 71, 79, 93–96, 98, 149
Berg, Nicholas, 144, 450
Berinato, Scott, 187
Bhopal, Union Carbide chemical release, India (1984), 159–160
bin Ladin, Usama, 16–17, 19, 30–31, 33, 44, 66, 71, 88–91, 93, 96–99, 104, 110, 391, 398, 406, 446, 448
    (See also al-Qaida)
Biological and Toxin Weapons Convention, 162, 163
Biological weapons, 161–168, 247, 291, 381
Biosecurity, 380–381, 465
Bioterrorism, 460
Black Liberation Army, 124
Black separatists, domestic, 124
Black September terrorists, 69–70
Bombing, 147–148
    air-based terrorism, xiii, 16, 56, 107, 108, 144–150, 393, 438
    airport terrorism, 14, 105, 106, 147
    embassy bombings, 28, 70, 71, 79, 93–94, 97, 149, 393
    high-yield explosives, 176–178
    LAX "millennial" bomber (2000-2001), 17, 23, 29–30, 97, 393
    Marine barracks, Lebanon (1983), 70, 71, 79, 93–96, 98
    Oklahoma City Federal Building (1995), 16, 56, 77, 122–123, 135, 149, 176–177, 375
    radiological weapons (dirty bombs), 168–172
    rail-based attacks, 143, 147
    residential, Saudi Arabia (1996), 98–99, 149, 392
    Shoe Bomber, 56, 149, 393
    suicide attacks, 31, 78–80, 149–150
    as tactic, 147–149
    threat preparedness, 360–361
    truck bombs, 16, 56, 77, 122–123, 135, 149, 169
    USS Cole, Yemen (2000), 97, 149, 392
    (See also Postal and shipping issues; additional specific incidents)

Booby traps, 148
Border and Transportation Security (BTS) Directorate, 217–218, 245–246
Briceno, Jorge, 430
Brooklyn Bridge threat, 139, 276
BTS (Border and Transportation Security) Directorate, 217–218, 245–246
Buckley, William, 144
Burnett, Tom, xiii
Burnham, Gracia and Martin, 394
Bush, George W., 41, 43, 44, 74, 92, 210, 213, 225, 240, 241, 242, 254–257, 285, 354
Bush administration, 17, 42, 43–46, 48, 258
Bush Doctrine, 43–46, 240
Business impact analysis, 338
    (See also Private sector preparedness)

Cadre, 137
Caliphates, 87, 90
Camp David Israel-Egypt Peace Treaty (1979), 93
Canada, 244, 345
Capacity, lack of, preparedness, 357–358
Car bombs, 149
Caracas, Molina, 111
Carnegie Mellon University's CERT Coordination Center, 198, 200
Carter, Jimmy, 122
Castano, Carlos, 432
Castro, Fidel, 431
Casualties (see specific incidents)
CBP (Customs and Boarder Protection, Bureau of), 218
CDC (Centers for Disease Control and Pevention), 164, 385, 454, 462, 463
Cells, terror organizations, 137–138
Centers for Disease Control (CDC), 164, 385, 454, 462, 463
Central Intelligence Agency (CIA), 15, 31, 53–54, 94–96, 99, 122, 144, 213, 225–226, 228, 262, 384
CERTs (Community Emergency Response Teams), 442
Chandler, Robert C., 331
Chechen terrorists, 144
Chemical Facilities Security Act (2003), 301
Chemical industry critical infrastructure, xvi, 293, 300–302
Chemical weapons, 155–161, 247, 292, 381
Chesimard, Joanne, 124, 434
China, 108, 198
Christ, 87
Christian Identify, 120, 124–125, 131
Christianity, 30, 78, 87, 90, 120, 124, 126, 131, 402
CIA (Central Intelligence Agency), 15, 31, 53–54, 94–96, 99, 122, 144, 213, 225–226, 228, 262, 384
Cigarette smuggling, fund raising, 274
Citizen Corps, 442, 443
Civic obligation, security preparation as, xvi–xvii

Civil liberties, 3, 5–8, 12–13, 15, 18, 274–275
Civil support team (CST), 327
Civil War, 5–8
Civilization, clash of, 91–92
Clash of Civilizations,The, (Huntington), 91
Clinton, Bill, 98, 122, 284
Clinton administration, 17
Clothing, emergency supplies, 366–367
Coast Guard, 189, 223–224, 246, 309
Cold War, 13–18, 20n14, 44, 155, 239, 244, 254, 384
Colonial view, 4
Color-coded DHS Advisory System, 220–223, 245, 326,
    354–355
Columbia, 108, 110–112, 430–433
Commerce, Department of, 196
Communication
    critical infrastructure, xvi, 293, 296–297
    effective, 358–359
    emergency management, 309–310
    family emergency planning, 367–368
    HSAS, 219–223
    NIMS, 321
    risk, 287, 289–290, 338–339, 345–346, 353–359
Communism, 8–10, 13–18, 20n14, 44, 93, 112, 123, 155, 239,
    244, 254, 376, 384
Communist Party of Philippines/New People's Army
    (CPP/NPA), 423–424
Communities (see State and local role)
Community Emergency Response Teams (CERTs), 442
Companies (see Private sector preparedness)
Computer security incident response teams (CSIRTs), 197
Computers (see Cyberterrorism)
Conflicts and extremist groups, 406–433
    ideological, 423–430
    nationalist, 412–419
    regional, 406–417, 424–427, 430–433
    religious, 419–423
    (See also specific countries and groups)
Congressional role, xvi, 4, 8, 9, 15, 17, 42, 49, 230–231
Consequence management, NRP, 317
Consistency, effective communication, 358
Constitution, 212, 231, 310
Consumer product tampering, 161, 167
Contingency plan
    disaster preparedness, 332–333, 336–345, 347–348
    information technology security, 347–348
    physical security, 346–347
    private sector preparedness, 333–334, 336–344
    supply chain security, 345–346
    testing, 343
Continuity
    business and private sector, 331, 333–342, 345, 347, 348
    of government, 311, 325–326, 328

Control of terrorists, 77–78, 79
Convention on Certain Conventional Weapons, 178
Convergence, 310, 378
Cooperation, international, 4, 46–48, 456
Correction, as preparedness measure, 341
Cost of terrorism, 32–35, 48, 55, 294, 332–337
Countermeasures, 146, 289–290
Countersurveillance, 272
Counterterrorism, 261, 264, 272
Counterterrorism Watch (CT Watch), 227
Countries (see specific countries and terrorist organizations)
Coupon fraud, fund raising, 273
Covenant, Sword and Arm of the Lord, The, (CSA), 190
CPP/NPA (Communist Party of Philippines/New
    People's Army), 423–424
CPTED (Crime Prevention through Environmental
    Design), 276
Creativity Movement, 119, 126
Crime, organized, 9, 108–112, 272–274
Crime Prevention through Environmental Design
    (CPTED), 276
Crime scene, first response, 279–280
Crisis management, NRP, 317
Critical infrastructure, 283–306
    defined, xvi, 284, 290
    Presidential Decision Directive (PDD), 284–286
    protection of, xvi, 247, 248, 253, 286–290, 326
    types of, 290–304
Cross-boarder terrorism (see International and transnational
    terrorism)
Crusades, 90
CSA (The Covenant, Sword and Arm of the Lord), 190
CSIRTs (computer security incident response teams), 197
CST (civil support team), 327
CT Watch (Counterterrorism Watch), 227
Cuba, 105, 107, 108, 124, 135, 433–435
Cultural war of ideas, 76, 91–92, 97–100, 241–242, 254–257
Customs and Boarder Protection, Bureau of (CBP), 218
Cyberspace, defined, 249
Cyberterrorism, 187–205
    computer system diagram, 190
    critical infrastructure, xvi, 293, 296–297
    cyberattacks, 190–193
    defined, 188
    future prospects, 202–203
    insider attacks, 188–189
    outsider attacks, 189
    preparedness and protection, 193–202, 249–250, 253

DCI (Director of Central Intelligence), 225–226
DEA (Drug Enforcement Administration), 110
Dean, Diana, 29
Deaths (see specific incidents)

Debs, Eugene V., 10
Decentralized terrorist structure, 27
Defeat/defend tenet, national terrorism strategy, 241, 242–243
Defense critical infrastructure, xvi, 293, 296
Defensive homeland security response, 12–13, 48–56, 193–199, 239, 241, 254, 257
Dehumanization, 77–78
Democracy and freedom, 44, 75, 89, 99, 241, 242, 254–257
Demographics of terrorists, 76, 89
Deny tenet, national terrorism strategy, 241, 242
Department of Agriculture (USDA), 230, 291, 293, 463, 466
Department of Commerce, 196
Department of Defense (DOD), 52, 54, 194, 195, 212, 214, 219, 224, 225, 228–229, 245, 267, 384
Department of Energy, 230, 293, 296, 298, 309
Department of Health and Human Services (DHHS), 53, 230, 293, 327, 385, 454, 462–463
Department of Homeland Security (DHS)
    critical infrastructure, 291, 293, 462
    cyberterror, 195–197
    domestic terrorism, 263, 264, 266
    emergency management, 315, 318–319, 321, 322
    future of, 315, 318–319, 321, 322, 385–386
    historical view, 48, 52–53, 56, 145
    jurisdiction, 214, 215, 217–228, 245–246, 263, 264, 266
    preparedness, 351, 354–355, 356, 453–454
Department of Interior, 293, 303
Department of Justice, 178, 226–227, 246, 250, 264, 267, 268–269, 443
Department of State, 54, 64–65, 81, 104, 225, 226, 239, 275–276, 313, 391
Department of Treasury, 250, 293, 300
Department of Veterans Affairs (VA), 455
Detection/deterrence, as preparedness measure, 341
Dev Sol, Turkey, 425
DHHS (Department of Health and Human Services), 53, 230, 293, 327, 385, 454, 462–463
DHKP/C (Revolutionary People's Liberation Party/Front), 425–426
DHS (see Department of Homeland Security)
Digital Research Inc., 334
Digital terrorism (see Cyberterrorism)
Diminish tenet, national terrorism strategy, 241–243
Directed energy technologies, 384
Director of Central Intelligence (DCI), 225–226
Dirty bombs, 168–172
Disaster medical assistance team (DMAT), 327, 385
Disaster mortuary operational response team (DMORT), 327, 385
Disaster preparedness (see Emergency management and response)
Disruption, domestic terrorism, 271–276
DMAT (disaster medical assistance team), 327, 385

DMORT (disaster mortuary operational response team), 327, 385
DNA, 171, 382–383
Doctrine, attack planning, 134–136
Documents, 275–276, 367
DOD (Department of Defense), 52, 54, 194, 195, 212, 214, 219, 224, 225, 228–229, 245, 267, 384
Domestic terrorism, 117–132, 261–282
    counterterrorism, 246
    defined, 118
    emergency management, 310–314
    evolving threats, 129–131
    FBI defined, 65
    future of homeland security, 374–376
    group profiles, 123–129
    historical view, 4–5, 8–18
    incidence and prevalence, 119–123
    resources and information sharing, 264–271
    state and local planning, 263–280
    (See also International and transnational terrorism)
Dostoyevsky, Feodor M., 63
Drug Enforcement Administration (DEA), 110
Drug-related terrorism, 108–112, 156–157, 250–251, 273

Earth Liberation Front (ELF), 375
EAS (Emergency Alert System), 355–356
Economic impact, 32–35, 48, 55, 294, 332–337
Eco-terrorism, 1, 123, 128–129, 375
Education and terrorism, 74–75, 76, 79, 89
Egypt, 26, 90, 93, 96, 397–398, 401
Egyptian Islamic Jihad (EIJ), 26, 401
EIJ (Egyptian Islamic Jihad), 26, 401
Electronics Industry Association, 200
ELF (Earth Liberation Front), 375
ELN (National Liberation Army), 143, 431
El Paso Intelligence Center (EPIC), 266
El Rukns, 107
EMAC (emergency management assistance compacts), 326
Embassy terrorism, 28, 70, 79, 92–94, 97, 149, 392–393
Emergency Alert System (EAS), 355–356
Emergency management and response, 307–330
    activities prior to emergency, 455–457
    agricultural security, 466–467
    all hazards disaster approach, 314–316
    catastrophic domestic management, 310–314
    challenge of, 308–310
    contingency planning, 332–333, 336–345, 347–348
    historical view, 4, 14, 34, 55–56
    national strategies, 247, 316–325
    New York preparedness and 9/11 attacks, 308
    physical security, 346–347
    private sector, 332–333

Emergency management and response (*Cont.*):
  state and local role, 231–233, 325–328, 455–460
  supply chain security, 345–346
Emergency management assistance compacts (EMAC), 326
Emergency Operations Center, NY, 378
Emergency operations center (EOC), 310, 316, 320, 325, 326, 328, 342–344
Emergency Preparedness and Response (EPR) Directorate, 218
Emergency response functions (ERFs), 317–318
Emergency service critical infrastructure, xvi, 293–295
Emergency supplies, 363–367
Emergency support functions (ESFs), 230
Encryption, computer (*see* Cyberterrorism)
Enemy combatants, 12–13
Energy, Department of, 230, 293, 296, 298, 309
Energy critical infrastructure, xvi, 293, 297–298
Entebbe airport highjacking, Uganda (1976), 147
Environmental Protection Agency (EPA), 158, 160, 292, 293, 301, 309, 335, 463
EOC (emergency operations center), 310, 316, 320, 325, 326, 328, 342–344
EPA (Environmental Protection Agency), 158, 160, 292, 293, 301, 309, 335, 463
EPIC (El Paso Intelligence Center), 266
Epidemics (*see* Biological weapons)
EPR (Emergency Preparedness and Response) Directorate, 218
Erambu, Mathivathani, 72
ERFs (emergency response functions), 317–318
ESFs (emergency support functions), 230
Espionage Act (1917), 9–10
Essabar, Zakaria, 31
ETA (Basque Fatherland and Liberty), 106, 109, 192, 421
Ethnic profiling, 274–275
Europe/European Union, 15, 47
  (*See also specific countries*)
Evacuation, 368–369
Evolving domestic threats, 129–131
Extremism *vs.* terrorism, 119–121

FALN (Fuerzas Armadas de Liberacion Nacional Puertorriquena), 105, 122
Family preparedness (*see* Public, personal and family preparedness)
FARC (Revolutionary Armed Forces of Columbia), 73, 110–112, 113, 143, 430–431
Faris, Iyman, 139, 276
Farmland security, 464–465
Fatwas, 87, 97
FBI (*see* Federal Bureau of Investigation)
FCC (Federal Communications Commission), 356, 357
FDA (Food and Drug Administration), 462, 463

Federal Bureau of Investigation (FBI)
  domestic terrorism, 118, 119–120, 122, 124, 128–129
  historical view, 8, 15, 18, 30, 31, 41, 53–54
  homeland security role, 225 –227, 245, 246, 262, 263, 265–272, 313, 317, 319, 362, 375, 390
  international terrorism, 65, 94–95, 103, 108, 112, 188
Federal Communications Commission (FCC), 356, 357
Federal Emergency Management Agency (FEMA), 14, 218, 230, 309, 315, 317, 322, 328, 333, 343–344, 442, 454
Federal power (*see specific topics*)
Federal Response Plan, 317, 318
FEMA (Federal Emergency Management Agency), 14, 218, 230, 309, 315, 317, 322, 328, 333, 343–344, 442, 454
Female terrorists, 76
Field intelligence group (FIG), FBI, 267
FIG (field intelligence group), FBI, 267
Financial Attack Center, 250, 251
Financial issues
  economic impact, 32–35, 48, 55, 294, 332–337
  finance and banking critical infrastructure, xvi, 293, 299–300
  money laundering, 48, 108, 250, 253, 273
Finney, Michael Robert, 124
First aid emergency supplies, 365, 366
First responders, 278–280, 323–325, 378–379, 457–460
Food
  and agriculture critical infrastructure, xvi, 290–293, 461–467
  emergency supply of, 364
  production facility security, 465–466
Food and Drug Administration (FDA), 462, 463
Food Safety and Inspection Service (FSIS), 465
Ford Motor Company, 345
Foreign Terrorist Tracking Task Force (FTTTF), 227
Fraud, document, 275–276
Freedom and democracy, 44, 75, 89, 99, 241, 242, 254–257
FSIS (Food Safety and Inspection Service), 465
FTTTF (Foreign Terrorist Tracking Task Force), 227
Fuerzas Armadas de Liberacion Nacional Puertorriquena (FALN), 105, 122
Funding terrorism, 28, 272–274
Furrow, Buford O., 119, 121, 130

Gaither Report, 13
GAO (General Accounting Office), 252, 253
Garber, Robert, 332
Garzon, Henry Castellanos, 112
Gender of terrorists, 76
General Accounting Office (GAO), 252, 253
Geneva Conventions, 67, 68–39
Gerena, Victor Manuel, 434
Germany, 9, 12–13, 25, 27, 70, 105, 106, 144, 238
GIA (Armed Islamic Group), 26, 410–411

Gilmore, James, III, 373
Gilmore Commission, 80–81, 373
Giuliani, Rudolph, 307
Globalization, xviii–xix, 25–26, 104
Goals, effective communication, 358
Goen, Earl, 111
Goldstein, Baruch, 65, 416
Gore, Al, 18
Government sector as critical infrastructure, xvi, 328
Great Britain, 47
Grenade attacks, 148
GSPC (Salafist Group for Call and Combat), 411–412
Guantanamo Bay prison, Cuba, 26
Guerilla war, 68–69, 73–74
Guevara, Che, 431
Gulf War I, 99
Guzman, Abimael, 424

Habash, George, 415
Habeas corpus, in Civil War, 6–7
Hackers (see Cyberterrorism)
HAMAS, 48, 103, 112, 412–413
Hammerskin Nation, 126
Hamza, Mustafa, 397
Handicapped, emergency preparedness and, 369–370
Hanjur, Hani, 31
Hanssen, Robert, 188
Harakat ul-Mujahidin (HUM), 26, 406–407
Hart-Rudman Commission Report, 153
Hate groups, 124–126
Hawala, 48
Hazardous materials critical infrastructure, xvi, 293, 300–302
HAZMAT, 279, 335
Hazmi, Nawaf al, 31
Health and Human Services, Department of (DHHS), 53, 230, 293, 327, 385, 454, 462–463
Hebrew University bombing, Jerusalem (2002), 147
Higgins, William "Rich," 144
Highjacking, xiii, 16, 56, 80, 106, 107, 108, 144–150, 147, 393, 438
(See also 9/11/2001 attacks)
High-yield explosives, 176–178
Hill, Charles, 124
Historical view
  al-Qaida and bin Ladin, 15–19, 25–36, 44, 47, 96
  CIA, 15, 31, 53–54
  Congressional role, xvi, 4, 8, 9, 15, 17, 42, 49, 230–231
  DHS, 48, 52–53, 56
  disaster preparedness and implementation, 4, 14, 34, 55–56
  DOD, 52, 54
  domestic terrorism, 4–5, 8–14, 16–18, 375–376

Historical view (Cont.):
  FBI, 8, 15, 18, 30, 31, 41, 53–54
  international attacks against U.S., 105–112
  Islam, 89–90
  mass destruction, 80–81
  9/11 attacks, 25–36, 308
  religious-inspired terrorism, 92–96
  state sponsorship, 28, 107–108
  terrorism, defined, 64
  (See also Traditional security)
Hizballah, 70, 86, 93–99, 113, 144, 147, 273, 274
HLS (Huntingdon Life Sciences), 129
Hoaxes, as technique, 150–151, 154
Holy Land Foundation, 48
Homeland defense, defined, 211
Homeland security, 42–56, 209–235, 373–389
  Bush Doctrine, 42–44
  creation of DHS, 210
  defensive response, 12–13, 48–56, 193–199, 239, 241, 254, 257
  defined, xiv–xv, 211
  federal role and responsibility, xiv–xv, 212–231
  international cooperation, 4, 46–48, 456
  media, 445–451
  national strategies for, 245–248
  offensive response, 14, 42–44, 239–241, 254
  organizing for, 211–212
  Patriot Act, 49–52, 227–228
  preemption, 43–46
  protection of U.S., 210–211
  resources, 247–248, 258, 264–271, 320
  roles and responsibilities, xv–xvi
  security structures, future of, 384–386
  state and local role, 212, 231–232
  strategic objectives of, xv
  and technology, future of, 380–384
  and terrorism, future of, 374–380
  (See also Department of Homeland Security [DHS]; National strategy; specific topics)
Homeland Security Act (2002), 53, 212, 215, 217, 218, 232–233, 311
Homeland Security Advisory System (HSAS), 220–223, 245, 326, 354–355
Homeland Security Council (HSC), 213–217
Homeland Security Information Network (HSIN), 223, 267
Homeland Security Operations Center (HSOC), 219, 223, 232, 266, 267, 318–319, 462
Homeland Security Presidential Directives (HSPD), 214, 220, 243, 285–286, 311–314, 316–319, 461
Hoover, J. Edgar, 8
Hostage-taking, 70, 92, 93, 147
Hot sites, 347
Hovey, Alvin P., 6

HSAS (Homeland Security Advisory System), 220–223, 245, 326, 354–355

HSC (Homeland Security Council), 213–217

HSIN (Homeland Security Information Network), 223, 267

HSOC (Homeland Security Operations Center), 219, 223, 232, 266, 267, 318–319, 462

HSPD (Homeland Security Presidential Directives), 214, 220, 243, 285–286, 311–314, 316–319, 461

Hudgins, A. J., 174–175

HUM (Harakat ul-Mujahidin), 26, 406–407

Human cost of 9/11 attacks, 32–33

Huntingdon Life Sciences (HLS), 129

Huntington, Samuel, 91

Hussein, Saddam, 88, 96, 97, 405, 426

IAEA (International Atomic Energy Association), 170, 184n41

IAIP (Information Analysis and Infrastructure Protection) Directorate, 219–220, 226, 245, 354

ibn Abd al Wahhab, 88

ICE (Immigration and Customs Enforcement, Bureau of), 218

ICS (incident command systems), 319–322

Ideology, 106, 134–136, 423–430
  of terrorism, 89–100

IEDs (improvised explosive devises), 148

IG (Al-Gama'a al-Islamiyya Group), 397–398

IIMG (Interagency Incident Management Group), 318

Immigration and Customs Enforcement, Bureau of (ICE), 218

Improvised explosive devises (IEDs), 148

IMU (Islamic Movement of Uzbekistan), 26, 399

Incident command systems (ICS), 319–322

India, 148, 159–160, 255

Individual preparedness (see Public, personal and family preparedness)

Individual terrorists "lone wolves," 65, 129–130, 150

Indoctrination of terrorists, 77–79

Indonesia, 147, 392, 400

Industrial critical infrastructure, xvi, 293, 296

Infectious disease (see Biological weapons)

Infidels, 25, 36, 77, 87, 90, 96

Information
  critical infrastructure, xvi, 293, 296–297
  effective communication and sharing of, 264–271, 321, 357–359

Information Analysis and Infrastructure Protection (IAIP) Directorate, 219–220, 226, 245, 354

Information Sharing Analysis Center (ISAC), 197, 284, 286–287, 288, 463–464

Information sharing environment (ISE), 269

Infrastructure (see Critical infrastructure)

Inhofe, James, 301

Initial National Response Plan, 318, 319

Insurance, 340

Intelligence cells, terror organizations, 137

Intelligence community, 225–227, 270–271
  (See also Central Intelligence Agency (CIA); Federal Bureau of Investigation [FBI])

Intelligence Reform and Terrorism Prevention Act (2004), 225, 226, 269

Interagency Incident Management Group (IIMG), 318

Interdiction, domestic terrorism, 271–276

Interior, Department of, 293, 303

International and transnational terrorism, 103–115
  cooperation with U.S., 4, 46–48, 456
  current threat, 112–113
  FBI defined, 65
  globalization and U.S. attacks, 104
  history of U.S. attacks, 105–112
  State Department predictions (pre-9/11), 104–405
  terrorism, defined, 105
  terrorist groups and locations, 114, 412–439
  traditional terrorism, 15–16
  worldwide terror organizations, 26–31
  (See also Domestic terrorism)

International Atomic Energy Association (IAEA), 170, 184n41

International Maritime Organization, 48

Internet Security Alliance, 200

Internet terrorism (see Cyberterrorism)

Interpol, 47

Intifadah, 404, 405, 413–415, 417

IRA (Irish Republican Army), 27, 106, 113

Iran, 15, 70, 86, 92–93, 96, 107, 135, 172, 176, 404–405

Iraq, 93, 99, 184n41, 198, 395–396, 426–428

Iraqi Kurdistan, 99, 395–396

Ireland, 27, 106, 112, 113, 418–419

Irish Republican Army (IRA), 27, 106, 113

ISAC (Information Sharing Analysis Center), 197, 284, 286–287, 288, 463–464

ISE (information sharing environment), 269

Islam and Islamic extremists, 85–101
  ideology of terrorism, 89–100
  monetary instruments, 48
  Muslim world, 86–89
  post-9/11 approach, 30, 242–243
  religious profiling, 274–275
  Shiite, 26, 88–89, 92–96, 98, 99
  suicide attacks, 79–80
  Sunni, 88, 92, 96, 98, 99, 391–403
  terrorist groups, 100, 391–412
  Wahhabi, 88
  vs. Western culture, 76, 91–92, 97–100
  (See also al-Qaida)

Islamaya al Gama'at, 113

Islamic Front, 97–98
Islamic Jihad, 26, 94, 401, 413
   (*See also* Hizballah)
Islamic Movement of Uzbekistan (IMU), 26, 399
Islamists, 88–89
Ismail, Mustafa Osman, 437
Isomoddin, Riduan bin, 400
Israel, 15, 69–70, 89, 91, 93, 96, 106–107, 112–113, 150, 242,
   403, 412–417
   (*See also* Jews, attacks on)
Israel-Egypt Peace Treaty (1979), 93
Israeli Boeing 757 missile attack (2002), 145, 299
Issue-oriented groups, 126–129
Italy, 27, 144
Izz-al-Din, Hasa, 403

Jabril, Ahmad, 416
Jaish-e-Mohammed (JEM), 407–408
Jakarta Marriott Hotel bombing, Indonesia (2003),
   392, 400
Jalandoni, Luis, 423
Jama'at al-Tawhid, 99
Janjalani, Abdurajak Abubakar, 394
Janjalani, Khadaffy, 394
Jannati, Ahmad, 405
Japan
   Aum Shinrikyo, 16–17, 23–25, 68, 80, 81, 113, 155, 156,
      166, 173, 419–421
   World War II, 13, 78, 150, 172–173, 255
Japanese Red Army (JRA), 106, 107, 262
JDL (Jewish Defense League), 105, 126
JEM (Jaish-e-Mohammed), 407–408
Jemaah Islamiya (JI), 399–400
Jerusalem, 90, 147
Jesus of Nazareth, 87
Jewish Defense League (JDL), 105, 126
Jews, attacks on, 85, 96, 97, 119, 124–125, 130, 149, 392
   (*See also* Israel)
JFO (joint field official), 318–319
JI (Jemaah Islamiya), 399–400
Jihad, 87, 88–89
John Paul II, Pope, 393
Johnson, Paul, 144
Joint field official (JFO), 318–319
Joint Intelligence Task Force, 267
Joint Operations Center, 319
Joint Regional Information Exchange System (JRIES), 223,
   267–268
Joint Terrorism Task Force (JTTF), 227, 265, 267
JRA (Japanese Red Army), 106, 107, 262
JRIES (Joint Regional Information Exchange System), 223,
   267–268
JTTF (Joint Terrorism Task Force), 227, 265, 267

Justice, Department of, 178, 226–227, 246, 250, 264, 267,
   268–269, 443

Kahande Chai/Kach, 416–417
Kahane, Meir, 416
Kamikazi attacks, 78, 150
Karimov, Islom, 399
Kashmir conflict, 26, 406–410
Kashmiri, Farooq, 406
Kerik, Bernard, 307
Key assets protection, xvi, 247, 248, 253, 293, 303
KGK (Kongra-Gel), 422–423
Khalil, Fazlur Rehman, 406
Khan, Q., 176
Khatami, Mohammad, 405
Khobar Towers bombing, Saudi Arabia (1996), 98–99, 149
Khomeini, Ayatollah, 92–93, 403, 405
Kidnapping, as technique, 143–144
Kikumura, Yu, 16, 107
Kim Jon Il, 436
KKK (Ku Klux Klan), 8, 14, 121, 125
Klinghoffer, Leon, 107, 414
Klug, Demetra, 107
Knowledge management, contingency plans, 346
Koizumi, Junichiro, 436
Kongra-Gel (KGK), 422–423
Korea, North, 13, 75, 107, 108, 172, 176, 436
Korea, South, 13, 148
Korean War, 13
Kosovo, 91
Krar, William, 130
Krueger, Alan B., 74–75
Ku Klux Klan (KKK), 8, 14, 121, 125
Kurdistan, Iraq, 99, 395–396
Kurdistan Workers Party (PKK), 422–423
Kuwait, 43, 91, 392

La Guardia Airport terrorism, NY (1975, 1976), 14, 105,
   106, 147
Lashkar-i-Jhangvi (LJ), 402
Lashkar-Tayyiba (LT), 408–410
Law Enforcement Online (LEO) Network, 268, 269
Law enforcement reforms, 53–54, 240
LAX "millennial" bomber (2000-2001), 17, 23, 29–30, 97,
   393
Layered defense, 257
Leaderless resistance, 65, 129–130, 137
Leadership, 136–139, 335–336
   (*See also specific persons*)
Leave-behind bombs, 147
Lebanon, 70, 71, 79, 93–96, 98, 99, 149, 396–397
Left-wing domestic extremists, 123–124
Legal issues, 264–265, 334–336

Legion of the Underground (LoU), 198–199
Legionnaries disease, Philadelphia (1976), 166
LEO (Law Enforcement Online) Network, 268, 269
Letters (*See* Postal and shipping issues)
Lewis, Bernard, 89–90
Liability, 335–336, 340
Liberation Tigers of Tamil Eelam (LTTE), 71–73, 79, 106,
    113, 150, 417–418
Library of Congress, 65–66
Libya, 15, 93, 96, 107–108, 438–439
Lincoln, Abraham, 6
LJ (Lashkar-i-Jhangvi), 402
Local (*see* State and local role)
"Logic bomb" cyberattack, 190
Logistics cells, terror organizations, 137
London Ambulance Service, 379
"Lone wolves," 65, 129–130, 150
Los Macheteros, 122, 434
LoU (Legion of the Underground), 198–199
LT (Lashkar-Tayyiba), 408–410
LTTE (Liberation Tigers of Tamil Eelam), 71–73, 79, 106,
    113, 150, 417–418

MACA (military assistance to civilian authorities), 455
Madrassas, 75
Mail (*see* Postal and shipping issues)
MANPADS, 144–146
Marine barracks bombed, Lebanon (1983), 70, 71, 79,
    93–96, 98
Markle, John, 8
Mass destruction, 80–81
    (*See also* Weapons of mass destruction [WMD])
MATRIX (Multistate Anti-Terrorism Information
    Exchange), 274–275
McDonald's attacks (2003), 140, 396–397
McKevitt, Michael, 418
McKinley, William, 8
McVeigh, Timothy, 16, 77, 122, 135, 140, 262
Mecca, Grand Mosque violence (1979), 93
Mechanical security, 346
Media, 445–451
    disaster information, 355–358
Medical Reserve Corps (MRC), 442
Medical services disaster planning and response, 363,
    453–460
MEK (Mujahedin-e Khalq Organization), 426–428
MEMS (microelectrical mechanical systems), 380–381
Mental health of terrorists, 76–77, 79–80
Merryman, John, 6
Metesky, George "Mad Bomber," 118
Metropolitan Medical Response System, 385, 386, 454
Mexico, 244
Microelectrical mechanical systems (MEMS), 380–381

Microsoft, 199
Middle East (*See specific countries*)
Middle East Partnership Initiative, 255
Military assistance to civilian authorities (MACA), 455
Military strategy, 228–230, 244
    (*See also* Department of Defense [DOD])
"Military Studies in the Jihad against the Tyrants"
    (al-Qaida manual), 31, 35, 90, 99, 133, 135, 138,
    141–142, 143, 178
Militia movements, domestic, 125
Miller, Zell, 301
Milligan, Lambdin P., 6–7
Milwaukee water supply contamination, WI (1993),
    166–167
Mind of terrorist (*see* Terrorist profiles)
Minimanual of the Urban Guerilla, 135
Missiles, antiaircraft, 144–147
Mitigation, all hazards disaster approach, 315–316
MKO (Mujahedin-e Khalq Organization), 426–428
Mohamed, Ali, 135
Money laundering, 48, 108, 250, 253, 273
Monitoring risk, contingency plans, 346
Montana Freeman, 125
Morales, William Guillermo, 434
Moro, Aldo, 144
Moro rebels, 26, 78, 394–395
Moscow theater attack, Russia (2002), 144
Moussaoui, Zacarias, 31
MRC (Medical Reserve Corps), 442
Muarulanda, Manuel, 430
Mubarak, Hosni, 398
Mueller, Robert S., 103
Mughniyah, 'Imad, 70, 93–96, 147, 403
Muhammad, 86–87
    (*See also* Islam and Islamic extremists)
Muhjin, Abu, 396
Mujahadeen, 37, 96, 97
Mujahedin-e Khalq Organization (MEK or MKO), 426–428
Mujahideen, 96, 97
Multistate Anti-Terrorism Information Exchange
    (MATRIX), 274–275
Munich Olympic hostages. Germany (1972), 70, 144
Muslim Brotherhood, 90
Muslims (*see* Islam and Islamic extremists)
Myth, in risk communication, 359

Nanotechnology, 380–381
Narco-terrorism, 108–112, 156–157, 250–251, 273
Nasrallah, Hassan, 99, 403–404
National Alliance, 130
National Commission on Terrorist Attacks (9/11
    Commission), 323–325
National Crime Information Center (NCIC), 188, 266, 270

National Criminal Intelligence Sharing Plan, 267
National Cyber Security Division (NCSD), 195–197
National Disaster Medical System, 385, 386, 454, 455
National Emergency Training Center (NETC), 269
National Fire Protection Association (NFPA), 333
National Governors Association, 231–232
National Guard, 229–230, 232, 327, 444
National Incident Management System (NIMS), 319–321, 326, 466–467
National Institute of Standards and Technology, 195, 196–197, 200
National Liberation Army (ELN), 143, 431
National Medical Disaster System (NMDS), 327
National Military Strategy, 244
National Money Laundering Strategy, 250
National monument protection, 293, 303
National nurse response team (NNRT), 327
National Oceanic and Atmospheric Administration (NOAA), 355
National pharmacist response team (NPRT), 327
National Plant Disease Recovery System (NPDRS), 461–462
National Response Plan (NRP), 218, 317–319
National security, defined, 210–211
National Security Act (1947), 212, 227, 384
National Security Agency (NSA), 194
National Security Council (NSC), 212–215, 384
National Security Strategy of the U.S., 43, 44–46, 237, 240, 241, 252
National Strategic Stockpile, 230, 292, 294, 327, 385, 386, 454
National strategy, 237–260
    to combat terrorism, 241–243
    to combat WMD, 243–244, 257
    cyberspace security, 249–250
    defined and purpose, 238–240, 257–258
    emergency management, 316–325
    fundamentals, 252
    for homeland security, 245–248
    military strategy, 244
    money laundering strategy, 48, 108, 250, 253, 273
    national drug control strategy, 250–251
    for physical protection of critical infrastructure and key assets, 248
    purpose of, 238–240, 257–258
    security strategy, 240–241
    for war on global terrorism, 237–260
National Strategy for Combating Terrorism, 241, 253
National Strategy for Homeland Security, xv, 52, 64, 211, 245–248, 252, 261
National Strategy for the Physical Protection of Critical Infrastructures and Key Assets, 248, 252
National Strategy to Combat Weapons for Mass Destruction, 243, 253
National Strategy to Secure Cyberspace, 249–250

National Veterinary Stockpile (NVS), 461
National Weather Service, 341, 355, 356
Nationalist conflicts, 74, 106–107, 412–419
NATO (North Atlantic Treaty Organization), 47, 384
Nazi Low Riders, 126
NCIC (National Crime Information Center), 188, 266, 270
NCSD (National Cyber Security Division), 195–197
Neighborhood Watch Program (NWP), 442–443
Neo-Nazi National Alliance, 125
NETC (National Emergency Training Center), 269
New Black Panter Party for Self-Defense, 124
New York City Emergency Operations Center, 308, 310
    (*See also* 9/11/2001 attacks)
NFPA (National Fire Protection Association), 333
NGOs (nongovernmental organizations), 47–48
NIMS (National Incident Management System), 319–321, 326, 466–467
9/11/2001 attacks
    first response, 308, 310, 323–325, 378–379
    historical view, xiii–xiv, 25–36, 308, 392
    national response to, 41–59, 345
    private sector effects, 332–333, 334
    traditional approach failure, 17–18
9/11 Commission (National Commission on Terrorist Attacks), 98, 323–325
911 telephone emergency system, 194, 357, 358
NMDS (National Medical Disaster System), 327
NNRT (national nurse response team), 327
NOAA (National Oceanic and Atmospheric Administration), 355
Nongovernmental organizations (NGOs), 47–48
NORAD (North American Aerospace Defense Command), 229
North American Aerospace Defense Command (NORAD), 229
North Atlantic Treaty Organization (NATO), 47, 384
North Korea, 13, 75, 107, 108, 172, 176, 436
NORTHCOM (U.S. Northern Command), 52, 229–230, 455
NPDRS (National Plant Disease Recovery System), 461–462
NPRT (national pharmacist response team), 327
NRP (National Response Plan), 218, 317–319
NSA (National Security Agency), 194
NSC (National Security Council), 212–215, 384
*N*th Country Experiment, 174–175
Nuclear facilities threat, 170, 171–172
Nuclear Nonproliferation Treaty, 176, 244
Nuclear weapons, 13–18, 20n14, 44, 154, 172–176, 246
NVS (National Veterinary Stockpile), 461
NWP (Neighborhood Watch Program), 442–443

Ocalan, Abdullah, 422
Occupational Safety and Health Administration (OSHA), 334–335

Offensive response, 14, 42–46, 239–241, 254
Office of Crisis Management, 462
Office of Management and Budget (OMB), 215
Oklahoma City Federal Building bombing (1995), 16, 56, 77, 122–123, 135, 149, 176–177, 375
Olympics (1972 and 1996), 70, 123, 144
OMB (Office of Management and Budget), 215
Operation TIPS, 56
Operational cells, terror organizations, 137
Operational phases and tactics, terrorist, 141–145
  (*See also* Attack planning and execution)
Operational priorities, contingency planning, 339–340
Operational security, 30–31, 138–139
Order, The, 122
Organization for emergency management, 309–310
Organization for Security and Cooperation in Europe, 47
Organization security, 346
Organized crime, 9, 108–112, 272–274
OSHA (Occupational Safety and Health Administration), 334–335
Outsider attacks, cyberterrorism, 189

Packages (*see* Postal and shipping issues)
Paine, Thomas, 3
Pakistan, 26, 37, 44, 75, 144, 176, 406–410
Palestine, 15, 69–70, 96, 106–107, 112, 135, 144, 150, 242, 412–417
Palestine Islamic Jihad (PIJ), 103, 112, 413
Palestine Liberation Front (PLF), 414–415
Palestine Liberation Organization (PLO), 69–70, 96, 106–107, 144
Pan Am Flight 103 bombing, Lockerbie, Scotland (1988), 16, 108, 148, 438
Pan Am raid by PLO, Rome (1973), 107
Pape, Robert A., 79
Papers, 275–276, 367
Password protection, 193, 199–202
PATRIOT Act, 49–52, 227–228
Patriotic Union of Kurdistan (PUK), 395
Patterns of Global Terrorism, 391
PDD (Presidential Decision Directive), 284–286
Pearl, Daniel, 144, 402, 406
Pentagon, xiii, 213
  (*See also* Department of Defense [DOD])
Personal preparedness (*see* Public, personal and family preparedness)
Personal protective equipment (PPE), 269
Personality-type of terrorist, 76
Peru, 424–425
PFLP (Popular Front for the Liberation of Palestine), 80, 415–416
PFO (principal federal official), 318, 322
Philippines, 26, 78, 394–395, 423–424

Phillips 66 plant explosion, Houston (1989), 159, 301
Physical damage, 9/11 attacks, 32
Pierce, William, 122, 125, 130, 135
PIJ (Palestine Islamic Jihad), 103, 112, 413
PKI (public key infrastructure), 194
PKK (Kurdistan Workers Party), 422–423
Planning
  contingency planning, 332–333, 336–345, 347–348, 457
  for domestic terrorism, 263–280
  family emergency planning, 367–368
  inter- and intrastate mutual aid agreements, 326–328
  sophistication of terrorist, 28–31
  (*See also* Attack planning and execution)
PLF (Palestine Liberation Front), 414–415
PLO (Palestine Liberation Organization), 69–70, 96, 106–107, 144
Political oppression, 75, 89
Popular Front for the Liberation of Palestine (PFLP), 80, 415–416
Posse Comitatus Act (1878), 8, 229, 230
Postal and shipping issues
  attack by mail, 32, 36, 48–49, 147–148, 150–151, 303
  postal service critical infrastructure, xvi, 293, 302–303
  shipping and postal services critical infrastructure, xvi, 293, 302–303
  suspicious, preparedness, 361–362
Posttraumatic stress disorder (PTSD), 32
Poverty and terrorism, 74–75, 79, 89
Powell, Colin, 437
POWs (prisoners of war), 12–13
PPE (personal protective equipment), 269
Prabhakaran, Velupillai, 71–72, 418
Practice, lack of, preparedness, 357
Preemption, policy of, 44–46
Preparedness (*see specific topics*)
Presidential Decision Directive (PDD), 284–286
Presidential role in homeland security, 212–217, 284–286, 290
Prevention, as preparedness measure, 341
Principal federal official (PFO), 318, 322
Prisoners of war (POWs), 12–13
Private sector preparedness, 331–349
  contingency planning, 333–334, 336–344
  critical infrastructure in, xvi
  cyberspace protection, 249
  cyberterrorism, 199–202
  exposure, 332–333
  information technology security, 347–348
  legal issues, 334–336
  as 9/11 attack response, 55–56
  physical security, 346–347
  public partnerships, 463–464
  standards for, 333

Private sector preparedness (*Cont.*):
  supply chain security, 345–346
  volunteer groups, 443
Production facilities, food, security of, 465–466
Profiles (*see* Terrorist profiles)
Prohibition, 9
Pro-life extremists, 120, 123, 126–128
Proliferation Security Initiative (PSI), 244
Property insurance, 340
PSI (Proliferation Security Initiative), 244
Psychological cost, 9/11 attacks, 32
Psychology of terrorists, 76
PTSD (posttraumatic stress disorder), 32
PTSN (Public Switch Telecommunications Network), 296–297
Public, personal and family preparedness, 351–372
  antiterrorism measures, 360–362
  attack indications, 370
  challenge of, 352–353
  communication of risk, 353–359
  emergency planning, 362–370
  public response to terrorism, 56
  resistance to, 352–353
Public health critical infrastructure, xvi, 292–294, 453–460
Public Health Security and Bioterrorism Preparedness and Response Act (2002), 291
Public key infrastructure (PKI), 194
Public Switch Telecommunications Network (PTSN), 296–297
Puerto Rican nationalists, 14, 105, 122, 124, 147
PUK (Patriotic Union of Kurdistan), 395

Qadhafi, Muammar, 96, 107–108, 438–439
Quick shipping, 348
Qur'an, 87

Radiological weapons (dirty bombs), 168–172
Rail-based attacks, 143, 147
Rajaei, Mohammad-Ali, 427
Rajneeshee cult biological acquisition (1984-1985), 163, 291
Rauf, Mohammad, 139
Ready Campaign, 56
Reagan, Ronald, 70, 93, 94, 98, 240, 255
Real IRA (RIRA), 418–419
Recovery, emergency management, xv, 316, 333–343, 346, 347
Red Brigade, 27, 144
Red Cross, 333, 341, 354, 363, 364–366, 368, 370, 441, 443
Red Scare, 8–9, 10
Red team techniques, 245
Reid, Richard, 393
Religious conflicts, 419–423
  (*See also specific religions*)
Religious profiling, 274–275

Remediation, contingency plans, 346
Republic of New Africa, 124
Republic of Texas, 125
Residential bombing, Saudi Arabia (1996), 98–99, 149, 392
Resources, homeland security, 247–248, 258, 264–271, 320
Response
  defensive, 12–13, 48–56, 193–199, 239, 241, 254, 257
  first responders, 278–280, 323–325, 378–379, 457–460
  to 9/11 attacks, 41–59, 308, 310, 323–325, 345, 378–379
  offensive response, 14, 42–46, 239–241, 254
  to weapons of mass destruction (WMD), 279–280
  (*See also* Emergency management and response)
Ressam, Ahmed, 17, 29
Revolutionary Armed Forces of Columbia (FARC), 73, 110–112, 113, 143, 430–431
Revolutionary Nuclei (RN), 428–429
Revolutionary People's Liberation Party/Front (DHKP/C), 425–426
Rice, Condoleezza, 71, 446
Ridge, Tom, 49, 209, 210
Right-wing domestic extremists, 124–130
RIRA (Real IRA), 418–419
Risk (assessment, management and communication), 287, 289–290, 338–339, 345–346, 353–359
RISS and RISSNET, 268–269
RN (Revolutionary Nuclei), 428–429
Ruby Ridge conflict, ID (1992), 122, 125
Rudolph, Eric, 123
Russia (former Soviet Union), 13–18, $20n14$, 30, 37, 44, 69, 75, $80n3$, 93, 96–97, 107, 135, 144, 155, 176, 188, 376, 383

Sabotage, as technique, 143
Sadat, Anwar, 93, 401
SAFECOM, 322
Saladin, 90
Salafist Group for Call and Combat (GSPC), 411–412
Salafist Islam, 88
Salvation Army, 443
SAMS, (surface-to-air-missiles), 144–146
Sarbanes-Oxley Act (2002), 335–336
Saudi Arabia, 30, 88, 96–99, 149, 392
SCADA (Supervisory Control and Data Acquisition), 190, 192
Science and Technology (S&T) Directorate, 219, 228, 321
Scotland, Pan Am Flight 103 bombing (1988), 16, 108, 148, 438
Secret Service, 223, 224, 266
Sector coordinating councils, critical infrastructure, 286
Security strategy, 240–241
Sedition Act (1918), 10–11

Sedky, Atef, 401
Select Agent Program, 247
Selection of terrorists, 77–78
Separatists, domestic, 124
September 11 Fund, 33
September 11, 2001 (*see* 9/11/2001 attacks)
17 November, Greece, 429–430
SHAC (Stop Huntingdon Animal Cruelty), 129
Shaffer, Jerel, 111
Shakur, Assata, 124
Sharia law, 87
Sharif, Nawaz and Shabaz, 402
Shaw of Iran, 92
Sheik, Ahmed Omar, 406
Shelter-in-place, 58, 60, 355, 363, 368–369
Shiite Islam, 26, 88–89, 92–96, 98, 99
   (*See also* Hizballah)
Shining Path (SL), 424–425
Shipping (*see* Postal and shipping issues)
Shoe Bomber, 56, 149, 393
Sison, Jose Maria, 423
6-Day War, Israel, 69
Skills of terrorists, 136
SL (Shining Path), 424–425
Sleeper cells, 138
Smallpox, 163, 164, 181n15
Smith, Benjamin, 119
Smuggling nuclear material, 173, 176
Sobero, Guellermo, 144
Social strife, and terrorism, 27–28, 73–76
Software (*see* Cyberterrorism)
Somalia, 71, 91, 97, 393
Sons of Gestapo, 143
South America, 113
South American, 424–425, 430–433
South Korea, 13, 148
Southeast Asia, 399–400
Southern Poverty Law Center, 120–121
Sovereign citizens, domestic terrorism, 125–126
Soviet Union, 13–18, 20n14, 30, 37, 44, 69, 75, 80n3, 93,
   96–97, 107, 135, 155, 176, 188, 376, 383
Spain, 5, 106, 109, 147, 192, 421
Spanish American War, 5
Spanish commuter train bombing (2004), 147
Special needs, emergency preparedness, 369–370
Spector, Arlen, 283
Sri Lanka, 71–73, 79, 106, 113, 150, 417–418
S&T (Science and Technology) Directorate, 219, 228, 321
Robert T. Stafford Disaster Relief and Assistance Act
   (1984), 218, 229
Standards, private sector preparedness, 333
State, Department of, 54, 64–65, 81, 104, 225, 226, 239,
   275–276, 313, 391

State and local role
   critical infrastructure protection, xv–xvi
   domestic terrorism planning, 263–278
   emergency management, 231–233, 325–328, 455–460
   federal HSAS communication, 219–223
   homeland security, 212, 231–232
   inter- and intrastate mutual aid agreements, 326–328
   as 9/11 attack response, 54–55
   state-managed defense forces, 443–444
   (*See also specific topics*)
State sponsorship of terrorists (*see specific countries*)
Stethem, Robert, 94, 147
Stop Huntingdon Animal Cruelty (SHAC), 129
Strategic National Stockpile, 230, 292, 294, 327, 385, 386,
   454
Strategic Research Corporation, 332–333
Strategy (*see* National strategy)
Suarez, Briceno, 111
Sudan, 28, 107, 436–438
Suicide attacks, 31, 78–80, 149–150
Sunni Islam, 88, 92, 96, 98, 99, 391–403
   (*See also* al-Qaida)
Supervisory Control and Data Acquisition (SCADA), 190,
   192
Supply kits, disaster, 363–367
Support organization for attacks, 137, 139
Surveillance system, medical, 456–457
Survivability, information technology, 347
Suspicious activities, 361–362
Symbolic value, target selection, 140–141
Syria, 15, 70, 93, 94, 107, 108, 435–436

Tactics, terrorist, 134
   (*See also* Attack planning and execution)
Taha Musa, Rifa'i, 397–398
Takfir Islam, 88
Taliban, Afghanistan, 28, 44, 110
Tamil Tigers (LTTE), 71–72, 73, 79, 106, 113, 150, 417–418
Taney, Roger B., 6
Target hardening, 276
Targeting and timing, attack, 140–141
Tavern bombing, NY (1975), 105, 122
Tear line, 271
Technology, 27–28, 136, 321–323, 347–348, 380–384
   (*See also* Cyberterrorism)
Telecommunication critical infrastructure, xvi, 293,
   296–297
Tenet, George, 99
Tenth Amendment, Constitution, 212, 231
Terrorism
   conditions for, 73–78
   defined, 64–67
   effectiveness, 68–72

Terrorism (*Cont.*):
  effects of, 31–35
  elements of, 66
  emergence of, 68–69
  vs. extremism, 119–121
  global goals, 25–26
  Islamic ideology, 89–100
  media as tool of, 446–447
  rise of modern, 23–40
  strategy to combat, 241–251, 253
  in twenty-first century, 24–25, 31–35
  WMD threats, 35–37
  worldwide organization, 26–31
  (*See also* al-Qaida; Attack planning and execution;
      Domestic terrorism; International and transnational
      terrorism; *specific topics*)
Terrorism Threat Integration Center (TTIC), 53–54,
  225–226
Terrorist profiles, 63–83, 391–439
  by country, 433–439
  domestic groups, 123–129
  groups, 73–78
  international and transnational issues, 114, 412–439
  international (non-Islamic), 412–433
  Islamic extremists, 100, 391–412
  mass destruction, 80–81
  reasons for terrorism, 66, 68–73
  suicide attacks, 78–80
  terrorism, defined, 64–67
  types of followers, 137
Terrorist Screening Center (TSC), 54, 225–226, 266
Terrorist's Handbook, The, 193
Testing contingency plan, 343
TIPOFF, 54, 226
Tools, emergency supplies, 366, 367
TOPOFF, 309
Torres, Felipe, 431
Traditional security, 3–21
  Civil War, 5–8
  Cold War, 13–18, 20n14, 44
  domestic threats, 4–5, 12–15
  early threats, 4–5
  emerging threats, 16–18
  international threats, 15–16
  9/11 attacks, 17–18
  pre-World War I, 9
  World War I, 9–10
  World War II, 11–14, 68, 78, 121, 150, 172–173, 238, 255
Train bombing, Spain (2004), 147
Training (*see* Planning)
Transnational terrorism (*see* International and
  transnational terrorism)
Transportation critical infrastructure, xvi, 293, 298–299

Transportation Security Agency (TSA), 53, 217
Treasury, Department of, 250, 293, 300
"Trojan Horse" cyberattack, 190
Truck bombs, 16, 56, 77, 122–123, 135, 149, 169
Truman, Harry, 14, 122
TSA (Transportation Security Agency), 53, 217
TSC (Terrorist Screening Center), 54, 225–226
TTIC (Terrorism Threat Integration Center), 53–54, 225–226
Turkey, 425–426
Turner Diaries, The, (Pierce), 122, 125, 130, 135, 137, 150
TWA Flight 840 bombing, Rome to Athens (1986), 107,
  147, 148
Tylenol tampering (1982), 161

UFF (United Freedom Front), 122
Uganda, 147
Unabomber, 65, 147
Union Carbide chemical release, India (1984), 159–160
United Freedom Front (UFF), 122
United Nations (UN), 47, 67, 70, 96, 125
United Self-Defense Forces of Columbia (AUC), 432–433
United States (*see specific topics*)
U.S. embassy bombings, 70, 79, 93–94, 149
U.S. Northern Command (NORTHCOM), 52, 229–230, 455
U.S. Pacific Command, 229
U.S. Postal Service, 302–303
  (*See also* Postal and shipping issues)
Urban search and rescue (US&R), 328
USA Freedom Corps, 56, 442
USA PATRIOT Act, 49–52, 227–228
US-CERT, 197, 198, 200
USDA (Department of Agriculture), 230, 291, 293, 463, 466
US&R (urban search and rescue), 328
USS *Cole* bombing, Yemen (2000), 97, 149, 392
Uzbekistan, 26, 399

VA (Department of Veterans Affairs), 455
Veterans Affairs, Department of (VA), 455
Veterinary medical assistance team (VMAT), 327, 385
Vietnam War, 14–15, 121, 375
VIPS (Volunteers in Police Service), 442
Virus cyberattack, 190, 192, 199
Visas required, 218
VMAT (veterinary medical assistance team), 327, 385
Volunteer services, 56, 278–280, 441–444
Volunteers in Police Service (VIPS), 442
von Clausewitz, Karl, 73
Vulnerabilities (*see specific topics*)

Waagner, Clayton, 126–127
Waco, TX, conflict (1993), 122, 125
Wahhabi Islam, 88
"Wall," between intelligence services, 8, 15, 16, 18, 49, 50

Wallace, J. D., 331
WAR (White Aryan Resistance), 120
War of 1812, 4–5
"War of ideas," 241, 242, 254–257
Warning system, 220–223, 271
Washington, George, 104
Washington Statewide Homeland Security Plan, 277–278
Wassenaar Arrangement (2002), 178
Water
    contamination of, 166–167
    critical infrastructure, xvi, 292, 293
    emergency supply of, 363–365
Weapons of mass destruction (WMD), 153–185, 243–244
    al Qaida's desire for, 35–36, 35–37
    biological weapons, 161–168
    chemical weapons, 155–161
    Clinton administration expenditures, 17
    first response, 279–280
    future of homeland security, 37, 376–380
    high-yield explosives, 176–178
    modern terrorism, 16–17, 35–37
    national defense against, 246–247
    nuclear weapons, 154, 172–176
    radiological weapons (dirty bombs), 168–172
    right-wing domestic, 130–131
    strategy to combat, 243–244, 253, 257
    (See also Postal and shipping issues)

Weather Underground Organization (WUO), 121–122
Web sites (see Cyberterrorism)
West, The, as perceived threat, 76, 91–92, 97–100, 241–242, 254–257
White Aryan Resistance (WAR), 120
White House role in homeland security, 212–217
White supremacists, 14, 119–121
WMD (see Weapons of mass destruction)
World Church of the Creator, 119, 126
World Islamic Front, 85
World Trade Center attack, New York (1993), 23, 97, 141, 178, 273
    (See also 9/11/2001 attacks)
World Trade Organization riot, Seattle (1999), 123–124, 375
World War I, 9–10
World War II, 11–14, 68, 78, 121, 150, 172–173, 238, 255
Worm cyberattack, 190
WUO (Weather Underground Organization), 121–122

Yap, Deborah, 394
Yassin, Ali Mohamed Osman, 437
Yemen, 71, 97, 149, 392
Yoldashev, Tohir, 399
Y2K, 54, 56, 194

Zubaydah, Abu, 193, 409

Mark Sauter serves as Chief Operations Officer of the Chesapeake Innovation Center, a public/private partnership that is America's first business accelerator for homeland security high technology. He has completed Community Emergency Response Team (CERT) training and is a member of his county's Citizen Corps Council, volunteer programs supported by the U.S. Department of Homeland Security. Formerly an award-winning investigative reporter, Sauter also served as an Army officer in Special Forces and light infantry units. He is a graduate of Harvard University, magna cum laude, and the Columbia University Graduate School of Journalism. Sauter witnessed the impact of terrorism first-hand as a resident of downtown Manhattan on 9/11.

Dr. James Jay Carafano is the Senior Fellow for Defense and Homeland Security at The Heritage Foundation in Washington, DC, and a recognized national expert on national security issues. Recognizing that the war against terrorism will be a protracted conflict, his research focuses on developing the national security that the nation needs to secure the long-term interests of the United States—protecting its citizens, providing for economic growth, and preserving civil liberties. A West Point graduate, Dr. Carafano is an historian and educator who has taught at U.S. Military Academy, Georgetown University, the U.S. Naval War College, and the National Defense University. Dr. Carafano serves as a member of the National Research Council's Committee on Army Science and Technology for Homeland Security and the National Defense Transportation Association's Security Practices Committee and is a 2005 Senior Fellow at the George Washington University's Homeland Security Policy Institute.

He is the coauthor of *Winning the Long War: Lessons from the Cold War for Defeating Terrorism and Preserving Freedom* (Heritage, 2005) and the author of *Waltzing into the Cold War* (Texas A & M: 2002), and *After D-Day* (Lynne Rienner: 2000), a Military Book Club selection.

Dr. Carafano joined Heritage after serving as a Senior Fellow at the Center for Strategic and Budgetary Assessments, a Washington Policy Institute, where he refined his defense analysis skills after a 25-year Army career. Before retiring as an Army Lt. Colonel he served as Executive Editor of *Joint Force Quarterly*, the Defense Department's premiere professional military journal.